Frommer's®

Buenos Aires

4th Edition

by Michael Luongo

WILEY
Wiley Publishing, Inc.

ABOUT THE AUTHOR

Michael Luongo has written about Argentina for the *New York Times, National Geographic Traveler, Bloomberg News, Out Traveler,* and many other publications. He is also a co-author of *Frommer's Argentina.* His debut novel, *The Voyeur,* was published by Alyson Books in 2007, and he has several other travel books. He has visited all seven continents and more than 80 countries, but few have stolen his heart like Argentina. Highlights of his travels include riding Juan Perón's coffin through the streets of Buenos Aires during his 2006 reburial, and wearing Evita's perfume to a dinner party. Visit him at www.michaelluongo.com and www.misterbuenosaires.com.

Published by:
WILEY PUBLISHING, INC.
111 River St.
Hoboken, NJ 07030-5774

ISBN 978-1-118-00964-2 (paper); ISBN 978-1-118-11548-0 (ebk); ISBN 978-1-118-11549-7 (ebk); ISBN 978-1-118-11550-3 (ebk)

Editor: Andrea Kahn
Production Editor: Jana M. Stefanciosa
Cartographer: Tim Lohnes
Photo Editor: Richard Fox
Production by Wiley Indianapolis Composition Services

Front cover: Cabildo and Clock Tower at Plaza de Mayo in Buenos Aires city center. ©Peter Barritt / Alamy Images
Back cover: Interior of Soul Café in Buenos Aires. ©Terry Carter / Lonely Planet Images / Alamy Images

For information on our other products and services or to obtain technical support, please contact our Customer Care Department within the U.S. at 877/762-2974, outside the U.S. at 317/572-3993 or fax 317/572-4002.

Wiley also publishes its books in a variety of electronic formats. Some content that appears in print may not be available in electronic formats.

Manufactured in the United States of America

5 4 3 2 1

CONTENTS

LIST OF MAPS

For Luis Formaiano and Lawrence Wheeler, who are like my two big brothers in Buenos Aires, and in honor of your 30th anniversary.

ACKNOWLEDGMENTS

Big thanks to my editors, Jamie Ehrlich and Andrea Kahn; to Kathleen Warnock for introducing me to the Frommer's bunch; and to Maureen Clarke, Ensley Eikenberg, Kelly Regan, P.J. Campbell, and everyone in the Hoboken office for their support during my work on this book. Thanks to Inés Segarra of the Argentina Tourism Office in New York for her endless help; to Consul General Jose Luis Perez Gabilondo, Verónica Garcia, and everyone in the New York Argentina Consular Office; to Eduardo Piva and staff in Miami; to Carlos Enrique Mayer and everyone at the Argentina Ministry of Tourism; and to the Buenos Aires City Tourism office. Thanks to Gabriel Miremont, Pablo Vazquez, Liliana and everyone at Museo Evita, and to Marta Granja, Carlos Francavilla and the "cat ladies" in Recoleta Cemetery. To Cristina Alvarez, Miguel Cuberos, and Juan Gandublia and Raul Zaffaroni for their support of my work, and to President Cristina Fernandez de Kirchner for her amusing mix of glamour and politics whenever I run into her in Argentina. To Luis Formaiano and Lawrence Wheeler, without whom I could achieve nothing in Argentina. To Juanita Pergamente and the Madres, to Tulio and the Islas Malvinas veterans for helping me better understand Argentina's deepest wounds, and to Cristian Bonaventura for insight on today's military. To Marcos Wolff for endless advice over the years. To Mario, for his friendship over the years. To my landlord Martin Routaboul and to Ruben and his family. To Sandra Borello of Borello Travel and Diego and staff. To Rafael Meyer and the Say Hueque staff, and Cecilia Nigro for advice. To Sorrel Moseley-Williams of the *Buenos Aires Herald,* Kristie Robinson of *Argentina Independent,* Soledad Vallejos of *Pagina 12,* Lorena Lemos of *Perfil,* Luciana Arias of *America,* and all the other local journalists for advice. For Rick Jarvie, Bill Faries, and everyone at Bloomberg Buenos Aires. Thanks to Caryn Carbonaro for introducing me to tango, and Eduardo, Nora, Suzanna, Michele, Marithe, and Laura Chummers for continuing, and for Marina Palmer too. To Jorge Arias for TangoModa's special world. To Helen Halldórsdóttir, Augustin, Mariana, Roxanna, and Edgardo of La Marshall, and Marcelo and Cesar of CHA and Maria Rachid of INADI. To Carlos Melia, Alfredo Ferreyra, Erik Hovinga, Gustavo Noguera, Gabriel Oviedo and Pablo De Luca. and Conyers Thompson, and to Marta Pasquali, Monika Varela, and Tamara Levinson, Carla and Julian of Dedios for advice, and to Ignacio Kliche, and David Goldfein for Punta advice. To Ambassador Vilma Martinez, Holly Murten, Shannon Farrell, Alex Delorey and staff of the U.S. Embassy in Buenos Aires and Montevideo. To Clarisa Poblete. Pedro Bevilacqua of the National Archives and Dr. Hipolito Barreriro for more on Juan and Evita. To Ingrid Breyer for being my eternal sounding board and to my roommate Harry in New York for taking care of things while I am gone. Thanks also to Richard Burnett in Canada for forwarding that e-mail that told me about the first Buenos Aires book, and to all my editors over the years for whom I have written on this wonderful city. Certainly I am missing many who have helped me and make Argentina special, but please know that you're loved and appreciated!

—Michael Luongo

HOW TO CONTACT US

In researching this book, we discovered many wonderful places—hotels, restaurants, shops, and more. We're sure you'll find others. Please tell us about them, so we can share the information with your fellow travelers in upcoming editions. If you were disappointed with a recommendation, we'd love to know that, too. Please write to:

Frommer's Buenos Aires, 4th Edition
Wiley Publishing, Inc. • 111 River St. • Hoboken, NJ 07030-5774
frommersfeedback@wiley.com

ADVISORY & DISCLAIMER

Travel information can change quickly and unexpectedly, and we strongly advise you to confirm important details locally before traveling, including information on visas, health and safety, traffic and transport, accommodation, shopping and eating out. We also encourage you to stay alert while traveling and to remain aware of your surroundings. Avoid civil disturbances, and keep a close eye on cameras, purses, wallets and other valuables.

While we have endeavored to ensure that the information contained within this guide is accurate and up-to-date at the time of publication, we make no representations or warranties with respect to the accuracy or completeness of the contents of this work and specifically disclaim all warranties, including without limitation warranties of fitness for a particular purpose. We accept no responsibility or liability for any inaccuracy or errors or omissions, or for any inconvenience, loss, damage, costs or expenses of any nature whatsoever incurred or suffered by anyone as a result of any advice or information contained in this guide.

The inclusion of a company, organization or Website in this guide as a service provider and/or potential source of further information does not mean that we endorse them or the information they provide. Be aware that information provided through some Websites may be unreliable and can change without notice. Neither the publisher or author shall be liable for any damages arising herefrom.

FROMMER'S STAR RATINGS, ICONS & ABBREVIATIONS

Every hotel, restaurant, and attraction listing in this guide has been ranked for quality, value, service, amenities, and special features using a **star-rating system.** In country, state, and regional guides, we also rate towns and regions to help you narrow down your choices and budget your time accordingly. Hotels and restaurants are rated on a scale of zero (recommended) to three stars (exceptional). Attractions, shopping, nightlife, towns, and regions are rated according to the following scale: zero stars (recommended), one star (highly recommended), two stars (very highly recommended), and three stars (must-see).

In addition to the star-rating system, we also use **seven feature icons** that point you to the great deals, in-the-know advice, and unique experiences that separate travelers from tourists. Throughout the book, look for:

🎁	Special finds—those places only insiders know about
💬	Fun facts—details that make travelers more informed and their trips more fun
😊	Best bets for kids and advice for the whole family
📷	Special moments—those experiences that memories are made of
✋	Places or experiences not worth your time or money
✎	Insider tips—great ways to save time and money
🏷	Great values—where to get the best deals

The following **abbreviations** are used for credit cards:

AE	American Express	**DISC**	Discover	**V**	Visa
DC	Diners Club	**MC**	MasterCard		

TRAVEL RESOURCES AT FROMMERS.COM

Frommer's travel resources don't end with this guide. Frommer's website, **www.frommers. com**, has travel information on more than 4,000 destinations. We update features regularly, giving you access to the most current trip-planning information and the best airfare, lodging, and car-rental bargains. You can also listen to podcasts, connect with other Frommers. com members through our active-reader forums, share your travel photos, read blogs from guidebook editors and fellow travelers, and much more.

THE BEST OF BUENOS AIRES

B uenos Aires is the capital of Argentina, on the east coast of South America where the Río de la Plata meets the Atlantic Ocean. Its neoclassical architecture, cafe culture, and international vibe give the city a strikingly European feel, earning it the nickname of "the Paris of South America." But Buenos Aires is also decidedly Argentine, with its tango salons, creative clothing boutiques, and culinary focus on local staples such as Pampas grass–fed beef. Whether you're looking for designer fashion, exquisite cuisine, or nightlife that doesn't stop, this vibrant metropolis leaves little room for disappointment.

THINGS TO DO Wander the purple-blossomed **Palermo** parks; take in Latin American and European art in the museums lining **Avenida del Libertador;** and marvel at the grand marble and bronze buildings lining **Avenida 9 de Julio,** the world's widest boulevard, and **Avenida de Mayo,** Buenos Aires's answer to Paris's Champs Elysées. Porteños, as the residents of Buenos Aires call themselves, love to be on display, and the city boasts countless outdoor activities—in parks, at outdoor markets, and on cafe-lined boulevards.

RESTAURANTS & DINING Buenos Aires restaurants are famous for their steaks, and excellent *parrillas* (Argentine steakhouses) can be found everywhere, from the **Puerto Madero** waterfront district to historic **Recoleta.** Also not to miss is Argentine fusion cuisine, in which chefs blend local ingredients with European and Asian flavors. Most of the city's best restaurants are in **Palermo,** where you can dine outdoors on cobblestone streets or indoors by romantic candlelight.

SHOPPING Buenos Aires is a shopper's paradise, whether you're seeking big-name design or local fashions found nowhere else. For the latter, head to **Palermo Viejo,** popular for its concentration of creative boutiques. On Recoleta's **Avenida Alvear** you'll find a mix of top European names and local designers, offering items ranging from antiques to wedding dresses. And what is a visit to Buenos Aires without a leather purchase? Find bargains on **Calle Florida** downtown, or in **Calle Murillo's** factory outlets.

NIGHTLIFE & ENTERTAINMENT Let the sexy kicks of tango mesmerize you at one of the city's show palaces, and then hit a *milonga* (tango salon) to try the dance yourself. The city by night offers more than just tango, from Broadway and West End–quality shows on **Avenida**

Corrientes to jazz clubs in **Palermo Soho** and **San Telmo.** Grab a drink at a cozy *bar notable,* then head to the **Costanera** district, where mega clubs blast techno music until the sun rises over the Río de la Plata.

THE most unforgettable
BUENOS AIRES EXPERIENCES

o **Best Tango Shows for Tourists:** Tango, a beautiful dance that tells the pained story of the city's early-20th-century immigrant poor, is the ultimate Buenos Aires–defining experience. For an authentic historical look, see the tango show **El Querandí,** Perú 302 (✆ **11/5199-1770**), which traces the dance from its origin in brothel slums, when it was only danced by men, to its modern-day leggy sexiness. **Señor Tango,** Vieytes 1655 (✆ **11/4303-0231**), employs Hollywood glamour and Fosse-esque moves, as well as horses trampling the stage, in the city's most popular show. A more elegant tango experience can be had at **Esquina Carlos Gardel,** Carlos Gardel 3200 (✆ **11/4867-6363**), in the Abasto neighborhood, where Carlos Gardel, the city's most famous tango crooner, lived and worked. A classical symphony accompanies traditional instruments in this show. See chapter 9.

o **Best Tango Hall for the Experienced or Those Who Want to Watch the Experienced:** If you're an expert tango dancer, or at least want to watch those who are, head to a *milonga* (tango salon). **El Niño Bien,** Humberto I no. 1462 (✆ **11/4483-2588**), will take you back in time as patrons whirl about under ceiling fans in an enormous Belle Epoque–era hall. The best dancers come here to show off, though you'll also find instructors in search of potential students watching from the sidelines. **Salón Canning,** Scalabrini Ortiz 1331 (✆ **11/4832-6753**), in Palermo Hollywood, has what many local dancers call the best tango floor in all of Buenos Aires—a hard, smooth, parquet surface perfect for the dance. The tight space, however, is less than ideal for the tango-challenged. See chapter 9.

o **Best Architecture Walks:** Buenos Aires abounds in beautiful architecture, thanks especially to its highly ambitious rebuilding project for Argentina's 1910 Centennial celebration of its independence from Spain. The plan was put into action in the 1880s, and by the turn of the 20th century, entire neighborhoods had been rebuilt. The French Beaux Arts movement was at the height of its influence then, meaning the city looks more like Paris than any other Latin American city. **Avenida de Mayo,** the world's widest boulevard and the city's official processional route linking the Presidential Palace (Casa Rosada) to the National Congress Building, is the longest and best-preserved example of this. (See p. 152 for a walking tour of this area.) The corner buildings along the wide **Diagonal Norte,** also known as **Avenida Sáenz Peña,** are all topped with fantastic neoclassical domes, from the street's origin at the Plaza de Mayo to where it intersects Avenida 9 de Julio at the **Obelisco,** Buenos Aires's defining monument. Don't miss the neighborhoods of **San Telmo** and **Monserrat** either, with their balconied late-19th and early-20th-century structures, most of which are gracefully decaying.

o **Best Park Strolls:** The Palermo park system runs along Avenida Libertador and includes some of the world's most beautiful parks. You could spend more than a day here, wandering amid trees and monuments, and still not see everything. Within the system are numerous small parks such as the **Rose Garden** and the **Japanese Gardens,** as well as museums such as the **MALBA** (Museo de Arte

Latinoamericano de Buenos Aires), Av. Figueroa Alcorta 3415 (✆ **11/4808-6500**), and the **Museo Nacional de Bellas Artes,** Av. del Libertador 1473 (✆ **11/4803-0802**). In the Argentine spring—late September and early October—the weather is at its best and the jacaranda trees here are in their full purple-bloomed glory, making this the perfect place for a stroll. In summer months, locals who can't escape the city come to jog, sunbathe, and while away the day beneath the trees. See chapter 6.

o **Best Bird-Watching:** Proof that nature is stronger than whatever humankind throws at it is just a brisk walk away from Buenos Aires's tallest office structures at the **Ecological Reserve** (along the Costanera, near Puerto Madero; ✆ **11/4893-1588**). In the 1960s and 1970s, demolished buildings and construction debris were dumped into the Río de la Plata. Nature responded by covering it with sediment and then grass and small plants, creating a home for myriad birds. Wander with caution if you're on your own, as some areas are still rough or unstable. Ask a tour company about bird-watching tours. See p. 118.

o **Most Heartbreaking Political Experience:** Argentina's political history is a long series of ups and downs. Perhaps the worst tragedy occurred between 1976 and 1982, when a military government, bent on destroying what it considered political enemies, ruled the country. During that period—referred to as the *Guerra Sucia,* or Dirty War—as many as 30,000 people, mostly college-age, were secretly murdered. Most of their bodies were never found, granting them the name *los desaparecidos,* meaning "the disappeared ones." The **Asociación Madres de Plaza de Mayo,** an organization formed by mothers of the victims that strives for justice for those murdered, marches on the Plaza de Mayo every Thursday at 3:30pm, giving speeches and handing out fliers. They also run a university with a store and library of books on this painful period of history that is still being dealt with emotionally and legally. See p. 108.

o **Best Evita Experiences:** Visit the **Plaza de Mayo,** the political heart of Argentina, and look toward the facade of the **Casa Rosada (Presidential Palace;** p. 99). The northern balcony is where Evita addressed her adoring fans, and now you too can stand here and sing "Don't Cry for Me Argentina": The Casa Rosada's free weekend tours now include the balcony, once reserved for visiting dignitaries. Others pay their respects at the **Recoleta Cemetery** (p. 111), where Evita was laid to rest in a tomb belonging to the family of her wealthy father. To understand why it has taken Argentina more than 50 years to come to terms with this controversial woman, visit **Museo Evita,** Calle Lafinur 2988 (✆ **11/4807-9433;** p. 122), in Palermo, where the story of her life is told through personal objects.

o **Best Museums:** The **MALBA** (Museo de Arte Latinoamericano de Buenos Aires), Av. Figueroa Alcorta 3415 (✆ **11/4808-6500;** p. 125), boasts an extensive and diverse modern art collection. The **Museo Nacional de Bellas Artes,** Av. del Libertador 1473 (✆ **11/4803-0802;** p. 124), was built into a former water-pump station and also houses an impressive art collection, including many European masterpieces and paintings depicting the history of Argentina.

o **Best Ethnic Neighborhoods:** With a population that is predominantly white and of either Spanish or Italian descent, Buenos Aires, on the surface, seems lacking in ethnic diversity. The neighborhood of **Once,** however, around Calle Tucumán in particular, is home to a still-thriving Jewish community. You'll find numerous kosher restaurants, synagogues, and Jewish businesses. For another neighborhood of cultural interest, head north to **Belgrano,** the city's Chinatown.

Most people in Buenos Aires know nothing of this neighborhood, a flourishing, busy community of Chinese restaurants, shops, and other businesses. If you're in town for the Chinese New Year, check out the Dragon Parade. See p. 32 and 33, respectively.

o **Best Outdoor Markets:** There's no market like the **San Telmo Antiques Fair,** held every Sunday in Plaza Dorrego, the old colonial heart of the San Telmo district. You'll find lots of small antiques and collectibles dealers here along with some kitschy souvenirs, local crafts, and free live tango dancing as good as anything that you might pay to see onstage. The **Feria de Plaza Francia,** in front of the Recoleta Cemetery, is another market you shouldn't miss, with crafts, live music, and a beautiful setting on a grassy knoll. See p. 163 and 167, respectively.

o **Best Shopping Experiences:** There's no shortage of top designer shops along **Avenida Alvear,** offering the same high quality and high style you find throughout North America and Europe at slightly lower prices befitting the Argentine economy. Leather shops abound on **Calle Florida** near Galerías Pacífico, and you can even have items custom-made at some of them. For top-quality high-design clothing and home items, my favorite shop is **Tienda Puro Diseño Argentino,** Gorriti 5953 (© 11/4776-8037; p. 179). For little boutiques specializing in the sexy styles Argentine women favor, wander the cobblestone streets of **Palermo Soho** and **Palermo Hollywood.** See chapter 8.

o **Best Vista Points:** Odd-looking as it might be, the **Palacio Barolo,** Av. de Mayo 1370 (© 11/4383-1065; p. 108), designed by an architect who took Dante's *Inferno* a little too literally, is finally open to the public for tours. Previously only accessible to those who worked here, the building's interesting interior is well worth a visit. Its tower, which once made it the tallest building in South America, provides a sweeping view of Avenida de Mayo and across the entire city. The **Torre Monumental,** Av. Libertador 49 (© 11/4311-0186; p. 115), better known by its old name, the British Clock Tower, has a fantastic view up and down Avenida Libertador and out to the Río de la Plata. So what if the tower represents a country with which Argentina has had some disagreements over the years? It's the view that counts now.

o **Best Oddball Museums:** Two modern-day necessities—taxes and toilets—are honored in two different small museums in Buenos Aires. The **Tax Museum,** Hipólito Yrigoyen 370, at Defensa (© 11/4347-2396), contains historical items relating to money, coins, and taxes throughout Argentine history. See p. 121. The **Museo del Patrimonio** in the Aguas Argentinas building; Av. Córdoba 1750 (museum entrance at Riobamba 750; © 11/6319-1882), better known as the Water Palace, is really about waterworks, but it contains what surely must be among the largest toilet collection in the world. Kids will have a blast here. See p. 124.

o **Best Museums for Kids:** Called **Museo de Los Niños (Children's Museum),** Av. Corrientes 3247 (© 11/4861-2325; p. 121), this is certainly a great place to bring the young ones. It's full of displays on various careers presented in an accessible and lighthearted way. In the **Museo Participativo de Ciencias,** Junín 1930 (inside the Centro Cultural Recoleta; © 11/4807-3260; p. 122), *not* touching the displays is forbidden. This place is full of scientific exhibits that are so much fun that kids will forget they're educational, too!

o **Best People-Watching:** Pedestrianized **Calle Florida** is not the elegant shopping stretch it might have been a generation ago, but all kinds of Porteños make their way here, especially at lunchtime. Day and night, musicians, tango dancers, broken-glass walkers, and comedians thrill crowds of tourists and locals alike. **Avenida Santa Fe** also remains busy and vibrant at night, with people popping into stores, gossiping at sidewalk cafes, and just checking each other out. See p. 132 and 163, respectively.

o **Best Nightlife Street:** Whether you want to eat at a *parrilla,* try some nouvelle cuisine, have some drinks, or do some dancing, **Calle Báez** in Las Cañitas is the place to go. This busy street in Palermo offers such excellent restaurant choices as **Novecento,** Báez 199 (© 11/4778-1900; p. 90), and **El Estanciero,** Báez 202 (© 11/4899-0951; p. 90). Afterwards, savor the night over drinks at trendy **Soul Café,** Báez 352 (© 11/4778-3115; p. 196). This street boasts some of the most densely packed nightlife in Buenos Aires.

THE best HOTEL BETS

o **Best Luxury Hotels:** These two hotels top my list of luxury accommodations in Buenos Aires, and they top the lists of numerous travel magazines as well. The **Alvear Palace Hotel,** Av. Alvear 1891 (© 11/4808-2100; p. 48), is a gilded confection of carved marble and ornate French furniture. It's the ultimate grand hotel experience in Buenos Aires, complete with butler service. The **Four Seasons Hotel,** Posadas 1086–88 (© 11/4321-1200; p. 49), offers subdued luxury (elegance without the flash), quiet pampering, and a refuge from the bustle of the city in the hotel's walled garden.

o **Best Historic Hotels:** The **Marriott Plaza Hotel,** Calle Florida 1005 (© 11/4318-3000; p. 39), is the oldest of the grand hotels still operating in Buenos Aires, and its location on Plaza San Martín can't be beat. The **Hotel Castelar** (© 11/4383-5000; p. 45) sits on Avenida de Mayo, once the city's most glamorous street. This hotel, adorned with Italian marble and bronze, was the favorite choice of Lorca and other Spanish writers in the 1930s, when Buenos Aires was the intellectual and literary capital of the Spanish-speaking world.

o **Best See-and-Be-Seen Hotels:** The **Faena Hotel and Universe,** Martha Salotti 445 (© 11/4010-9000; p. 38), located in the Puerto Madero district, is the fashionista's see-and-be-seen choice. The hotel was designed with several bars in the lobby and a pool out front, so that any new arrivals would know exactly who else was around. In Recoleta, the new **Buenos Aires Park Hyatt,** Av. Alvear 1661 (© 11/5171-1234; p. 48), built into the old Palacio Duhau, has the best garden in the city. It's here that fashionable ladies come to lunch and be seen and businesspeople make decisions over drinks alfresco.

o **Best Boutique Hotels:** With the tourism boom, boutique hotels have become all the rage in Buenos Aires. These are some of the best, and the newest. **Home** in Palermo Viejo, Honduras 5860 (© 11/4778-1008; p. 55), offers a home away from home that's both trendy and welcoming, and has kept prices reasonable in spite of its popularity. Nearby, **Legado Mítico,** Gurruchaga 1848 (© 11/4833-1300; p. 52), has large rooms, each named and designed after a famous Argentine; a book- and wing-back-chair-filled English-style lobby; and pampering wine-based toiletries. **Bo-Bo** in Palermo, Guatemala 4882 (© 11/4774-0505; p. 52), is housed in a European-style mansion from 1920, and each of the seven rooms follows a different design aesthetic.

- **Best Budget Hotel:** A property of the French miracle chain **Hotel Ibis,** Hipólito Yrigoyen 1592 (✆ **11/5300-5555**), wins in this category. The efficient service and location overlooking Congreso make this an excellent choice. See p. 51.

- **Best Hotel Gyms:** The gym in the **Pan Americano,** Carlos Pellegrini (9 de Julio) 551 (✆ **11/4348-5000;** p. 42), must be seen to be believed. It sits in a rooftop 3-story glass box, so that you feel as if you're floating over Avenida 9 de Julio while running on the treadmills. The **Marriott Plaza Hotel,** Calle Florida 1005 (✆ **11/4318-3000;** p. 39), also has an enormous gym with an abundance of equipment.

- **Best Hotel Pools:** In the hot summer months of the Southern Hemisphere (Dec–Mar), any hotel pool is a welcome treat in Buenos Aires, but two really stand out. The **Pan Americano,** Carlos Pellegrini (9 de Julio) 551 (✆ **11/4348-5000;** p. 42), has a combination indoor-outdoor pool on its roof, so that you can gaze out over the city while you're swimming. The **Four Seasons,** Posadas 1086–88 (✆ **11/4321-1200;** p. 49), has the best garden swimming pool in Recoleta. Lounging poolside in the walled garden complex, you'll forget that you're in the heart of the city.

- **Best Business Hotel:** With its location away from the noise of the city in Puerto Madero, and with one of the largest convention centers in all of Buenos Aires, the **Hilton Buenos Aires,** Av. Macacha Güemes 351 (✆ **11/4891-0000**), is a logical choice for travelers on business. Its business center, complete with translation services, is also one of the largest in Buenos Aires. See p. 39.

THE best DINING & CAFE BETS

- **Best *Parrilla*:** For fear it might become overrun, I am almost afraid to explain how much I love **El Obrero,** Agustin R. Caffarena 64 (✆ **11/4362-9912**), opened decades ago in La Boca by two brothers from Barcelona. It's not just how thick the steaks are, or how inexpensive. It's the wonderful family atmosphere here and how quick the owners' children are to attend to customers. See p. 96.

- **Best Cafe Experiences: Café Tortoni,** Av. de Mayo 825 (✆ **11/4342-4328;** p. 71), might not offer the best service in town, but its history and beauty more than make up for this. The cafe was and still remains Argentina's intellectual coffee spot of choice, and tourists have yet to overrun it. Sit outside at **La Biela,** Av. Quintana 596 (✆ **11/4804-0449;** p. 78), in glamorous Recoleta, overlooking the world-famous Recoleta Cemetery. From the view of Iglesia Pilar to the wonderful trees, this is Buenos Aires at its best. In San Telmo, visit **La Poesía,** Chile 502 (✆ **11/4300-7340;** p. 75), a recently reopened *café notable* that sat abandoned for decades. More than just beautiful, it has a romantic, intellectual air.

- **Best Authentic Old Buenos Aires Dining:** Buenos Aires is full of trendy new eateries, but the surefire bets are where Porteños have eaten for decades. Ham hangs from the rafters and the steaks are as thick as the crowds at the Spanish eatery **Plaza Asturias,** Av. de Mayo 1199 (✆ **11/4382-7334;** p. 80). **Palacio Español,** Bernardo de Yrigoyen 180 (✆ **11/4334-4876;** p. 72), in the Club Español, is an orgy of bronze, marble and stained glass, with waiters fussing over you in a formal but friendly way.

- **Best Seafood:** Argentina has a long coastline, but the turf, not the surf, has always been the centerpiece of the country's culinary scene. Still, check out **Puerto Cristal,** Av. Alicia Moreau de Justo 1082 (✆ **11/4331-3669;** p. 67), which offers friendly service and an inexpensive executive menu in Puerto Madero. Or head to **Olsen,** Gorriti 5870 (☎ **11/4776-7677;** p. 86), in Palermo Viejo, where seafood is served Scandinavian style under the direction of super-chef Germán Martitegui.

o **Best Italian Restaurant:** With more than half the residents of Buenos Aires of Italian immigrant stock, it's easy to find good Italian food: most *parrillas* serve an excellent array of pastas, usually homemade on the premises. The best formal Italian dining experience in the city, however, is **Piegari,** Posadas 1042 (☎ **11/4328-4104**), in the Recoleta la Recova area, near the Four Seasons hotel. The selection of northern Italian dishes is superb, with a stunning assortment of risottos. See p. 76.

o **Best French Restaurant: La Bourgogne,** Av. Alvear 1891 (☎ **11/4805-3857**), in the Alvear Palace, is hands down the best French restaurant in Buenos Aires and the recipient of numerous awards. Yes, it's very formal and very expensive, but what else would you expect from such a place? See p. 76.

o **Best Restaurant for Kids: Garbis,** Scalabrini Ortiz 3190, at Cerviño (☎ **11/4511-6600**), is an Armenian restaurant with what one British expat loves to call a "jumpee castle" for kids. Adults can eat in peace while kids entertain themselves on this indoor playground. See p. 90.

o **Best Value Restaurants: Juana M,** Carlos Pellegrini (9 de Julio) 1535 (☎ **11/4326-0462;** p. 78), a little-known, family-run *parrilla* in the Recoleta district on the very end of Avenida 9 de Julio, wins this distinction. They offer great cuts of meat and an unlimited salad bar. If you're in Puerto Madero, head straight to **La Bistecca,** Av. Alicia Moreau de Justo 1890 (☎ **11/4514-4996;** p. 67), which has an all-you-can-eat menu offering high-quality steaks and a generous salad bar. It's a huge space, but the seating arrangements create a sense of intimacy; at this price, it can't be beat.

BUENOS AIRES IN DEPTH

What the traveler sees in Buenos Aires today is the result of a confluence of factors. The glorious but at times decrepit city is the greatest artifact of Argentina's hopes to rise as a world power on the global stage. The city is the capital of what was once among the world's wealthiest countries, and South America's most powerful, drawing its strength from the bounty of its agricultural hinterland, the labor of its immigrants, and its commercial and political ties with European powers. The architecture, culture, and sense of nostalgia that characterize Buenos Aires today are all vestiges of its physical and spiritual transformation at the turn of the 20th century. Its wide boulevards lined with Parisian-style buildings, its government headquarters of European marble, its fashion boutiques and art galleries, and its conversation-filled cafes represent what the city once was, what it could have been, and what it still longs to be in the eyes of the world.

BUENOS AIRES TODAY

The past few years have seen Argentina recover from its worst economic tumble, the 2001–02 peso crisis, and enter a period of hopeful buoyancy, floating on apparent prosperity thanks to a tourism boom, a new political era, and high prices for Argentine commodities on the global market. In December 2001, the Argentine peso, once on a par with the U.S. dollar, collapsed to less than a third of its former value. (At press time, the dollar-to-peso ratio is about 4 to 1.) Unemployment rose to more than 20%, businesses shut down, and many people who had trusted the banking system lost their entire life savings overnight. News networks across the world showed images of social unity, such as members of the middle class banging pots in the streets and shouting at police officers, followed by social breakdown, when those same police officers shot rioters on the pedestrianized shopping streets in the city's downtown.

While no one watching the news at the beginning of 2002 could have guessed that Buenos Aires would experience a tourism boom as a result of the peso crisis, that was exactly what happened. With hotels, restaurants, and shopping at barely a third of their former prices, the most expensive capital in South America suddenly became a bargain destination. Tourism is now the third-most-important sector of the country's economy. The peso crisis also forced locals to make do with their own resources— to cook with Argentine ingredients, to design clothes made from local

materials, and to turn to elements of their own culture, particularly the tango, for entertainment. Argentine culture was revived in Buenos Aires, rendering it a more vibrant city for tourists.

Politics changed dramatically when Peronist Néstor Kirchner was elected president in 2003. At the same time, the commodities Argentina has always been famous for—grain and beef—rose in value throughout the world, particularly with the growth of China and other Asian nations. The same was true of petroleum, another major Argentine export, the price of which rose substantially in the first decade of the millennium. The turnaround of the economy of Buenos Aires, and the nation as a whole, was spectacular.

The new economic situation led to inflation, however, with tourism a major driver. Much of the recent residential high-rise construction in Buenos Aires, particularly in Palermo and Puerto Madero, was speculated on the premise that foreigners would buy apartments to rent to other foreigners, hardly sustainable.

In the wake of her husband's success in revitalizing the country's economy, former First Lady and Buenos Aires province Senator Cristina Fernandez de Kirchner was elected president in 2007. The election was met with delight both around the world and within the country, but her immense popularity soon crashed. Her administration began to publish false inflation figures, claiming inflation was held at various points between 1% and 7% when it was as high as 25%. The government also enacted price controls and tariffs on grain and beef exports, causing international trade of these commodities to plummet at a time of high demand. Argentina's chance to grow wealthy from its natural bounty, as it had 100 years before, was lost. Meat production declined, causing the rise in prices that both Kirchners had been trying to avoid.

In anticipation of the 2010 Bicentennial, Buenos Aires spiffed itself up. The city renovated historical buildings, repaved and replanted boulevards, and expanded its subway system. Yet even this dramatic makeover was not without its controversies. The restoration of the Teatro Colón, the most important symbol of Buenos Aires's golden period, was years behind schedule and fraught with corruption on every level. If, at the 1910 Centennial, Teatro Colón represented the city in its most glorious period, the process of its restoration showed what it had become 100 years later—a city of opportunity lost, but one that still longs to return to its former glory.

The years ahead are marked by political uncertainty. Néstor Kirchner died in October 2010. Argentine law limits presidents to two consecutive terms but allows unlimited terms if they are not consecutive. The Kirchners' plan was that each would run for office every 4 years, creating a new Peronist dynasty. Cristina Kirchner plans to run in 2011, and if she wins, she won't be able to run in the following election. Furthermore, the Peronists have already begun to splinter into various factions, meaning it should prove a brutal race.

LOOKING BACK: BUENOS AIRES HISTORY

In 1880, 300 years after the final, permanent founding of Buenos Aires, the city was made the official capital of Argentina. For decades afterward, Buenos Aires experienced a period of wealth and explosive growth, laying the foundation for the glory days that Argentines recall. Trade with Europe expanded, with cattle and grain from the newly conquered hinterlands as the main exports. Millions immigrated from Italy, Spain, and other countries, filling the city's slums, primarily in the southern sections of La Boca and San Telmo. To this day, there are almost as many Italian surnames as Spanish in Argentina. Even the Spanish spoken in Argentina seems to resemble Italian in its rhythm and pitch, and Lunfardo, the street dialect associated with tango, owes many of its words to immigrant Italian. The exponential growth of this time means that Buenos Aires—unlike Salta, Córdoba, and other old Argentine cities—retains few colonial buildings besides its churches.

Today, as a visitor mindful of Argentina's past several decades of political and economic chaos, it is difficult to make sense of the ostentatious infrastructure that remains from this earlier time. Built at tremendous expense, Buenos Aires was the imperial capital of a country hungry to assert its importance as a global power. Indeed, at the turn of the 20th century, Argentina was one of the 10 wealthiest countries in the world.

The Cultural Growth of the 1920s & 1930s

Argentina's wealth, economic expansion, and sense of power at the turn of the 20th century laid the groundwork for the cultural growth it experienced in the 1920s and 1930s. During this period, traditions that had always existed among the lower classes began to draw international attention. Tango had always been associated with the lower classes, but one man changed all of that. In 1917, Carlos Gardel, who began his career singing as a child in Buenos Aires's Abasto Market, recorded what is considered the first important tango song—"Mi Noche Triste"—which launched him into stardom. Throughout the 1920s, Gardel toured in France. Seeing Parisians accept and even embrace tango, Argentina's upper classes embraced it as well. By the middle of the 1920s, tango had become the country's most important musical form; its history is akin to the rise of jazz in the United States. Gardel died at the age of 44, on June 24, 1935, in a plane crash in Colombia, but only after having solidified his status as one of Argentina's most important cultural icons.

The same period saw a flowering of literature and theater. Jorge Luis Borges published short stories on the gangsters and lower classes of Buenos Aires. By the 1930s, with the Civil War and resulting repression in Spain, Buenos Aires became the preeminent center of Spanish-language culture. Federico García Lorca lived in Buenos Aires between 1933 and 1934, staying at the Castelar Hotel on Avenida de Mayo.

The 1930s were also a golden age for radio and cinema. Many stars came of age at this time, including Tita Morello and Libertad Lamarque. The Argentine film industry's only South American rival was Rio de Janeiro. Even there, however, stars such as Carmen Miranda, long before Hollywood discovered her, emulated the style of Buenos Aires. With the widening of Avenida Corrientes in the 1930s, many theaters opened here, making it the Broadway of Buenos Aires.

Buenos Aires glittered as the cultural capital of Argentina, pulling fame-seeking young men and women from the provinces. In 1934, one teenage girl from the city of Junín in the Province of Buenos Aires would come to do just that, changing Argentine history forever. Though accounts differ as to exactly how, we know that Maria Eva Duarte came to Buenos Aires for the first time at the tender age of 15. With little but looks, charm, and persistence, Ms. Duarte moved through a succession of jobs and men, in theater, radio, and film. Eventually, with her success as an actress, she would meet her most powerful boyfriend of all.

The Perón Years

Juan Perón's popularity was anchored by an earthquake that occurred on January 15, 1944, in San Juan, a city near Mendoza, while he served as the head of the country's labor division. About 10,000 people died and nearly half the city was left homeless. The event was Perón's ultimate public relations opportunity. He arranged a fundraiser for the victims of the earthquake with a star-studded concert in Luna Park, a stadium in Buenos Aires. Though they actually met earlier, legend cites the gala as the point at which Perón and Evita met.

Fearing his rise to power, the military government arrested Perón and imprisoned him on Juan García Island in the Tigre Delta. A near revolt occurred in Buenos Aires, and the government quickly released him. On October 17, 1945 (the most important date in the Peronist calendar), Perón spoke to a crowd from a balcony at the Casa Rosada and announced that elections would be forthcoming. Feeling the need to legitimize their relationship, Eva and Perón married secretly in Los Toldos, the town of her birth, using the civil registry, and later held a Catholic ceremony in La Plata, the provincial capital of Buenos Aires Province, overseen by a priest relative of Perón's.

Perón became president in 1946 in an election marked by fraud and brutality on both sides. Though Juan technically had the power, he could not have retained his popularity without Eva. With their power based in workers' unions, the couple launched numerous economic and work initiatives, many along the lines of Communist-style 5-year plans. Employment and wages spiked. Argentina's middle class owes its existence to this period.

After Evita's long insistence, women received the right to vote in 1947, and the presidential elections of 1951 were the first in which women participated. Wanting to legitimize her power within the government, Evita sought vice presidential candidacy in the 1951 election, a move that was met with anger from many powerful political leaders but immense support from the working class. Juan ultimately forced her to renounce the nomination. Stricken with cervical cancer, Evita was dying, and forfeiting this final fight worsened her health. She voted in the elections from her hospital bed. She was so weak during the inaugural parade through Buenos Aires that she had to be doped up on painkillers and strapped to a wood frame, hidden by an oversized fur coat, so she could wave to crowds.

On July 26, 1952, Evita finally died. A 2-week mourning period ensued, and millions poured into Buenos Aires to pay their final respects. Knowing that without Evita his days might soon be over, Perón commissioned a monument to her, which was never completed, and had her body embalmed so that it would be preserved forever.

A period of economic instability ensued, exacerbated by Perón's own policies. In 1955, the military deposed him and stole Evita's body, sending it on a journey lasting 17 years. Images of the Peróns were banned by the military government; even uttering their names was an offense.

Juan Perón bounced through various countries—Paraguay, Panama, Venezuela, the Dominican Republic—before settling in Spain, ruled by longtime ally Francisco Franco. In Panama, he met his future third wife and vice president, nightclub dancer Isabel Martínez. While Perón was in exile, Evita's body was returned to him, and his power base in Argentina strengthened, enabling him to return to the presidency in 1973. Still, his arrival was fraught with chaos. Gun battles broke out at Ezeiza Airport when his plane landed. When he died in 1974, Isabel replaced him as president. Neither as strong as her husband nor his previous wife, Isabel could not hold the country for very long. She took on the nickname Isabelita to bring back the memory of her predecessor and she is said to have held séances over Evita's coffin to absorb her power. Despite her efforts, on March 24, 1976, she was deposed in a military coup headed by Jorge Rafael Videla.

The Dirty War & Its Aftermath

The regime of Jorge Rafael Videla, established as a military junta, carried out a campaign to weed out anybody suspected of having Communist or Peronist sympathies. (Ironically, it was in this period that Evita was finally laid to rest in her current tomb in Recoleta Cemetery.) Congress was closed, censorship was imposed, and unions were banned. Over the next 7 years, during this "Process of National Reorganization"— a period now known as the *Guerra Sucia* (Dirty War) or El Proceso—between 10,000 and 30,000 intellectuals, artists, and activists were tortured or executed by the Argentine government. The mothers of these *desaparecidos* (the disappeared ones) began holding Thursday afternoon vigils in front of the presidential palace in Buenos Aires's Plaza de Mayo as a means of calling international attention to the plight of the missing, a ritual that continues to this day. President Videla finally relinquished power to Roberto Violo in 1981. Violo would only serve as an interim president before being ousted by yet another military dictator, Leopoldo Galtieri, at the end of 1981.

In 1982, seeking a political distraction for an Argentine population growing increasingly vocal about human rights abuses and the worsening economy, President Galtieri invaded the Falkland Islands (known in Argentina as Islas Malvinas), which the British had taken from Argentina in 1833. The disastrous war, in which more than 900 died, ended the military regime. An election in 1983 restored constitutional rule and brought Raúl Alfonsín, of the Radical Civic Union, into power. In 1989, political power shifted from the Radical Party to the Peronist Party (established by Juan Perón), the first democratic transition in 60 years. Carlos Saúl Ménem, a former governor from the province of La Rioja, won the presidency by a surprising margin.

A strong leader, Ménem pursued an ambitious but controversial agenda, with the privatization of state-run institutions as its centerpiece. With the peso pegged to the dollar, Argentina enjoyed unprecedented price stability, allowing Ménem to deregulate and liberalize the economy. For many Argentines, it meant a kind of prosperity they had not seen in years. Ménem's policies, however, devastated manufacturing, and the export market virtually ended. The chasm between rich and poor widened, squeezing out much of the middle class and eroding social support systems. This destroyed investor confidence, and the national deficit soared.

After 10 years as president, Ménem left office. By that time, an alternative to the traditional Peronist and Radical parties, the center-left FREPASO political alliance, had emerged on the scene. The Radicals and FREPASO formed an alliance for the October 1999 election, and the alliance's candidate, running on an anti-corruption campaign, defeated his Peronist competitor.

Less charismatic than his predecessor, President Fernando de la Rúa was forced to reckon with the recession. In an effort to eliminate Argentina's ballooning deficit, de la Rúa followed a strict regimen of government spending cuts and tax increases recommended by the International Monetary Fund (IMF). However, crippled economic growth and political infighting prevented de la Rúa from implementing other reforms to stimulate the economy. An economic crisis loomed.

The meltdown arrived with a run on the peso in December 2001. Government efforts to restrict the run by limiting bank withdrawals fueled anger and Argentines took to the streets in sometimes violent demonstrations. De la Rúa resigned on December 20, as Argentina faced the worst economic crisis of its history. A series of interim governments did little to improve the situation. Peronist President Eduardo Duhalde unlocked the Argentine peso from the dollar on January 1, 2002, and the currency's value quickly tumbled. Within a few months, several presidents came and went, and people died in street protests. The country's IMF default was the largest in history.

Argentina's economic crisis severely eroded the population's trust. Increased poverty, unemployment exceeding 20%, and inflation hitting 30% resulted in massive emigration. *Piqueteros* and *cartoneros,* the protestors and the homeless, became a visible presence throughout Buenos Aires and other large cities, as the unemployed in rural areas picked garbage for a living. Ironically, those who could not flee built a stronger nation. Under Ménem, Argentina idolized Europe and the United States, but now citizens had to look to their own historical and cultural models, things authentically Argentine. The tango—long expected to die out as a dance for the older generation—found new enthusiasts among the young.

The country further stabilized by 2003, with the election of Néstor Kirchner, the governor of the Province of Santa Cruz in Patagonia, a province made wealthy by oil exploration. Kirchner had proven his economic savvy by sending the province's investments overseas just before the peso collapsed. A left-wing Peronist, he had seen many of his friends disappear under the military regime. He reopened investigations into this dark period in Argentina's history and also went after the most corrupt figures of Ménem's regime. He and his senator wife, Cristina Fernandez de Kirchner, became the country's most important political couple. Economic stability returned, with exports of soy, oil, and meat pumping the economy and a cheap peso. An overall global boom meant there was a hungry market for the Argentina's raw material exports, especially in the Chinese and other Asian economies. Tourism became the third-most-important economic sector under his administration, with many well-off foreigners deciding to stay and invest in property and business.

Yet Kirchner was hardly a reformist and Argentine politics remained mired in bitter rivalries, exacerbated by a weak bureaucratic civil service and compromised judiciary. Corruption scandals, such as public works backhanders and a Venezuelan cash-in-suitcase election donation, failed to dent the president's popularity, buoyed by a consumer boom and relative prosperity. Sure to win a second term, Kirchner surprised everybody when he put his wife forward instead. She won the presidency in October 2007 with 45% of the vote, making her the country's first elected female leader.

ART & ARCHITECTURE

The vast majority of what visitors see in Buenos Aires today was built in the explosive period between 1880 and 1910, just after the city became the capital of Argentina, and in preparation for the country's Centennial. As a result, very little of Buenos Aires's colonial heritage exists today, save for **Cabildo** and **Catedral Metropolitana** surrounding **Plaza de Mayo,** both of which have been altered dramatically over time, and several churches within Monserrat and San Telmo.

Redesigning Streets

Instead of Spain, it was France to which Argentina looked when re-envisioning Buenos Aires. The idea was to adopt the principles that Baron Georges-Eugène Haussmann used in Paris to create a new Argentine capital. The Parisian concepts of diagonals, grand structures, parks, and vista points found their place all over the city.

Developers laid new boulevards over the original Spanish colonial grid. The most important was **Avenida de Mayo,** which opened in 1893 to serve as the government procession route, linking the Casa Rosada or Presidential Palace on its eastern end with the new **Congreso** on its western terminus. Lined with Beaux Arts and Art Nouveau buildings, according to the styles of the time, it became the cultural and nightlife center of the city. **Diagonal Norte** and **Diagonal Sur** were also built. Diagonal Norte was completed in the 1930s and, as such, its buildings represent a mix of neoclassical and Art Deco elements. Each building is capped with a corner dome, creating a sweeping skyline meant to connect the **Plaza de Mayo** and the **Casa Rosada** to the **Tribunales Building** in Plaza Libertad. The sprawling design of Diagonal Norte and Avenida de Mayo was meant to provide philosophical and physical connections between the executive, judicial, and legislative branches of government. This point was lost to a degree with the erection of the **Obelisco,** which blocked the view of the Tribunales, in 1936, marking the 400th anniversary of the first founding of the city. The Obelisco sits in the oval **Plaza de República,** which was once the site of **Iglesia de San Nicolás** where the Argentine flag was first displayed on August 23, 1812. Like the Eiffel Tower in Paris, the Obelisco was hated by many when it was first built but has become the most important symbol of the city. The grand architectural plans for Diagonal Sur never came to fruition. Though it began grandly, with the **City Legislature Building,** over time it became lined with buildings lacking distinction, and it has no vista point.

The widest boulevard in the world, **Avenida 9 de Julio,** was planned in 1888, but its construction didn't begin until the 1930s. It was built in stages, beginning with the center portion that exists today, and then widened by a street block on each side. What appears to be the grand entrance of **Teatro Colón** today was once the back of the structure facing what was at the time only an obscure street.

Technically, Avenida 9 de Julio is incomplete. The grand expansion of the street that created the underground portions of Teatro Colón was to extend all the way to Avenida del Libertador. Ironically, the plan to redesign Buenos Aires to look like Paris would have meant the destruction of the Belle Epoque French Embassy. France refused to sell the structure, and today this building remains a beautiful vista point at the boulevard's northern terminus and is a reminder of the neighboring neoclassical buildings that were destroyed here. At the southern end of the boulevard, the Health Department building was too large a structure to demolish, so the boulevard simply circumvents it. It was from this building, looking out over Avenida 9 de Julio, that Evita gave the speech in which she renounced her candidacy for the vice presidency. From one end to the other, with the Obelisco as its fulcrum, the grand boulevard seems out of kilter, the low-rise buildings that line it out of balance with its expanse, remaining to this day a testament to ambitious plans that could never be entirely fulfilled.

Grand Architecture

As the streets were rebuilt, grand plans were announced to build what were to become the city's most iconic structures. The first of these was the **Water Palace,** originally designed in 1877 to provide the city with a clean water supply, in response to the yellow fever epidemic raging through San Telmo. But as wealthy residents erected mansions adjacent to the site and the city poised itself to become the capital of the country, what had been meant merely as a structure for water pumps was transformed into an exquisite, high-Victorian-style edifice, built with more than 300,000 glazed Royal Doulton bricks shipped from Britain and interior workings from Belgium. Completed in 1887, it is the earliest example of how, for the next several decades, Buenos Aires would continue to outdo itself architecturally.

Perhaps the grandest of all was the **Congreso** building. Opened in 1906 after nearly 9 years of work, and built in a Greco-Roman style with strong Parisian Beaux Arts influences, Congreso is the city's most imposing building. One of the main architects was Victor Meano, who was also involved in designing the Teatro Colón but was murdered before completion of either building. Certain elements within the structure call to mind the Argentine desire to emulate other countries. The overall scheme of the building, with its wings and central dome, mimics the U.S. Capitol in Washington, D.C. The bronze ornamentation at the roofline simulates that of the Paris Opera House, and the grand entrance, capped by bronze horses, is almost a direct copy of the Brandenburg Gate in Berlin. Though the exterior walls are made of Argentine granite, the building's interior is lavishly decorated with woods, tiles, marbles, bronzes, and other material imported from Europe. The **Teatro Colón** opened in 1908 and was perhaps the grandest example of Buenos Aires's desire to compete with the capitals of Europe. It, too, is filled with exquisite imported materials. After its opening, Italy's greatest opera stars, such as Enrico Caruso, graced its stage.

Yet for all its desire to transform itself architecturally to rival Europe, Buenos Aires was more the Dubai or Beijing of its time. The city had the wealth to pay for the massive rebuilding, but it lacked the know-how and had to import talent, labor, and materials from Europe. Buenos Aires needed the countries it competed with in order to transform itself in their image, something that to this day remains a sticking point.

BUENOS AIRES IN POP CULTURE

Recommended Books

Book-lovers will rejoice at Argentina's rich body of literature. **Jorge Luis Borges** is considered the grandfather of Argentine writers, having combined symbolism, fantasy, and reality into metaphysical narratives that have been translated all over the world. *Labyrinths* and *A Universal History of Iniquity* are just two collections of short stories from his prolific career; he is also famous for his poetry and nonfiction essays. **Julio Cortázar** is another giant of letters who, like Borges, was very much influenced by European ideas and lived abroad for many years in Paris. His unconventional novel *Hopscotch* suggests two possible orders in which its chapters can be read, each resulting in a different version of the story. His short story "The Droolings of the Devil" was adapted into the famous art-house movie *Blowup,* directed by Michelangelo Antonioni. Another Borges-influenced writer is **Ernesto Sábato,** whose novel *On Heroes and Tombs* is one of the most thorough artistic expressions of Buenos Aires ever written. *The Tunnel,* also by Sábato, is the compelling narrative of an obsessed painter. Less lauded abroad but more indicative of Argentine rural life is the work of **Horacio Quiroga.** A tragic figure (he committed suicide in 1937), Quiroga set most of his work in the jungle frontier of Misiones and combined the supernatural and bizarre in stories that are enjoyed by both young and old and can be seen as a predecessor to magical realism. *The Decapitated Chicken* and *The Exiles* are his two short-story collections currently available in English. A seminal book in Argentine literature is the 19th-century gaucho poem *Martin Fierro* by **José Hernández,** a compulsory read for all Argentine students.

Popular modern writers include **Manuel Puig,** whose novel *Kiss of the Spider Woman* was adapted into a movie by the same name. It deals with sex and repression and frequently references movies and popular culture. Puig's background as a screenwriter can also be seen in his other novels, such as *Betrayed by Rita Hayworth* and *Heartbreak Tango.* The biography *Manuel Puig and the Spider Woman,* by academic **Suzanne Jill Levine,** provides excellent insight into Puig's life and work. **Osvaldo Soriano's** *Shadows* and *A Funny Dirty Little War* are popular critiques of Argentine society, while **Federico Andahazi's** novel *The Anatomist* is an entertaining and somewhat bawdy work of historical fiction.

For an outsider's take on Argentine culture, read *In Patagonia* by **Bruce Chatwin,** one of the most famous travelogues ever written. *Chasing Che,* by **Patrick Symmes,** is an eloquent description of the writer's attempt to retrace the road trip of the famous revolutionary. **Miranda France's** *Bad Times in Buenos Aires* is an excellent impression of an expat's frustrating experience of living in Argentina. For something a bit lighter, read *Kiss and Tango* by **Marina Palmer:** the confessions of a tango-dancing gringa. Women should take note that as exciting and romantic as tango men may seem in this book, when Palmer finally settled down, she married a man who couldn't dance.

Recommended Films

Despite limited funding and very little exposure, the Argentine movie industry has a prodigious output, from slick mainstream features to grim independent films, with the occasional award-winning gem in between. Themes such as the breakdown of society, the Dirty War, the Malvinas War, and the sex wars provide rich pickings for young creative directors with little money but lots of talent. Many actors move back and forth among TV, film, and theater production in Buenos Aires, often starring in the live shows in Corrientes theatres, so if you have a favorite Argentine actor, it might be easy to catch him or her live.

Maria Luisa Bemberg is probably the most famous of late-20th-century Argentine filmmakers. She specialized in period dramas. Her *Camila* (1984), which was Argentina's selection for the Oscars, and *Miss Mary* (1986) both deal with the feminine experience in Argentina, with **Julie Christie** starring in the latter. *The Official Story* (1985), directed by **Luis Puenzo,** and *The Night of the Pencils* (1986), directed by **Hector Olivera,** are two powerful dramas about the military dictatorship and how the repression affected the nation's children. *Man Facing Southeast* (1986) and *The Dark Side of the Heart* (1992) are two compelling movies directed by **Eliseo Subiela,** the former a sci-fi drama and the latter an intriguing love story.

The Italian neorealist style of filmmaking has a strong influence in Argentine cinema, and nowhere is it more evident than in the movies of **Pablo Trapero.** *Crane World* (1999) and *El Bonaerense* (2002) are two gritty working-class features, the former about a crane operator and the latter a stark portrait of police corruption. Another master of everyday themes and deadpan comedy is **Carlos Sorin.** *Historias Mínimas* (2003) and *Bombon the Dog* (2004) deal with love, life, and dogs. For something more mainstream but just as hilarious, *Tiempo de Valientes* (2008), directed by **Dámian Szifron,** concerns two favorite Argentine topics—crime and psychoanalysis. *Blessed by Fire* (2004), directed by **Tristán Bauer,** is possibly one of the best movies ever made about the Falklands War, while grifter movie *Nine Queens* (2001), directed by **Fabián Bielinsky,** is so good it was remade in Hollywood.

One of the first Hollywood movies made about Buenos Aires is a lighthearted musical called *Down Argentine Way* (1940), directed by **Irving Cummings** and starring Brazilian **Carmen Miranda. Robert Duvall's** *Assassination Tango* (2002) is almost a personal project, and he stars in it along with his Argentine wife **Luciana Pedraza.** It is a slow movie but highlights his obsession with Argentina and the tango, letting the city serve as a backdrop. **Christopher Hampton's** *Imagining Argentina* (2003), based on the book by **Lawrence Thornton,** details the Dirty War, and stars **Emma Thompson** and **Antonio Banderas.** More than likely, you've seen **Alan Parker's** *Evita* (1996), starring **Madonna.** While the film is often criticized and not completely accurate, its cinematography is fantastic. So is its use of real Buenos Aires sites, such as the balcony of the Casa Rosada where Evita once stood and entranced millions, as well as its use of Budapest as a stand-in in other scenes. For a more authentic depiction of Evita's life, however, see the Argentine film *Eva Perón,* starring **Esther Goris,** which was produced almost as a response to the Madonna film.

Music

When it comes to music in Argentina, it's all about the tango. The most famous tango crooner of all is **Carlos Gardel.** He performed and recorded dozens of songs, and you're likely to hear many of them while in Buenos Aires, even if you never step foot in a *milonga* or go to a tango show. Among his most memorable are "Mi Buenos Aires Querido" and "Por una Cabeza." One of the best known tango composers of all time is **Astor Piazzolla,** for whom the tango show **Piazzolla Tango** is named (see p. 201). The music of Gardel and Piazzolla is readily for sale throughout Buenos Aires (see chapter 8). Today, Rock Nacional (Spanish-language rock by Argentine artists) is popular; the best-known musician of this genre is **Charly Garcia,** who has had a decades-long career and is regarded as a living treasure. Argentine-American **Kevin Johansen** is a popular performer on the Argentine scene, with a following among locals and expats alike, representing a new hybrid in Argentine music.

EATING & DRINKING

Buenos Aires is one of the world's most important food cities. Its cuisine derives from a mix of influences, using beef from cows raised on the Pampas, Italian staples such as pastas and rich sauces, and even underlying native Indian ingredients like *choclo* (a form of corn). With the Argentines' growing wealth and desire to emulate what they saw as they traveled the rest of the world, French and other European influences entered the cuisine. The go-go Ménem years of the 1990s, in particular, saw the rise of sushi and other Japanese specialties throughout Buenos Aires.

The most important Argentine staple is beef, and the world-famous Argentine steak should be at the top of every visitor's list of foods to try as soon as possible. Sidewalk restaurants and cafes throughout Buenos Aires sell a multitude of meat-based snacks such as *milanesas* (filet in bread crumbs) and *lomitos* (steak sandwiches). The ultimate steak experience is the epic Argentine *asado,* an event for which the translation "barbecue" does no justice, as there is not a hot dog or hamburger in sight. Instead, you get a mouth-watering parade of every meat cut imaginable, from *costillas* (ribs) to *bife de chorizo* (tenderloin). Offal is popular in the form of *mollejas* (sweetbread) and *chimchullinis* (intestine). A weekend invitation to a family *asado* should not be missed and, as you travel around, you will see such gatherings in the most unlikely places such as freeway curbs, street steps, and high-rise balconies. When Argentines want to celebrate, it is nearly always with an *asado*. If such an invite is not forthcoming, settle for an *asado de tira* (rack of grilled beef ribs) in any *parrilla* (grillhouse restaurant), with the ubiquitous empanadas for starters. You'll find wonderful choices all over the city; the family-run La Boca favorite **El Obrero** (p. 96) and Puerto Madera's upscale **Cabaña Las Lilas** (p. 66) represent just a few.

The neighborhood of **Palermo Viejo** reigns supreme in food experimentation. It is here that some of the most interesting examples of Argentine–nouvelle cuisine were born, largely in response to the peso crisis. Look to such restaurants as **Meridiano 58, Te Mataré Ramírez,** and **Casa Cruz** for this type of cuisine (p. 86, 89, and 82, respectively). In addition, some restaurants have turned to ancient Argentine staples now popular in neighboring regions such as Peru. These include **Bio** (p. 92), a vegetarian restaurant that uses quinoa, the grain of the Incas, in some of its dishes; and **De Olivas i Lustres** (p. 89), serving dishes containing quinoa, *yacare* (river alligator), and llama, many cooked in a Mediterranean fashion—a fantastic fusion of continents. Even beyond the gourmet re-creations of star chefs, the Indian heritage of Buenos Aires remains in other staples, such as *locro,* a heavy winter stew of meats and *chocla.*

With more than half the population of Italian descent, Italian food can hardly be considered an ethnic specialty in Buenos Aires, or anywhere in Argentina for that matter. Italian food is Argentine food. However, Middle Eastern influences exist in the city—a remnant of the immigrants who moved here after the disintegration of the Ottoman Empire—in such restaurants as **Viejo Agump** and **Garbis** (p. 93 and 90, respectively). Similarly, kosher restaurants, particularly with Sephardic and Mizrahi influences, exist in the neighborhoods of **Abasto** and **Once.** If you're craving peanut butter, kosher shops will stave the craving. Asian food can be found all over the city, particularly sushi. Sushi's popularity during the Ménem years continued during the presidency of Fernando de la Rúa, whose economic advisors were nicknamed "the Sushi Club" because of their consumption of the dish during meetings. In Buenos Aires, head to such restaurants as **Asia de Cuba** (p. 63) and **Sushi Club** (p. 91) if you're craving raw fish. Recently, the sushi trend has resulted in another cultural fusion, born of immigration from Peru during the economic boom and the rise of Japanese-Argentine star chefs. Peruvian cuisine, itself based on raw fish and now often served by Japanese sushi chefs, can be best enjoyed in Palermo's **Ceviche** (p. 83).

Mate tea is a national obsession, with groups of people consuming this bitter green infusion on street corners and at soccer games. Scan the city's parks on a hot day and you'll see it carried by nearly everyone out enjoying the sun. Coffee is popular and served strong. For something different, try a *submarino*—a lump of dark chocolate (often in the shape of a submarine) dunked in a glass of hot milk. Ice cream is indulged in at all hours, with many parlors open until early morning and offering a bewildering range of flavors topped by the national pride, *dulce de leche* (caramelized milk).

The Italian digestif Fernet has taken on a new life as the alcoholic drink of the young and is popular in late-night bars and discos. Argentine wine is some of the best in the world: The powerful red Malbec from Mendoza is the perfect companion for beef, and the aromatic white Torrontes from Salta and La Rioja is excellent with fish or pasta.

WHEN TO GO

The seasons in Argentina are the reverse of those in the Northern Hemisphere. The weather in Buenos Aires is ideal in fall (Mar–May) and spring (Sept–Nov). The best travel deals are between April and June. The most beautiful time to visit, however, is in October and November when the jacaranda trees are in bloom. "High season" is the period from December through February; "low season" is from June to August. In July and August, there's a slight rise in tourism because of North American summer and the South American ski season (tourists stop in Buenos Aires before heading to nearby ski resorts like Bariloche). In December, weather is pleasant for the most part. However, you won't find over-the-top Christmas decorations and rituals, in spite of the fact that the city's population is overwhelmingly Catholic. In January and February, much of the city is abandoned by locals who flock to beach resorts in Mar del Plata or Uruguay. January is a time when many tourists do visit, resulting in over-booked hotels, yet many restaurants and museums have limited hours during this time period, often closing entirely from January 1 to January 15. Call ahead to make sure places are open.

Weather

Except for a small tropical area in northern Argentina, the country lies in the temperate zone, characterized by cool, dry weather in the south, and warmer, humid air in the center. Buenos Aires in January and February can be terribly hot and humid—often in the high 90s to more than 100°F (38°C)—while winter (approximately June–Aug) can be overcast, chilly, and rainy, though you won't usually find snow. As in the rest of the world, global warming is shifting these trends, and sometimes odd heat waves or cold spells happen.

Average Daytime Temperature (°F & °C) in Buenos Aires

	JAN	FEB	MAR	APR	MAY	JUNE	JULY	AUG	SEPT	OCT	NOV	DEC
Temp (°F)	75	73	69	62	56	51	50	53	56	61	66	72
Temp (°C)	24	23	21	17	13	11	10	12	13	16	19	22

HOLIDAYS

Public holidays are January 1 (New Year's Day), Islas Malvinas (Falkland Islands) Day (Apr 2, or the first Mon after), the Monday and Tuesday before Ash Wednesday (Carnival), Good Friday, May 1 (Labor Day), May 25 (First Argentine Government), June 10 (National Sovereignty Day), June 20 (Flag Day), July 9 (Independence Day), August 17 (anniversary of the death of General San Martín), October 12 (Día de la Raza), December 8 (Immaculate Conception Day), and December 25 (Christmas). Most tourist businesses and restaurants, however, will remain open during all holidays except Christmas and New Year's. Christmas itself is also celebrated on December 24, and many places will be closed that day.

Calendar of Events

A few holidays and festivals are worth planning your trip around. The best source of information about these events is your local Argentina tourism office (see "Recommended U.S.-Based Operators," below). The **Buenos Aires Tourism Office** (© **11/4313-0187;** www. bue.gov.ar) also provides information on all of these events. For an exhaustive list of events beyond those included in this chapter, check **http://events.frommers.com**, where you'll find a searchable, up-to-the-minute roster of what's happening in cities all over the world.

FEBRUARY

Fiesta de las Murgas. Buenos Aires's version of Carnaval or Mardi Gras is not quite as colorful as Rio de Janeiro's but is still a lot of fun. Various neighborhoods have costumed street band competitions full of loud music and dancing. Every weekend in February.

Chinese Lunar New Year. Belgrano's Chinatown is small, but the dragon-blessing parade is a fun, intimate event that kids and adults are certain to enjoy. Beware of irresponsible firecracker users. The actual date of this holiday follows a lunar calendar. First Sunday of February.

Buenos Aires Fashion Week. Fashionistas will certainly enjoy this event. Design is important in the city, the first ever designated by UNESCO as a world design capital. Visit **www.bafweek.com** for more information. Last week of February.

APRIL

Feria del Libro (Book Festival). This is one of the world's largest book festivals. Visit **www.el-libro.org.ar** for exact dates and the event schedule or call ✆ **11/4370-0600.** Late April to early May.

JULY

Buenos Aires Querible. Literally "lovable Buenos Aires," this event celebrates the history and neighborhoods of the city, with events spread throughout town. Visit **www.buenosairesquerible.gov.ar** for more information. Mid-July.

Exposicion Rural. Gaucho and *estancia* culture invades the urban center during this livestock and agricultural show. It's held in La Rural, an exposition center built expressly for the event. It also stars artisanal food purveyors. Visit **www.exposicionrural.com.ar** for more information. Late July.

AUGUST

Buenos Aires Fashion Week. In August, you'll find the fashionistas gathering once again, this time for the spring and summer collections. Visit **www.bafweek.com** for more information. Late August.

SEPTEMBER

Festival Internacional de Buenos Aires. Theater lovers should try to visit during this 2-week event of international theater programs. Visit **www.festivaldeteatroba.gov.ar** or call ✆ **11/4374-2829** for more information. September or October.

OCTOBER

World Tango Festival. This celebration consists of a number of events across the city but is concentrated in the neighborhood of San Telmo. See **www.mundialdetango.gov.ar** for more information and exact dates. Early to mid-October.

NOVEMBER

National Gay Pride Parade. The parade route is along Avenida de Mayo. Visit the Comunidad Homosexual de Argentina website at **www.cha.org.ar** for updated information. **Diversa,** the national gay and lesbian film festival, usually occurs around this time. Check **www.diversa.com.ar** for the schedule. First Saturday in November.

Argentine Open Polo Championships. The world's biggest polo event, the **Argentine Open Polo Championships,** is held at the polo grounds in Palermo, near the Las Cañitas neighborhood. It attracts moneyed crowds from around the world, who get to mingle with visiting British royalty. Call the Argentine Polo Association (✆ **11/4343-0972**) for more details. Late November to early December.

DECEMBER

El Día Nacional de Tango. Always on December 11, this festival celebrates the birth of Carlos Gardel, the world's most famous tango crooner. Avenida 9 de Julio and Avenida de Mayo are blocked off for live tango concerts and tango dancing in the street. This is Buenos Aires at its most magical.

Midnight Mass on Christmas Eve (Noche Buena). Though Argentina has little in the way of Christmas rituals, the mass at the Catedral Metropolitana (p. 103) is a beautiful spectacle. It is usually held at 10pm on Christmas Eve. In Argentina, December 24 is a more important day than December 25, and family dinners are held on Christmas Eve rather than Christmas Day.

RESPONSIBLE TRAVEL

Sustainability is still catching on in Buenos Aires; for a long time, the most widespread attempts at responsible tourism in the city were hotels' requests that visitors reuse towels and sheets. Since 2009, however, Buenos Aires has begun developing a network of bicycle paths, including many in tourist areas, particularly in the **Ecological Reserve** (p. 118). Biking is a convenient, enjoyable way of seeing the city without drastically increasing your carbon footprint. See "Bike Tours" (p. 24).

The company **Travel Native** (© 11/15-4419-3467; www.travelnative.com) offers tours as well as a Web portal of information on Argentine hotels and companies that use environmentally conscious methods of operation. It's run by French expat Olivier Dufeu, who recommends for instance that travelers to Argentina dedicate more time to their trip and not fly vast distances across the country using jets, using other means of transit or staying in one place. Also visit **www.reddeturismoresponsable.org** for lists of responsible operators and companies throughout Argentina, or see **www.frommers.com/planning** for more tips on responsible travel.

TOURS

Recommended U.S.-Based Operators

The following U.S.-based tour companies offer solid, well-organized tours in various price categories based on years of experience. All can arrange tours of Buenos Aires, the surroundings, and other parts of Argentina and South America.

Borello Travel & Tours, 7 Park Ave., Ste. 21, New York, NY 10016 (© 800/405-3072 or 212/686-4911; www.borellotravel.com; info@borellotravel.com), is a New York–based travel firm specializing in upscale travel. The owner, Sandra Borello, has run the company for nearly 20 years and is a native of Buenos Aires. They also have an office in Buenos Aires, at Perú (9 de Julio) 359 (© 11/5031-1988). **Travel Dynamics International,** 132 E. 70th St., New York, NY 10021 (© 800/257-5767 or 212/517-0076; www.traveldynamicsinternational.com), is a luxury cruise operator that specializes in educational enrichment programs aboard small cruise ships. TDI voyages include expert guided land tours and onboard lectures by distinguished scholars and guests. **Limitless Argentina,** 135 Willow St., #907, Brooklyn, NY 11201 (© 202/536-5812; www.limitlessargentina.com), is a boutique travel company dedicated to designing authentic, personalized journeys for the discerning traveler. Itineraries include fine arts, regional culture and history, food and wine, the great outdoors, and shopping. The company earned the distinction of top travel specialist for Argentina 2006 from Condé Nast's *Traveler* magazine.

Recommended Buenos Aires–Based Operators

The following companies are all excellent and have English-speaking staff members. All can also arrange trips to other parts of Argentina and the rest of South America.

Say Hueque Tourism, Viamonte 749, Office 601 (© 11/5199-2517, -2518, -2519, or -2520; www.sayhueque.com) organizes various themed city tours, adventure tours to the Tigre Delta, and longer trips to Patagonia and Iguazú that focus on remote, often overlooked destinations. **Euro Tur,** Viamonte 486, 1053 Buenos Aires (© 11/4312-6077; www.eurotur.com), one of the largest and oldest travel companies in Argentina, specializes in inbound travel but can also accommodate travelers directly in Buenos Aires, arranging city tours as well as trips throughout South America. **Les Amis,** Maipú 1270, 1005 Buenos Aires (✆ **11/4314-0500;** www. lesamis.com.ar), is another large Argentine tour company with offices throughout Buenos Aires and Argentina. **South America Travel Advisor** (✆ **11/5275-5280** or 11/15-3232-8600 [cell] in Buenos Aires and 646/233-1152 in the U.S. and Canada; www.southamericanadvisor.com; info@southamericanadvisor.com) is a travel advisor for Argentina, Brazil, Uruguay, Chile, and Peru. For a flat fee, travelers can contact them with a tentative plan and budget, and they will suggest customized itineraries. They also run cuisine and restaurant tours of Buenos Aires.

Private Tour Guides

You can hire guides through your hotel, any travel agency, or **AGUITBA** (Asociación de Guías de Turismo de Buenos Aires), Carlos Pellegrini (9 de Julio) 833 (✆ **11/4322-2557;** aguitba@sion.com), a professional society of tour guides. Its offices are open Monday to Friday from 1 to 6pm. I also recommend private guides **Marta Pasquali** (✆ **11/15-4421-2486;** marpas@uolsinectis.com.ar), **Monica Varela** (✆ **11/15-4407-0268;** monyliv@hotmail.com or varmonica@gmail.com), **Rubén Forace** (✆ **11/15-4410-8234** [cell] or 11/4866-6193; rudarifo@yahoo.com.ar), and **Francisco Martoccia** (✆ **011/4803-0950;** franmarto@hotmail.com).

Specialized Tours of Buenos Aires

ACADEMIC TRIPS & LANGUAGE CLASSES

Argentina I.L.E.E., Callao 339 (3rd floor at Sarmiento; ✆ **11/4782-7173;** www.argentinailee.com) opened in 1986 and offers a cultural immersion program. They can arrange housing with families for students who attend their classes. All teachers have a master's degree in education or literature from the University of Buenos Aires. They also offer tango classes and other local outings.

Español Andando (✆ **11/5278-9886;** www.espanol-andando.com) uses a cultural immersion program in a 4-day crash course and fights what it calls "boring" ways to learn Spanish. Rather than a classroom, students travel around Buenos Aires with professors to also use their new language skills in real situations. The school doesn't have an office for drop-by visits, but the first class meetings are at a cafe in San Telmo. **World Class Language School,** Ciudad De La Paz 2476, 1A (at Monroe, in Belgrano; ✆ **11/4781-5891;** www.wclass.com.ar) is a great choice whether you know Spanish well or not at all; you'll find several levels of classes with this school. The school is open to tourists and also has many business clients.

ART TOURS

GraffitiMundo (✆ **11/15-3683-3219** [cell]; www.graffitimundo.com) was among the first of the street art tours, with a focus on the Palermo district. They offer a variety of tour themes and locations, looking at artists from Jazz to PumPum and many others.

Juanale (✆ **11/15-3120-9255** [cell]; www.juanele.me) runs art tours focusing on young, emerging contemporary galleries, street art, history, and culture, particularly in San Telmo. Tours depart Tuesday and Thursday 3pm from Balcarce 1150 (Centro Cultural de España Buenos Aires) and run for a few hours. Other times can be arranged.

BIKE TOURS

Buenos Aires Urban Biking (© **11/4568-4321** or 11/15-5165-9343 [cell]; www. urbanbiking.com) has four different biking themes, including Buenos Aires by night and the Tigre Delta region. Trip lengths vary from half-days to full 8-hour days. Equipment is provided. The organization also operates in La Plata, capital of the Buenos Aires province. Guides speak English, Spanish, French, and Portuguese.

La Bicicleta Naranja (© **11/4362-1104**; www.labicicletanaranja.com.ar) has two offices and four route formats. One begins in San Telmo and looks at the origins of the city in its southern section; another focuses on the northern area, another on the Palermo park system, and a fourth, called "Aristocratic Buenos Aires," is a comprehensive tour of Recoleta.

Lan and Kramer Bike Tours (© **11/4311-5199**; www.biketours.com.ar) leads group tours, which generally meet and start their trips in Plaza San Martín. There are several tour routes, some of which pass through the Ecological Reserve along the Puerto Madero waterfront. Rates vary, depending on the length of the itinerary.

BOAT TOURS

Buenos Aires Boats, La Boca Docks, at the base of Caminito (© **11/4303-1616**; www.bueboats.com), leaves four times daily from the port in La Boca near where Caminito hits the waterfront. Trips last about 1½ hours and go from La Boca to the Río de la Plata. Tours cost about $4 for adults, $2.50 for seniors and children, and are free for children under 3. Group discounts are available. Only cash is accepted.

Puro Remo Boats and Kayaks (© **11/15-6397-3545** [cell] or 11/15-3218-6540 [cell]; www.puroremo.com.ar) leaves from the Puerto Madero Yacht Club and offers various tours in which you do all the paddling. Tours vary in length, price, and required skill. Only cash is accepted.

Sturla Viajes (© **11/4314-8555**; www.sturlaviajes.com.ar) offers boat trips between Puerto Madero and Tigre, a river resort near Buenos Aires. Trips by boat allow for a beautiful daytime view of Buenos Aires's waterfront, and a spectacular view of the waterfront by night.

In addition, La Boca also has small **ferry boats** at the base of the now-closed Puente N. Avellaneda (that big rusty bridge locals insist is a UNESCO heritage site, but is not). These are the boats used by locals to cross the river to and from Buenos Aires from the very poor suburbs in Avellaneda. Costing only a peso, they are fun to ride, but I suggest crossing and coming back instead of exploring the other side of the river, because Avellaneda is considered dangerous if you don't know it well. Few tourists take these boats, so you will be especially welcomed onboard by locals who rarely meet foreigners. Though it seems far-fetched considering the setting, some locals half-jokingly call these boats the *La Boca Gondolas*. Whatever you do, do not touch the heavily polluted water full of industrial waste and sewage. Only cash is accepted.

BUS TOURS

Travel Line (© **11/4393-9000**; www.travelline.com.ar) offers more than 20 tours with various themes in Buenos Aires and its suburbs. Participants are picked up at their hotels and tours can last anywhere from 4 hours up to a full day; some include meals. Themes include Eva Perón, tango, gaucho culture (including trips to *estancias*), the city by night, and the Tigre Delta, among others.

Buenos Aires Bus, Av. Roque Sáenz Peña 846, 10th floor (© **11/5239-5160**; www.buenosairesbus.com), inaugurated in May 2009, is a private tour bus system with 12 designated stops that uses the Hop-On-Hop-Off method. Tickets range from

$18 to $23, with various discounts, and can be purchased on the bright yellow and black buses, at the stops, in their office, online, and at city tourism kiosks. Information about sites near the stops is provided in English, and the 24-hour or 48-hour bus passes are good for unlimited rides.

CUSTOMIZED & INDIVIDUAL TOURS

BA Local (✆ 11/15-4870-5506 [cell]; www.balocal.com) is run by Christina Wiseman, a young, glamorous American expat from New York, who is also the force behind the *puerta cerrada* restaurant **Cocina Sunae** (p. 87). Her tours range from off-the-beaten-path neighborhoods to art galleries, shopping, and other themes. They are particularly good for seeing the city from a young woman's perspective.

CiceroneBA Tours (✆ 11/15-5654-9032 [cell]; www.cicereneba.com.ar) is run by Buenos Aires native Marcello Mansilla. He offers highly customized and individualized tours on many themes, including gay tourism.

Diva Tours/Bitch Tours (✆ 11/15-6157-3248 [cell]; www.bitchtours.blogspot. com) are run by sassy Buenos Aires–born Agustina Menendez, who also works as an actress and dancer. She'll take you on tours with a twist, to sites from the Casa Rosada to a slaughterhouse.

DISABLED, HANDICAPPED & LOW-MOBILITY TOURS

BA Cultural Concierge (✆ 11/4777-0581 or 11/15-5457-2035 [cell]; www. BACulturalConcierge.com) is run by Madi Lang, an American from Bethesda, Maryland. She works with those who are low-mobility, are disabled, or have other issues making travel difficult. Easily reachable by cell or Blackberry, she can order special car services, breathing apparatuses, and additional services.

TTS Viajes Independent Living Tourism Division (✆ 11/5941-9694 or 11/15-5646-6269 [cell]; www.ttsviajes.com/viajes-turismo-con-discapacidad.php) is a division of TTS Viajes, overseen by travel specialist Nelida Barbeito, an Argentine native fluent in English. She can arrange all aspects of a trip, advising also on how accessible properties actually are, and assist with emergencies. She also runs a blog (www.nelidabarbeito.blogspot.com) on accessible travel.

DINING TOURS

Dine at Home Tours (✆ 11/4801-3182, 11/15-6051-9328 or 11/15-5564-9846 [all cells]; www.dineathome.com.ar) organize dinners for tourists in the homes or locals, and are a good way to get to meet English-speaking locals. Edward Goedhart started the tours, which clients can select depending on an occupation. So, for instance, if you're an architect and want to know a local architect, this is a way to do it. Book through an agent or directly with the organization.

See also our note on *puertas cerradas,* private dining at chefs' homes (p. 87).

FOOD & WINE TRIPS

The best wine tours in Argentina are in the Mendoza winegrowing region, in the western part of the country near the Andes. For wine tastings in Buenos Aires, see "Wine Tasting" in chapter 5 (p. 66). In addition, virtually all tour companies we list above can help organize wine tastings or hire a guide to take you to specialized restaurants. In chapter 5, we also list *puertas cerradas,* in which groups dine at the home of a chef (p. 87). Most chefs who run *puertas cerradas* will also offer cooking classes in their homes. In addition, the restaurant **Pampa Picante** (p. 87) runs an *asado* cooking class, where you can learn to cook Argentine beef like a native.

FREE BUENOS AIRES CITY TOURISM OFFICE TOURS

The **Buenos Aires City Tourism Office** (© 11/4114-5734 or 11/4114-5791 for tours) offers an excellent array of free city tours. Participants are taken through the city on buses or meet at a designated point and walk through a neighborhood as a guide explains the highlights. Most of the tours are conducted in Spanish; however, a few are in Spanish and English. The possibility of an English-speaking guide being on hand can change at the last minute, but I encourage you to sign up for a tour anyway and see what happens. You can always leave if the tour ends up being in a language you don't understand, or someone will more than likely be able to translate.

Ask for information about tours at the many **Visitor Information** kiosks (p. 270). You can also ask for self-guided tour maps at these kiosks, or call the tourism office during its hours, Monday to Friday 10am to 4pm. The direct number for the tour guides division is © **11/4114-5791.** Tours are on a space-available basis, so you'll have to register for them.

Another interesting, free, self-guided city tour service offered by the Buenos Aires City Tourism Office is the **Cellular Telephone Tours.** Ask for the brochure *Audio Guía Móvil* (currently only available in Spanish). It details itineraries and provides a number that you can call to hear information (in either English or Spanish) about the various attractions. While this information service is free, don't forget that you will be charged for cellphone usage, making the cost of using this service possibly significant. Still, the system's complete flexibility and ability to allow you to hear recordings from the past certainly makes this different from any other tour option out there.

BA Free Tour (© 11/15/6395-3000; www.bafreetour.com) offers a variety of 2- to 3-hour tours. The individuals who provide the tours make their living on tips. The company can also arrange private tours.

GAY TOURS

BueGay (© 11/4805-1401 or 11/15-4184-8290 [cell]; www.buegay.com.ar), run by Alfredo Ferrerya, is one of the oldest gay travel companies in Argentina, with tours in Spanish and English. They can arrange all aspects of your trip to Buenos Aires and other parts of Argentina, as well as day tours.

Carlos Melia Travel (© 11/15-5760-6959 [cell] in Argentina and 347/944-0026 in the U.S. and Canada; www.carlosmelia.com), run by Carlos Melia, specializes in luxury gay travel and can arrange all aspects of your trip to Buenos Aires and other parts of Argentina, as well as day tours. Carlos has the distinction of having been Mr. Gay Argentina, and Mr. Gay World.

Duques del Plata (© 11/3221-2629 or 11/15-6144-9639 [cell]; www.duques delplata.com), run by Damian Gatto, offers full-service tourism booking and various city tours, from wine tasting to tango.

Mister Papi Tours (© 11/4372-4578 or 11/15-5995-8531 [cell]; www.mister papi.com.ar), run by Fabian Fuentes, offers tours in Spanish and English. He only does them for individuals or very small groups of friends, in a combination of walking, taxi, or rent-a-car, depending on what people want.

The **Royal Family Argentina** (© 11/5353-2047; www.theroyalfamily.com.ar), run by Dutchman Erik Hovenga, offers a variety of tours, along with full service tour booking, and a language school catering to gay and lesbian and other travelers. He also runs **PinkPoint,** Lavalle 669 (© 11/5353-2046; www.pinkpointbuenosaires. com), a private gay tourism information center.

Gay travel agencies that organize trips to Buenos Aires include San Francisco–based **Now, Voyager** (© 800/255-6951; www.nowvoyager.com); Chicago-based **Zoom Vacations** (© 866/966-6822; www.zoomvacations.com); New York–based **Steele Travel** (© 646/688-2274; www.steeletravel.com) and California-based **David Travel** (© 949/723-0699; www.davidtravel.com).

HORSEBACK RIDING TOURS

Caballos a la Par (Lima [9 de Julio] 549, 2E; © 11/4384-7013; www.caballosala par.com) organizes horseback riding tours in Parque Provincial Pereyra Iraola, about half an hour from Buenos Aires, allowing a quick half-day trip. They work with various tour companies, including **Tangol Tours** (© 11/4312-7276; www.tangol.com). See also the section on San Antonio de Areco and the Pampas in chapter 10 (p. 243).

JEWISH-THEMED TOURS

TravelJewish (© 877/TANGO-SI [826-4674] in the U.S. or 11/5258-0774 in Buenos Aires; www.traveljewish.com; info@traveljewish.com) will plan trips from beginning to end, including flights, high-end hotels, adventure kayaking, and a day in Tigre, or simply Jewish-themed day tours. They also organize South American trips and tango and Spanish instruction.

Susana Alter (© 11/15-3214-4432 [cell] or 11/4555-7297; altersusana@ yahoo.com.ar or altersusana@gmail.com), a native of Argentina who spent several years in Israel, is a private tour guide who conducts Jewish-themed and other tours for individuals and groups. She speaks several languages, and offers tours in English, Spanish, and German.

SHOPPING TOURS

Al TunTunno Tours (© 11/15-4197-2381 [cell] or 11/4806-7115; www.altun tunno.com) is run by Argentine natives Julieta Caracoche and Sofia Lanusse. They'll take you shopping for anything, especially shoes.

SPANISH-LANGUAGE TOURS

While **Conocer Buenos Aires** (© 11/15-5565-0348 [cell]; www.conocerbue. com.ar) only offers tours in Spanish, its in-depth themes are not found in most English-language tours. They cover major cultural figures in Argentina, immigration, off-the-beaten-path neighborhoods where tourists rarely venture, and other themes, using a combination of walking and minibuses, depending on the tour. Check the website for new tours, which are definitely worth taking if you understand Spanish.

SPORTS TOURS

Go Football Tours (© 11/4816-2681 or 11/15-4405-9526 [cell]; www.gofootball. com.ar) will help you purchase tickets to various sporting events (not just football) and provide round-trip transportation between your hotel and the stadium. Visit their website to find out which games fit into your travel schedule. Visa and cash are accepted. Prices vary, beginning at about $60, including tickets and transportation.

Argentine Golf (© 11/15-6892 9451 or 877/753-3155 from the U.S.; www. argentinegolf.com.ar) is perfect for busy executives who don't have the time to plan a day of golf but want to squeeze in a few holes before leaving Buenos Aires. This company will pick you up, take you to a local golf course, provide lunch, and then bring you back to your hotel.

TANGO TOURS

There are dozens of tours for people interested in tango here in Buenos Aires, the city where it all began. For more information, see "Tango Tours" in chapter 9, p. 204.

VOLUNTEER TOURISM

Voluntario Global (© 11/15-6206-9639 [cell]; www.voluntarioglobal.org.ar) is an association that promotes responsible tourism. It offers visitors a chance to see how the other half lives, with trips to *villas miserias,* or slums, surrounding Buenos Aires, where you work alongside nongovernmental agents helping the poor. In some cases, you see where the *cartoneros,* or garbage pickers, live—the ones you've avoided during your trip—and can better understand their lives.

WALKING TOURS

See chapter 7 for walking tours. See "Free Buenos Aires City Tourism Office Tours," above, for a description of walking tours provided by the Buenos Aires Tourist Office.

Buenos Tours (© 11/3221-1048; www.buenostours.com) offers various walking tours, calling themselves "The Private Walking Tour Specialists in Buenos Aires." Tours range from downtown walking tours to barhopping adventures.

IN VIP Visit BA (© 11/15-5063-6602 [cell]; www.invisitba.4t.com) also offers customized tours, some of which are strictly walking, others of which are bus-and-walking combinations. Prices vary by itinerary, but can range from $20 to $40 or more per person, depending on the group size and itinerary.

BUENOS AIRES NEIGHBORHOODS & ITINERARIES

After a few days, most tourists wish they could spend a lifetime in Buenos Aires. Of course, that's not realistic for most people! Here, we highlight the most important neighborhoods to help you plan your trip, no matter the length. Then we suggest a 5-day itinerary, which you can easily tailor for a longer or shorter stay.

Neighborhoods in Brief

Buenos Aires is an enormous metropolis, with over 12 million inhabitants in the city and its suburbs. Most of what you'll be interested in, however, is in a compact area near the center of the city's historic core, around Plaza de Mayo. Below I list the neighborhoods you'll most likely see as a tourist, including the general boundaries of each. Keep in mind, though, that even in Buenos Aires, some people and maps call the same areas by different names, so use these descriptions only as a general guide. For more detailed descriptions, see "Neighborhoods Worth a Visit," p. 126.

Plaza de Mayo Area This is not so much a district as the historical and political heart of Buenos Aires, laid out by Don Juan de Garay in 1580 during the second founding of the city. The plaza is surrounded by government buildings and the **Catedral Metropolitana** (p. 103), which dates back to the late colonial era. The plaza's defining feature is the **Casa Rosada** (**Presidential Palace;** p. 99), home to Evita's famous balcony. This plaza is the main site of political demonstrations and a shelter area for the homeless and the *piqueteros* (demonstrators) who often camp out here at night. The most important ongoing demonstration is that of the **Madres de Plaza de Mayo** (p. 108), which occurs every Thursday at 3:30pm and is a must-see for understanding the country's tragic history.

Puerto Madero Once a dilapidated port, the area northeast of Plaza de Mayo is now filled with an abundance of restaurants in renovated warehouses. Offices, high-rise residences, and luxury hotels are gradually popping up as well. The district can feel cold and antiseptic by day because of its vast expanses and new construction, so you might want to come at sunset when the water in the port glows a fiery red and the city skyline is silhouetted. The closest *subte* stop is Alem, on the B line, and a new tourist train runs the length of Puerto Madero, but walking is generally the fastest means of getting around.

Microcentro This is Buenos Aires's busy downtown core, home to many of the hotels, banks, and services that make the city tick. The area's defining feature is the pedestrianized **Calle Florida,** which runs from Avenida de Mayo to **Plaza San Martín.** The plaza provides a restful respite from this very compact center. On its edge sits **Retiro Station,** once among the most important points of entry into Buenos Aires from the provinces.

Monserrat Sitting between San Telmo and the Plaza de Mayo, this area is often grouped with San Telmo, though it's a proper district of its own. It's home to some of the city's oldest churches, and many government buildings have been constructed here as well. Some are beautiful old Beaux Arts structures; others, built in the mid–20th century, exemplify South American Fascist architecture, with their smooth, massive walls of dark polished marble and granite and heavy, pharaonic bronze doors. Many unions have headquarters here so they can more easily speak with government officials. To some Porteños, this neighborhood extends up the historic **Avenida de Mayo** toward Congreso; others call this area **San Cristóbal.** Parts of Monserrat are desolate and possibly dangerous at night.

San Telmo If you think of tango, romance, and a certain unexpressed sensual sadness when you think of Buenos Aires, then you're thinking of San Telmo. This is one of the city's oldest neighborhoods, once the home of the very wealthy until the 1877 outbreak of yellow fever caused many to flee to newly developing areas north of the city center. The heart of San Telmo is **Plaza Dorrego,** the city's second-oldest plaza (after the Plaza de Mayo). This neighborhood is my favorite, and I like it most at

sunset when the buildings glow gold and their ornamental tops become silhouetted against the sky. Many Porteños still think of the neighborhood as dangerous, but rapid gentrification has changed it drastically in recent years. Still, take caution at night, just as you should anywhere.

La Boca Historically, La Boca is Buenos Aires's Little Italy, the home of Italian immigrants who came to Buenos Aires in the late 19th and early 20th centuries. The focal point of La Boca is **El Caminito,** a pedestrianized roadway lined with buildings painted in brilliant colors, plaques and statues explaining neighborhood history, and stores selling souvenirs. La Boca is my least favorite neighborhood because it so overdoes its efforts to draw tourists that it has little authentic to offer. Be aware that the area is considered exceedingly dangerous at night. When the shops close up, you should head out. There is no convenient subway access to La Boca.

Barracas This emerging neighborhood in the south of Buenos Aires borders La Boca and San Telmo. For years, tourists visited only for its famous tango show hall **Señor Tango** (p. 201). The neighborhood has the reputation of being dangerous, though the recent influx of artists and young people due to rising housing prices in surrounding areas has caused gentrification. A number of the warehouses and barracks from which the neighborhood takes its name are being converted into luxury apartments and art centers. Businesses here often claim to be in San Telmo.

Recoleta The name of this neighborhood comes from an old Spanish word meaning "to remember." Its history dates to the late colonial period and the establishment of a convent where Recoleta Cemetery, Evita's final resting place, now sits. Once on the edge of Buenos Aires, Recoleta is now one of its most exclusive shopping and residential neighborhoods. Marble buildings reminiscent of Paris and green leafy streets characterize this area. **Avenida Alvear,** crowned by the city's most famous hotel, the **Alvear Palace,** is lined with luxurious showrooms (some in buildings that were

Buenos Aires at a Glance

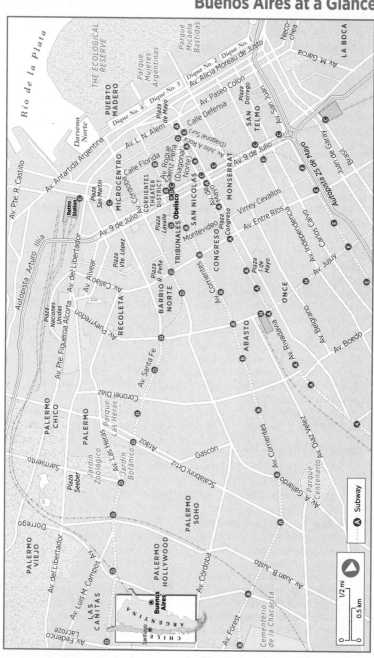

once the homes of the city's wealthiest residents) from the most impressive designers. There is no convenient subway access to this neighborhood.

Barrio Norte This neighborhood borders Recoleta, and many consider it to be part of Recoleta. However, while the two are physically similar, Barrio Norte is busier and more commercialized, with shops primarily aimed at a middle- and upper-middle-class clientele. If anyone ever describes to you a place allegedly in Recoleta but with convenient subway access, it's actually in this neighborhood. Most shops are located on **Avenida Santa Fe,** which is serviced by the D subway line. This area was historically home to much of the city's gay population and services, but that is changing over time as venues spread across the city, especially to San Telmo.

Palermo This broadly defined district actually includes a number of smaller neighborhoods: **Palermo** proper or **Alto Palermo,** home to the city's extensive park system; **Palermo Chico,** an exclusive neighborhood of elegant mansions located off of Avenida Alcorta; up-and-coming **Palermo Viejo,** encompassing **Palermo Soho** to the south and **Palermo Hollywood** to the north; and **Las Cañitas,** a trendy area of restaurants, bars, and shops next to the city's famous polo field. See "Palermo Neighborhoods," p. 127.

Congreso The western end of the Avenida de Mayo surrounds the massive Congreso building overlooking Plaza Congreso. Though the building and plaza are important and popular attractions, the neighborhood itself has a run-down feel. Things are beginning to change, however, and numerous hotels have opened in this area, though they are not as well known as those in some of the more glamorous parts of the city. To the north along Callao, you'll come across blocks of decaying marble and stucco neoclassical buildings that call to mind Buenos Aires's glory days and Argentina's desire to rise as a global power.

Corrientes Theater District The Obelisco at the intersection of Avenida Corrientes and Avenida 9 de Julio is the defining feature of this flashy neighborhood. Avenida Corrientes, widened in the 1930s on both sides of Avenida 9 de Julio, is lined with the city's most important theaters and movie palaces, Buenos Aires's answer to New York's Broadway. The world-famous **Teatro Colón** (p. 112) sits a block away. Though most of the action is at night, some theaters are worth wandering into during the day as well, in particular the **Teatro San Martín** (p. 189), which has ongoing exhibits. Starry-eyed hopefuls from the provinces still come to the area on their quest for fame, just as Evita once did (her first Buenos Aires apartment was in this district).

Abasto On first glance, this working- and middle-class neighborhood seems to offer little of interest to tourists. However, it's steeped in Buenos Aires history. This is where tango crooner Carlos Gardel grew up and lived as an adult. Vestiges of that time period include the **Abasto Shopping Center** (p. 167), once an open-air market, on Calle Corrientes, where Gardel sang to the vendors as a child and first became famous. The tango show palace **Esquina Carlos Gardel** (p. 200) was built over a bar he frequented, and his home on Calle Jean Jaures is now a museum (p. 122).

Once The name of this neighborhood is short for **Once de Septiembre,** taken from a train station that honors the death of Domingo Faustino Sarmiento, President of Argentina from 1868 to 1874. Once borders Abasto (see above) and has a similar history and feel. It is a historically Jewish neighborhood, and Calle Tucumán in particular still retains many Jewish businesses and kosher restaurants.

Tribunales The defining feature of this neighborhood is the **Argentine Supreme Court,** from which the area takes its name. This massive building, overlooking **Plaza Lavalle,** is not generally open to the public, but if you can sneak in, it's worth a look. For tourists, the most important feature of this neighborhood is what sits across the plaza, **Teatro Colón,** the city's supreme cultural center, also in the midst of a serious and terribly delayed overhaul.

Belgrano You'll probably be in Buenos Aires for a long time before you venture out to Belgrano, a well-to-do neighborhood in the north of the city, beyond Palermo. Its main feature is its *barrancas,* a series of hills in the center of the neighborhood and an enormous waterfront park,

which is an extension of those in Palermo. While tiny, this is where you'll find Buenos Aires's Chinatown, near the intersection of Arribeños and Mendoza, close to the Belgrano train station.

THE BEST OF BUENOS AIRES IN 5 DAYS

No length of time ever seems like enough in a city as wonderful as Buenos Aires. This itinerary takes you through 5 days in the capital—ideally a Wednesday to a Sunday. The route guides you through the best features of various neighborhoods. I've scheduled in plenty of downtime, too, in case you want to tango all night long and take it easy the following day (Buenos Aires, like New York, is a city that doesn't sleep).

1 Relaxing & Settling In

More than likely, you've arrived early in the morning after an all-night flight. Before you head out for the day, make reservations at **Cabaña Las Lilas** ★★★ (p. 66) for dinner tonight. Afterward, head to Calle Florida to check out the shops at **Galerías Pacífico** ★★★ (p. 168) and have a snack at **Il Gran Caffe** ★ (p. 72). Wander down to **Plaza de Mayo** ★★ (p. 104) and take a look at historic sites such as the **Cabildo** ★★★ (p. 99), Buenos Aires's original city hall, the **Catedral Metropolitana** ★★ (p. 103), and the **Casa Rosada** ★★★ (p. 99), with Evita's famous balcony. Head back to the hotel for a much-needed nap before heading out to Cabaña Las Lilas for dinner. Certainly you've admired the view of Puerto Madero from your table, so have a wander dockside.

2 Historical Buenos Aires

I recommend exploring the historic center of Buenos Aires with a professional guide, my favorite of which are listed in chapter 2 (see "Tours," p. 22). As they lead you through the historic center of Buenos Aires, past the **Plaza de Mayo** ★★ (p. 104) and the turn-of-the-20th-century marvel **Avenida de Mayo** to **Congreso,** they'll explain how centuries of history and culture are reflected in the streets of Buenos Aires. Ride the wooden trains of the **A line** *subte* ★★★ (p. 98) to station Avenida de Mayo. Have a coffee and *medialunas* at **Café Tortoni** ★★★ (p. 115), one of the city's most historic and scenic cafes, and try to catch the conversation of Buenos Aires locals discussing the latest issues. If it's a Thursday, return to Plaza de Mayo at 3:30pm for **Madres of Plaza de Mayo,** a weekly protest held by the mothers of the 30,000 young people who disappeared during the military regime between 1976 and 1982. Then head back to the hotel. In the evening, have dinner in the glorious gilded dining hall of **Palacio Español** ★★ (p. 72).

3 A Day in Recoleta

Sleep in and have a late breakfast at your hotel. Have your hotel make dinner reservations at **La Bourgogne** ★★★ (p. 76), a fine French restaurant in the **Alvear Palace Hotel** ★★★ (p. 48). Then head to **Recoleta Cemetery** ★★★ (p. 111)

Buenos Aires in 5 Days

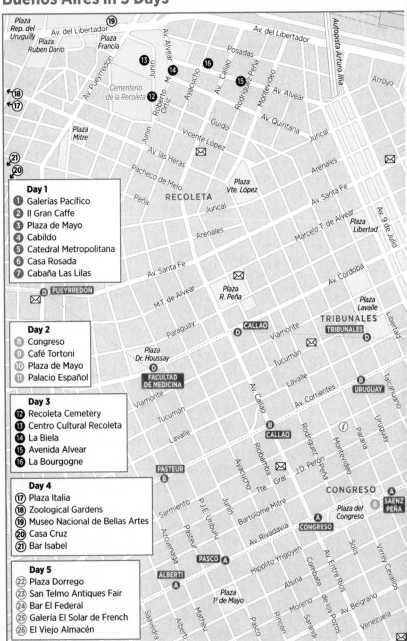

Day 1
1. Galerías Pacífico
2. Il Gran Caffe
3. Plaza de Mayo
4. Cabildo
5. Catedral Metropolitana
6. Casa Rosada
7. Cabaña Las Lilas

Day 2
8. Congreso
9. Café Tortoni
10. Plaza de Mayo
11. Palacio Español

Day 3
12. Recoleta Cemetery
13. Centro Cultural Recoleta
14. La Biela
15. Avenida Alvear
16. La Bourgogne

Day 4
17. Plaza Italia
18. Zoological Gardens
19. Museo Nacional de Bellas Artes
20. Casa Cruz
21. Bar Isabel

Day 5
22. Plaza Dorrego
23. San Telmo Antiques Fair
24. Bar El Federal
25. Galería El Solar de French
26. El Viejo Almacén

to pay homage to the most famous tomb in the city, Evita's. Be sure to wander around and see many of the other tombs, all glorious works of art. Around the corner from the cemetery, head to the **Centro Cultural Recoleta** ★★ (p. 188) and check out the newest art exhibit. If you've brought the kids along or you're feeling young at heart, don't forget to visit the children's section with its interactive science exhibits. Afterward, head across Plaza Francia and grab a coffee at **La Biela** ★★★ (p. 78), one of the most famous cafes in the city. After this much-needed break, it's time to do some shopping along Avenida Alvear. Stop into such stores as **Polo Ralph Lauren** (p. 177), built into a grand mansion. If you've been shopping for hours, you're just in time for your reservation at La Bourgogne.

4 Palermo

After breakfast, head to Plaza Italia and take a walk around, enjoying the contrast of the green trees against the white-marble buildings lining this part of Avenida Santa Fe. Head to the **Zoological Gardens** ★★★ (p. 133) and check out the animals, after buying special food to feed them. Afterward, wander the parks along Avenida Libertador, heading toward **Museo Nacional de Bellas Artes** ★★ (p. 124). Swing by the hotel, freshen up, and head out again for dinner at **Casa Cruz** ★★ (p. 82), in Palermo Viejo, one of the city's best places to be seen on a night out. Then visit **Bar Isabel** ★ (p. 193) next door, a watering hole popular among models.

5 San Telmo & Tango

Head to **Plaza Dorrego** ★★ (p. 105) for the Sunday **San Telmo Antiques Fair** ★★ (p. 163), one of the most enjoyable highlights of Buenos Aires. In this open-air bazaar, you can buy small antiques and souvenirs to bring home, while watching live tango performances. (Keep an eye on your pockets while you watch.) Then grab a late lunch at the atmospheric **Bar El Federal** ★★ (p. 74). Head up **Calle Defensa** to take a look at more antiques in the numerous shops lining the street, such as **Galería El Solar de French** (p. 170). Head back to the hotel and freshen up. You're having dinner tonight at **El Viejo Almacén** (p. 200). Watching their show is a great way to end your 5-day stay in Buenos Aires.

WHERE TO STAY

You love Buenos Aires and so does everyone else. Inflation and the massive influx of tourists to the city have made hotel bargains hard to find. Most hotel prices have bounced back to what they were before the peso crisis or even climbed higher. Still, bargains can be found, especially at off-the-beaten-path hotels, and at locally owned rather than international hotel chains. Hotels often fill up in high season, so you should book ahead, even if only for your first night or two. Then, if you're not happy, you can change accommodations once you're on the ground.

4

Most four- and five-star hotels in Buenos Aires provide in-room safes, 24-hour room service, cable TV, direct-dial phones with voice mail, in-room modem access or Wi-Fi, and many other amenities. The competition between hotels on this level can be intense, so they renovate and add amenities often. Many also have superb health clubs, pools, and spas. Even if you are on a budget, I recommend splurging for 1 or 2 nights if you find a five-star property you really like.

If you're trying to save money, you will need to compromise, as not all two- and three-star hotels have the above-mentioned amenities (though air-conditioning and even lobby-based Wi-Fi access have become virtually standard in hotels throughout Buenos Aires, regardless of rating). At less expensive hotels, ask to see a few rooms to help you choose the best option available. Many recently renovated hotels have a lot of internal variation, with huge and small rooms sometimes going for the same price.

Local hotels, especially if they are family run, have a certain charm that is rarely rivaled by four- and five-star properties. Be aware, however, that while many people in Buenos Aires's travel industry speak English, fewer will at the less expensive or family-run hotels. While rooms in these hotels might not have certain amenities, such as hair dryers, irons, or coffeemakers, you can usually request them at the concierge. Safes, too, are often kept at the front desk. Always ask for a receipt when leaving valuable items at the front desk (or at least find out the name of the person who locked them), and whether keys for access are only available during certain hours of the day.

Hostels offer individual spots in shared bunk-bed-filled rooms and are usually booked by the young, budget-minded, and adventurous. However, some also have private rooms with attached bathrooms, so ask before you decide a hostel isn't for you. All of the hostels listed in this chapter provide sheets and towels and have 24-hour access, with no shutout periods.

Choosing a location is a matter of deciding what you want out of your Buenos Aires vacation. In this chapter, I have given a brief description of each neighborhood in which I've listed hotels. For a more thorough discussion of neighborhoods, see "Neighborhoods in Brief" in chapter 3.

Prices listed below are rack rates in high season and include the 21% tax levied on hotel rooms countrywide. Discounts are almost always available on weekends at business-oriented hotels and during low season at all hotels, and may even be available during high season in some cases. Web packages and specials can also be found on various hotel websites. Check **www.priceline.com** or Spanish-language **www.despegar.com** for bargains, and always ask hotels if there is a better rate than the first offered, or if your AAA card, student ID, or other discounts might apply. Most hotels offer valet parking for an additional fee or can recommend self-parking facilities close by. You should avoid parking on the street long-term. Few hotels have tour desks, but all concierges and front desks can arrange tours, offer advice, and rent cars, bicycles, and other things you might need.

I've given exact prices for hotels and placed them within general price categories by neighborhood. **Very Expensive** refers to hotels costing $400 or more per night. Keep in mind that some hotels in this category do not serve free breakfasts, which can increase your costs even more. **Expensive** hotels go for roughly $250 to $399 per night. **Moderate** hotels run from about $100 to $249 per night. **Inexpensive** hotels are $99 per night and less; this category also includes hostels, which may charge as little as $12 per night for a bed. Quality and offerings vary considerably in this price category.

For long-term stays, I have also listed apartment rental services. Prices will vary according to company, location, and length of stay, but this is generally a cheaper option than staying in a hotel.

PUERTO MADERO

Puerto Madero is home to some of the more expensive hotels in Buenos Aires. With its new construction and wide expanses, it feels somehow isolated from the rest of the city. The hotels in this neighborhood are near the restaurants of Puerto Madero's historic dock district, so you'll never want for places to dine at night. The sunset in Puerto Madero is a magnificent sight: The water in the port turns a fiery red and the city's skyline is magically silhouetted, adding a touch of romance to an area that by day can seem clinical and desolate. A drawback is that the neighborhood lacks good *subte* access—Alem on the B Line is the only metro stop close by—so taxis are the most convenient means of getting around. For a map of the hotels listed in this section, see the "Hotels in Central Buenos Aires" map on p. 40.

Very Expensive

Faena Hotel and Universe ★★★   The Faena opened to much fanfare among fashionistas in 2004, with its Philippe Starck design and handsome owner Alan Faena. The hotel, built into El Porteño, a 1902 grain silo, feels like a resort within the city. In public spaces, decayed Edwardian elegance meets country kitsch—tin metal sheeting, peeling paint, and unicorn wall ornaments. Oversized rooms have white Empire-style furnishings and cut-glass mirrors reminiscent of colonial Mexico, and each has a home entertainment center. Rooms facing the city skyline have incredible vistas; others overlook the nearby Ecological Reserve. The spa is spacious and unique, using the round silos to great effect, with a Turkish-style *hammam* bath and a stone Incan-style sauna shaped like an igloo.

Martha Salotti 445 (at Av. Juana Manso), 1107 Buenos Aires. www.faenahotelanduniverse.com. ✆ **11/4010-9000.** Fax 11/4010-9001. 103 units, including 14 suites and 20 apts of varying size, space, and price. From $514 double; from $841 suite. Rates include continental breakfast. AE, MC, V. Parking $24. No metro access. **Amenities:** 3 restaurants; 3 bars; large health club; outdoor heated pool; room service; large sauna w/unique elements; spa w/extensive treatments. *In room:* A/C, home theater TV, high-speed Internet, minibar, individualized bath treatments, Wi-Fi.

Hilton Buenos Aires ★★   The Hilton opened in mid-2000 as the first major hotel and convention center in Puerto Madero. Within easy walking distance of some of the best restaurants in Buenos Aires, it's an excellent choice for steak and seafood connoisseurs. The strikingly contemporary hotel—a sleek silver block hoisted on stilts—features a seven-story atrium with more than 400 well-equipped guest rooms. Spacious rooms offer multiple phone lines, walk-in closets, and bathrooms with separate showers and tubs. Those staying on the executive floors receive complimentary breakfast and have access to a private concierge. The lobby restaurant, **El Faro**, serves California cuisine with a focus on seafood. The hotel has the largest in-hotel convention center in the city.

Av. Macacha Güemes 351 (at Malecón Pierina Dealessi), 1106 Buenos Aires. www.buenos.hilton.com. ✆ **800/445-8667** in the U.S. or 11/4891-0000. Fax 11/4891-0001. 418 units. From $329 double; from $409 suite. AE, DC, MC, V. Parking $24. No metro access. **Amenities:** Restaurant; bar; babysitting; concierge; modern gym facility w/open-air pool and a service of light snacks and beverages; room service. *In room:* TV, minibar, Wi-Fi.

MICROCENTRO

The Microcentro is an ideal place to stay if you want to be close to Buenos Aires's shopping, and because of the many *subte* lines in this area. Theater buffs will also appreciate this location because most performance spaces, including Teatro Colón, are within walking distance. Many local travel agencies seem to cluster in the vicinity, which can be convenient if you want to make last-minute changes to your itinerary. Low-cost Internet and telephone centers are everywhere, too. If you arrive in Buenos Aires without any reservations, come to this neighborhood; the density of hotels means you won't have to wander long before finding something. For a map of the hotels listed in the section, see the "Hotels in Central Buenos Aires" map on p. 40.

Very Expensive

Marriott Plaza Hotel ★★   The historic Plaza was the Buenos Aires grande dame for most of the 20th century. The intimate lobby, decorated in Italian marble, crystal, and Persian carpets, is a virtual revolving door for Argentine politicians, foreign diplomats, and business executives. Twenty-six rooms overlook Plaza San Martín, providing dreamlike views of the green canopy of trees in spring and summer. The **Plaza Grill** (p. 69) remains a favorite spot for business lunches and offers a reasonably priced multicourse dinner menu. The **Plaza Bar** (p. 195) is among the most famous in the city. The hotel's enormous health club has a large heated indoor pool and specialized dance and aerobics rooms. The hotel lobby has free Wi-Fi access, but in-room Internet access costs about $16 a day, decreasing with additional days. The hotel also offers free high-quality historical tours of Buenos Aires.

Calle Florida 1005 (at Santa Fe overlooking Plaza San Martín), 1005 Buenos Aires. www.marriottplaza buenosaires.com. ✆ **11/4318-3000.** Fax 11/4318-3008. 318 units. $385 double; from $445 suite. Rates

Hotels in Central Buenos Aires

WHERE TO STAY | Microcentro

include buffet breakfast. AE, DC, MC, V. Valet parking $20. Metro: San Martín. **Amenities:** 2 restaurants; cigar bar; concierge; exercise room; health club w/outdoor pool; massage; room service; sauna; Wi-Fi in lobby. *In room:* A/C, TV, high-speed Internet, minibar.

Pan Americano ★★★   The enormous Pan Americano faces the Obelisco and the Teatro Colón, offering convenient access to tourist sites as well as many *subte* lines. The South Tower rooms are a good size, but the North Tower rooms are even larger, and bathrooms have whirlpool tubs and separate shower units. All rooms in both towers come with desks, extra side chairs, and ample closet space. The three-story glass rooftop health club, spa, and sauna will give you the sense that you're floating above Avenida 9 de Julio. The health club restaurant, **Kasuga,** becomes a sushi bar at night. Two other restaurants are located in the lobby: **Lucíernaga,** the main lobby bar where breakfast is served, and **Tomo Uno** (p. 68). Both spaces serve international, Argentine, and Italian cuisine. The Pan Americano is sometimes called the Crowne Plaza, though it is no longer part of that chain.

Carlos Pelligrini (9 de Julio) 551 (at Corrientes), 1009 Buenos Aires. www.panamericano.us. © **11/4348-5000.** Fax 11/4348-5250. 386 units. $346 double; from $550 suite. Rates include buffet breakfast. AE, DC, MC, V. Free valet parking. Metro: Lavalle or Diagonal Norte. **Amenities:** 3 restaurants; babysitting; concierge; exercise room; enormous health club w/indoor/outdoor pool; massage; room service; sauna; spa. *In room:* A/C, TV, high-speed Internet, minibar.

Sofitel ★★★   This classy French hotel near Plaza San Martín joins two seven-story buildings to a 20-story neoclassical tower dating from 1929, linked by a glass atrium lobby resembling an enormous gazebo, with ficus trees, a giant iron-and-bronze chandelier, and an Art Nouveau clock. Adjacent to the lobby, you'll find an elegant French restaurant, **Le Sud** (p. 68), and the early-20th-century-style **Buenos Aires Café.** These rooms vary in size; ask for one of the "deluxe" rooms or suites if you're looking for more space. Beautiful marble bathrooms have separate showers and bathtubs and feature Roger & Gallet amenities. Rooms above the eighth floor offer the best views, and the 17th-floor suite, *L'Appartement,* covers the whole floor. Many of the staff members speak Spanish, English, and French.

Arroyo 841-849 (at Juncal), 1007 Buenos Aires. www.sofitel.com. © **11/4131-0000.** Fax 11/4131-0044. 144 units. From $531 double; from $605 suite. AE, DC, MC, V. **Amenities:** Restaurant; cafe; bar; concierge; fitness center; indoor swimming pool; room service. *In room:* A/C, TV, high-speed Internet, minibar.

Expensive

Esplendor ★★   Esplendor is built into the Galerías Pacífico shopping gallery, in a spectacularly renovated old hotel. If you want a stylish boutique hotel and don't want to sacrifice a convenient location, this is the place for you. Rooms have high ceilings and interesting decor by the Tramando Design House of Martin Churba. The lobby has a restaurant, **Rouge,** and a gift shop full of design-oriented items. Double-insulated windows keep out the noise. Many rooms also have balconies.

San Martín 780 (btw. Viamonte and Córdoba), 1004 Buenos Aires. www.esplendorbuenosaires.com. © **11/5256-8800.** Fax 11/5256-8800. 51 units, including 25 suites and 3 VIP suites. $156 double; from $167 suite. Rates include breakfast buffet. Parking $12 a day. AE, MC, V. Metro: San Martín. **Amenities:** Restaurant; bar; babysitting; bikes; concierge; health club; Internet in business center; room service; sauna. *In room:* A/C, TV, Internet, minibar.

Hotel Reconquista Plaza ★   Near busy Calle Florida, this hotel is a good option for business travelers who do not need full services and want a convenient, central location and clean, modern amenities. All rooms have enormous, rounded windows looking out onto the street. Desks provide ample workspace. Suites are merely oversized rooms partially separated by a large wardrobe unit with a sleeper couch. Some suites have enormous terraces, with views overlooking the Microcentro. All rooms have tub/shower combinations, but the tubs are small in standard rooms. Suite bathrooms are equipped with whirlpools. Double-glazing on the windows blocks out noise, an important consideration in this area. Staff is exceptionally friendly and helpful.

Reconquista 602 (at Tucumán), 1003 Buenos Aires. www.hotelesreconquista.com.ar. ℰ 11/4311-4600. Fax 11/4311-3302. 60 units. From $206 double; from $315 suite. Rates include breakfast buffet. AE, MC, V. Parking $12. Metro: Florida. **Amenities:** Restaurant; bar; concierge; small health club; Internet in business center; room service; sauna. *In room:* A/C, TV, Internet ($8 a day), minibar.

Sheraton Buenos Aires Hotel and Convention Center ★★

Across from the Retiro train station and the British Clock Tower, the Sheraton is ideally located for business travelers and tourists alike. Rooms are large and comfortable. The hotel boasts four restaurants that it shares with the Park Tower, including **Crystal Garden,** serving refined international cuisine in an atrium dining room overlooking Alem; **El Aljibe,** serving Argentine beef fresh from the grill; **Cardinale,** offering Italian specialties; and **Café Express,** a fast-food and pastry shop off of the lobby. Its "Neptune" pool and fitness center are among the best in the city. The entire pool and spa complex is set in a garden. One pool has a pressurized current to boost your workout during your swim.

Av. San Martín 1225 (at Leandro N. Alem), 1104 Buenos Aires. www.sheraton.com. ℰ 11/4318-9000. Fax 11/4318-9346. 742 units. $308 double; from $526 suite. AE, DC, MC, V. Metro: Retiro. **Amenities:** 3 restaurants; snack bar; piano bar; babysitting; concierge; fitness center; massage; 2 pools; putting green; room service; wet and dry saunas; 2 lighted tennis courts. *In room:* A/C, TV, high-speed Internet, minibar.

Moderate

Amerian Buenos Aires Park Hotel ★★

One of the best four-star hotels in the city, the modern Amerian is a good bet for tourists as well as business travelers. The warm atrium lobby looks more like California than Argentina, and the highly qualified staff offers personalized service. Rooms are elegant and include wood, marble, and granite details. All have comfortable beds, chairs, and work areas. The Argentine-owned hotel is just blocks away from Calle Florida, Plaza San Martín, and the Teatro Colón, very convenient for both business travelers and tourists.

Reconquista 699 (at Viamonte), 1003 Buenos Aires. www.amerian.com. ℰ 11/5171-6500. Fax 11/5171-6501. 152 units. $133 double; from $284 suite. Rates include buffet breakfast. AE, DC, MC, V. Parking $16 a day. Metro: Florida. **Amenities:** Restaurant; pub; concierge; exercise room; room service; sauna. *In room:* A/C, TV, high-speed Internet, minibar.

Howard Johnson Florida Street ★★

The Howard Johnson has a prime location on Calle Florida near Plaza San Martín and is accessed through a ground-level shopping-and-restaurant gallery. Guest rooms are equipped with sleeper chairs (in addition to beds), large desks and dressers, and well-appointed bathrooms. Room size is above average for this category. Each room has two phones, and local calls and Internet use are free. There's a small, airy lobby cafe and bar, with additional food served in the gallery below. There is no pool or health club on premises, but access is offered free of charge at a nearby facility. Wi-Fi is free in the lobby.

Calle Florida 944 (at Alvear), 1005 Buenos Aires. www.hojoar.com. ℰ 11/4891-9200. Fax 11/4891-1200. 77 units. $169 double. Rates include buffet breakfast. AE, DC, MC, V. Metro: San Martín. **Amenities:** Restaurant; bar; room service; Wi-Fi in lobby. *In room:* A/C, TV, high-speed Internet, minibar.

Inexpensive

V&S Hostel ★★ 🎒 This conveniently located hostel is privately owned but part of an Argentine network. It's inside a gorgeous turn-of-the-20th-century apartment building, with lavish touches like curved doorways, stained-glass ornamentation, and balconies. Six private bedrooms with attached private bathrooms are also available. A kitchen is available for preparing meals. Guests can mingle in the quiet library, TV sitting room, or patio. Several computers are also available for Internet access. Service is exceptionally friendly. This place is a great value, with air-conditioning throughout the rooms. Except for same-day reservations, the hostel prefers that reservations be made by e-mail at **reservas@hostelclub.com**.

Viamonte 887 (at Suipacha), 1053 Buenos Aires. www.hostelclub.com. 📞 **11/4322-0994.** 60 bed spaces, including 10 in 6 bedrooms with attached bathroom. From $13 per bed; $66 per private room. Rates include continental breakfast. No credit cards. Metro: Lavalle. **Amenities:** Concierge; high-speed Internet; shared kitchen; lockers; Wi-Fi. *In room:* A/C (for a small fee), Wi-Fi (select rooms).

4 MONSERRAT

Monserrat borders San Telmo but is more easily accessed by subway than the latter neighborhood. Monserrat is distinguished by old, turn-of-the-20th-century buildings similar to those in San Telmo, as well as enormous mid-century, Fascist-style government buildings along its border with the Plaza de Mayo. While Monserrat, like San Telmo, is rapidly gentrifying, parts of it can be desolate and a little dangerous at night, so use caution and avoid empty streets. For a map of the hotels listed in this section, see the "Hotels in Central Buenos Aires" map on p. 40.

Expensive

InterContinental ★★★ This luxurious tower hotel in one of the city's oldest districts is decorated in 1930s style. The marble lobby is beige and apricot, with heavy black and brass accents and handsome carved-wood furniture and antiques inlaid with agates and other stones. The lobby's small **Café de las Luces** sometimes offers evening tango performances. The **Restaurante y Bar Mediterráneo** (p. 73) serves healthful, gourmet Mediterranean cuisine on an outdoor patio under a glass-in trellis. Stop by the **Brasco & Duane** wine bar for an exclusive selection of Argentine vintages. Guest rooms continue the 1930s theme, with elegant black woodwork, king-size beds, marble-top nightstands, large desks, and black-and-white photographs of the city. Marble bathrooms have separate showers and bathtubs, and extensive amenities.

Moreno 809 (at Piedras), 1091 Buenos Aires. www.buenos-aires.interconti.com. 📞 **11/4340-7100.** Fax 11/4340-7119. 312 units. $192 double; from $345 suite. AE, DC, MC, V. Parking $20. Metro: Moreno. **Amenities:** Restaurant; wine bar; lobby bar; concierge; executive floors; exercise room; health club w/indoor pool; massage; room service; sauna; sun deck. *In room:* A/C, TV, high-speed Internet, minibar.

Moreno ★ This all-suite hotel says it is located in San Telmo, but it's really in Monserrat, on the border of the two neighborhoods. It opened in 2007 and is an incredible reuse of a 1920s Art Deco building. Inside, you'll find fantastic preserved details such as stained-glass windows. The suites are huge and graced with Art Deco furniture. The extra-large suites all have chaise longues and are some of the largest rooms at hotels in this category. Loft rooms also come with Jacuzzis. A rooftop lounge has a Jacuzzi and views to the dome of the nearby San Francisco church, and is where the small gym sits. The hotel also contains a restaurant and theater/tango lounge, currently home to the **Evita Vive** tango show (p. 200).

Moreno 376 (btw. Balcarce and Defensa), 1091 Buenos Aires. www.morenobuenosaires.com. ℰ **11/6091-2000.** Fax 11/6091-2001. 39 units. $109 suite; from $336 loft. AE, DC, MC, V. Parking $12. Metro: Bolívar, Catedral, or Plaza de Mayo. **Amenities:** Restaurant; bar; babysitting; concierge; exercise room; Internet in business center; room service. *In room:* A/C, TV, minibar, Wi-Fi.

Moderate

Hotel Castelar   The 1929 Hotel Castelar was a stopping point for Spanish literary stars during the golden years of the 1930s. Federico García Lorca lived here in 1934, and his room is preserved as a museum. The lobby retains many original brass, marble, and heavy plaster elements, including in the dining area, which was once a *confitería* (cafe) as important as Café Tortoni. Mario Palanti, eccentric architect of nearby Palacio Barolo, designed the Castelar. The spa in the basement is free for guests (men and women are separated), with fees for various services. Even if you're not staying here, it's worth paying the $15 entrance to see the Turkish-style, white Carrara marble space. Rooms were renovated in 2005, but 1920s wooden touches, speckled glass, and tiled bathroom floors remain. The rooms are not large, but have a small antechamber adding a sense of privacy. Suites have an added living area.

Av. de Mayo 1152 (at Lima and Av. 9 de Julio), 1152 Buenos Aires. www.castelarhotel.com.ar. ℰ **11/4383-5000.** Fax 11/4383-8388. 151 units, including 70 suites. $127 double; $163 suite. Rates include buffet breakfast. AE, DC, MC, V. Metro: Lima. **Amenities:** Restaurant; bar; small health club; room service; rooms for those w/limited mobility (minimal accommodation); extensive spa; Wi-Fi. *In room:* A/C, TV, high-speed Internet, minibar.

NH City Hotel ★★   The Spanish-owned NH hotel chain opened this property in the old City Hotel, a Jazz Age masterpiece. Its lobby has been meticulously renovated, a combination of Art Deco and collegiate Gothic, with earth-tone furnishings offsetting the stained-glass ceiling and honey-colored marble floors. A new building was also added in 2006. The rooftop, with its small outdoor heated pool, offers a view all the way to Uruguay on a clear day, and there's a small health club, with a spa, sauna, and Jacuzzi. The downside is many back rooms have no view. There's a casual restaurant and a formal one, **Clue,** which serves Spanish cuisine in a 1930s minimalist space.

Bolívar 160 (at Alsina), 1066 Buenos Aires. www.nh-hotels.com. ℰ **11/4121-6464.** Fax 11/4121-6450. 369 units, including 38 suites. From $153 double; from $248 suite. Rates include generous buffet breakfast. AE, DC, MC, V. Parking $13. Metro: Bolívar or Plaza de Mayo. **Amenities:** 2 restaurants; bar; babysitting; concierge; executive floor; small gym facility w/open-air pool; Jacuzzi; room service; sauna; spa. *In room:* TV, high-speed Internet or Wi-Fi, minibar.

SAN TELMO

I find San Telmo the most romantic and Porteño of Buenos Aires's touristy neighborhoods. San Telmo is rapidly gentrifying, so it's not as dangerous as in the past, but you still need to be cautious here at night. Most hotels here are hostels, B&Bs, or boutique hotels, an expanding category. The area is most easily accessed by stations on *subte* line C, which runs along Avenida 9 de Julio, and these can be a slightly long walk from some accommodations. For a map of the hotels listed in this section, see the "Hotels in Central Buenos Aires" map on p. 40.

Expensive

The Axel Hotel ★★   A Spanish chain, this is a hotel for gays, billing itself as "hetero-friendly." Most of its clientele are gay men from around the world; the rest are lesbians and heterosexuals, usually from the fashion world. Naturally, style is important here. The chic but small rooms look like space-station pods, with their interior portholes and bathrooms set in glass cubes. The hotel has two pools, one set in an outdoor garden, with its own bar, and the site of summer Sunday pool parties open to the public. Most unique is the glass-bottom pool set on the top floor of the building inside the combination sauna and lounge—you can watch people swimming from below within the combination atrium and lobby. The dining area is called **Kitchen,** and even if you don't stay here, it's worth coming to dine or socialize.

Venezuela 649 (btw. Perú and Chacabuco), 1095 Buenos Aires. www.axelhotels.com. © **11/4136-9393.** Fax 11/4136-9394. 48 units. $189–$429 double. Rates include continental breakfast. AE, MC, V. Metro: Belgrano. **Amenities:** Restaurant; 2 bars; exercise room; Internet in business center; Jacuzzi; indoor and outdoor pools; room service; sauna. *In room:* A/C, TV, minibar, Wi-Fi.

Mansion Vitraux Hotel ★   This hotel opened in 2009, bringing trendy glamour to San Telmo. The lobby has a cascading waterfall, leading down to the sunken wine-tasting room, where every afternoon, from 6 to 9pm, there is a wine tasting included in the services for guests. Breakfast is also included in the rates. The uniquely designed rooms have various themes, like the sensual red-and-white Marilyn room. Some rooms have views of the nearby San Telmo church, and two open directly onto the interior courtyard. Lower-level Spa Bleu has mood lighting, a heated pool with a waterfall, a Jacuzzi, a wet and dry sauna, massage rooms, and a small gym. A large wraparound sun deck on the roof overlooks the outdoor heated pool. Spa and sun deck day passes for those not staying here cost $30. All rooms are nonsmoking.

Carlos Calvo 369 (btw. Defensa and Balcarce). 1102 Buenos Aires. www.mansionvitraux.com. © **11/4300-6886.** 12 units. $248–$351 double. Rates include continental breakfast. AE, DC, MC, V. Metro: Independencia. **Amenities:** Restaurant; bar; babysitting; gym; Jacuzzi; massage; indoor and outdoor pools; room service; wet and dry sauna. *In room:* A/C, projection TV, hair dryer, minibar, Wi-Fi.

Moderate

Babel ★   This is a charming, small boutique hotel with a *conventillo* feel to it, built around a glass-covered, light-filled central courtyard in a century-old house. The rooms are simply furnished, with king- or queen-size beds or two twins, rustic brick walls, neutral coloring, and hardwood floors. Bathrooms are shower-only. The ground level contains an art gallery, with rotating art for sale. The lobby is full of rich woods, and there's a lounge full of shelves heaping with books. There's no elevator in this two-story hotel, and no pool or gym, but service is excellent and intimate, and it's a bargain choice among boutiques, with a convenient San Telmo location.

Balcarce 946 (btw. Carlos Calvo and Estados Unidos), 1064 Buenos Aires. www.hotelbabel.com.ar. © **11/4300-8300.** 9 units. $100–$132 double. Rates include continental breakfast. AE, MC, V. Metro: Independencia or Plaza de Mayo. **Amenities:** Bar; babysitting; bikes; room service. *In room:* A/C, TV, hair dryer, Wi-Fi.

The Cocker ★   Tucked away in an unassuming part of San Telmo, this boutique hotel is a fantastic Art Nouveau house and takes its name from the former owners' cocker spaniel. The structure has 16-foot-high ceilings and a variety of public spaces, including a sitting room graced by a piano and a rooftop garden with fantastic views. The decor in the five guest rooms varies—some are modern and stark; others have

French touches. If you are looking for romance, choose the rooftop room with its own private patio. Guests can use the shared kitchen. Be aware that the staircases throughout this hotel make it a difficult choice for people with limited mobility.

Av. Juan de Garay 458 (btw. Defensa and Bolívar), 1153 Buenos Aires. ✆ **11/4362-8451.** 5 units. $90–$135 double. Rates include continental breakfast. No credit cards. No parking. Metro: Constitución. *In room:* A/C, Wi-Fi.

Inexpensive

El Lugar Gay ★   This is Buenos Aires's first exclusively gay hotel, open only to men. It's inside a historic turn-of-the-last-century building less than a block from Plaza Dorrego. It has a homey feel, with industrial chic well blended into a century-old interior. Ask for the rooms in the back with the beautiful views of the Church of San Telmo. Rooms are small and sparse. Some share bathrooms with adjacent rooms; one group has a Jacuzzi. Several flights of narrow stairs leading to the lobby and rooms might be a problem for people with limited mobility. The hotel becomes a de facto gay community center at times, with its small cafe and Sunday evening tango lessons at 7pm, conducted by the gay tango group La Marshall. These are open to the public, so even if you don't stay here, you can still visit (though only if you're male; sorry ladies).

Defensa 1120 (at Humberto I), 1102 Buenos Aires. www.lugargay.com.ar. ✆ **11/4300-4747.** 7 units, some with shared bathrooms. $45–$70 double. Rates include continental breakfast. No credit cards. Metro: Independencia. **Amenities:** Restaurant; bar. *In room:* A/C, TV.

Hostel Carlos Gardel ★   If you can't get enough of Gardel in tango clubs, stay here, where a red wall plastered with his photos is the first thing to greet you. This hostel is built into a renovated house, and though it was severely gutted, a few marble staircases, wall sconces, and stained-glass windows remain. Two rooms with private bathrooms (but few other amenities) are available, reasonably priced at $40, and a nearby apartment is available beginning at $43 per day. The staff is friendly, and there's a large TV room where you can chat with them and other patrons. A shared kitchen and an *asado* on the rooftop terrace provide more spaces for socializing.

Carlos Calvo 579 (at Perú), 1102 Buenos Aires. www.hostelcarlosgardel.com.ar. ✆ **11/4307-2606.** 45 bed spaces, including 10 in 2 rooms with private bathroom. From $12 per bed; $40 for room; $43 for apt. Rates include continental breakfast. No credit cards. Metro: Independencia. **Amenities:** Concierge; self-service drink station; free high-speed Internet; shared kitchen; TV room. *In room:* Lockers.

Lina's Tango GuestHouse ★★★ 🛏   If you want to immerse yourself in the tango scene, this is the place. Owner Lina Acuña, who lives in the hotel, hails from Colombia and is a tango dancer. The hotel is also great for women traveling alone; Lina often makes informal trips to the *milongas* with her guests. While the facade of the hotel dates from the 1960s, the building is turn-of-the-last-century and some rooms retain original elements, with kitschy colors reminiscent of La Boca. The back garden, overgrown with vines and trees, adds to the authentic Porteño atmosphere. Guests and Lina's friends gather here for conversation, impromptu tango lessons, and *asados* on holidays and weekends. Three of the eight guest rooms share bathrooms. Breakfast is included, and guests can use the small kitchen and a washing machine. There's a TV in a shared living room, and the courtyard can get noisy with people talking and dancing.

Estados Unidos 780 (at Piedras), 1011 Buenos Aires. www.linatango.com. ✆ **11/4361-6817** or 11/4300-7367. 8 units, 5 with private bathroom. $45–$70 double. 20% added for 1-night stays. Rates include continental breakfast. No credit cards. Metro: Independencia. **Amenities:** Continental breakfast; self-service kitchen; tango tours. *In room:* Wi-Fi.

RECOLETA

Most of the best hotels in Buenos Aires are in Recoleta, a very scenic, Parisian-style neighborhood. But if you stay here, you'll probably find yourself spending more money on cabs; the neighborhood is not conveniently accessible by any of the *subte* lines, except in areas bordering nearby Barrio Norte. (Of course, if you can afford to stay in Recoleta, then the extra cost of taxis might not be an issue for you!) Public transportation aside, Recoleta is exceedingly beautiful, and staying here puts you close to the Recoleta Cemetery and Evita's grave, as well as the parks and museums of nearby Palermo, which are best accessed by cab to begin with, no matter where you are coming from in the city. For a map of the hotels in this section, see the "Hotels in Central Buenos Aires" map on p. 40.

Very Expensive

The Algodon Mansion   The newest luxury Recoleta property, the Algodon boutique hotel is built into a mansion, offering only 10 very spacious suites, with your own available on-call butler. The lobby has a cognac bar and restaurant open to the public. Rooms retain original details, with marble and rich burl woods, but have added electronic elements like remote control–automated shantung silk curtains and lighting systems. The royal suite is 140 sq. m (1,507 sq. ft.), with a dining room, living room, and wine room. Bathrooms are enormous and have both showers and tubs, and his and her sinks. Some rooms have small balconies opening onto the mansion's back garden. The spa is a delight of its own, offering wine-based treatments, a Scottish shower, and a wet and dry sauna. A heated pool sits on the rooftop.

Montevideo 1647 (btw. Guido and Quintana), 1021 Buenos Aires. www.algodonmansion.com. © **11/3530-7777.** 10 units, all suites. $800–$1,600 suite. Rates include luxurious buffet breakfast. AE, MC, V. Metro: Callao. **Amenities:** Restaurants; bar; private butler service; concierge; health club; massage; room service; spa. *In room:* A/C, TV, minibar, Wi-Fi.

Alvear Palace Hotel ★★★   Among the world's top hotels, this gilded classical confection of marble and bronze combines Empire- and Louis XV–style furniture with exquisite French decorative arts. Past guests include Antonio Banderas, Donatella Versace, the emperor of Japan, and Robert Duvall. Modern conveniences are combined with luxurious comforts such as chandeliers, Egyptian cotton linens, and silk drapes. All rooms come with personal butler service, cellphones that can be activated on demand, fresh flowers and fruit baskets, and daily newspaper delivery. Large marble bathrooms contain Hermès toiletries, and most have Jacuzzi tubs. The formal hotel provides sharp, professional service, and the concierges go to great lengths to accommodate guests' requests. The Alvear Palace is home to one of South America's best French restaurants, **La Bourgogne** (p. 76) and offers an excellent, expensive Sunday brunch and afternoon tea in **L'Orangerie.** Kosher dining is also available.

Av. Alvear 1891 (at Ayacucho), 1129 Buenos Aires. www.alvearpalace.com. © **11/4808-2100.** Fax 11/4804-9243. 197 units (100 palace rooms and 97 suites). From $581 double; from $690 suite. Rates include luxurious buffet breakfast. AE, DC, MC, V. Valet parking $23. No metro access. **Amenities:** 2 restaurants; bar; private butler service; concierge; small health club; massage; room service; spa. *In room:* A/C, TV, high-speed Internet, minibar.

Buenos Aires Park Hyatt ★★★   This hotel combines a modern tower with the Palacio Duhau, the Duhau family mansion. Mansion rooms mix modern and classical details. Some tower rooms have breathtaking Río de la Plata views. Restaurant/bars include the French-style **Piano Nobile; Oak Bar,** with panels from a medieval Normandy castle; **Gioia,** offering modern Italian cuisine for breakfast, lunch, and dinner; and **Duhau Restaurant,** Argentine high-end cuisine overseen by chef Federico Heinzmann. The layered garden, with gently cascading waterlily-filled pools, is a pleasant place for a drink. The underground wine-and-cheese bar stocks about 45 artisanal Argentine cheeses. The spa, called Ahin, offers a broad range of treatments, and the gym has a large heated swimming pool. Internet is available in all rooms, beginning at $12 a day. The multicourse breakfast is not always included in rates and goes for about $20 per day.

Av. Alvear 1661 (at Montevideo), 1014 Buenos Aires. www.buenosaires.park.hyatt.com. ℂ **11/5171-1234.** Fax 11/5171-1235. 165 units, including 23 mansion units, 23 suites in both towers. $599 double; from $780 suite; from $1,143 select suites. AE, DC, MC, V. Valet parking $24. No metro access. **Amenities:** 3 restaurants; lobby bar; babysitting; concierge; exercise room; health club; massage; heated indoor pool; room service; sauna; Wi-Fi. *In room:* A/C, TV/VCR, high-speed Internet, minibar, Wi-Fi.

Four Seasons Hotel ★★★ ☺   This landmark hotel consists of two parts—the 12-story "Park" tower housing most of its guest rooms, and the 1916 French-style "La Mansión," with seven elegant suites and private-event rooms. A French-style garden and a pool separate the buildings, and a well-equipped health club contains a spa offering various treatments, including wine massages and facials. The hotel's restaurant, **Le Mistral** (p. 77), serves excellent Mediterranean cuisine in a casual setting. Spacious guest rooms have walk-in closets, wet and dry bars, stereo systems, cellphones, and large marble bathrooms with water-jet bathtubs. Executive Library Floor guests enjoy a private lounge and additional in-room amenities including a printer, fax machine, Argentine wine, complimentary breakfast, and evening cocktails. Kids receive bedtime milk and cookies. A favorite hotel of many celebrities, it's most famous as Madonna's choice during the filming of *Evita* and again on her 2008 tour.

Posadas 1086–88 (at Av. 9 de Julio), 1011 Buenos Aires. www.fourseasons.com. ℂ **11/4321-1200.** Fax 11/4321-1201. 165 units, including 49 suites (7 suites in La Mansión). $599 double; from $1,022 suite; $3,500 mansion suite. Prices include breakfast. AE, DC, MC, V. Valet parking $22. No metro access. **Amenities:** Restaurant; lobby bar; babysitting; concierge; executive level; exercise room; health club; massage; heated outdoor pool; room service; sauna. *In room:* A/C, TV/VCR, high-speed Internet, minibar.

Moderate

Etoile Hotel ★ 🍴   In the heart of Recoleta, steps from the neighborhood's fashionable restaurants and cafes, the 14-story Etoile is an older hotel with Turkish flair. It's not as luxurious as the area's other five-star venues, but it's not as expensive, either. Colored in gold and cream, guest rooms are fairly large—although they're not really "suites," as the hotel describes them. Executive rooms have separate sitting areas, large tile-floor bathrooms with whirlpool tubs, and balconies. Rooms facing south have balconies overlooking Plaza Francia and the Recoleta Cemetery.

Roberto M. Ortiz 1835 (at Guido overlooking Recoleta Cemetery), 1113 Buenos Aires. www.etoile.com.ar. ℂ **11/4805-2626.** Fax 11/4805-3613. 96 units. $135 double; from $160 suite. AE, DC, MC, V. Free parking. No metro access. **Amenities:** Restaurant; concierge; exercise room; rooftop health club w/indoor pool; room service. *In room:* A/C, TV, high-speed Internet, minibar.

Inexpensive

The Recoleta Hostel ★ 🎒   This is a great inexpensive choice for young people who want to be in a beautiful neighborhood close to everything but wouldn't ordinarily be able to afford such a location. Accommodations are simple, with 22 bunk bed–filled rooms for 8 to 12 people each. Two double rooms with private bathrooms can also be rented, but they have bunk beds, too, so couples wishing to cozy up will have to get really cozy. Rooms are simple, with decor reminiscent of a convent. The hostel has a public kitchen, a TV room, laundry service, lockers, and an outdoor patio. It's also a Wi-Fi hotspot.

Libertad 1216 (btw. Juncal and Arenales), 1012 Buenos Aires. www.trhostel.com.ar. © **11/4812-4419.** Fax 11/4815-6622. 75 bed spaces, including 4 in 2 double bedrooms with private bathrooms. From $12 per bed; from $48 private room. Rates include continental breakfast. No credit cards. Metro: Lavalle. **Amenities:** Concierge; high-speed Internet; shared kitchen; lockers; outdoor patio; Wi-Fi.

BARRIO NORTE

Barrio Norte borders Recoleta, though some people—especially real estate agents and hotel owners—claim it is actually a part of it. However, the area is distinctly busier and more commercialized, with more of a middle-class feel than upscale Recoleta. Its main boulevard is busy Santa Fe, full of shops, restaurants, and cafes. This can make staying in Barrio Norte noisier than Recoleta, but still less so than the Microcentro. You also have easy metro access in this neighborhood. For a map of the hotels listed in the section, see the "Hotels in Central Buenos Aires" map on p. 40.

Moderate

Art Hotel ★ This was among the earliest of the boutique hotels to open in Buenos Aires during the tourism boom in 2004, and the owners have maintained the historical nature of the property. You'll find high ceilings, rich wood details on the doors, and even "Viva Perón" etched into the mirrors of the 100-year-old elevator. Some rooms are on the small side, but all have such interesting details such as polished concrete floors with embedded ornamental tiles. Bathrooms are small and shower-only. The public areas on each floor are spacious. A rooftop solarium also has great views, and two guest rooms are located here as well. The extensive stairs throughout make this hotel a difficult choice for anyone with limited mobility. The hotel describes itself as being in Recoleta, but it is truly in Barrio Norte.

Azcuénaga 1268 (btw. Beruti and Arenales), 1115 Buenos Aires. www.arthotel.com.ar. © **11/4821-4744.** Fax 11/4821-6248. 36 units. $95–$155 double. Rates include breakfast buffet. AE, MC, V. Parking (off-site) $12 a day. Metro: Pueyrredón. **Amenities:** Babysitting; concierge; Internet in business center; room service. *In room:* A/C, TV, minibar, Wi-Fi.

CONGRESO

Congreso is a historic district that surrounds the building Congreso, at the western terminus of the Avenida de Mayo. In addition to Congreso, the neighborhood contains other grand and imposing buildings, some almost imperial in scale and design. While there is a lot to see in the area, it can seem desolate and seedy at night, especially in the Congreso Plaza, which serves as a hangout for the homeless. The intense government police presence in the area, however, means that, in spite of appearances, it is relatively safe at night. With increased tourism to Buenos Aires, many hotels and other establishments are beginning to move into this neighborhood. For a map of the hotels listed in the section, see the "Hotels in Central Buenos Aires" map on p. 40.

Moderate

The Golden Tulip Savoy Ever since Dutch Crown Prince William married the beautiful Argentine Maxima in 2002, the Dutch have flocked to Argentina.

Dutch-owned Golden Tulip, opened in the historic hotel Savoy, catches that traffic. The original hotel opened in 1910, part of the glamorous rebuilding of Avenida Callao in the aftermath of the opening of nearby Congreso. The hotel was renovated completely in 2010, but maintains original details such as gorgeous moldings and stained-glass decoration. Rooms are large and those facing the street have tiny French balconies, but half of the hotel faces an interior courtyard with no views. All rooms are soundproof and have Wi-Fi. Suite bathrooms include a whirlpool bathtub. The hotel's **Madrigales** restaurant offers interesting Latin American fusion cuisine.

Av. Callao 181 (at Juan Perón), 1022 Buenos Aires. www.savoyhotel.com.ar. © **11/4370-8000.** Fax 11/4370-8020. 174 units, including 15 suites. From $133 double; $213 suite. Rates include buffet breakfast. AE, DC, MC, V. Parking $18 a day. Metro: Congreso. **Amenities:** Restaurant; bar; concierge; access to nearby health club; room service; spa. *In room:* A/C, TV, minibar, Wi-Fi.

Hotel Ibis ★★ ☺ ⚑   This hotel is conveniently located on Plaza Congreso, and all rooms have street views, many facing the plaza. Rooms are a good size for this price range. All are identical doubles, with an extra bed available for a few dollars more. Some rooms connect, ideal for families or groups of friends. The basic Argentine restaurant is a good value at about $10 for a prix-fixe dinner, and $1 to $3 for most lunch items a la carte. Breakfast is not included in the rates but costs about $5 per person. The hotel is popular with French tourists and college-age backpackers, and the staff speaks Spanish, English, and French.

Hipólito Yrigoyen 1592 (at Ceballos), 1089 Buenos Aires. www.ibishotel.com. © **11/5300-5555.** Fax 11/5300-5566. 148 units. From $88 double. AE, DC, MC, V. Parking $18 in a nearby garage. Metro: Congreso. **Amenities:** Restaurant; bar; concierge; high-speed Internet; Wi-Fi. *In room:* A/C, TV, Wi-Fi.

TRIBUNALES

Tribunales encompasses the area surrounding the Supreme Court building and Teatro Colón, which borders the Corrientes theater district. It's full of government buildings and is close to the Microcentro's shopping, but is far less noisy than this neighboring area. Its most important feature is Plaza Lavalle. For a map of the hotels listed in the section, see the "Hotels in Central Buenos Aires" map on p. 40.

Moderate

Dazzler Hotel Libertad ★   This hotel, built in 1978, is virtually unknown to the North American market. The majority of clients come from South America, though all staff members speak English. The hotel is conveniently situated overlooking Plaza Libertad, set against Avenida 9 de Julio, a few blocks from Teatro Colón (p. 112). Front rooms have excellent views, but they can be noisy. All rooms are on the small side, but they're exceptionally bright, with floor-to-ceiling windows that make them feel larger. Corner rooms offer the most space. Ask about connecting rooms if you're traveling in a group or with a family. The small smoke-glass-mirrored lobby has a staircase leading to the large and bright restaurant, where breakfast is served.

Libertad 902 (at Paraguay), 1012 Buenos Aires. www.dazzlerhotel.com. © **11/4816-5005.** 87 units. From $114 double. Rates include buffet breakfast. AE, MC, V. Parking garage across from hotel. Metro: Tribunales. **Amenities:** Restaurant; bar; concierge; small health club; room service; sauna; Wi-Fi. *In room:* A/C, TV, Internet, minibar.

PALERMO VIEJO

Palermo Viejo is divided into two sections: Palermo Soho and Palermo Hollywood, with Juan B. Justo as the dividing line. This is the trendiest part of Buenos Aires, yet it still retains a small-neighborhood feel, with its old low-rise houses, cobblestone streets, and oak-tree-shaded sidewalks. This is where the newest and most fashionable boutique hotels are located, and for the young and chic, it can be a great place to stay. Subway access is not the best, however. For a map of the hotels listed in the section, see the "Hotels & Restaurants in Palermo" map on p. 84.

Expensive

Bo-Bo ★★ Bo-Bo is short for Bourgeois Bohemian, whatever that contradictory term is supposed to mean. This little boutique hotel is high on charm and gives you the sense that you've stepped back in time. The rooms have modern touches, though, with bold colors and white surfaces. Some have terraces. Each room has a different theme and name, such as the Angelina Room, which has a Jacuzzi and balcony. One room is also available for travelers with disabilities and, though this is a turn-of-the-20th-century building, an elevator has been added for the convenience of all. Children under 14 are generally not allowed. The excellent restaurant is overseen by Chef Adrian Sarkassian. You might also just want to come by for drinks at the bar, an enjoyable place to meet before going to dinner at one of the many great restaurants in Palermo.

Guatemala 4882 (btw. Borges and Thames), 1425 Buenos Aires. www.bobohotel.com. (C) **11/4774-0505.** Fax 11/4774-9600. 7 units. $200–$275 double. Rates include buffet breakfast. AE, MC, V. Free parking. Metro: Plaza Italia. **Amenities:** Restaurant; bar; bikes; concierge; Internet (in lobby); room service. *In room:* A/C, TV, Wi-Fi.

The Glu ★ Taking its name from the family that owns it—the Glusmans—this is one of the newest boutique hotels in Palermo, opened at the end of 2008. Rooms have a simple decor, with neutral and dark tones and hardwood floors, but with a splash of color via a floral wall pattern. What makes the hotel special, in addition to service, is how quiet it is compared to other boutique hotels in Palermo Soho, which strive to be social centers. Walls and windows are specially insulated, so when you're done having your fun on the town, this will be a quiet respite. The rooftop sun deck has a Jacuzzi.

Godoy Cruz 1733 (btw. Gorriti and Honduras), 1414 Buenos Aires. www.thegluhotel.com. (C) **800/405-3072** in the U.S. or Canada or 11/4831-4646. Fax 11/4831-4646. 11 units. $260–$375 double. Rates include breakfast buffet. AE, MC, V. No parking. Metro: Plaza Italia. **Amenities:** Concierge; health club and spa w/massage room; Internet in business center; Jacuzzi; room service; sauna. *In room:* A/C, TV/DVD, microwave, minibar, robes, Wi-Fi.

Legado Mítico ★ This luxurious boutique hotel was opened by owners Javier Figueroa and Horacio Menendez in November of 2007. Each room is named for a "mythical" Argentine, from Che to Borges to Evita, with art and decor hinting at the namesake. One nod to macho icon Che is that his is the only room with just a shower; all others come with tub/shower combinations. Bathrooms come with generous amenities, including wine-based Terra shampoos and crèmes. The lobby lounge, with its library and leather wing-back chairs, recalls an English gentleman's club and opens onto a patio. The rooftop patio has a Jacuzzi and a special mist cooling system, and can be blocked for specific periods by individual patrons for privacy.

B & B in Buenos Aires = Beautiful & Bargain-Priced

Buenos Aires has a growing number of intimate, chic bed-and-breakfast-type guesthouses for $40 to $100 a night. Unlike American B&Bs—which are so often fusty and cluttered with bric-a-brac and cats—those in Buenos Aires tend to have hip, young owners with clean, cosmopolitan taste. While you won't get five-star luxury, private guesthouses are often nicer than hotels charging three or four times the price. You can also get to know the owners and other guests. Many offer weekly or monthly rates. We recommend **Che Lulu,** Emilio Zolá 5185 (www.luluguest house.com; ✆ **11/4772-0289**), the lovely **La Otra Orilla,** Julian Alvarez 1779 (www.otraorilla.com.ar; ✆ **11/4863-7426**), and **Cabrera Garden,** Cabrera 5855 (www.cabreragarden. com; ✆ **11/4777-7668**). See individual websites for additional information and prices.

Gurruchaga 1848 (btw. Costa Rica and Nicaragua), 1414 Buenos Aires. www.legadomitico.com. ✆ **11/4833-1300.** 11 units. From $290 double. Rates include breakfast buffet. AE, MC, V. No parking. Metro: Plaza Italia. **Amenities:** Babysitting; bikes; concierge; Jacuzzi; massage; room service. *In room:* A/C, TV/DVD, minibar, robes, Wi-Fi.

Malabia House ★ Opened in 1998 in a former convent house 100 years old at the time, the Malabia House was among the first boutique hotels in Palermo. It still retains its antique essence, even with a 2010 renovation adding a sleek layer of silvers and purples to the interior. The heart of the place is a tiny garden atrium with a Saint Anthony sculpture. Rooms are decorated in light colors: beiges and creamy whites, some with cowskin leather accent rugs. All rooms have shower-only bathrooms, but three have private bathrooms (though they're outside of the room). The multi-level space has no elevators and might be problematic for someone with low mobility.

Malabia 1555 (btw. Honduras and Gorriti), 1414 Buenos Aires. www.malabiahouse.com.ar. ✆/fax **11/4833-2410.** 15 units. From $230 double. Rates include breakfast buffet. AE, DC, MC, V. Metro: Scalabrini Ortiz. **Amenities:** Babysitting; bikes; concierge; massage; room service. *In room:* A/C, TV-DVD, minibar, Wi-Fi.

Soho All Suites ★★★ "Chic" is the word that sprang to mind when I first stepped into this new boutique hotel. The lobby is modern and clean, and the staff in all-black uniforms is immediately attentive. The fashionable lobby bar and its adjacent patio lounge are often the site of parties and special events for Buenos Aires's young media crowd. The majority of the hotel's clients are between 25 and 45 years old. All rooms have kitchens and complete apartment accessories, including dishes, microwaves, and irons. Guest rooms are different sizes, some with extra bedrooms or terraces, so ask when booking. There is a rooftop solarium with a wonderful view of the neighborhood.

Honduras 4762 (btw. Malabia and Armenia), 1414 Buenos Aires. www.sohoallsuites.com.ar. ✆ **11/4832-3000.** 21 units. $236–$448 suite. Rates include breakfast buffet. AE, DC, MC, V. Parking $8. Metro: Palermo or Ortiz. **Amenities:** Restaurant; bar; concierge; room service; spa. *In room:* A/C, TV, kitchenette, minibar, Wi-Fi.

Vitrum ★ The Vitrum, opened in October 2008, is a stylish addition to the Palermo scene. Its decor has a '70s pop-art retro feel, with polka-dot wallpaper and acid greens and oranges with red accents. Bathrooms have creative ceramic flower-shaped sinks with brilliant glazes in yellow and red. The lobby is home to an art gallery, events room, and Sushi Club restaurant, where breakfast is also served. Pass-keyed elevators ensure room security. Rooms are large, especially the two-floor suites, with kitchenettes and microwaves. A backyard garden has a hidden seating area, and the rooftop contains a 24-hour gym and a spa with a wet and dry sauna, and massage rooms, including one with an outdoor view. Up here, you'll also find an open air sun deck complete with a Jacuzzi and *asado* grill.

Gorriti 5641 (btw. Bonpland and Fitzroy), 1414 Buenos Aires. www.vitrumhotel.com. ℂ/fax **11/4776-5030.** 16 units, including 12 duplex suites. From $278 double; $363 suite. Rates include breakfast buffet. AE, MC, V. No Parking. Metro: Palermo. **Amenities:** Restaurant; bar; babysitting; bikes; children's center; concierge; Jacuzzi; room service; spa w/wet and dry sauna. *In room:* A/C, TV/DVD, kitchenette (suites only), microwave (suites only), minibar, Wi-Fi.

Moderate

Craft   Looking as if it were constructed from wood from a shipwreck, Craft has a makeshift, country-rough feel to it, with mismatched colors, white surfaces, and patched-together clapboard. Popular with hipsters and independent travelers, the hotel opened in 2008, and the staff would not look out of place in Williamsburg, Brooklyn, or an artist enclave in East Berlin. White, small, and with a lot of shelf space, rooms look like dorms for grown-ups, and many have white tiled tub/shower combinations that are next to the bed, rather than in a separate bathroom. Vintage touches include a 45-RPM record player in the Music Room. The rooftop lounge, with its elegant, private sunbathing spaces, is the most adult part of the hotel and also has a rescued wood kitchen table and an *asado* barbecue space that guests can use. There are no elevators, and no pets are allowed, nor are children under 13.

Nicaragua 4583 (btw. Armenia and Malabia), 1414 Buenos Aires. www.crafthotel.com. ℂ **11/4833-0060.** Fax 11/4832-4464. 9 units. $121–$172 double. Rates include breakfast buffet. AE, MC, V. No parking. Metro: Scalabrini Ortiz. **Amenities:** Bikes; concierge; massage; room service. *In room:* A/C, TV/DVD, Wi-Fi.

Fierro Hotel ★   Calling itself "The Hotel for the Gourmand Visiting Buenos Aires" because of its **HG Restaurant ★** (p. 83) and its Palermo Hollywood location close to the restaurant scene, Fierro is a fiery new devil red-and-black presence that opened in September 2010. Art adorns each of the simply furnished rooms, most of which are extremely large (up to 59 sq. m/635 sq. ft.), and some of which have balconies or patios. The comfortable beds have Egyptian cotton sheets, and the large bathrooms have heated mirrors to prevent fogged surfaces after showers. Some rooms are shower-only; others have Jacuzzis and showers. Double-glazed windows keep out noise.

Soler 5862 (btw. Ravignani and Carranza), 1425 Buenos Aires. www.fierrohotel.com. ℂ **11/3220-6800.** Fax 11/3220-6801. 126 units. From $206 double. Rates include breakfast buffet. AE, MC, V. Parking $10. Metro: Carranza. **Amenities:** Babysitting; bikes; concierge; gym w/wet and dry sauna; Internet; small outdoor heated pool w/whirlpool; room service. *In room:* A/C, TV, cabled Internet, minibar, robes, extra sink, Wi-Fi.

Five Cool Rooms ★   The name of this hotel is somewhat misleading—there are actually 16 rooms, "five" referring to the number of owners. It's a little hard to find; look for its small metal sign. There are no restaurants or bars inside, but breakfast is served on the delightful rooftop terrace. The terrace also has an *asado* and the owners periodically have barbecues for hotel patrons. Overall, for a small hotel, it has a lot of public space, including a lobby with leather sofas leading to an outdoor patio garden. Rooms can be on the small side but are filled with light, making them feel larger.

"Bohemian chic" characterizes the design throughout this place. Some rooms have Jacuzzis. One room is available for travelers with disabilities.

Honduras 4742 (btw. Malabia and Armenia), 1414 Buenos Aires. www.fivehotelbuenosaires.com. ✆ **11/5235-5555.** Fax 11/4833-3600. 126 units. From $140 double. Rates include breakfast buffet. AE, MC, V. Parking (off-site) $12. Metro: Palermo or Ortiz. **Amenities:** Bikes; children's programs; concierge; Internet (in lobby); room service. *In room:* A/C, TV, minibar, Wi-Fi.

Home ★★★ This is one of Palermo's most popular boutique hotels due to the young couple behind it, Irish-Argentine Patricia O'Shea and her British husband Tom Rixton. She grew up a few blocks away and he is a former DJ, giving the place both anchor and soul. On Fridays, there's a DJ in the lobby bar, and it's a great place for drinks, even if you're not staying here. There's a real backyard with an ironic suburban edge, with grass and an outdoor heated pool. Rooms are high-design, and some suites come with Jacuzzis or kitchens. One room is available for travelers with disabilities. A two-level apartment with its own entrance is attached to the property. There's an excellent spa sunken into the courtyard, open to the public, with day-rate packages costing about $200, which includes breakfast and lunch.

Honduras 5860 (btw. Carranza and Ravignani). 1414 Buenos Aires. www.homebuenosaires.com. ✆ **11/4778-1008.** Fax 11/4779-1006. 21 units. From $157 double; from $351 suite; $399 apt. Rates include breakfast buffet. AE, MC, V. Metro: Palermo. **Amenities:** Restaurant; bar; babysitting; bikes; concierge; health club and spa; Internet in business center; heated outdoor pool; room service. *In room:* A/C, TV, kitchen (in some), minibar.

Krista Hotel ★ This small one-story boutique hotel, built into a long chorizo or sausage house, has a romantic, antique feel. Each room is named for an Argentine artist. This was the former home of Raúl Matera, a doctor to Juan Perón and a politico of his own, and was among the places the U.S. Bush twins stayed during their infamous Buenos Aires romp. Rooms are small, even the oversized one that's billed as a suite. Service is intimate, and there are many public spaces, including a dining room, courtyard, and back patio with a Jacuzzi. There's an appointment-only massage room and the hotel has agreements with other hotels, whose services you can use for an additional fee. Pets are allowed, but call ahead.

Bonpland 1665 (btw. Honduras and Gorriti), 1425 Buenos Aires. www.kristahotel.com.ar. ✆ **11/4771-4697.** Fax 11/4776-4650. 10 units, including 1 suite. $182–$236 double; $260 suite. Rates include breakfast buffet. AE, MC, V. Parking $10. Metro: Palermo. **Amenities:** Babysitting; bikes; Jacuzzi; room service. *In room:* A/C, TV, minibar (most rooms), Wi-Fi.

ABASTO

Abasto lies outside of the city center: along Corrientes, but beyond the theater district. Historically, it's associated with singer Carlos Gardel, the country's greatest tango star of the 1920s and 1930s. The area, along with the bordering neighborhood of Once, is also the historic home of Buenos Aires's Jewish communities. This neighborhood is anchored by the enormous **Abasto Shopping Center,** which is home to many places of interest to families with kids, such as the **Museo de los Niños** (p. 121). For a map of the hotels listed in the section, see the "Abasto & Once" map on p. 95.

Expensive

Abasto Plaza Hotel ★ A block away from this hotel are both the **Abasto Shopping Center** and **Esquina Carlos Gardel,** sites dedicated to the tango crooner.

An estimated 25,000 to 50,000 American expats live in Buenos Aires, along with a nearly equal number of Brits, and a smaller number of Canadians, Australians, and New Zealanders. A number of websites can help you connect with other expats and find out about local parties, including **www.LandingpadBA.com, www.baexpats.org, www.expat-argentina.blogspot.com, www.discoverbuenosaires.com, www.yanquimike.blogspot.com, www.everydayinbuenosaires.com, www.movingtoargentina.typepad.com, www.**

gaysawayinba.multiply.com, and **www.expat-connection.com. Spanglish** or **Beerlingual (© 11/15-4042-5001;** www.spanglishexchange.com) offers social networking and language-learning events. If you're planning on moving to Buenos Aires long-term, the apartment recommendations in this section can help you take the plunge, but if you plan to set up a business or buy property, be sure to contact your local Argentine Embassy or Consulate for proper paperwork.

The hotel takes this to heart, with a tango shop for shoes, dresses, and other *milonga* accessories. Free tango lessons and shows take place Thursday evenings at 9pm in the lobby. There's also a free tango show every night at 8pm in the restaurant. Rooms are a decent size, and thematic suites have a tango decor. Superior rooms come with whirlpool bathtubs. The restaurant, **Volver,** is named for a Gardel song. The small heated outdoor pool sits on the rooftop, with access through a small gym.

Av. Corrientes 3190 (at Anchorena), 1193 Buenos Aires. www.abastoplaza.com. © **11/6311-4466.** Fax 11/6311-4465. 120 units including 26 suites. From $115 double; from $266 suite. Rates include buffet breakfast. AE, DC, MC, V. Parking $12. Metro: Carlos Gardel. **Amenities:** Restaurant; bar; concierge; small health club; heated outdoor pool; room service; 1 room for those w/limited mobility. *In room:* A/C, TV, high-speed Internet, minibar, Wi-Fi.

APARTMENT SERVICES IN BUENOS AIRES

Hotels are not for everyone. Maybe you want a place where you can come and go as you please. Maybe you want a space where you can throw parties while you're in town. Maybe you're independent-minded and want a better idea of what it feels like to live in Buenos Aires as a local, especially if you're thinking of making the big leap and moving here like tens of thousands of expats. Apartments allow you the opportunity to do all of that. Contact each company directly for exact terms, prices, payments, and services. A few words of caution: Recently, crime targeting foreign apartment-renters has gone up, especially coming from the airport, as most apartment-rental companies demand a huge amount of cash up front. It's a good idea to work out payment by credit card or PayPal, or in installments. Also, keep in mind that hotels have concierges and guards, and many buildings, unless they have a doorman, do not, so there is a certain amount of vulnerability involved in living in an apartment. That said, this is a great window into living like a local.

BA Apartments This is a full-service rental company with apartments in many neighborhoods throughout Buenos Aires. Paraguay 2035 (btw. Ayacucho and Junín). www.baapartments.com.ar. © **11/4864-8084.**

Best Rentals Buenos Aires This service is run out of the El Firulette youth hostel in downtown Buenos Aires. It offers inexpensive long-term and short-term rentals, many catering to the budget-conscious. Some of their prices are significantly lower than those offered by other companies, but the sizes of apartments differ. Maipu 208 (at Perón). www.bestrentalsba.com. © **11/5031 2215** in Buenos Aires, or 646/502-8605 in the U.S. and Canada.

Buenos Aires Apartment This is a reasonably priced apartment in Barrio Norte, rented by owner Debora Pucheta, who has lived in the United States. www.buenosaires apt.com.ar. © **291/15-5727238** (cell) or debotwister@gmail.com.

ByT Argentina This apartment service has apartments all over Buenos Aires, focusing on up-and-coming Palermo Viejo. www.bytargentina.com. © **11/4876-5000.**

Friendly Apartments This apartment service concentrates on Barrio Norte and serves a gay clientele. It combines short-term rentals with hotel services, offering concierge and almost-daily maid service. The company also represents foreigners purchasing apartments as investments. **Temporary Apartments,** listed below, is the company's non-gay face. Callao 1234 (at Juncal). www.friendlyapartments.com. © **11/4816-9056,** 11/4811-0279 in Buenos Aires, or 619/841-0054 in the U.S. and Canada.

Loft & Arte This is a boutique apartment hotel complex just off of Avenida de Mayo. Apartments range from efficiencies to double-level apartments. Many have balconies and washing machines. The complex provides breakfast, a cleaning service, and a concierge. There's also a pleasant central patio. Hipólito Yrigoyen 1194 (btw. Cerrito [9 de Julio] and Libertad). www.loftyarte.com.ar. © **11/4381-3229** or 11/4115-1770.

My Apartment Abroad A small, personal apartment service run by Buenos Aires native Sebastian Avila. He works closely with his foreign clients, and personally knows most apartment owners he represents. Sebastian can also arrange tours. www.myapartmentabroad.com. © **11/3964-2065** or 11/15-2157-2612 (cell).

Temporary Apartments This is the mainstream face of Friendly Apartments; buildings, offerings, and prices are the same. Callao 1234 (at Juncal in the Concord Building). www.temporaryapartments.com.ar. © **11/4816-9056,** 11/4811-0279 in Buenos Aires, or 619/841-0054 in the U.S. and Canada.

WHERE TO DINE

Buenos Aires offers world-class dining and cuisine at a variety of Argentine and international restaurants. While the bargains available in the wake of the collapse of the peso are long gone, restaurants in Argentina are still a great value compared to similar establishments in North America and Europe.

Buenos Aires's most fashionable eateries are in **Palermo Hollywood** and **Palermo Soho,** where fine dining and a bohemian atmosphere meet in small, renovated, turn-of-the-20th-century houses. **Puerto Madero's** docks are cluttered with excellent restaurants with water views. The **Microcentro** and **Recoleta** offer many outstanding restaurants and cafes, some of which have been on the map for decades. **Calle Báez** in **Las Cañitas** has one of the most happening restaurant scenes in the city, and restaurants and bars that serve food surround **Plaza Serrano** in Palermo Soho, with many good choices for the young and bargain-minded. Both of these neighborhoods have plenty of nearby places for after-dinner drinks and dancing, so you won't have to go all over for a night out.

Buenos Aires's cafe life, in which friends meet over coffee, is as sacred a ritual to Porteños as it is to Parisians. Excellent places to enjoy a *cafe con leche* (coffee with milk) include **La Biela** in Recoleta, across from the world-famous Recoleta Cemetery, and **Café Tortoni,** one of the city's most beautiful and traditional cafes, on Avenida de Mayo close to Plaza de Mayo. Both are among the city's protected *cafés notables*.

Porteños eat breakfast up until 10am, lunch between noon and 4pm, and dinner late—usually after 9pm, though some restaurants open as early as 7pm. If you are an early diner in the North American and British style, look for restaurants in my listings that remain open between lunch and dinner. If you can make a reservation, I highly recommend doing so. If you do not want to commit, go to a restaurant at the typical 8pm opening time, when you will almost always arrive to find it nearly empty. By 9pm, however, virtually every table at the best restaurants will be full.

If you want to dine in an atmosphere recalling the glory days of Buenos Aires's past, choose one of dozens of *bares* and *cafés notables*—historic restaurants, cafes, and bars that have been specially protected by a law stating that their interiors cannot be changed. Known as Law No. 35, this special protection granted by the city of Buenos Aires was passed in 1998 and updated in 2002. I list many of these special establishments in this chapter, including **Café Tortoni, La Biela,** and **Bar El**

Federal. Naturally, based on age, these *notables* cluster in Monserrat, Congreso, La Boca, and San Telmo, the city's oldest areas. Ask the tourism office for the map *Bares y Cafés Notables de Buenos Aires,* which lists them all and includes photographs of their interiors. If you really like the atmosphere in these unique spots, you can bring a part of them home with you in a coffee-table book with photos from these wonderful places that some of the venues sell.

Many restaurants close between lunch and dinner, and some close completely on Sunday or Monday, or only serve dinner. In late December, January, and February, many restaurants have limited hours and service, or close entirely, as this is when Porteños flee the city for the beach resorts. Call ahead so you're not disappointed.

Executive lunch menus (usually fixed-price three-course meals) are served at many restaurants beginning at noon, but most dinner menus are a la carte. There is sometimes a small "cover" or "service" charge for bread and other items placed at the table, which can add a few dollars to a final bill. In restaurants that serve pasta, the pasta and its sauce are sometimes priced separately. Standard tipping is 10% in Buenos Aires, but you should leave more for exceptional service. When paying by credit card, you will often be expected to leave the *propina* (tip) in cash.

If you can't make up your mind, visit **www.restaurant.com.ar**, which has English-language and Spanish-language information on restaurants in Buenos Aires and elsewhere, searchable by neighborhood and cuisine. Check out **www.guiaoleo.com.ar** (Spanish only) and **www.gastronomique.com.ar**, which provides an overview of Argentine cuisine, and the *Buenos Aires Herald,* especially Dereck Foster's food and wine reviews. Once in Buenos Aires, look for the **De Dios** map company's excellent restaurant map in bookstores everywhere, or order it ahead of time at **www.dediosonline.com**. Many Palermo restaurants are on a special Palermo dining map available in Palermo businesses. A similar map exists for San Telmo.

I list exact prices for main courses and group restaurants into general price categories. **Very Expensive** restaurants have main courses costing about $25 and up. **Expensive** restaurants have main courses from about $15 to $25. **Moderate** restaurants have prices ranging from around $10 to $20. **Inexpensive** restaurants have main courses ranging from under $3 to about $15. Tips, drinks, desserts, other menu items, as well as table service and the unavoidable charge for bread and spreads, will add costs. While English is becoming more and more prevalent in Buenos Aires, less expensive restaurants have fewer English speakers.

RESTAURANTS BY CUISINE

AMERICAN

McDonald's Kosher ★★ (Abasto, $, p. 94)

ARGENTINE

Al Galope ★ (Once, $$, p. 94)

Bar El Federal ★★ (San Telmo, $$, p. 74)

Bien Porteño ★ (Congreso, $, p. 81)

The Brighton ★★★ (Microcentro, $$$, p. 68)

Cabaña Las Lilas ★★★ (Puerto Madero, $$$, p. 66)

Caseros ★ (Barracas, $$, p. 96)

Café de la Ciudad (Microcentro, $$, p. 69)

Café Retiro ★★ (Microcentro, $, p. 71)

Campo Bravo ★★ (Palermo, $$, p. 89)

Clásica y Moderna ★★ (Barrio Norte, $$, p. 79)

Club Social ★ (Barracas, $$, p. 97)

Cluny ★★★ (Palermo, $$$, p. 83)

Confitería del Botánico (Palermo, $, p. 92)

De Olivas i Lustres ★★ (Palermo, $$, p. 89)

El Obrero ★★★ (La Boca, $$, p. 96)

El Palacio de la Papa Frita (Microcentro, $$, p. 70)

Gardel de Buenos Aires ★ (Abasto, $, p. 93)

Gran Parrilla del Plata ★★★ (San Telmo, $$, p. 74)

Gran Victoria ★ (Plaza de Mayo area, $$, p. 63)

HG Restaurant ★ (Palermo, $$$, p. 83)

Inside Resto-Bar ★★ (Congreso, $$, p. 80)

La Americana ★★ (Congreso, $, p. 82)

La Brigada ★★ (San Telmo, $$, p. 75)

La Cabaña ★ (Puerto Madero, $$$, p. 66)

La Cabrera ★★ (Palermo, $$$, p. 86)

La Chacra ★ (Microcentro, $$, p. 70)

La Clac ★ (Congreso, $$, p. 80)

La Coruña ★★ (San Telmo, $, p. 75)

La Perla (La Boca, $$, p. 96)

La Poesía ★★ (San Telmo, $S, p. 75)

La Salamandra ★ (Palermo,$$, p. 90)

Las Choclas ★★ (Palermo, $, p. 92)

Las Cuartetas ★★★ (Microcentro, $, p. 72)

Las Nazarenas ★ (Microcentro, $$, p. 68)

Macondo Bar ★★ (Palermo, $, p. 92)

Meridiano 58 ★★ (Palermo, $$$, p. 86)

Pampa Picante ★ (Palermo, $$$, p. 87)

Patagonia Sur ★ (La Boca, $$$$, p. 95)

Plaza Asturias ★★ (Congreso, $$, p. 80)

Plaza del Carmen (Congreso, $$, p. 81)

Richmond Cafe ★★ (Microcentro, $$, p. 71)

Rio Alba ★ (Palermo, $$$, p. 88)

Sucath David ★ (Once, $$, p. 94)

Sullivan's Drink House (Palermo, $$$, p. 88)

T-Bone Bar & Grill ★ (Palermo, $$, p. 91)

36 Billares ★★ (Congreso, $$, p. 81)

Utopia Bar (Palermo, $$, p. 91)

ASIAN

Asia de Cuba ★ (Puerto Madero, $$$, p. 63)

Empire ★ (Microcentro, $$, p. 70)

Sudestada ★ (Palermo, $$$, p. 88)

Tandoor ★ (Barrio Norte, $$, p. 79)

CAFES/CONFITERIAS

Bar El Federal ★★ (San Telmo, $$, p. 74)

Bien Porteño ★ (Congreso, $, p. 81)

Café de la Ciudad (Microcentro, $$, p. 69)

Café de Madres de Plaza de Mayo ★★ (Congreso, $, p. 81)

Café Retiro ★★ (Microcentro, $, p. 71)

KEY TO ABBREVIATIONS:
$$$$** = Very Expensive   **$$$** = Expensive   **$$** = Moderate   **$ = Inexpensive

Café Tortoni ★★★ (Microcentro, $, p. 71)

Café Victoria ★ (Recoleta, $$, p. 77)

Confitería del Botánico (Palermo, $, p. 92)

Gran Victoria ★ (Plaza de Mayo area, $$, p. 63)

Il Gran Caffe ★ (Microcentro, $, p. 72)

La Biela ★★★ (Recoleta, $, p. 78)

La Coruña ★★ (San Telmo, $, p. 75)

La Moncloa ★ (Congreso, $$, p. 80)

La Perla (La Boca, $$, p. 96)

Plaza del Carmen (Congreso, $$, p. 81)

Richmond Cafe ★★ (Microcentro, $$, p. 71)

CHILEAN

Los Chilenos ★ (Microcentro, $$, p. 70)

CHINESE

Buddha BA ★ (Belgrano, $$$, p. 96)

FRENCH

Brasserie Petanque ★★ (San Telmo, $$$, p. 73)

La Bourgogne ★★★ (Recoleta, $$$$, p. 76)

Le Sud ★★ (Microcentro, $$$, p. 68)

Ligure ★★ (Microcentro, $$, p. 70)

Te Mataré Ramírez ★★★ (Palermo, $$$, p. 89)

INDIAN

Tandoor ★ (Barrio Norte, $$, p. 79)

INTERNATIONAL

Bien Porteño ★ (Congreso, $, p. 81)

The Brighton ★★★ (Microcentro, $$$, p. 68)

Casa Cruz ★★ (Palermo, $$$$, p. 82)

Caseros ★ (Barracas, $$, p. 96)

Clark's ★ (Recoleta, $$, p. 78)

Club Social ★ (Barracas, $$, p. 97)

Cluny ★★★ (Palermo, $$$, p. 83)

HG Restaurant ★ (Palermo, $$$, p. 83)

Inside Resto-Bar ★★ (Congreso, $$, p. 80)

La Poesía ★★ (San Telmo, $$, p. 75)

La Vineria de Gualterio Bolivar ★ (San Telmo, $$$, p. 73)

La Salamandra ★ (Palermo, $$, p. 90)

Lola ★ (Recoleta, $$$, p. 77)

Macondo Bar ★★ (Palermo, $, p. 92)

Meridiano 58 ★★ (Palermo, $$$, p. 86)

Milion ★★ (Barrio Norte, $$$, p. 79)

Mute (Palermo, $$$, p. 86)

Novecento ★★★ (Palermo, $$, p. 90)

Osaka ★ (Palermo, $$$, p. 87)

Pampa Picante ★ (Palermo, $$$, p. 87)

Patagonia Sur ★ (La Boca, $$$$, p. 95)

Plaza Grill ★★ (Microcentro, $$$, p. 69)

Prodeo ★★ (Palermo, $$$, p. 88)

Prologo ★ (Palermo, $, p. 92)

Puerto Cristal ★ (Puerto Madero, $$, p. 67)

647 Club ★★ (San Telmo, $$$, p. 74)

T-Bone Bar & Grill ★ (Palermo, $$, p. 91)

Tegui ★★★ (Palermo, $$$$, p. 82)

Te Mataré Ramírez ★★★ (Palermo, $$$, p. 89)

Tomo Uno (Microcentro, $$$$, p. 68)

Utopia Bar (Palermo, $$, p. 91)

ITALIAN

Broccolino ★ (Microcentro, $$, p. 69)

Casa Cruz ★★ (Palermo, $$$$, p. 82)

El Obrero ★★★ (La Boca, $$, p. 96)

Filo ★ (Microcentro, $, p. 72)

Gardel de Buenos Aires ★ (Abasto, $, p. 93)

Il Fiume (Puerto Madero, $$$, p. 66)

Il Gran Caffe ★ (Microcentro, $, p. 72)

La Americana ★★ (Congreso, $, p. 82)

La Baita ★★ (Palermo, $$$, p. 86)

Las Cuartetas ★★★ (Microcentro, $, p. 72)

Ligure ★★ (Microcentro, $$, p. 70)

Piegari ★★ (Recoleta, $$$$, p. 76)

Plaza Asturias ★★ (Congreso, $$, p. 80)

Sorrento del Puerto ★★ (Puerto Madero, $$$, p. 67)

Sottovoce ★★ (Puerto Madero, $$$, p. 67)

JAPANESE

Asia de Cuba ★ (Puerto Madero, $$$, p. 63)

Ceviche ★★ (Palermo, $$$, p. 83)

Osaka ★ (Palermo, $$$, p. 87)

Sushi Club (Palermo, $, p. 91)

KOSHER

Al Galope ★ (Once, $$, p. 94)

McDonald's Kosher ★★ (Abasto, $, p. 94)

Sucath David ★ (Once, $$, p. 94)

MEDITERRANEAN

Bio ★★ (Palermo, $, p. 92)

De Olivas i Lustres ★★ (Palermo, $$, p. 89)

HG Restaurant ★ (Palermo, $$$, p. 83)

Le Mistral ★★ (Recoleta, $$$, p. 77)

Le Sud ★★ (Microcentro, $$$, p. 68)

Restaurante y Bar Mediterráneo ★★ (Monserrat, $$, p. 73)

647 Club ★★ (San Telmo, $$$, p. 74)

Tegui ★★★ (Palermo, $$$$, p. 82)

MEXICAN

Lupita ★★ (Palermo, $$, p. 90)

Tazz ★ (Palermo, $, p. 93)

MIDDLE EASTERN

Al Galope ★ (Once, $$, p. 94)

Garbis ★★ (Palermo, $$, p. 90)

Sucath David ★ (Once, $$, p. 94)

Viejo Agump ★ (Palermo, $, p. 93)

PARRILLAS

Al Galope ★ (Once, $$, p. 94)

Campo Bravo ★★ (Palermo, $$, p. 89)

El Desnivel ★ (San Telmo, $$, p. 74)

El Estanciero ★ (Palermo, $$, p. 90)

El Mirasol ★★ (Recoleta, $$$, p. 76)

El Obrero ★★★ (La Boca, $$, p. 96)

El Palacio de la Papa Frita (Microcentro, $$, p. 70)

Gran Parrilla del Plata ★★★ (San Telmo, $$, p. 74)

Juana M ★★ (Recoleta, $$, p. 78)

La Bistecca ★★ (Puerto Madero, $$, p. 67)

La Brigada ★ (San Telmo, $$, p. 75)

La Cabaña ★ (Puerto Madero, $$$, p. 66)

La Cabrera ★★ (Palermo, $$$, p. 86)

La Chacra ★ (Microcentro, $$, p. 70)

La Clac ★ (Congreso, $$, p. 80)

Las Choclas ★★ (Palermo, $, p. 92)

Pampa Picante ★ (Palermo, $$$, p. 87)

Patagonia Sur ★ (La Boca, $$$$, p. 95)

Rio Alba ★ (Palermo, $$$, p. 88)

Sucath David ★ (Once, $$, p. 94)

T-Bone Bar & Grill ★ (Palermo, $$, p. 91)

PERUVIAN

Ceviche ★★ (Palermo, $$$, p. 83)

Osaka ★ (Palermo, $$$, p. 87)

PIZZA

Filo ★ (Microcentro, $, p. 72)

Las Cuartetas ★★★ (Microcentro, $, p. 72)

Prologo ★ (Palermo, $, p. 92)

SCANDINAVIAN

Olsen ★★ (Palermo, $$$, p. 86)

SEAFOOD

Ceviche ★★ (Palermo, $$$, p. 83)

La Vineria de Gualterio Bolivar ★ (San Telmo, $$$, p. 73)

Los Chilenos ★ (Microcentro, $$, p. 70)

Olsen ★★ (Palermo, $$$, p. 86)

Osaka ★ (Palermo, $$$, p. 87)

Prodeo ★★ (Palermo, $$$, p. 88)

Puerto Cristal ★ (Puerto Madero, $$, p. 67)

SPANISH

HG Restaurant ★ (Palermo, $$$, p. 83)

La Tasca de Plaza Mayor ★★ (Recoleta, $$$, p. 77)

Palacio Español ★★ (Monserrat, $$, p. 72)

Plaza Asturias ★★ (Congreso, $$, p. 80)

PLAZA DE MAYO AREA

For a map of the restaurants listed in this section, see the "Restaurants in Central Buenos Aires" map on p. 64.

Moderate

Gran Victoria ★ CAFE/ARGENTINE   Watch the political world of Argentina pass by your window at this great cafe overlooking Plaza de Mayo. This cafe sits in the middle of one of the country's most important historic areas, with stunning views of the Cabildo, Plaza de Mayo, Casa Rosada, and the Metropolitan Cathedral, in addition to excellent people-watching opportunities. Food is basic Argentine with Italian touches, and there's a great dessert selection. I'd recommend coming here for a break after sightseeing in the area. What's more, the waitresses have a pleasant sense of humor (I guess they'd have to, dealing with so many politicians).

Hipólito Yrigoyen 500 (at Diagonal Sur). © **11/4345-7703.** Main courses $4–$15. AE, MC, V. Mon–Sat 7am–9pm. Metro: Bolívar.

PUERTO MADERO

Not all of Puerto Madero has convenient metro stops, but all restaurants are, at most, a 20-minute walk from a metro station.

For a map of the restaurants listed in this section, see the "Restaurants in Central Buenos Aires" map on p. 64.

Expensive

Asia de Cuba ★ ASIAN/JAPANESE   Though not associated with the other Asia de Cubas around the world, this place offers an exciting environment in which to dine. Renovated in 2008, the space is chic, with black and dark brown decor, gold-gilded carved columns decorated with lotuses, and a golden reclining Buddha over the bar. In the back, there's a sushi bar and a VIP lounge. It's very glamorous at dinnertime; lunch is a more casual affair. A table sushi menu, with 110 different items, is about $180. Dinner comes with all kinds of exotic entertainment, such as Arabian belly dancers. Asia de Cuba is also one of the most important clubs in the Puerto Madero area, ideal for a more mature crowd because a large portion of its clientele is older than 40. Dancing begins at about 1am Tuesday to Saturday, and there is no admission charge if you're already dining. If you do not eat here, admission ranges from $15 to $20.

Pierina Dealessi 750 (at Güemes on Dique 3). © **11/4894-1328** or 11/4894-1329. www.asiadecuba.com. ar. Reservations recommended. Main courses $10–$20. AE, MC, V. Daily 1pm–5am, often later on weekends. Metro: L. N. Alem.

Restaurants in Central Buenos Aires

5

Puerto Madero

WHERE TO DINE

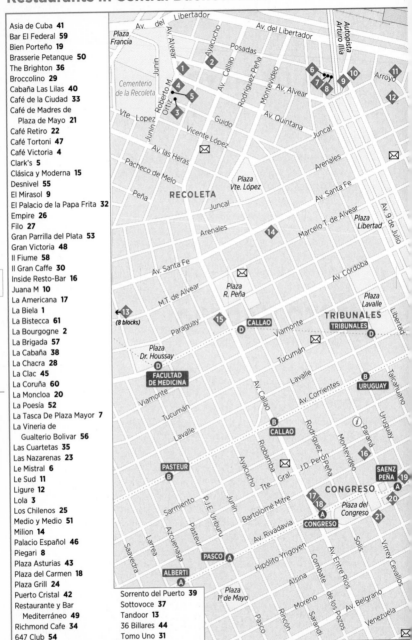

wine TASTING

Part of what makes meals in Buenos Aires so outstanding is the fine wine selection. Most Argentine wine comes from the Mendoza region, bordering the Andean mountains. If you know nothing about wine, you may want to take a wine-tasting class to make sense of the selections you'll encounter on your trip. One of the best is run by the Hotel Alvear's **Cave de Vines** (© **11/4805-3857;** www.alvearpalace.com), which takes place Monday through Friday at 7pm and costs $78 per person. You'll get about 45 minutes with a sommelier who will explain the grape-growing process, the harvest, and how the wine is actually produced as you sample wine and appetizer pairings from various regions. You'll learn what to look for in every glass, how to pair wines with food, and how to hold a glass without damaging its contents with your hand's warmth.

The Palermo Viejo wine shop **Lo De Joaquin Alberdi,** Borges 1772 at Costa Rica (© **11/4832-5329;** www.lodejoaquinalberdi.com.ar), offers tastings by appointment, which cost about $43 for four wines. In early 2010, the winery **Fin del Mundo** opened the chic Experiencia Bodega Fin del Mundo in Palermo, Honduras 5673 between Fitzroy and Bonpland (© **11/4852-6661;** www.bodegadelfindelmundo.com), offering a variety of wine-tasting options.

La Cabaña ★ ARGENTINE/PARRILLA This is the third incarnation for one of Buenos Aires's most legendary eateries. A computer lets you track where your beef came from, even the date the cow was killed (cool or creepy depending on your view). Besides beef—served in portions as large as a kilogram (2.2 lb.)—there's chicken, fish, and a large salad selection. This place is often confused with its main competitor, Cabaña Las Lilas, also in Puerto Madero, which has similar prices but is less formal.

Alicia Moreau de Justo 380 (at Corrientes). © **11/4314-3710.** www.lacabanabuenosaires.com.ar. Main courses $14-$50. AE, DC, MC, V. Daily noon–1am. Metro: L. N. Alem.

Cabaña Las Lilas ★★★ ARGENTINE Widely considered the best *parrilla* in Buenos Aires, the 400-seat Cabaña Las Lilas is always packed. The menu pays homage to Argentine beef, which comes from the restaurant's private *estancia* (ranch). The table "cover"—which includes dried tomatoes, mozzarella, olives, peppers, and delicious garlic bread—nicely whets the appetite. Clearly, you're here to order steak: The best cuts are the rib-eye, baby beef, and thin skirt steak. Order sautéed vegetables, grilled onions, or Provençal-style fries separately. The enormous eatery offers indoor and outdoor seating. In spite of its high prices, it's casual and informal; patrons come in suits or shorts. They also offer a good salad selection, so even vegetarians can share a table with friends. As they don't close between lunch and dinner, the restaurant is ideal for early dining in the North American or British style.

Alicia Moreau de Justo 516 (at Villaflor in Dique 3). © **11/4313-1336.** www.laslilas.com. Reservations recommended. Main courses $12-$30. AE, DC, V. Sun–Thurs noon–12:30am; Fri–Sat noon–1am. Metro: L. N. Alem.

Il Fiume ITALIAN This Italian restaurant is ideally located directly on the Puerto Madero waterfront, on the eastern bank of the port, and has a combination of indoor and outdoor seating. You'll find scaloppine, rabbit alla Genovese with portobello mushrooms and cherry tomatoes, *pollo* (chicken) de Capri, cod Venetian style, and several kinds of risotto. Desserts are decadent, from vanilla *panna cotta* (cream custard), to *baba au rhum* (yeast cake in rum) with gelato. Sometimes, there is also live modern Italian music and jazz in the outdoor dining area.

Olga Cossetini 1651 (at Ezcurra, in Dique 1). © **11/5787-3097.** Main courses $12–$20. AE, DC, V. Daily 12:30pm–1am. No metro access.

Sorrento del Puerto ★★ ITALIAN

When the city decided to reinvigorate Puerto Madero in the mid-1990s, this was one of the first five restaurants opened (today you'll find more than 50). The sleek modern dining room boasts large windows, modern blue lighting, and tables and booths decorated with white linens and individual roses. The outdoor patio accommodates only 15 tables, but the inside is enormous. People come here for two reasons: great pasta and even better seafood. Choose your pasta and accompanying sauce: seafood, shrimp scampi, pesto, or four cheeses. The best seafood dishes include trout stuffed with crabmeat, sole with a Belle Marnier sauce, Galician-style octopus, paella Valenciana, and assorted grilled seafood for two. A three-course lunch menu with a drink costs $16.

Av. Alicia Moreau de Justo 410 (at Guevara on Dique 4). © **11/4319-8730.** www.sorrentorestaurant. com.ar. Reservations recommended. Main courses $10–$25. AE, DC, MC, V. Mon–Fri noon–4pm and 8pm–1am; Sat 8pm–2am. Metro: L. N. Alem.

Sottovoce ★★ ITALIAN

One of the city's best Italian restaurants, Sottovoce provides great dining with a view to the port. Look for various *lomos* (sirloin cuts), rabbit dishes, saltimbocca, shrimp with a curry red-wine sauce, and over 17 kinds of pasta dishes. The wine list, with local, French, and Italian vintages, is more than 10 pages long.

Alicia M. De Justo 176 (at Tucumán, on Dique 4). © **11/4313-1199.** www.sottovoceristorante.com.ar. Main courses $12–$25. AE, MC, V. Daily noon–4pm; Mon–Thurs 8pm–midnight; Fri–Sat 8pm–1am. Metro: L. N. Alem.

Moderate

La Bistecca ★★ 🍴 PARRILLA

This Puerto Madero eatery offers a wide range of meal choices at an incredible value. This is an all-you-can-eat establishment, locally called a *tenedor libre*. A three-course lunch is about $12, and dinner ranges from about $12 to $20. If you came to Argentina for beef, definitely stop here. The high quality of the meat surprised me, considering the price and bottomless portions. For vegetarians, there is also a diverse salad bar. In spite of the restaurant's large size, the lighting and seating arrangements create small intimate spaces. At lunchtime, the place is full of businesspersons, while at night you'll find a mix of couples, friends, and families.

Av. Alicia Moreau de Justo 1890 (at Peñaloza on Dique 1). © **11/4514-4996.** www.labistecca.com. Main courses $8–$12. AE, DC, MC, V. Daily noon–4pm and 8pm–1am. Metro: L. N. Alem.

Puerto Cristal ★ INTERNATIONAL/SEAFOOD

The menu here has everything, but fish is why patrons choose this restaurant over others in Puerto Madero. The place is enormous, with friendly hostesses and theatrical waiter service; a constant flurry of fresh silverware and dishes will cross your table between courses, befitting a much pricier establishment. Windows overlooking the port and glassed-in central garden lend tranquillity to the industrial-chic design. Great lunch specials are part of the draw here; their executive menu costs about $15 and usually includes a glass of champagne (though other drinks and the table cover will be additional charges).

Av. Alicia Moreau de Justo 1082 (at Villaflor in Dique 3). © **11/4331-3669.** www.puerto-cristal.com.ar. Main courses $6–$20. AE, MC, V. Sun–Fri 6:30am–midnight; Sat 6:30am–2am. Metro: L. N. Alem.

MICROCENTRO

For a map of the restaurants listed in this section, see the "Restaurants in Central Buenos Aires" map on p. 64.

Very Expensive

Tomo Uno INTERNATIONAL   Tomo Uno has been around in various incarnations for decades, and now is in the Pan Americano Hotel's mezzanine, its windows opening onto Avenida 9 de Julio. It was started by sisters Ada and Ebe Concaro, though sadly, Ada died in December 2010. Her son, Federico Fialayre, is manager and chef, and has insisted on carrying on his mother's work. This is a quiet, business-like place, especially at lunchtime, its burlap walls and carpeting keeping down the noise of ladies-who-lunch and office workers wheeling and dealing. Food is quickly prepared, and choices include traditional beef items and a range of fish dishes, such as rainbow trout with lemon sauce and almonds. There's an excellent wine list, chosen by Federico, who has also written a book on Argentine wine.

Carlos Pellegrini (9 de Julio) 521 (btw. Tucumán and Lavalle in the Pan Americano Hotel). ✆ **11/4326-6698.** www.tomo1.com.ar. Main courses $25–$65. AE, DC, MC, V. Mon-Fri noon–3pm; Mon-Sat 7:30pm–12:30am. Metro: Carlos Pellegrini.

Expensive

The Brighton ★★★ ARGENTINE/INTERNATIONAL   The Brighton, a bar and café notable, is one of the most stunningly situated restaurants in Buenos Aires. The restaurant interior dates from 1908 and was originally a tailor shop patronized by British royalty. The decor is elegantly Edwardian, with stained glass and wood paneling ornamented with carved symbols of the Prince of Wales. The atmosphere is jovial, with a very active bar, especially during their happy hour from 5 to 8pm. The cuisine is a mix of international and traditional Argentine dishes, from lomo cooked in various sauces to an extensive array of fish dishes, including lobster. The restaurant is also open for breakfast, offering crepes, coffee, and croissants. There is also a beautiful wine room in the back, and a professional sommelier for wine tastings.

Sarmiento 645 (btw. Florida and Maipu). ✆ **11/4322-1515** or 11/4325-9126. www.thenewbrightonsrl. com.ar. Main courses $10–$30. AE, DC, MC, V. Mon-Sat 8am–2am, sometimes later. Metro: Florida.

Las Nazarenas ★ ARGENTINE   This is not a restaurant, an old waiter will warn you; it's an *asador*. More specifically, it's a steakhouse with meat on the menu, not a pseudo-*parrilla* with vegetable plates or some froufrou international dishes for the faint of heart. You have two choices: cuts grilled on the *parrilla* or meat cooked on a spit over the fire. Argentine presidents and foreign ministers alike have made their way here. The two-level dining room is handsomely decorated with cases of Argentine wines and abundant plants. Service is unhurried, allowing you plenty of time for a relaxing meal. The location near high-rise office complexes means it is very busy during lunch.

Reconquista 1132 (at Leandro N. Alem). ✆ **11/4312-5559.** www.lasnazarenas.com.ar. Main courses $15–$25. AE, DC, MC, V. Daily noon–1am. Metro: San Martín.

Le Sud ★★ FRENCH/MEDITERRANEAN   Executive Chef Thierry Pszonka earned a gold medal from the National Committee of French Gastronomy and gained experience at La Bourgogne before opening this gourmet restaurant in the new Sofitel Hotel. His simple, elegant cooking style embraces spices and olive oils from Provence, to create delicious entrees such as stewed rabbit with green pepper and tomatoes, polenta with Parmesan and rosemary, and spinach with lemon ravioli. Le Sud's dining room is as sophisticated as the cuisine: The design is contemporary, with chandeliers and black-marble floors, tables of Brazilian rosewood, and large windows overlooking Calle Arroyo. After dinner, consider a drink in the adjacent wine bar.

Arroyo 841-849 (at Suipacha in the Sofitel Hotel). **☎ 11/4131-0000.** Reservations recommended. Main courses $15-$25. AE, DC, MC, V. Daily 6:30–11am, 12:30–3pm, and 7:30pm–midnight. Metro: San Martín.

Plaza Grill ★★ INTERNATIONAL   For nearly a century, the Plaza Grill dominated the city's power-lunch scene, and it remains the first choice for government officials and business executives. The dining room is decorated with dark oak furniture, the owners' 90-year-old Dutch porcelain collection, Indian fans from the British Empire, and Villeroy & Boch china place settings. Tables are well spaced, allowing for intimate conversations. Order a la carte from the international menu or off the *parrilla*—the steaks are perfect Argentine cuts. Order the marinated filet mignon with gratinéed potatoes, or the venison with crispy applesauce—served during the November and December holiday season, though seemingly incongruous in the heat of Buenos Aires's summer. The "po parisky eggs" form another classic dish dating back to the hotel's Belle Epoque opening. The kitchen is overseen by Chef Donato Gabriel Mazzeo, and the restaurant's wine list spans seven countries, with the world's best Malbec coming from Mendoza. There is a very reasonable $40 executive lunch menu.

Marriott Plaza Hotel, Calle Florida 1005 (at Santa Fe overlooking Plaza San Martín). **☎ 11/4318-3070.** Reservations recommended. Main courses $12-$25. AE, DC, MC, V. Daily noon–4pm and 7pm–midnight. Metro: San Martín.

Moderate

Broccolino ★ ITALIAN   The name of this restaurant doesn't mean little broccoli; it's a corruption of Italian immigrant slang for New York's biggest and once most heavily Italian borough (notice the Brooklyn memorabilia filling the walls and the mural of Manhattan's skyline). This casual trattoria near Calle Florida is popular with North Americans. Many of the waiters speak English, and the restaurant has a distinctly New York outer-borough feel. Three small dining rooms are decorated in quintessential red-and-white-checkered tablecloths, and the smell of tomatoes, onions, and garlic fills the air. The restaurant is known for its spicy pizzas, fresh pastas, and, above all, its sauces (salsas in Spanish). The restaurant also serves 907 kilograms (2,000 lb.) per month of baby calamari sautéed in wine, onions, parsley, and garlic.

Córdoba 820 (at Esmeralda). **☎ 11/4322-9848.** www.broccolino.com. Reservations recommended. Main courses $5-$15. AE, DC, MC, V. Daily noon–4pm and 7pm–1am. Metro: Lavalle.

Café de la Ciudad CAFE/ARGENTINE   The city's only restaurant with outdoor dining directly overlooking the Obelisco, Café de la Ciudad opened more than 40 years ago on one of the corners around the landmark, on Avenida 9 de Julio. It's like Buenos Aires's Times Square or Piccadily Circus, where you can watch flashing electronic ads while you eat. Sure, it's noisy, and, sure, you're a target for beggars, but you'll be dining under the symbol of the city. The food comes in large portions; sandwiches, pizzas, and specially priced executive menus are made fast, so it's a great stop if you're short on time. On nights after the Boca Juniors have won a game, it's a great free show, when locals gather to cheer under the Obelisco, as cars and taxis hurtle by, honking at the crowd. The cafe is also open 24 hours, so you can stop by after clubbing or a show at one of the nearby theaters, and watch the parade of Porteños passing by.

Corrientes 999 (at Carlos Pellegrini [9 de Julio]). **☎ 11/4322-8905** or 11/4322-6174. Main courses $4-$15. AE, DC, MC, V. Daily 24 hr. Metro: Carlos Pellegrini.

El Palacio de la Papa Frita ARGENTINE/PARRILLA   You'll definitely notice this fun, kitschy place, part of a chain of Argentine restaurants, when walking around the Microcentro. Literally, it means the French Fry Palace, but it's much more of course. Their fries are made in such a way that they puff when cooked, creating a sort of thick but light potato chip. Mostly though, this is an excellent *parrilla*, with very thick, well-cooked steaks. The decor is a mix of Argentine memorabilia celebrating the various provinces, '70s disco glitz, and soccer paraphernalia.

Lavalle 735 (btw. Esmeralda and Maipu). ℂ **11/4394-7060** or 11/4393-5849 www.elpalacio-papafrita. com.ar. Main courses $10–$30. AE, DC, MC, V. Daily noon–midnight. Metro: Lavalle.

Empire ★ ASIAN/THAI   This interesting eatery is on a tiny street behind Harrods that was pedestrianized in 2009, making it an ideal outdoor dining and happy hour spot. Enter the dark interior, with paintings of elephants and mosaic decorations made from broken mirrors on its columns, and you'll feel as though you've stepped into some kind of funky club. For vegetarians seeking a break from meat-heavy menus, it's an ideal stop, with many all-vegetable and noodle offerings. Many come for drinks alone and sit at the large bar with shelves of backlit bottles casting a warm glow. Empire's symbol is the Empire State Building, but there's nothing New York–like about it. It's also one of the city's most popular restaurants among gay locals.

Tres Sargentos 427 (at San Martín). ℂ **11/4312-5706.** www.empirethai.net. Main courses $10–$12. AE, MC, V. Mon–Fri noon–1am; Sat 7:30pm–3am. Metro: San Martín.

La Chacra ★ ARGENTINE/PARRILLA   Your first impression from outside this place will be either the stuffed cow begging you to go on in and eat some meat, or the open-fire spit grill glowing through the window. Professional waiters clad in black pants and white dinner jackets welcome you into what is otherwise a casual environment, with deer horns and wrought-iron lamps adorning the walls. Dishes from the grill include sirloin steak, T-bone with red peppers, and tenderloin. Barbecued ribs and suckling pig call out from the open-pit fire, as do a number of hearty brochettes. Steaks are thick and juicy. Get a good beer or an Argentine wine to wash it all down.

Av. Córdoba 941 (at Carlos Pelligrini [9 de Julio]). ℂ **11/4322-1409.** Main courses $5–$12. AE, DC, MC, V. Daily noon–1:30am. Metro: San Martín.

Ligure ★★ 🍴 FRENCH/ITALIAN   Painted mirrors look over the long rectangular dining room, which, since 1933, has drawn ambassadors, artists, and business leaders by day and a more romantic crowd at night. A nautical theme prevails, with fishnets, dock ropes, and masts decorating the room; captain's wheels substitute for chandeliers. Portions are huge and meticulously prepared—an unusual combination for French-inspired cuisine. Seafood options include the Patagonian tooth fish sautéed with butter, prawns, and mushrooms, and trout glazed with an almond sauce. The Châteaubriand is outstanding, and the *bife de lomo* (filet mignon) is prepared seven different ways (pepper sauce with brandy, made at your table, is delightful).

Juncal 855 (at Esmeralda). ℂ **11/4393-0644** or 11/4394-8226. Reservations recommended. Main courses $6–$10. AE, DC, MC, V. Daily noon–3pm and 8pm–midnight. Metro: San Martín.

Los Chilenos ★ SEAFOOD/CHILEAN   A taste of the long country next door is what you'll find here, and because of that, this restaurant is popular with Chileans who live here or are visiting. It's a simple place, with a home-style feeling. The dining room has long tables where everyone sits together and is decorated with posters of Chilean tourist sites and draped with Chilean flags. Fish is one of the restaurant's fortes; one of the most popular dishes is abalone in mayonnaise.

Suipacha 1024 (at Santa Fe). ✆ **11/4328-3123.** Main courses $3–$10. V. Mon–Sat noon–4pm and 8pm–1am. Metro: San Martín.

Richmond Cafe ★★ CAFE/ARGENTINE   Enter this place and find the pace and atmosphere of an older Buenos Aires. The Richmond Cafe, a *café notable*, is all that is left of the Richmond Hotel, an Argentine-British hybrid that opened in 1917 and once catered to the elite. The cafe sits in the lobby of the former hotel, whose upstairs area has been converted into offices. The menu here is traditionally Argentine, and there is a confitería section in the front, serving as a cafe and fast-food eatery. You'll find locals of all kinds, from workers grabbing a quick bite to well-dressed seniors who recall Calle Florida's more elegant heyday. The decor is that of a gentlemen's club, full of wood, brass, and red-leather upholstery. Patrons can still let loose downstairs, in a bar area full of billiard tables. The restaurant offers hearty basics such as chicken, fish, and beef. A la carte, the food tends to be expensive, but three-course executive menus with a drink included are a good bargain, running about $20.

Calle Florida 468 (at Corrientes). ✆ **11/4322-1341** or 11/4322-1653. http://restaurant.com.ar/richmond. Main courses $6–$10. AE, DC, MC, V. Mon–Sat 7am–10pm. Metro: Florida.

Inexpensive

Café Retiro ★★ 👔 CAFE/ARGENTINE   This cafe is part of a chain, the Café Café consortium. As such, there is nothing spectacular about the food, but it is high quality, consistent, and inexpensive. The main point of dining here is to enjoy the restored elegance of the original cafe, which was part of Retiro Station when it was built in 1915. The place had been closed for many years but was restored in 2001 and is now one of the cafés notables, the interiors of which are considered historically important to the nation and thus protected. The marble has been cleaned, the bronze chandeliers polished, and the stained-glass windows have been restored, filling the place with luminescent light. This cafe is ideal if you are taking a train from here to nearby parts of Argentina, such as Tigre, or if you came to admire the architecture of Retiro and the other classical stations in this enormous transportation complex.

Ramos Meija 1348 (at Libertador, in the Retiro Station Lobby). ✆ **11/4516-0902.** Main courses $2–$6. No credit cards. Daily 6:30am–10pm. Metro: Retiro.

Café Tortoni ★★★ 📷 CAFE   You cannot come to Buenos Aires without visiting this Porteño institution. The artistic and intellectual hangout of Buenos Aires since 1858, this historic cafe has served guests such as Jorge Luis Borges, Julio de Caro, Cátulo Castillo, and José Gobello. Its current location opened in the 1890s, when Avenida de Mayo was built as the main thoroughfare of a rich and powerful emerging Buenos Aires. Wonderfully appointed in woods, stained glass, yellowing marble, and bronzes, the place itself exudes more history than any of the photos and artifacts on its walls. It's the perfect place for a coffee or a small snack after wandering along Avenida de Mayo. Twice-nightly tango shows in a cramped side gallery, in which the performers often walk through the crowd, are worth attending, though tight seating means you'll get to know the patron next to you almost too well. Tourists and locals once existed side by side quite comfortably, but tour buses have come to fill the venue with gawkers. Try to visit in the morning, or very late at night. However, do not expect great service from the indifferent waiters. And management seems to be limiting who gains entry, disallowing quick peaks inside at the architecture. All told, it's a beautiful, historic place, but service and treating people well are not the Tortoni's forte.

Av. de Mayo 825 (at Piedras). ✆ **11/4342-4328.** www.cafetortoni.com.ar. Main courses $2–$10. AE, DC, MC, V. Mon–Thurs 8am–2am; Fri–Sat 8am–3am; Sun 8am–1am. Metro: Av. de Mayo.

Filo ★ 🍴 ITALIAN/PIZZA   Popular with young professionals, artists, and anyone looking for cause to celebrate, Filo presents its happy clients with pizzas, more kinds of pasta than you can imagine, salads with an Italian touch, and potent cocktails. The colorfully decorated and crowded bar hosts occasional live music, and tango lessons take place downstairs a few evenings per week. There are also rotating displays of art in the restaurant.

San Martín 975 (at Alvear). ✆ **11/4311-0312.** www.filo-ristorante.com. Main courses $4–$10. AE, MC, V. Daily noon–4pm and 8pm–2am. Metro: San Martín.

Il Gran Caffe ★ CAFE/ITALIAN   As its name implies, this Italian restaurant sells an extensive selection of pastries, pastas, and panini, as well as more traditional Argentine fare. On a busy corner across the street from Galerías Pacífico, it is also one of the best perches to watch crowds passing on Calle Florida. A covered canopy on the Córdoba side also provides further outdoor seating, rain or shine. In fact, the people-watching is so good that the restaurant charges about 10% more for outdoor dining. If that bothers the budget-conscious spy in you, the best compromise is to sit inside on their upper-floor level, with its bird's-eye view of the street and the Naval Academy, one of the city's most beautiful landmarks. Mixed drinks start at about $5 each. They have an excellent Italian pastry menu; the Neapolitan *sfogliatella* is especially good.

Calle Florida 700 (at Córdoba). ✆ **11/4326-5008.** Main courses $4–$15. AE, MC, V. Daily 7am–2am. Metro: Florida.

Las Cuartetas ★★★ 🍴 ITALIAN/PIZZA/ARGENTINE   I can't say enough about this wonderful pizzeria in the middle of the theater district, yet it's one of those places travel writers fear telling too many people about, worried it might become overrun by tourists. It's that good. It's a sprawling place, opened decades ago, and little has changed since the beginning, including the waiters. Pizzas are heaping with creamy mozzarella. They have special combinations, many with large green olives, and a pizza made with a hearty mix of wheat and ground chickpeas. Salads, steaks, and other Argentine fast food items complement the pizza menu. They also do take-away, so you can always order extra to bring back to your hotel.

Corrientes 838 (btw. Esmeralda and Suipacha). ✆ **11/4326-0171.** Main courses $2–$10. No credit cards. Mon–Sat 11am–midnight; Sun 11am–7pm. Metro: Florida.

MONSERRAT

For a map of the restaurants listed in this section, see the "Restaurants in Central Buenos Aires" map on p. 64.

Moderate

Palacio Español ★★ SPANISH   This restaurant has one of the most magnificent dining rooms in Buenos Aires. It's located in the Club Español, one of the grandest buildings along 9 de Julio. An orgy of brass, marble, agate lighting fixtures, carved oak bas-reliefs, and molded plaster ornaments surrounds you. Interspersed are Spanish paintings of major battles and graceful Art Nouveau maidens who stare down from the tops of pilasters. Despite the restaurant's architectural grandeur, the atmosphere is surprisingly relaxed and often celebratory; don't be surprised to find a table of champagne-clinking Argentines next to you. Tables have beautiful silver place settings, and tuxedo-clad waiters offer friendly but formal service. Although the menu is a tempting sample of Spanish cuisine—including paella and Spanish omelets—the fish dishes are best. The wine list is pages long, with a large selection of whites to complement the fish offerings. Bills include a table service charge of about $1.50.

Bernardo de Yrigoyen 180 (at Alsina). (ℂ **11/4334-4876.** www.palacioespanol.com.ar. Reservations recommended. Main courses $5–$12. AE, DC, MC, V. Daily noon–4pm and 8pm–midnight (sometimes until 1am Fri–Sat). Metro: Lima.

Restaurante y Bar Mediterráneo ★★ MEDITERRANEAN   The InterContinental hotel's exclusive Mediterranean restaurant and bar were built in colonial style, resembling the city's famous Café Tortoni. The downstairs bar, with its hardwood floor, marble-top tables, and polished Victrola playing tango music, takes you back to Buenos Aires of the 1930s. A spiral staircase leads to the elegant restaurant, where subdued lighting and well-spaced tables create an intimate atmosphere. Mediterranean herbs, olive oil, and sun-dried tomatoes are among the chef's usual ingredients. Dishes might include carefully prepared shellfish bouillabaisse; black hake served with ratatouille; chicken casserole with morels, fava beans, and potatoes; or duck breast with cabbage confit, wild mushrooms, and sautéed apples. Express menus (items ready within minutes) are available at lunch.

Moreno 809 (at Piedras in the InterContinental). (ℂ **11/4340-7200.** Reservations recommended. Main courses $8–$15. AE, DC, MC, V. Daily 7–11am, 11:30am–3:30pm, and 7pm–midnight. Metro: Moreno.

SAN TELMO

For a map of the restaurants listed in this section, see the "Restaurants in Central Buenos Aires" map on p. 64.

Expensive

Brasserie Petanque ★★ 🄾 FRENCH   The Swiss-born owner of this restaurant, Pascal Meyer, is always on hand, personally seeing to his clients. It feels like an old spot, though it opened in the past few years; the walls are soft yellows with old advertising posters and other decorations such as French flags politely tucked into corners. The stunning tile floor has been redone in a turn-of-the-last-century style. The menu offers specialties like steak tartare, lemon chicken, trout with almonds, and beef bordelaise. Chef Sebastian Fouillade worked with Alain Ducasse. While it's on the pricey side for dinner, lunch is reasonable, especially the three-course menu for $12.

Defensa 596 (at México)). (ℂ **11/4342-7930.** www.brasseriepetanque.com. Main courses $8–$25. AE, DC, MC, V. Sun–Fri 12:30–3:30pm; Tues–Sun 8:30pm–midnight. Metro: Independencia.

La Vineria de Gualterio Bolivar ★ INTERNATIONAL/SEAFOOD   Among the most unusual dining venues in Buenos Aires, this restaurant is the work of chef Alejandro Digilio, who has been called by *Food & Wine* magazine one of the world's top 20 rising chefs to watch for. The cuisine is what he calls rational, though some also call it molecular cooking, based on principles behind the balance of one food with another. The space is tiny, with just a few tables and an open view of the kitchen. Their offerings range from a delectable pizza topped with fish and spices, to octopus with potatoes and wine sauce, as well as various specials each day.

Bolívar 865 (btw. Independencia and Estados Unidos). ✆ **11/4361-4709.** www.lavineriadegualterio bolivar.com. Main courses $8–$25. AE, DC, MC, V. Tues–Sun 1–4pm and 9pm–midnight. Metro: Independencia.

647 Club ★★ 📷 INTERNATIONAL/MEDITERRANEAN   Tucked away in an obscure part of San Telmo, 647 Club is among the most romantic of Buenos Aires restaurants. Crystal chandeliers, red walls, and marbleized, gold-flecked mirrors give the place a retro, nightclub atmosphere. The cuisine is a mix of European influences, heavy on French and Italian. Look for such creative starters as the duck strudel layered with brie cheese and smothered in a molasses sauce, or goat sweetbreads drizzled in truffle oil with tomato chimichurri. Main dishes are elaborate, such as a risotto made from corn, held together with mascarpone and dotted with sautéed portobello mushrooms, beans, and broccoli; and veal ravioli with toasted almonds. Argentine standbys, such as rib-eye steak, are reinvented as kabobs with a special sauce. You might also just come for drinks to check out the atmosphere.

647 Tacuari (at Chile). ✆ **11/4331-3026.** www.club647.com. Reservations recommended. Main courses $15–$20. AE, V. Mon–Thurs 8pm–1am, later on Fri–Sat. Metro: Independencia.

Moderate

Bar El Federal ★★ 📷 ARGENTINE/CAFE   This bar and restaurant, on a quiet corner in San Telmo, represents a step back in time. Fortunately, as a *bar notable,* it will stay that way forever. The first thing that strikes you is the massive, carved-wood and stained-glass ornamental stand over the bar area. Local patrons sit at the old tables chatting, or reading a book and drinking tea or espresso. The original tile floor remains, and old signs, portraits, and small antique machines decorate this space. In business since 1864, Bar El Federal is among the most Porteño of places in San Telmo, a neighborhood with more of these establishments than any other area. Some of the staff has been here for decades on end, and they're very proud of this distinction. The menu is a collection of small, simple items: mostly sandwiches, steaks, and *lomos* (sirloin cuts), with a very large salad selection. High-quality pastries are also served.

Corner of Perú and Carlos Calvo. ✆ **11/4300-4313.** Main courses $3–$10. AE, MC, V. Sun–Thurs 7am–2am; Fri–Sat 7am–4am. Metro: Independencia.

El Desnivel ★ PARRILLA   The name of this venue means "disorganized" in Spanish, and with its haphazard layout it's certainly aptly named. Serving mostly thick, well-cooked, and fatty steaks, this is one of San Telmo's best *parrillas*. Once almost a secret, it has become very popular with tourists. Authenticity abounds, however, on Sundays or on the day of a game, when large local crowds come to watch and eat under the blaring TV screen suspended over the dining area. The decor in this two-level restaurant is unassuming and home style; it's full of mismatched wooden chairs, tablecloths, and silverware. Unlike many other local restaurants that have inflated their prices in recent years, this *parrilla* has maintained its reasonably priced menu.

Defensa 855 (at Independencia). ✆ **11/4300-9081.** Main courses $5–$12. No credit cards. Daily noon–4pm and 8pm–1am. Metro: Independencia.

Gran Parrilla del Plata ★★★ ARGENTINE/PARRILLA   One of the city's best *parrillas*, this small, corner place in San Telmo often has lines out the door. Get there early or you will have to wait awhile. The decor is simple: green walls, tiles, and wood, with hams hanging from the ceilings and seats made of rustic cowhide. The waitstaff is bilingual, but that does not mean the place feels touristy at all. The beef is served in slabs, with a delicious, smoky, mesquite flavor. You'll find other Argentine specialties, salads, and pastas, along with an extensive wine list, which even includes a few whites. Order dessert, like the chocoholic's delight Torta Guilt.

Chile 594 (at Perú). ✆ **11/4300-8858** or 11/4362-5748. Reservations recommended. Main courses $4-$15. AE, MC, V. Daily noon-4pm and 8pm-midnight, sometimes later. Metro: Independencia.

La Brigada ★★ ARGENTINE/PARRILLA   Known as one of the best *parrillas* in San Telmo, La Brigada is reminiscent of the Pampas, with gaucho memorabilia filling the restaurant. White-linen tablecloths and tango music complement the atmosphere. An upstairs dining room faces an excellent walled wine rack. The best choices include the *asado* (short rib roast), *lomo* (sirloin steak, prepared with a mushroom or pepper sauce), baby beef (an enormous 850g/30 oz., served for two), and the *mollejas de chivito al verdero* (young goat sweetbreads in a scallion sauce). The waiters are exceedingly nice and professional. For a period of time, management seemed unhappy that tourists had flooded this venue, driving locals away from this San Telmo favorite. A compromise seems to have been reached, however, with tourists often shunted to the lower floor near the bar, and locals in the old portion of the restaurant and upstairs.

Estados Unidos 465 (at Bolívar). ✆ **11/4361-5557.** Reservations recommended. Main courses $4-$25. AE, DC, MC, V. Daily noon-3pm and 8pm-midnight. Metro: Constitución.

La Poesía ★★ ARGENTINE/INTERNATIONAL   This is a strikingly beautiful, romantic corner cafe in San Telmo, and one of the *bares y cafés notables*. It reopened in 2009 after being closed for decades. It's a step back in time, with its wood interiors, black-clad waiters, and brick walls hung with various old signs and knickknacks. They have a varied menu, from breakfast to sandwiches, to grilled meats and salads, along with an artisanal beer menu. It's a great place to sit and read a book—they even have a small library in English—or to dine outdoors and watch San Telmo pass by.

Chile 502 (at Bolívar). ✆ **11/4300-7340.** Main courses $4-$12. No credit cards. Sun-Thurs 8am-2am; Fri-Sat 8am-4am. Metro: Independencia.

Inexpensive

La Coruña ★★ ◙ CAFE/ARGENTINE   This extremely authentic old cafe and restaurant bar, another of the *cafés notables* protected by law, is the kind of place where you'd expect your grandfather to have eaten when he was a teenager. This neighborhood hub draws young and old alike, who catch soccer games on television or quietly chat away as they order beer, small snacks, and sandwiches. The TV seems to be the only modern thing in here. Music plays from a wooden tabletop radio that must be from the 1950s, and two wooden refrigerators, dating from who knows when, are still used to store food. José Moreira and Manuela Lopéz, the old couple who own the place, obviously believe that if it ain't broke, there's no reason for a new one.

Bolívar 994 (at Carlos Calvo). ✆ **11/4362-7637.** Main courses $2-$6. No credit cards. Daily 9am-10pm. Metro: Independencia.

Medio y Medio ★ URUGUAYAN   This place serves Uruguayan chivitos, which are *lomo* sandwiches. *Lomo* takes on a different meaning in Uruguay than in Argentina. In Argentina, it is only a cut of beef; in Uruguay, it can be steer, pork, or chicken, cut flat as a filet, served as a hot sandwich with a slice of ham, cheese, and an egg, with a garnish of tomatoes and lettuce. This is a crowded, busy place, especially at night when patrons sit outside under a canopy, at tables painted with *fileteado,* an Italian art of painted filigree borders that has become quintessentially Argentine. Occasionally, there are live music and folkloric dance shows.

Chile 316 (at Defensa). © **11/4300-7007.** Main courses $4–$10. No credit cards. Mon–Tues noon–2am; Wed noon–3am; Thurs noon–4am; Fri noon–8am; Sat 24 hr. Metro: Independencia.

RECOLETA

For a map of the restaurants listed in this section, see the "Restaurants in Central Buenos Aires" map on p. 64. There are no convenient metro stops in this neighborhood.

Very Expensive

La Bourgogne ★★★ FRENCH   The only Relais Gourmand in Argentina, Chef Jean Paul Bondoux serves the finest French and international food in the city here. *Travel + Leisure* magazine rated La Bourgogne the number-one restaurant in South America, and *Wine Spectator* called it one of the "Best Restaurants in the World for Wine Lovers." Decorated in elegant pastel hues, the formal dining room serves the city's top gourmands. Begin your meal with a warm foie gras scallop with honey-wine sauce or the succulent *ravioli d'escargots.* The kitchen's fresh vegetables, fruit, herbs, and spices originate from Bondoux's private farm. Downstairs, **La Cave** offers a less formal experience, with a different menu, though the food comes from the same kitchen. Wine tastings are offered Monday through Friday at 7pm in the restaurant's wine-cellar area, called **Cave de Vines** (p. 66); contact La Bourgogne for details.

Av. Alvear 1891 (at Ayacucho in the Alvear Palace Hotel). © **11/4805-3857.** www.alvearpalace.com. Reservations required. Jacket and tie required for men. Main courses $25–$35. AE, DC, MC, V. Free valet parking. Mon–Fri noon–3pm; Mon–Sat 8pm–midnight. Closed Jan. No metro access.

Piegari ★★ ITALIAN   This is a fine Italian restaurant under the highway overpass in a part of Recoleta dubbed "La Recova," near the Four Seasons Hotel. Piegari has two restaurants located across the street from each other; the more formal focuses on Italian dishes, while the other, **Piegari Vitello e Dolce,** is mainly a *parrilla.* Both restaurants are excellent, but visit the formal Piegari for outstanding Italian cuisine, with an emphasis on seafood and pastas. Homemade spaghetti, six kinds of risotto, pan pizza, veal scaloppine, and black salmon ravioli are just a few of the mouthwatering choices. Huge portions are made for sharing, and an excellent eight-page wine list accompanies the menu. If you decide to try Piegari Vitello e Dolce instead, the best dishes are the short-rib roast and the leg of Patagonian lamb.

Posadas 1042 (at Av. 9 de Julio in La Recova, near the Four Seasons Hotel). © **11/4328-4104.** Reservations recommended. Main courses $25–$45. AE, DC, MC, V. Daily noon–3:30pm and 7:30pm–1am. No metro access.

Expensive

El Mirasol ★★ PARRILLA   One of the city's best *parrillas,* this restaurant serves thick cuts of fine Argentine beef. Like **Piegari** (see above), El Mirasol is located in Recoleta's La Recova under the highway overpass, but the glassed-in dining area with plants and trellises gives the impression of outdoor dining. A mammoth 2½-pound serving of tenderloin is a specialty. The best dessert is an enticing combination of meringue, ice cream, whipped cream, dulce de leche, walnuts, and hot chocolate sauce. The wine list pays tribute to Argentine Malbec, as well as Syrah, merlot, and cabernet sauvignon. Frequented by business executives and government officials at lunch and a more relaxed crowd at night, this restaurant remains open in the afternoon, and is thus ideal for travelers who wish to dine early.

Posadas 1032 (at Av. 9 de Julio in La Recova, near the Four Seasons Hotel). ℂ **11/4326-7322.** www.elmirasol.com.ar. Reservations recommended. Main courses $8–$40. AE, DC, MC, V. Daily noon–2am. No metro access.

La Tasca de Plaza Mayor ★★ SPANISH   We list the full name of this restaurant, but most people call it just Plaza Mayor, the name for Madrid's main square. Decorations on the rough brick walls, like Spanish fans, let you know you've entered the mother country, and the aproned waitstaff give old-fashioned service. Highlights of the menu include *pollo Plaza Mayor* (chicken in a wine sauce), several kinds of paella, and lots of steak and pastas as you'd find all over Argentina. There is plenty of exotic fruit of the sea, from octopus to crabs, and an excellent Bacalao a la Gallega.

Posadas 1052 (at Av. 9 de Julio in La Recova, near the Four Seasons Hotel). ℂ **11/4393-5671.** www.plaza-mayor.com.ar. Reservations recommended. Main courses $15–$30. AE, MC, V. Daily noon–1am, sometimes later Sat–Sun. No metro access.

Le Mistral ★★ MEDITERRANEAN   This elegant yet informal restaurant in the Four Seasons Hotel serves Mediterranean cuisine with Italian and Asian influences, overseen by chef Matthias Zumstein. The executive lunch menu includes an antipasto buffet with seafood, cold cuts, cheese, and salads followed by a main course and dessert. From the dinner menu, the aged Angus New York strip is an excellent choice. All grilled dishes come with béarnaise sauce or chimichurri (a thick herb sauce) and a choice of potatoes or seasonal vegetables. Organic chicken and fresh seafood are also on the menu, along with terrific desserts. Enjoy an after-dinner drink in **Le Dôme,** the split-level bar adjacent to the lobby featuring live piano music and occasional tango shows. The Sunday brunch, which runs about $35, is one of the best in Buenos Aires.

Posadas 1086 (at Av. 9 de Julio, in the Four Seasons Hotel). ℂ **11/4321-1730.** Reservations recommended. Main courses $13–$25. Sun brunch $35. AE, DC, MC, V. Daily 7–11am, noon–3pm, and 8pm–1am. No metro access.

Lola ★ INTERNATIONAL   Among the best-known international restaurants in Buenos Aires, Lola has a brilliantly lit, contemporary dining room. Caricatures of major personalities adorn the walls, and fresh plants and flowers give Lola's dining room a springlike atmosphere. The menu features dishes such as chicken fricassee with leek sauce, grilled trout with lemon-grass butter and zucchini, and beef tenderloin stuffed with Gruyère cheese and mushrooms. The kitchen is overseen by the Argentine chef Gonzal Vidal, who studied in France's Cordon Bleu school.

Guido 1985 (at Ortiz). ℂ **11/4804-5959.** www.lolarestaurant.com. Reservations recommended. Main courses $10–$20. AE, DC, MC, V. Daily noon–4pm and 7pm–1am. No metro access.

Moderate

Café Victoria ★ CAFE   Perfect for a relaxing afternoon in Recoleta, the cafe's outdoor patio is surrounded by flowers and shaded by an enormous tree. Sit and drink a coffee or enjoy a complete meal. The three-course express lunch menu offers a salad, main dish, and dessert, with a drink included. Afternoon tea with pastries and scones is served daily from 4 to 7pm. The cafe remains equally popular in the evening, with excellent people-watching opportunities, when live music enlivens the patio. It's a great value for the area—the Recoleta Cemetery and cultural center are next door.

Roberto M. Ortiz 1865 (at Quintana). © **11/4804-0016.** Main courses $5–$12. AE, DC, MC, V. Daily 7:30am–11:30pm. No metro access.

Clark's ★ INTERNATIONAL   The dining room here is an eclectic mix of oak, yellow lamps, live plants, and deer antlers. A slanted ceiling descends over the English-style bar with a fine selection of spirits; in back, a 3m-high (9¾-ft.) glass case displays a winter garden. Booths and tables are covered with green-and-white checkered tablecloths and are usually occupied by North Americans. Specialties include tenderloin steak with goat cheese, sautéed shrimp with wild mushrooms, and sole with a sparkling wine, cream, and shrimp sauce. A number of pasta and rice dishes are offered as well. A large terrace attracts a fashionable crowd in summer.

Roberto M. Ortiz 1777 (at Guido). © **11/4801-9502.** Reservations recommended. Main courses $8–$14. AE, DC, MC, V. Daily noon–3:30pm and 7:30pm–midnight. No metro access.

Juana M ★★ 🍴 PARRILLA   This *parrilla* is hard to find but worth the effort, and remains one of my favorite dining spots in the city. A family-owned affair, it takes its name from its chic matriarch owner and is known almost solely by Porteños who want to keep this place all to themselves. Juana Marty and her husband Enrique can often be seen floating from table to table, checking in on customers. Located in the basement of a former orphanage, which was once part of the city's Catholic University, this neoclassical building is one of the few saved from the highway demolition that created the nearby La Recova area, where Avenida 9 de Julio intersects with Libertador. This cavernous industrial-chic space can seat over 200 patrons. At night, when the space is lit only by candlelight, trendy young patrons flood in. The menu is simple, high quality, and inexpensive, with a free unlimited salad bar with the *parrilla*.

Carlos Pellegrini (9 de Julio) 1535 (basement; at Libertador). © **11/4326-0462.** www.juanam.com. Main courses $6–$14. AE, MC, V. Sun–Fri noon–5pm and 7:30pm–1am; Sat 8pm–2am. No metro access.

Inexpensive

La Biela ★★★ CAFE   Originally a small sidewalk cafe and grocery opened in 1850, La Biela earned its distinction as the rendezvous choice of race-car champions and early car-owning pioneers. *Biela* itself is a Spanish word referring to an engine's connecting rod. Black-and-white photos of early Argentine car enthusiasts and racers decorate the huge dining room. Today artists, politicians, and neighborhood executives (as well as a very large number of tourists) all frequent La Biela, which serves breakfast, informal lunch plates, ice cream, and crepes. The outdoor terrace sits beneath an enormous 19th-century ombu tree, opposite the Church of Nuestra Señora del Pilar and the adjoining Recoleta Cemetery. You'll often see live street tango under the tree on weekends. This place ranks among the most important cafes in the city and is a protected *bar notable*. It has some of the best sidewalk viewing anywhere in Recoleta, but I also love looking into La Biela's windows at night, when the place takes on a sepia glow. You might just feel like you're in Paris when you come here.

Av. Quintana 596 (at Alvear). © **11/4804-0449.** www.labiela.com. Main courses $3–$12. V. Daily 7am–3am. No metro access.

BARRIO NORTE

For a map of the restaurants listed in this section, see the "Restaurants in Central Buenos Aires" map on p. 64.

Expensive

Milion ★★ 💼 INTERNATIONAL   This is one of the most stunningly situated restaurants in Buenos Aires, and yet despite this and the fact that it's been around for a decade, it remains hard to find. You must pass through the marble-lined former carriage entrance of a beautiful Belle Epoque mansion, and then make the choice of dining in the garden or upstairs in a room with dark-wood-paneled walls with bronze sconces and beveled-glass windows. Beef is served in large, hearty portions, and lighter menu items include fish, especially in the summer months, as well as creative salads and tapas. Many people come here just for drinks and socializing, which spreads to all the floors of the five-level mansion. If you hear about any of the local art or media parties that sometimes happen here, be sure to find a way to get invited.

Paraná 1048 (at Santa Fe). ⓒ **11/4815-9925.** www.milionargentina.com.ar. Main courses $15–$20. AE, MC, V. Mon–Wed noon–2am; Thurs noon–3am; Fri noon–4am; Sat 8pm–4am; Sun 8pm–2am. Metro: Callao.

Moderate

Clásica y Moderna ★★ 💼 ARGENTINE   This restaurant helped save an important bookstore from extinction. The bookstore opened in this location in 1938, though the company dates from 1918. Emilio Robert Díaz was the original owner, and now his grandchildren run the place. In 1988, books were relegated to the back to make way for diners, but this remains among the best bookstores for English-speaking tourists. While this is a protected *café notable,* the interior has been stripped down to the exposed brick, giving the place a dark, industrial feel. Decorations overhead include old bicycles and signs. It is a pleasant, relaxed space, where it's easy to chat with the staff as you dine or sit at the bar. The menu includes light, healthful choices such as salads and soy burgers. Mixed drinks start at about $6. Events of all kinds are held here too, from literary readings to plays, dance shows, and art exhibitions. Shows are held Wednesday to Saturday around 10pm, and there are sometimes two shows, the second one beginning after midnight.

Callao 892 (at Córdoba). ⓒ **11/4812-8707** or 11/4811-3670. www.clasicaymoderna.com. Reservations recommended for shows. Main courses $5–$15. AE, MC, V. Daily 8am–1am, sometimes closing later on Fridays and Saturdays. Bookstore hours: Mon–Sat 9am–1am; Sun 5pm–1am. Metro: Callao.

Tandoor ★ 💼 ASIAN/INDIAN   If you're looking for an overdone, Bollywood-inspired dining experience, you won't find it at Tandoor. You will, however, enjoy fine dining in an elegant French neoclassical building. Owners Shahrukh and Belli are Indian expats; Shahrukh originally came to Argentina to tango in 2004, and then opened Tandoor in 2007. All of the menu items come mildly spiced, but you can have anything spiced to taste. The philosophy behind the restaurant is to offer various regional dishes, many cooked in the styles families use at home. Choose such staples as the classic Tandoori curry chicken dish, *tikka masala;* or lamb biryani, cooked the old-fashioned way in a sealed pot for a few hours. Several kinds of *nan* (flatbread) can accompany the meal. Finish with basmati rice pudding, mango ice cream, or a fusion dessert.

Laprida 1293 (at Charcas). ⓒ **11/4821-3676.** www.tandoor.com.ar. Main courses $8–$15. AE, MC, V. Daily noon–4pm and 8pm–1am, sometimes later. Metro: Aguero.

CONGRESO

For a map of the restaurants listed in this section, see the "Restaurants in Central Buenos Aires" map on p. 64.

Moderate

Inside Resto-Bar ★★ INTERNATIONAL/ARGENTINE This place draws a largely gay clientele, though anyone is welcome. The waitstaff and owner Diego provide great, attitude-free service. The decor is low-key: red and black with dim, moody lighting, and a loft level of tables that opens up when it gets crowded. The flavorful dishes exhibit a mix of French and Italian influences. You can also go just for drinks at the small bar, where many locals gather for conversation. There are special tango shows on weekends and male strippers virtually every day, too, usually after 11pm. Reservations are accepted and recommended for weekends. Make sure to ask for pepper on your food; the way they grind it is an unforgettable experience.

Bartolomé Mitre 1571 (at Montevideo). *©* **11/4372-5439.** www.restaurantinside.com.ar. Main courses $9-$20. AE, MC, V. Daily 8pm-2am, later Sat-Sun, depending on the crowds. Metro: Congreso.

La Clac ★ PARRILLA/ARGENTINE If you're looking for a fun, kitschy place with a lot of local color, this is the right spot. This is a theater restaurant, decorated with all manner of things on the walls and ceiling, from pictures of 1960s Argentine comedians, to currency from all over the country, to bottles of all kinds and some things indescribable. As you're eating, you may begin to notice lines forming all around you, but people aren't gathered to keep an eye on your table manners. The basement of the restaurant plays host to unusual plays and comedy routines, usually starting at 9pm. Food is basic Argentine, from steaks to salads, sandwiches, and pastas.

Av. de Mayo 1156 (at Salta). *©* **11/4382-6529** or 11/4115-3510. Main courses $8-$12. MC. Daily 8am-2am, sometimes later Sat-Sun. Metro: Lima.

La Moncloa ★ 🍴 CAFE The trees surrounding this place lend a sense of calm to sidewalk eating in what is normally a busy area on a street just off Plaza Congreso. La Moncloa takes its name from a famous Spanish palace. Basic Argentine fare such as empanadas, steaks, and salads is on offer, along with croissant sandwiches and an extensive dessert menu. There is also a large selection of pork dishes, including the tempting pork in white-wine sauce. Still, for the diet-conscious, there is also a low-calorie menu with vegetarian offerings. Whatever you order, I recommend taking the time for a break in this restaurant's parklike setting. Flavored and alcoholic coffees, one of their specialties, are about $5. They also deliver to local hotels.

Av. de Mayo 1500 (at Sáenz Peña). *©* **11/4381-3357** or 11/4382-7194. Main courses $4-$12. AE, DC, MC, V. Daily 7:30am-2am. Metro: Sáenz Peña.

Plaza Asturias ★★ 🍴 SPANISH/ITALIAN/ARGENTINE This decades-old eatery on Avenida de Mayo is about as authentic as it gets, packed mostly with Porteños who want to keep this place to themselves. Food has touches of Italian, Argentine, and, most importantly, authentic Spanish cuisine. The place is so busy and has to keep so much food on hand that there are legs of cured ham hanging from the rafters over diners' heads. Steaks are as thick as the crowds waiting to get in, and among their specialties are Spanish casseroles and lots of food with various sauces. Fish is also a big highlight. ***Be warned:*** The staff is so busy yelling out orders to the kitchen and rushing food to the tables that you can get hurt trying to find the bathroom.

Av. de Mayo 1199 (at Salta). ✆ **11/4382-7334.** Main courses $6–$12. No credit cards. Daily noon–3am. Metro: Sáenz Peña.

Plaza del Carmen CAFE/ARGENTINE   Part of a chain, this cafe is clean and slightly sterile. The best part of this place is not the interior but the view of Congreso. It's generally open 24 hours, and no matter what time of day it is you can find people having nothing more than croissants and coffee here. On weekdays, the outdoor seating area is a little overwhelming, as there is a huge amount of traffic flowing by this corner. Choose to eat inside, protected from the noise and car fumes, or wait until the weekends, when the sidewalk is less busy and the outdoor area becomes ideal. This restaurant offers standard Argentine cuisine in addition to a selection of salads and other light items. Pizzas, pastas, and other Italian items round out the menu.

Rivadavia 1795 (at Callao). ✆ **11/4374-8477.** Main courses $5–$8. AE, MC, V. Daily 7am–2am. Metro: Congreso.

36 Billares ★★ ARGENTINE   This restaurant opened in 1894, but was reborn in 2005 in a more exciting incarnation. Originally part of a gambling and gaming hall (*billares* is Spanish for billiards), it has been revamped with new food and nightly entertainment, ranging from tango to flamenco. Most patrons are old-time Porteños who even sing along to the music. Some of the best nights are Thursdays, when there's a tango show. It's a historic bar, with a beautiful interior of oak paneling and a Movado clock from the 1920s. Below ground, the billiards-and-games hall remains, with some of the oldest equipment around. The dishes are reasonably priced, with large portions. Try the *lomo de la Avenida,* a steak with Patagonian mushrooms, or any of the chicken or pasta dishes. There's no charge for the show, held every night but Monday.

Av. de Mayo 1265 (btw. Libertad and Talcahuano). ✆ **11/4381-5696.** www.los36billares.com.ar. Main courses $4–$12. AE, DC, MC, V. Mon–Thurs 8am–1am; Fri–Sat 8am–5am; Sun 3pm–midnight. Metro: Lima.

Inexpensive

Bien Porteño ★ CAFE/INTERNATIONAL/ARGENTINE   Known largely by Argentines who tango, this small cafe, opened in 2006, has exposed-brick walls and an old-time atmosphere. The food is basic Argentine staples, such as grilled-beef *picadas* (tartlets), enhanced with sandwiches and salads, and many people come just for coffee and to while away the time chatting. The main highlight of the restaurant is its emphasis on tango and folkloric shows on Fridays and Saturdays, which sometimes means a small entry fee of about $8 to $12, or sometimes none at all. Ask about the schedule of tango classes also held on Monday, Wednesday, and Friday. Owner Ceferina de Jesus Orzuza speaks English, and with her piercing green-hazel eyes, is an engaging woman with whom to hold a conversation. The name of the restaurant is an expression meaning "very Buenos Aires," and it is to the core.

Rivadavia 1392 (at Uruguay). ✆ **11/4383-5426.** www.bienporteno.com. Main courses $3–$10. AE, MC, V. Mon–Fri noon–9:30pm without show, until 2am or later with show. Sat–Sun hours depend on showtimes. Metro: Sáenz Peña.

Café de Madres de Plaza de Mayo ★★ 📷 CAFE   This place is officially called Café Literario Osvaldo Bayer, after an Argentine political intellectual. It's in the lobby of the headquarters and teaching center of the Madres de Plaza de Mayo, just off of Plaza Congreso. What makes the place so special is its left-wing political atmosphere. In few other places in Buenos Aires can you speak so freely with those who had family members disappear during Argentina's military dictatorship, or with young students who have come to study here and seek justice in the cause. The Madres bookstore is just to the side of the cafe, and it's full of books and newspapers on liberal causes throughout Latin America, including one of the largest collections of books on Che Guevara anywhere in the world. An Argentine native, he is a hero of many of the Madres, and his image adorns walls throughout the building. The restaurant offers light Italian fare, and has an outdoor seating area in the summer.

Hipólito Yrigoyen 1584 (at Ceballos). ✆ **11/4382-3261.** www.madres.org. Main courses $3–$8. No credit cards. Mon–Fri 8:30am–10:30pm; Sat (and some Sun) 11am–5pm. Metro: Congreso.

La Americana ★★ ARGENTINE/ITALIAN   This place calls itself "La Reina de las Empanadas" (the Queen of Empanadas), and that indeed it is. It offers an enormous range of empanadas, all made with a light dough and slightly burned edges; they're never heavy or greasy. The place is busy and loud, the constant din of conversation bouncing off the tile-and-stone walls and plate-glass windows looking out to Callao. There are tables and an area for standing and eating—some people can't be bothered to sit and simply scarf down these delicious creations once they get them. Waiters are frantic, scurrying from table to table. You'll have to keep reminding them of what you ordered if you feel it's taking too much time, but don't blame them: It's just too busy for normal humans to keep up with the pace of the place. Excellent Italian specialties such as calzones and pizzas round out the menu.

Callao 83 (at Bartolomé Mitre). ✆ **11/4371-0202.** Main courses $1–$7. No credit cards. Sun–Thurs 7am–2am; Fri–Sat 7am–3am. Metro: Congreso.

PALERMO

Both Palermo Viejo and Las Cañitas are near the D subway line, but restaurants are often quite far from the metro stations. The long walk and the fact that the *subte* closes at 11pm mean you are better off taking a cab.

For a map of the restaurants listed in this section, see the "Hotels & Restaurants in Palermo" map on p. 84.

Very Expensive

Casa Cruz ★★ 🍴 ITALIAN/INTERNATIONAL   Casa Cruz is one of the city's chicest restaurants. With its enormous polished-brass doors, it gives you the impression that you're entering a nightclub, and inside, the dark, modern interior maintains the theme. The impressive round bar, always decorated with fresh flower arrangements, is the first thing you'll see before continuing on into the spacious dining area full of polished woods and red upholstery. The place takes its name from its original owner, Juan Santa Cruz. The menu here is eclectic and interesting, overseen by the creative chef Germán Martitegui, who oversees Olsen and Tegui. Rabbit, sea bass, Parma ham rolls, and other exotic ingredients go into the many flavorful dishes.

Uriarte 1658 (at Honduras). ✆ **11/4833-1112.** www.casacruz-restaurant.com. Reservations highly recommended. Main courses $25–$45. AE, MC, V. Mon–Thurs 8:30pm–3am, later on Fri–Sat. Closed Sun. No metro access.

Tegui ★★★ 🍴 MEDITERRANEAN/INTERNATIONAL   Tegui is star chef Germán Martitegui's latest venture in Buenos Aires dining, a place he pretends to want to hide. Opened in January 2009, it's a virtually unreadable name on a door of a building covered in graffiti. The menu is a mix of Mediterranean influences, along with skillfully crafted retakes of Argentine basics, like veal tenderloin covered in Brazilian manioc flour nestling an egg, matched with potatoes and chimichurri. The place is tiny, seating only 45, the ebony-and-cream vertically striped walls creating an optical illusion leading to the brilliantly lit open kitchen where the staff watch your reaction to the dishes they have created. It's an especially romantic option for couples visiting Buenos Aires. The menu can be ordered a la carte, or in a tiered system of courses.

Costa Rica 5852 (at Ravignani). (C) **11/5291-3333.** www.tegui.com.ar. Reservations highly recommended. Main courses $15–$40. AE, MC, V. Tues–Sat 12:30–4pm, 8:30pm–12:30am, later on Fri–Sat. Metro: Ministro Carranza.

Expensive

Ceviche ★★ JAPANESE/PERUVIAN/SEAFOOD

A trend has developed in Buenos Aires, which some say is the result of the worldwide sushi trend coupled with an increase in the Peruvian population in Buenos Aires. Peruvian restaurants have sprouted, with Japanese-Argentine chefs blending Japanese and Peruvian cuisine. Ceviche is among the newest and most elegant locations, with exposed blood-red brick walls and antique posters, and a hint of the Andean nation in its Peruvian textile accents. The sushi bar sits at the front of the restaurant, with the dark, moody, candlelit dining area towards the back, and an open-air patio decorated with cactus and other desert plants. Chef Roberto Nishida oversees the menu and preparation of the various offerings, from sushi to ceviche to an array of other seafood dishes. Desserts are also a highlight, from Peruvian flan to dulce de leche (caramel) cheesecake.

Costa Rica 5644 (at Fitzroy). (C) **11/4776-7373.** www.ceviche.com.ar. Reservations recommended. Main courses $12–$20. AE, DC, MC, V. Mon–Fri 12:30–3pm and 8pm–1am; Sat 8pm–1am. Metro: Palermo.

Cluny ★★★ INTERNATIONAL/ARGENTINE

Casual but elegant, this restaurant looks more like a modernist living room than a dining room. A filtered-air loft space, where smoking is allowed, is excellent for private conversations. Some choose to dine outside in the patio garden. Sinatra tunes and bossa nova add to the relaxed atmosphere. The menu emphasizes fish and fowl, from prawn risotto to spider crabs and duck magret. There are many salmon and codfish dishes, as well as "lamb cooked in two different ways." Beef seems to be a second thought, unlike in other Argentine restaurants, though it is well prepared. The extensive wine list runs more than eight pages, including the finest Argentine vintages from Catena Zapata as well as French imports at more than $250 a bottle. In the afternoon, there's a fine British tea service.

El Salvador 4618 (at Malabia). (C) **11/4831-7176.** Reservations highly recommended. Main courses $15–$20. AE, MC, V. Mon–Sat 12:30–4pm, 4–7:30pm for teatime, and 8pm–1am, sometimes later. Metro: Plaza Italia.

HG Restaurant ★ MEDITERRANEAN/INTERNATIONAL/ARGENTINE/SPANISH

HG Restaurant, in the **Fierro Hotel** (p. 54), takes its name from chef Hernan Gipponi, who trained in Valencia, Spain. The dinner is served as a 3-hour tasting menu, with nine courses for about $50, though you can order individual items. Many dishes are served in Spanish tapas style, with a rounded proportion of meats, fish, and rice dishes. Try the veal with quinoa or the rabbit comfit with barbecued pumpkin. One of the best desserts is the lychee yogurt foam with caramelized pumpkin seeds and tack cream.

Soler 5862 (btw. Ravagnini and Carranza in Fierro Hotel). (C) **11/3220-6820.** Reservations recommended. Main courses $8–$12. AE, MC, V. Daily 8am–4pm; Tues–Sat 8pm–midnight. Metro: Carranza.

Hotels & Restaurants in Palermo

RESTAURANTS ◆
Bio **11**
Campo Bravo **5**
Casa Cruz **27**
Ceviche **13**
Cluny **42**
Confitería del Botánico **23**
De Olivas i Lustres **43**
El Estanciero **7**
Garbis **44**
HG Restaurant **10**
La Baita **28**
La Cabrera **31**
La Salamandra **36**
Las Choclas **1**
Lupita **3**
Meridiano 58 **21**
Mute **2**
Novecento **4**
Olsen **17**
Osaka **14**
Pampa Picante **25**
Prodeo Lounge & Suites **29**
Prologo **32**
Rio Alba **8**
Sudestada **12**
Sullivan's Drink House **22**
Sushi Club **6**
Tandoor **45**
Tazz **35**
T-Bone Bar & Grill **33**
Te Mataré Ramírez **37**
Tegui **15**
Utopia Bar **34**
Viejo Agump **39**

HOTELS ■
Bo-Bo **20**
Craft **26**
Fierro Hotel **9**
Five Cool Rooms **41**
The Glu **30**
Home **16**
Krista Hotel **18**
Legado Mítico **24**
Malabia House **38**
Soho All Suites **40**
Vitrum **19**

La Baita ★★ ITALIAN   This is one of the best Italian restaurants you'll find in Palermo Viejo. It's upscale and yet very family style, so much so that manager Guido Bioloi often has his grandchildren in his arms as he leads you to your seat. Traditional homemade pastas and sauces, seafood of the day, and saltimbocca alla Romana are served in the Pompeian red interior space. Wine is served by the glass and the bottle, and an upstairs loft has seating under a skylight. This restaurant is often exceedingly crowded, but for good reason.

Thames 1603 (at Honduras). ✆ **11/4832-7234.** www.labaita-restaurante.com.ar. Main courses $10–$17. AE, MC, V. Tues-Fri noon-3pm; Mon-Fri 8pm-2am; Sat-Sun noon-2am, sometimes later. Metro: Plaza Italia.

La Cabrera ★★ ARGENTINE/PARRILLA   This restaurant has become so well known among tourists visiting Buenos Aires that the owners have also opened another branch up the street for spillover patrons, called **La Cabrera Norte,** at Cabrera 5127 (✆ **11/4832-5754**). Both places deserve their superb reputations. The meat is excellent and comes in such huge portions that it's impossible to finish. One of the specialties is *pamplona,* a sausage made of various meats and sauces, or try the pork ribs with a sauce of dried tomatoes and pesto. All meals come with a spread of olives, sauces, breads, and other appetizers, which is a meal in itself. The restaurant sits on a corner and is a beautiful setting for outdoor dining, or you can eat inside in the charming dining room with exposed brick walls and antique posters.

Cabrera 5099 (at Thames). ✆ **11/4831-7002.** www.parrillalacabrera.com.ar. Main courses $8–$18. AE, DC, MC, V. Wed-Sun 12:30-4pm; Sun-Thurs 8:30pm-1am, later Sat-Sun. No metro access.

Meridiano 58 ★★ 🏠 ARGENTINE/INTERNATIONAL   This moody restaurant has an aura of Zen chic. During the day, you'll notice its Argentine touches, such as Salta Indian designs, leather lounge sofas, and dark leather place mats. At night, when the staircase is lit with candles and the water fountain is on, you're in a new romantic world. The restaurant has three levels, plus a torch-lit terrace, all overseen by waiters in gauzy outfits with Nehru collars. In spite of these Asian touches, Chef Gustavo Soria prepares largely Argentine food. The desserts alone are worth a trip here; try the chocolate mousse with passion fruit or the orange flan with ginger and coconut. Prix-fixe lunch and dinner menus run from $15 to $20, Monday to Thursday. The restaurant's name refers to Buenos Aires's location on the globe.

J.L. Borges 1689 (at El Salvador). ✆ **11/4833-3443.** Main courses $10–$20. AE, DC, MC, V. Daily noon-1am, later Sat-Sun. Metro: Plaza Italia.

Mute INTERNATIONAL   Open from late breakfast into the wee hours, Mute has dining on two levels in its dark, chic space. The place really comes alive at night, though, when a DJ spins electronica. Technically there's no dancing, but people have been known to move to the music while eating. The selection is varied, from Argentine beef staples to fish to a vegetarian selection and different pastas. Top it off with interesting desserts, such as ice cream with ginger sauce, or take a risk and try their huge chocolate volcano, a multilayered confection.

Báez 243 (btw. Arguibel and Arévalo). ✆ **11/4776-6883.** www.mute.com.ar. Main courses $12–$20. AE, MC, V. Mon-Tues 10am-3am; Wed-Sat 10am-5am. Metro: Carranza.

Olsen ★★ SCANDINAVIAN/SEAFOOD   A bit of Scandinavia has landed in Argentina. Built into what was once a warehouse, this restaurant soars to churchlike proportions and has a mezzanine overlooking the main dining area. The interior, complete with a central round metal fireplace, has a 1960s mod feel to it. There's also

puertas cerradas: CLOSED-DOOR DINING IN A CHEF'S HOME

In the past few years, a trend has developed in Buenos Aires in which chefs invite small groups of diners into their homes. Ranging anywhere from 12 to 30 per group, participants dine together under the guidance of a chef who explains the several-course meal he or she has prepared. In a way, it's a little like a group blind date between you, your travel companions, and whomever else has booked that night.

More than 30 *puertas cerradas* operate in Buenos Aires. Some of the best include **Casa Salt Shaker** (✆ 11/15-6132-4146; www.casasaltshaker.com), started by the American chef Dan Perlman and his partner Henry Tapia; **Cocina Sunae** (✆ 11/15-4870-5506;

www.cocinasunae.com), run by the American Christina Sunae Wiseman who uses Asian fusion in her cooking; and **Casa Felix** (✆ 11/4555-1882; www.diegofelix.com), run by the Argentine chef Diego Felix. Most dining sessions are on weekends, but chefs can arrange additional sessions for private groups, along with cooking classes. Most *puertas cerradas* are cash-only, but you can often arrange payment via PayPal. My experience has been that that dining this way allows you to witness interactions among locals, expats, and travelers from various countries, and often leads to a group night out exploring the city after the dinner is over.

a tranquil patio garden overgrown with vines. Starters are fun and meant to be shared, such as an excellent selection of bagels, tiny pancakes, smoked salmon, smoked herring, caviar, and flavored cheeses and butters. Fish is the focal point of this place, and a few of the meat dishes, though flavorful, tend to be on the dry side. Many people come just for the bar, with its enormous vodka selection kept in special super-cold freezers. Absolut rules this part of the restaurant and is available by the shot or the bottle. On Sunday, try their brunch, which begins at 10am. The restaurant is overseen by Germán Martitegui, who also oversees **Casa Cruz** (p. 82) and **Tegui** (p. 82).

Gorriti 5870 (at Carranza). ✆ **11/4776-7677.** restaurantolsen@netizon.com.ar. Reservations recommended. Main courses $12–$25. AE, MC, V. Tues-Thurs noon–1am; Fri-Sat 12:30pm–2:30am (sometimes later); Sun 10am–1am. No metro access.

Osaka ★ JAPANESE/PERUVIAN/INTERNATIONAL/SEAFOOD Osaka has long been considered one of the best Japanese restaurants in Buenos Aires. The restaurant has a tranquil feeling, with its intimate spaces and warm, neutral tones. The cuisine is a mix of Japanese and Peruvian, with raw fish as the star, whether ceviche—served in a variety of creative ways—or sushi. You can still get your Argentine beef fix here; it's just presented in a lighter way.

Soler 5608 (at Fitzroy). ✆ **11/4775-6964.** www.osaka.com.pe. Reservations recommended. Main courses $12–$25. AE, MC, V. Mon-Sat 12:30–4pm and 8pm–1am, sometimes later. Metro: Palermo.

Pampa Picante ★ ARGENTINE/PARRILLA/INTERNATIONAL This *parrilla* in Palermo, overseen by owner Claudia Iluane, has a wonderful take on Argentine cooking, using country methods associated with the Pampas and Patagonia. Hearty vegetables, like potatoes, pumpkin, squash, and carrots, are used in the preparation of many of the starters and as sides. The beef here is fantastic, and the smell of the *asado* permeates the surrounding street. There are fresh pastas and interesting desserts, like peach "soup" with chocolate ice cream. For $100 a person, they offer a 4-hour cooking class in *parrilla* and other Argentine cooking.

Nicaragua 4610 (at Armenia). ✆ **11/4833-7251.** www.pampapicante.com.ar. Main courses $8–$20. AE, MC, V. Tues–Sun 6pm–1am, sometimes later. Metro: Plaza Italia.

Prodeo Lounge & Suites ★★ INTERNATIONAL/SEAFOOD

Prodeo Lounge & Suites is in Palermo Soho, opened in mid-2010 by New Jersey native Michael Abridello. The interior is sleek industrial gray, with a lighted glass block pathway leading to white leather booths, an outdoor poolside dining patio, and a second floor level with an open atrium overlooking the bar. There's a fountain at the entrance and a carp pond with a submerged Buddha. Some weekends, there are DJs and the place gets packed for drinks. Dutch chef Jeroen Van den Bos, who has worked throughout Europe and most recently in Aruba, oversees the kitchen. The menu offers creative and playful combinations, such as grilled bass with soba noodles flavored with leeks, sesame, and peanuts; along with pineapple, cilantro, and jalapeno salsa. There are beef, lamb, and chicken dishes, as well as many vegetarian options and a special menu for the gluten-intolerant. Every Thursday at 7pm, there's a $30 2-hour bartending class with bartender Robert Kala. The "Suites" portion of the name refers to a hotel that's planned to be opened above the restaurant, still in the works at the time of this writing.

Gorriti 5374 (btw. Godoy Cruz and Altacalco). ✆ **11/4831-4471.** www.prodeolounge.com. Reservations recommended. Main courses $10–$15. AE, MC, V. Tues–Sat 7pm–3am (sometimes later); Sun brunch noon–4pm. Metro: Palermo.

Rio Alba ★ PARRILLA/ARGENTINE

Tucked away in the neighborhood behind La Rural, this great high-end *parrilla* is easy to overlook. Its location makes it a favorite of the embassy crowd. There's a certain old-fashioned flavor to the place, with its white-linen tablecloths, rustic chairs, yellow walls, wheat-stalk bouquets, and legs of ham hooked to the rafters, mixing a touch of elegance with a touch of the countryside. Cuts of meat are massive and juicy, from the *ojo de bife* to the *lomo*. Or choose pork, chicken, or fish, all in hefty portions. Wine from 10 different *bodegas* is served, and there's a great selection of desserts to top it all off.

Cerviño 4499 (at Oro). ✆ **11/4773-5748.** Main courses $12–$25. AE, DC, MC, V. Daily noon–4pm and 8pm–1am. Metro: Plaza Italia.

Sudestada ★ VIETNAMESE/ASIAN/THAI

Inside this simple restaurant with its Zen-like white-and-black decor, you'll find some of the best Asian food in Buenos Aires. Sudestada is a mix of Vietnamese, Thai, and other Asian cuisines. Look for the special wok menu, or choose pork with lemon grass, rabbit with rice and vegetables, or interesting desserts such as lychee pie. Argentine beef is great, but if you're looking to try something different, this will be a wonderful change.

Guatemala 5602 (at Fitzroy). ✆ **11/4776-3777.** www.sudestadabuenosaires.com. Main courses $12–$20. AE, MC, V. Mon–Sat noon–3:30pm; Mon–Thurs 8pm–midnight; Fri–Sat 8pm–1am. Metro: Palermo.

Sullivan's Drink House IRISH/ARGENTINE

Sullivan's still retains its green Emerald Isle decor but has overhauled its menu, bringing it more in line with traditional Argentine fare. That means more beef and other *parrilla* items, and just a smattering of traditional Irish food. Sandwiches and children's meals are also on the menu. Windows to the street provide great views, and a VIP lounge decorated in Old English style is upstairs, serving as a cigar bar. On the rooftop there's a covered terrace offering even more dining space. In spite of the change in food, if you have come to drink as the Irish do, well, you're definitely in luck. Sullivan's has one of the most extensive imported whiskey menus in town, beginning at about $5 per serving. The luck of the Irish is indeed evident in the history of this restaurant: They opened on December 20, 2001, just days before the peso crisis, yet they have survived. If you're in Buenos Aires on St. Patrick's Day, come have a drink and share the luck.

El Salvador 4919 (at Borges). © **11/4832-6442.** Main courses $7-$12. AE, DC, MC, V. Mon-Thurs 10:30am-2 or 3am; Fri-Sat 10:30am-5am; Sun noon-2:30am. Metro: Scalabrini Ortiz.

Te Mataré Ramírez ★★★ 🍴 INTERNATIONAL/FRENCH   This is perhaps the most interesting and creative dining experience in Buenos Aires. Its symbol, a fork with an extended and upright prong, gives you a clue as to the erotic nature of the restaurant. The name of the restaurant means "I am going to kill you, Ramírez." It comes from the threats that the owner's Casanova-esque friend would hear from husbands with whose wives he was having affairs. It's an erotic restaurant, both in food and decor. Sensual combinations include garlic and sun-dried tomatoes mixed with sweet elements and poured over sautéed or marinated meats. The ceilings are decorated with paintings of naked men and women wearing nothing more than high-heeled shoes, mixed with naughty cherubs. Erotic art, for sale, hangs on the walls. The lighting is boudoir red, and wine is consumed from antique cut-crystal glasses that cast red sparkles on the table. Black-clothed actors perform playfully racy shows on a small stage here, using hand-held puppets that do naughty things.

Gorriti 5054 (btw. Thames and Serrano). © **11/4831-9156.** www.tematareramirez.com. Reservations recommended. Main courses $17-$25. AE, MC, V. Daily 8:30pm-1am, sometimes later on weekends. Metro: Scalabrini Ortiz.

Moderate

Campo Bravo ★★ 🍽 PARRILLA/ARGENTINE   This restaurant serves as the virtual center of the Las Cañitas dining scene. It's relaxed during the day but insane at night. Dining on the sidewalk here, you'll have a great view of the glamorous crowds emerging from taxis to kick off their night in this happening neighborhood. The *parrilla* serves up basic Argentine cuisine, and the enormous slabs of meat are served on wooden boards. A large, efficient waitstaff will take care of you, but there's often up to an hour wait for an outdoor table on weekends (they don't accept reservations). While you wait, do as the locals do: Get a glass of champagne and sip it on the street amid what looks like a well-dressed and over-age frat party. A limited wine selection and imported whiskeys are also part of the drink menu. Can't handle the late dinners in Argentina? Well, then you're in luck—they don't close between lunch and dinner, so you can enjoy a great meal here without having to wait until 9pm.

Báez 292 (at Arévalo). © **11/4514-5820.** www.campobravo.com.ar. Main courses $8-$15. AE, MC. Mon 6pm-4am; Tues-Sun 11:30am-4am (often later on weekends). Metro: Ministro Carranza.

De Olivas i Lustres ★★ MEDITERRANEAN/ARGENTINE   This magical restaurant was opened in the 1990s by Miguel Moreno, along with his business partner and chef, Sebastián Tarica, building the foundation for the gastronomic paradise the neighborhood would soon become. The dining room displays eccentric antiques, olive jars, and wine bottles. The reasonably priced menu celebrates Mediterranean cuisine, with light soups, fresh fish, and sautéed vegetables as its focus. The breast of duck with lemon and honey is mouthwatering, and there are also a number of *tapeos* (appetizer-size dishes). For about $32 per person, you and your dining partner can share 15 sensational small plates—brought out individually, and building in adventurousness—over the course of a couple of hours. What I find most unique about this restaurant beyond the Mediterranean fare is the use of native and Incan ingredients in various dishes. If you've ever wanted to try alligator or llama, this is the place to do it.

Gorriti 3972 (at Medrano). ✆ **11/4867-3388.** www.deolivasilustres.com.ar. Reservations recommended. Main courses $8–$12. AE, MC, V. Mon–Thurs 8:30pm–midnight; Fri–Sat 8:30pm–1am. Metro: Scalabrini Ortiz.

El Estanciero ★ 🏠 PARRILLA   In most of the restaurants in the Las Cañitas district of Palermo, it's all about the glamour. In this *parrilla*, however, it's all about the beef, which I would argue is the best in the neighborhood. The cuts are amazingly flavorful, with just the right mix of fat to add tenderness. If you order the steak rare (*jugoso*), they know not to serve it nearly raw. The restaurant has two levels, with sidewalk seating at the entrance and a covered open-air terrace above. Both floors have subtle gaucho-accented decor. Never as crowded as the other restaurants on this street, it's a great option when lines get long at nearby hot spots.

Báez 202 (at Arguibel). ✆ **11/4899-0951.** Main courses $6–$15. AE, MC, V. Daily noon–4pm and 8pm–1am (until 2am weekends). Metro: Ministro Carranza.

Garbis ★★ ☺ MIDDLE EASTERN   If you're looking for great Middle Eastern food at reasonable prices or a spot to entertain the kids, Garbis has the answer. The menu includes kabobs, falafel, lamb, and other Middle Eastern treats, including some served as kid-size portions, and service is excellent and friendly. The desert kitsch—in the form of tiled walls and brilliant colors—makes you think you've wound up far away from Argentina. A children's entertainment center will keep the kids happy while you dine. Tarot card readings on select days add fun for the adults. Call for the mystic's schedule. This is a chain, with additional restaurants in Belgrano and Villa Crespo.

Scalabrini Ortiz 3190 (at Cerviño). ✆ **11/4511-6600.** www.garbis.com.ar. Main courses $6–$15. AE, MC, V. Daily 11am–3pm and 7–11:30pm. Metro: Scalabrini Ortiz.

La Salamandra ★ ARGENTINE/INTERNATIONAL   Not for the lactose intolerant, this Palermo eatery is a delicious dairy bar. You'll find some of Argentina's best dulce de leche, mozzarella, and other dairy products, along with light snack items. It's largely meant as a place to buy items to eat later, but they have a small sit-down section, so you can eat right away, deciding what exactly to buy more of.

El Salvador 4761 (btw. Gurruchaga and Armenia). ✆ **11/4831-1600.** www.lasalamandra.com.ar. Main courses $2–$10. AE, MC, V. Daily 10am–9pm. Metro: Plaza Italia.

Lupita ★★ MEXICAN   Modern Mexican cuisine awaits at Lupita, an almost religious experience with its giant image of the Virgin of Guadalupe (hence the name) overlooking the bar. This dinner-only restaurant has nine kinds of guacamole, various combination platters, and delicious gourmet tacos and quesadillas. Desserts are a riot of creativity, from pastries mixing peaches and corn to chocolate flan with banana topping. At night, the restaurant is lit with candles, and the menu of alcoholic drinks comes out (adorned in Virgins, plastic Day of the Dead skeletons, and tiny sombreros), listing an enormous tequila collection, as well as other liquors.

Báez 227 (btw. Arguibel and Arévalo). ✆ **11/5197-5149.** www.lupitaweb.com.ar. Main courses $8–$15. AE, MC, V. Sun–Tues 8pm–1am; Wed 8pm–2am; Thurs–Sat 8pm–3am. Metro: Carranza.

Novecento ★★★ INTERNATIONAL   With a sister location in New York's SoHo, Novecento was a pioneer restaurant in Las Cañitas. Fashionable Porteños pack the New York–style bistro by 11pm, clinking wineglasses under a Canal Street sign or

Gelato in Buenos Aires

With such a rich Italian heritage, you'll find a lot of places in Buenos Aires to enjoy the Italian take on ice cream: gelato. Virtually every corner will have at least one of the many chain options, along with individually owned shops. Stop in and try some and then debate like a Porteño which is best. Each company's website will list some of their branches, but you'll easily find them on your own. **Freddo** (www.freddo.com. ar), **Persicco** (www.persicco.com), and the Patagonian company **Abuela Goye** (www.abuelagoye.com) are just a few.

opting for the busy outdoor terrace. The pastas and risotto are mouthwatering, but you may prefer a steak au poivre or a chicken brochette. Top it off with an Argentine wine. At night, by candlelight, it makes a romantic choice for couples. A large, separate, slightly sterile side room is available for spillover or to rent for private parties.

Báez 199 (at Arguibel). *©* **11/4778-1900.** www.novecento.com. Reservations recommended. Main courses $10–$18. AE, DC, MC, V. Daily noon–4pm and 8pm–2am; Sun brunch 8am–noon. Metro: Ministro Carranza.

Sushi Club JAPANESE   This restaurant is part of a very popular chain, with many locations throughout the city, but this is one of its nicest outlets. The Sushi Club serves sushi and other Japanese cuisine in a modern club-like interior, with a chic, creamy monotone color and moody lighting. Fish is a major highlight of the menu, as is beef with Japanese seasonings. The sushi roll selection is enormous and creative; many of the offerings pay tribute to other international cuisines, using ingredients to match.

Báez 268 (at Arévalo). *©* **0-810/222-SUSHI** (78744; toll-free) or 11/4772-5270. www.sushiclubweb. com.ar. Main courses $6–$15. AE, DC, MC, V. Sun–Wed noon–1am; Thurs noon–1:30am; Fri–Sat noon–2am. Metro: Carranza.

T-Bone Bar & Grill ★ PARRILLA/INTERNATIONAL/ARGENTINE   If you want authentic Argentine meat by *parrilla* experts who have worked for more than 20 years, then come here, where huge portions weigh in at 500 grams, more than a pound of meat. T-Bone has two restaurants in Palermo, combining modern ambience with specialties from land and sea. Interesting starters include grilled provolone cheese with oregano, olive oil, tomato slices and arugula, and fresh sashimi salmon. T-Bone's signature steak and Patagonian rack of lamb are accompanied by rustic potatoes. The table service includes homemade bread, sauces, and an ice-cream shot. The wine list includes more than 60 wines.

Armenia 2479 (at Av. Santa Fe). *©* **11/4833-6565.** www.tbone.com.ar. Reservations recommended. Main courses $8–$15. AE, MC, V. Daily 8am–1am. Metro: Plaza Italia.

Utopia Bar ARGENTINE/INTERNATIONAL   Cozier and calmer than the other bars that surround Plaza Serrano, this is an excellent place to grab a bite in this trendy and busy neighborhood. Yellow walls and rustic wooden tables add a sense of calm, though the live music, scheduled on an irregular basis, can be loud. There is an emphasis on drinks here, and breakfast comes with a large selection of flavored coffees, some prepared with whiskey. At night, pizza and sandwiches are the bulk of the offerings. The upstairs, open-air terrace on the roof is one of the best places to sit.

Serrano 1590 (at Plaza Serrano). *©* **11/4831-8572.** Main courses $2–$8. AE, MC, V. Daily 24 hr. Metro: Plaza Italia.

Inexpensive

Bio ★★ 🎁 VEGETARIAN/MEDITERRANEAN   In a nation where meat reigns supreme, finding an organic vegetarian restaurant is a near impossibility. Bio is the exception. Their "meat" is made on the premises from wheat, then marinated to add flavor, making for an elevated, tasty variation on a hamburger. All ingredients are organic and grown or produced in Argentina. Piles of organic cheese line the counters near the chefs, who are happy to explain their processes. Quinoa, the ancient Incan grain, is used in many dishes. You must try the quinoa risotto, one of the restaurant's specialties, though everything here is delicious. Chairs and tables are painted a spring green, and, on warm days, a few tables are scattered on the sidewalk outside. This is also a great place for veg-heads to buy snacks to bring back to their hotel. They have a small shop inside selling organic chips, teas, cheeses, and even organic wine. Best of all, they offer organic cooking classes; check the website for details.

Humboldt 2199 (at Guatemala). ✆ **11/4774-3880.** www.biorestaurant.com.ar. Main courses $8-$10. No credit cards. Mon 9am-5pm; Tues-Sun 9am-1am (often later on weekends). No metro access.

Confitería del Botánico CAFE/ARGENTINE   Stop here after visiting the nearby zoo or Botanical Gardens. It's on a pleasant corner on busy Santa Fe, but its enormous windows onto the green spaces of the gardens and Plaza Siria give it a tranquil feel. Continental breakfast is inexpensive, and you can also order from the full menu at any time of day (omelets from the dinner menu make a hearty breakfast). Lunch specials run from $6 to $10. You can also grab takeout here for a picnic in the park or zoo.

Av. Santa Fe 3799 (at República Siria). ✆ **11/4833-5515.** Main courses $4-$8. AE, MC, V. Sun-Fri 6:30am-midnight; Sat 6:30am-2am. Metro: Plaza Italia.

Las Choclas ★★ ARGENTINE/PARRILLA   Rustic tables, a casual atmosphere, wonderful and inexpensive food, and a great corner location come together in this Las Cañitas restaurant. The main emphasis is on beef, and tons of it, with *bife de chorizo, ojo de bife,* and other beef cuts served in large portions. Filled with the scent of charred wood used in the ovens, the place is always very busy. It doesn't close between lunch and dinner, so it's a great choice for getting your *parrilla* fix at any time of day.

Arce 306 (at Arevolo). ✆ **11/4899-0094.** Main courses $4-$10. No credit cards. Sun-Thurs noon-1am; Fri-Sat noon-2am. Metro: Carranza.

Macondo Bar ★★ INTERNATIONAL/ARGENTINE   Macondo Bar is one of the stars of Plaza Serrano, with sidewalk seating and lots of levels overlooking the action. Inside, the low-ceilinged restaurant twists around several staircases. Sandwiches, pizzas, salads, and *picadas* (masa tartlets) make up the menu. DJs blast music of all kinds throughout the bar, from folkloric to techno to electronica. Technically, there's no live music, but sometimes people come around and play on the street in front of the bar. It's a loud and busy place, for sure, but the setup creates a sense of intimacy.

Borges 1810 (at Plaza Serrano). ✆ **11/4831-4174.** Main courses $3-$8. No credit cards. Mon-Thurs 6pm-4am; Fri-Sat 5pm-7am; Sun 5pm-3am. Metro: Plaza Italia.

Prologo ★ PIZZA/INTERNATIONAL   Whether you're looking for a bar or a great place to eat inexpensively, Prologo's theme is "Let it Beer," and there are more than 70 local and international beers on the menu. To go along with that is a great selection of food, from breakfast omelets to heavy German sandwiches, as well as homemade pastas, hamburgers, salads, and Argentine staples such as beef from the grill. There's even a children's menu. Walls are covered with all sorts of bric-a-brac and posters, and there are tiny booths with high wooden backs, so you can sit cozily with friends and chat away, forgetting the world around you. Upstairs, dine with a view of Plaza Serrano and the exciting nightlife of Palermo Soho.

Serrano 1580 (at Borges, on Plaza Serrano). ☎ **11/4833-0447.** Main courses $3–$8. No credit cards. Sun–Thurs 8:30am–4am; Fri–Sat 24 hr. No metro access.

Tazz ★ MEXICAN   In an old house, like so many other restaurants in Palermo Viejo, Tazz is among the best spots for outdoor seating on Plaza Serrano. Step inside, though, and you'll think you've entered the dining hall of a spaceship, with its blue glowing lights and walls, mod aluminum panels, and billiard table after billiard table. The booths look like emergency space capsules ready to be released if the mother ship gets attacked. The bulk of the menu is Mexican, with sangria and margaritas adding to the fun. More bar than restaurant, it's very popular with a young clientele.

Serrano 1556 (at Plaza Serrano). ☎ **11/4833-5164.** www.tazzbars.com. Main courses $6–$12. No credit cards. Sun–Thurs noon–3am; Fri–Sat noon–6am. Metro: Plaza Italia.

Viejo Agump ★ 🍴 MIDDLE EASTERN   In the heart of the old Armenian section of Buenos Aires, owner Elizabeth Hounanjian offers authentic Middle Eastern cuisine and a new hub for her compatriots ("agump" means "club" or "meeting place" in Armenian), in the shadows of the Armenian church and the community center. The exposed-brick interior of the old house adds a touch of comfort to the dining area, where mainstays include kabobs and baklava. Sidewalk seating on this tree-lined street is a delight in warm weather. A special menu is offered for about $14, which includes an appetizer, a main dish, and a drink. On weekends, Arabic belly dancing and coffee-bean readings heighten the exotic atmosphere. To arrange a reading, contact the mystic Roxana Banklian and schedule an appointment (☎ **11/15-4185-2225** [cell]; roxanabanklian@arnet.com.ar).

Armenia 1382 (at José Antonio Cabrera). ☎ **11/4773-5081.** www.viejoagump.com.ar. Main courses $6–$12. No credit cards. Mon–Thurs 8am–midnight; Fri 8am–2am; Sat 11am–2am. Metro: Scalabrini Ortiz.

ABASTO & ONCE
Abasto

For a map of the restaurants listed in this section, see the "Abasto & Once" map on p. 95.

INEXPENSIVE

Gardel de Buenos Aires ★ ARGENTINE/ITALIAN   You won't see tango here, but this cafe celebrates the famous tango singer Carlos Gardel in other ways. A clock, with his hands at the 12 o'clock position, overlooks the dining area, with its brilliant red tablecloths and rich wood trim. Gardel photos adorn the place, a papier-mâché mannequin of his likeness juts out from one of the walls, and his songs play nonstop from loudspeakers. And in spite of the overwhelming kitsch, the food is good. The menu offers Argentine standards such as beef and empanadas, as well as salads, pastas, desserts, sandwiches, pizzas, and Italian specialties. The house specialty is *fugazzata*, a kind of stuffed pizza. Service is fast and friendly, so this is a great place to grab a quick coffee or a sandwich. It's open 24 hours Friday and Saturday, so come by and toast Gardel after a night of tangoing, with a drink from the extensive liquor selection.

Entre Ríos 796 (at Independencia). ☎ **11/4381-4170.** Main courses $3–$10. AE, MC, V. Sun–Thurs 6am–1am; Fri–Sat 24 hr. Metro: Entre Ríos.

Kosher McDonald's ★★ 📷 AMERICAN/KOSHER   I wouldn't ordinarily advise a traveler to eat at McDonald's on vacation, but this location is clearly unique: it's the only kosher McDonald's in the world outside of Israel, underscoring Buenos Aires's reputation as one of the world's great Jewish centers. Rabbi supervision makes sure that kosher rules are strictly followed here. It's typical McDonald's fare—burgers, fries, salads, fish sandwiches—except that no dairy at all is served here, and the meat is charcoal-grilled, rather than fried. They also sell souvenir mugs and other items to bring home. Locals of all kinds, Jewish or not, patronize the place. If you only came to gawk but still end up craving a Big Mac without cheese, a total kosher no-no, fret not: You're in the Abasto Shopping Center's Food Court, so all you have to do is turn around and walk to the regular McDonald's on the other side.

Abasto Shopping Center Food Court, Av. Corrientes 3247 (at Agüero). © **11/4959-3709** or 0800/777-6236 for McDonald's Argentina information hot line. Main courses $2–$6. No credit cards. Sun–Thurs 10am–midnight; Fri 10am–2pm; Sat 9pm–midnight, but times will vary seasonally depending on sunset and Jewish holidays. Metro: Carlos Gardel.

Once

For a map of the restaurants listed in this section, see the "Abasto & Once" map on p. 95.

MODERATE

Al Galope ★ ARGENTINE/PARRILLA/MIDDLE EASTERN/KOSHER   This is one of Buenos Aires's most popular kosher restaurants, located in what was once the epicenter of Buenos Aires's Jewish community. This place is best described as an Argentine *parrilla* with Middle Eastern accents. It serves wonderfully juicy and yet still kosher slabs of beef, made tender through a special marinating process replacing moisture in the meat after the blood has been removed. The interior is simple, wood-paneled, and home style. The family that owns the restaurant oversees its operations; sometimes they argue right in front of you. The menu also features a selection of kosher Argentine wines, and you can take a bottle home with you if you like. Middle Eastern fare—such as pitas and hummus as starters or sides, and baklava desserts—is also on hand, as well as fast food such as pastrami sandwiches and salads.

Tucumán 2633 (at Pueyrredón). © **11/4963-6888.** Main courses $5–$14. AE, DC, MC, V. Sun–Fri noon–4pm; Sun–Thurs 8pm–1am; Sat 9pm–midnight, but times will vary seasonally depending on sunset and Jewish holidays. Metro: Pueyrredón.

Sucath David ★ ARGENTINE/PARRILLA/MIDDLE EASTERN/KOSHER   Run by the Levy family, who moved to Buenos Aires from Damascus more than 60 years ago, Sucath David serves traditional Argentine food with Middle Eastern touches. Try their brisket in a garlic tomato sauce, or their pastrami, served as a slab. Grilled steaks are generously cut and deliciously pink, tender, and juicy. Make sure to try the starters: hummus, tabbouleh made with a tangy tomato sauce, black and green olives, baba gannouj, and pickled cabbage, served with toasted pita bread. They also offer kosher wines from the San Juan vintner Tariag 613.

Tucumán 2349 (btw. Pasteur and Azcuenaga). © **11/4952-8878.** www.sucathdavid.com. Main courses $5–$14. AE, DC, MC, V. Sun–Fri noon–3:30pm; Sun–Thurs 8pm–midnight; Sat 9pm–midnight, but times will vary seasonally depending on sunset and Jewish holidays. Metro: Pueyrredón.

LA BOCA

While I highly recommend the restaurants below, note that you should arrive by cab if you're coming for dinner and have the restaurant call a cab for you when you leave.

Abasto & Once

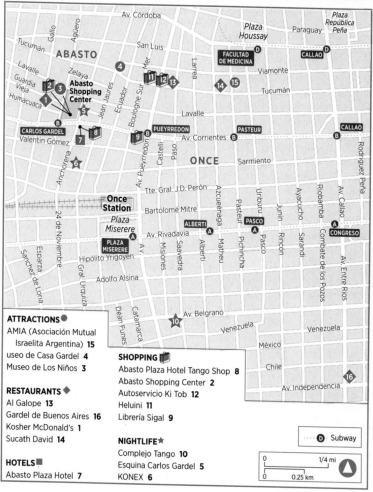

ATTRACTIONS ●
AMIA (Asociación Mutual
   Israelita Argentina) **15**
useo de Casa Gardel **4**
Museo de Los Niños **3**

RESTAURANTS ◆
Al Galope **13**
Gardel de Buenos Aires **16**
Kosher McDonald's **1**
Sucath David **14**

HOTELS ■
Abasto Plaza Hotel **7**

SHOPPING 🛍
Abasto Plaza Hotel Tango Shop **8**
Abasto Shopping Center **2**
Autoservicio Ki Tob **12**
Heluini **11**
Librería Sigal **9**

NIGHTLIFE ★
Complejo Tango **10**
Esquina Carlos Gardel **5**
KONEX **6**

····ⒹⓁ Subway

0   1/4 mi
0   0.25 km

The area is considered dangerous at night and you should not wander around. For a
map of the restaurants listed in this section, see the "La Boca" map on p. 97.

Very Expensive

Patagonia Sur ★ PARRILLA/INTERNATIONAL/ARGENTINE   One of the
most expensive restaurants in all of Buenos Aires is in an unlikely setting overlooking
the waterfront in working-class La Boca. The brainchild of Argentine superstar chef
Francis Mallmann, the author of the book *Seven Fires*, it's a tiny sliver of a place with
a country-chic interior just off Caminito. The three-course menu goes for just over
$100, and by the time you add wine and extras, you're looking at $200 each. The food
is creative, however, bursting with flavor and contrast, like the salad starter of arugula

with grapefruit, Parmesan, and toasted almonds, served with a simple main of the Argentine staple beef rib-eye with chimichurri and roasted potatoes.

Rocha 801 (at Pedro de Mendoza, overlooking La Boca harbor). ℭ **11/4303-5917** or 11/4303-5918. www.restaurantepatagoniasur.com. Set 3-course menu for $101. AE, DC, V, MC. Tues–Sat noon–3pm and 8–11pm. No metro access.

Moderate

El Obrero ★★★ ☺ PARRILLA/ITALIAN/ARGENTINE   Two brothers from Barcelona, Marcelino and Francisco Castro, started this wonderful institution in 1954 in a remote, hard-to-find part of La Boca. Marcelino's children, Juan Carlos, Pablo, and Silvia, have since taken over and give the restaurant their loving care, personally waiting tables along with the staff. Here, you'll dine on thick, juicy, perfectly cooked steaks. There's also Italian food, including excellent calamari, fish, and chicken. Ask about half portions, which are perfect for kids. Lots of Boca Juniors and other sports memorabilia hanging on the walls remind you that you're in one of the most important *fútbol* (soccer) neighborhoods in the world. This is one of the best places in La Boca, but tables fill up rapidly around 9pm, so reserve or come earlier.

Agustin R. Caffarena 64 (at Caboto). ℭ **11/4362-9912.** www.bodegonelobrero.com.ar. Main courses $6–$15. No credit cards. Mon–Sat noon–4pm and 8:30pm–midnight (sometimes later). No metro access.

La Perla CAFE/ARGENTINE   This ancient cafe and bar is one of Buenos Aires's *cafés notables*. It dates from 1899 and has a beautiful interior, loaded with photos of the owners mingling with important visitors from around the world who came to La Boca and this important stop on the tourist circuit. U.S. President Bill Clinton is among the luminaries, and his image is among those most highlighted. Pizzas, *picadas*, and a range of coffees and drinks are on offer. If you're in La Boca, it's a great place to stop for a drink and to soak up atmosphere.

Pedro de Mendoza 1899 (at Caminito). ℭ **11/4301-2985.** Main courses $4–$12. No credit cards. Daily 7am–9pm. No metro access.

BELGRANO

Expensive

Buddha BA ★ CHINESE   In the heart of Belgrano's Chinatown, this very elegant, two-level Chinese teahouse and restaurant is built into a house, with an adjacent garden and art gallery selling fine Asian art and antiques. The interesting and creatively named menu includes items such as Dragon Fire, a mix of spicy chicken and curried *lomo*, and Buddha Tears, squid in a soy-and-chicken broth sauce with seasoned vegetables. The atmosphere is very welcoming, so this makes a great rest stop if you're exploring this neighborhood in depth.

Arribeños 2288 (at Mendoza). ℭ **11/4706-2382.** www.buddhaba.com.ar. Main courses $8–$15. AE, MC, V. Tues–Sun 12:30–3:30pm and 8pm–midnight; tea service Tues–Sun 4–7:30pm. Metro: Juramento.

BARRACAS

Moderate

Caseros ★ ARGENTINE/INTERNATIONAL   Opened in 2008, this restaurant has become a mainstay in the emerging Barracas dining scene. Look for rich comfort foods like roast suckling pig and lamb, as well as beef served in interesting ways and

La Boca

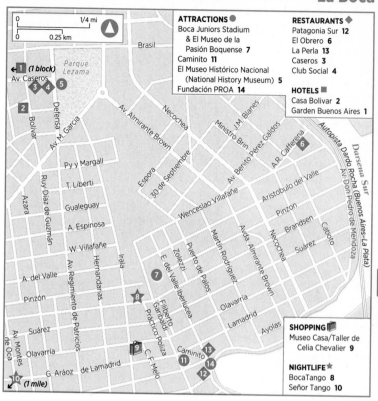

ATTRACTIONS ●
Boca Juniors Stadium
  & El Museo de la
  Pasión Boquense **7**
Caminito **11**
El Museo Histórico Nacional
  (National History Museum) **5**
Fundación PROA **14**

RESTAURANTS ◆
Patagonia Sur **12**
El Obrero **6**
La Perla **13**
Caseros **3**
Club Social **4**

HOTELS ■
Casa Bolivar **2**
Garden Buenos Aires **1**

SHOPPING 🛍
Museo Casa/Taller de
  Celia Chevalier **9**

NIGHTLIFE ★
BocaTango **8**
Señor Tango **10**

a number of vegetarian options. The decor is country chic with an English touch, much of the wood salvaged from other buildings, lending a makeshift air to the place.

Av. Caseros 486 (btw. Defensa and Bolívar). ✆ **11/4307-4729.** Main courses $8–$15. AE, MC, V. Mon noon–5pm; Tues–Sat noon–12:30am, sometimes later. Metro: Constitución.

Club Social ★ ARGENTINE/INTERNATIONAL   The charming decor in this place makes it seem like a *café notable,* but it's actually quite new; the owner, Ezequiel Arslanian, decorated it with salvaged tiles and turn-of-the-last-century relics to create the impression of an old bistro. Stop in for breakfast while exploring Barracas or San Telmo, or try the delicious dinner entrees, including wok-prepared chicken and cappelletti stuffed with pumpkin and brie.

Av. Caseros 442 (btw. Defensa and Bolívar). ✆ **11/4307-1919.** www.restaurantclubsocial.com. Main courses $8–$15. AE, MC, V. Mon 9:30am–5pm; Tues–Thurs 9:30am–2am; Fri–Sat 9:30am–3am; Sun 9:30am–6pm. Metro: Constitución.

5

WHERE TO DINE

Barracas

EXPLORING BUENOS AIRES

The beauty of Buenos Aires is evident the moment you set foot on its streets. The city's most impressive historical sites surround Plaza de Mayo, although you will certainly experience Argentine history in other neighborhoods, such as La Boca and San Telmo. Be sure not to miss a waterside walk in Puerto Madero and the adjacent Ecological Reserve or an afternoon among the plazas and cafes of Recoleta or Palermo. Sidewalk cafes offer respite for weary feet, and there's good public transportation to carry you from neighborhood to neighborhood.

One thing to remember when exploring Buenos Aires's attractions is their historical legacy. Under the Spanish Empire, Buenos Aires was an unimportant backwater, with other Argentine cities, such as Córdoba, regarded as more significant and culturally sophisticated. With the 1880 movement of the capital to Buenos Aires, however, the city sought to overcome its inferiority complex with grand architectural plans, and indeed, for almost the entire first half of the 20th century, this was one of the wealthiest cities in the world. Within the descriptions of these buildings, I include, wherever possible, the history behind their impressive beauty. They are not mere baubles; they are the physical remnants of a lost opportunity for glory on the world stage.

FAMOUS ATTRACTIONS

Plaza de Mayo Area

A Line Subte ★★★ ☺ ◙ This was the first subway line in Buenos Aires, and it still retains its original cars. The line was opened in 1913, making the Buenos Aires *subte* the 13th-oldest subway system in the world, the oldest in South America, and the fourth-oldest in the Americas as a whole (after New York, Boston, and Philadelphia). The A line runs under Avenida de Mayo, beginning at Plaza de Mayo, through Congreso, its original terminus, though it now continues much farther. The old cars are wooden and rickety, and as they proceed along the bends underground, you can watch the whole car shimmy and shake. The cars' wooden side panels are made to bend and slip into each other. Windows are still wooden, with leather pulls. Rings, now plastic, are also held by leather straps. Be aware that, unlike those on the cars of the other subway lines, the doors on this line do not always open and close automatically. The system has begun adding new cars to this line, meaning fewer wooden trains are running, but about every third car passing will be one of these historical treasures. It's worth the wait to ride one. Stations between Plaza de Mayo and Congreso still retain most of their early ornamentation as well; the best station is Perú.

The A Line begins at Plaza de Mayo and travels along Av. de Mayo to Congreso and beyond. www.subte.com.ar. Admission 30¢.

Cabildo ★★★

This small, white, colonial-style building with a central bell tower was the original seat of city government established by the Spaniards. The building was completed in 1751, but parts of it were demolished to create space for Avenida de Mayo and Diagonal Sur in the late 1800s and early 1900s. The remainder of the building was remodeled in 1939. The most important site of meetings related to Argentina's declaration of independence against Spain, the building underwent another renovation for the 2010 Bicentennial, expanding its exhibit spaces. The small, informal museum displays paintings and furniture from the colonial period, and its ledges and windows allow some of the best views of the Plaza de Mayo. The Cabildo is the only remaining government building on the Plaza de Mayo dating back to colonial times. Many people come here just for the changing of the guard that happens every hour at the front of this building (see "Men in Uniform: The Changing of the Guard," p. 104). On Thursday and Friday from 11am to 6pm, the Cabildo's back patio is home to a crafts fair.

Bolívar 65 (at Rivadavia). ☎ **11/4334-1782.** www.cultura.gov.ar. Free admission. Wed–Fri 10:30–5pm; Sat–Sun 11:30–6pm. Metro: Bolívar, Catedral, or Plaza de Mayo.

Casa de Cultura & Palacio de Gobierno ★★

On a street lined with impressive structures meant to rival the Champs-Elysées, these two buildings, grouped together on tours, are standouts that should not be missed. The Palacio de Gobierno, on the corner of Rivadavia and San Martín, is the new City Hall. The working office of the mayor of Buenos Aires, it is a white Beaux Arts building fronting the Plaza de Mayo on the block opposite the Cabildo, the old city hall. The building was originally constructed between 1891 and 1902, and it was expanded 10 years later.

The adjoining Casa de Cultura, a sumptuous gray granite building with bronze ornamentation, is the former home of the newspaper *La Prensa*, at one time the most important paper in Argentina. The paper was started by the Paz family, former owners of the palace on San Martín now occupied by the **Círculo Militar** (p. 113). The Casa de Cultura is topped by a statue representing freedom of the press (suppressed in Argentina under many regimes). The clientele of the paper were largely wealthy oligarchs, and the building's beauty reflects this. The dark lobby even has extremely ornate payment-window stands. The most impressive room is the Salón Dorado, a French neoclassical masterpiece of gilded columns, painted ceilings, an ornate parquet floor, and a performance stage. Tours take visitors through this room and others throughout the building, but you should also ask for schedules of the various functions hosted here in the evenings, which are usually free. The building is now headquarters of the city's Office of Culture, and there's no finer home for it.

Av. de Mayo 575 (at San Martín, near Plaza de Mayo). ☎ **11/4323-9669.** www.buenosaires.gov.ar. Free guided tours Sat 4 and 5pm; Sun every hour 11am–4pm. Metro: Catedral, Bolívar, or Plaza de Mayo.

Casa Rosada & The Presidential Museum (Museo del Bicentenario) ★★★

Perhaps the most photographed building in Buenos Aires, the Casa Rosada is the main presence on the Plaza de Mayo. The Argentine president does not live here, contrary to what many tourists think, but she does work here. (She lives in a mansion in Los Olivos, a suburb north of the city.) It is from a balcony of the north wing of

this building that Eva Perón addressed adoring crowds. Hoping for star-quality glamour, former President Carlos Ménem allowed Madonna to use it for the 1996 movie *Evita*, to the shock of many Porteños. Most Argentines, however, associate the balcony with the announcement of military dictator Leopoldo Galtieri's ill-fated war in 1982 against the United Kingdom over the Falkland Islands, known here as the Islas Malvinas. Girl power aside, the color pink has nothing to do with the female president. Two theories explain the color. One is political: At the time of its construction in the late 1800s, two warring parties, one represented by the color red, the other by white, are said to have created a truce by painting the building a color combining both shades. The other, rather revolting theory is more practical: In days past, the building was painted with cow blood that later dried in the sun to a deep pink color. At night, hot pink floodlights now also illuminate the building.

You can watch the changing of the guard in front of the palace every hour on the hour. In the back of the building, you'll find the Presidential Museum, with information on the history of the building and items owned by various presidents over the centuries. Portions of the museum extend underground into basements of former buildings, including a 2011 extension to house a mural by Mexican artist José David Alfaro Siqueiros. Make sure to step outside to look at excavations on the Customs house and port area, which existed along the Río de la Plata at this point until landfill projects pushed the shore farther east. The Casa Rosada is now also open to the public on weekends, with free tours on the hour Saturdays and Sundays from 10am to 6pm. If you're going on one, bring identification and expect to have personal items X-rayed to help ensure the security of the president. The tour will take you through ornate chambers, many overseen by marble busts of past presidents. You even get to stand on Evita's balcony and tell Argentina not to cry for you.

Casa Rosada overlooking Plaza de Mayo on Calle Balcarce (btw. Rivadavia and Hipólito Yrigoyen). Museum entrance at Yrigoyen intersection with Paseo Colón Av. © **11/4344-3802.** Free admission. Tues–Sun 10am–6pm. Casa Rosada public tours Sat–Sun 10am–6pm. Free admission. Metro: Plaza de Mayo.

Legislatura de la Ciudad (City Legislature Building) ★

This striking neo-classical building houses exhibitions in several of its halls. Ask about free tours, offered on an informal basis by guide Alejandra Javier in English or Spanish, Monday through Friday. She will take you into the impressive bell tower that, according to legend, was made as high as it is so that the city could keep an eye on the president in the Casa Rosada. Portions of the building were also built around an old mansion that once faced the Plaza de Mayo. The view from the corner balcony of this part of the building calls to mind how powerful, wealthy families, at a time before the city began to grow so rapidly, could oversee the entire town from their living-room window. Around the corner from Legislatura on Diagonal Sur, you'll see a bronze statue of Julio A. Roca. He is considered one of Argentina's greatest generals, but one of his legacies is the slaughtering of tens of thousands of Indians in the name of racial purity within the province of Buenos Aires. It's because of him that Argentina, unlike most of Latin America, reflects at first glance a largely white, rather than mestizo, society.

Calle Perú 130 and Hipólito Yrigoyen. © **11/4338-3167** or 11/4338-3000. www.legislatura.gov.ar. Free admission. Mon–Fri 10am–5pm. Metro: Bolívar.

Manzanas de las Luces (Blocks of Enlightenment) ★★

Manzana is an old name for a city block (as well as the Spanish word for "apple"), and the name "las Luces" refers to this area being the intellectual center, or "light," of the city in the 17th and 18th centuries. This land was granted in 1616 to the Jesuits, who built San

Ignacio, the city's oldest church, which still stands at the corner of calles Bolívar and Alsina. San Ignacio has a beautiful altar carved in wood with baroque details. It was renovated in 2007 after years of neglect. It was also nearly destroyed in the revolution that took Perón out of power in 1955, in which he sought to reduce the power of the Catholic Church (something that Evita might not have permitted him to do, had she still been alive). Also located here is the Colegio Nacional de Buenos Aires (National High School of Buenos Aires). Argentina's best-known intellectuals have gathered and studied here, and the name "block of lights" honors the school's graduates and their work in achieving Argentina's independence in the 19th century.

English-language tours are usually Saturday and Sunday at 3 and 4:30pm and include a visit to the Jesuits' underground tunnels, which connected their churches to strategic spots in the city (admission $2). Speculation remains as to whether the tunnels also served a military purpose or funneled pirated goods when the city was a colonial smuggling center. The full extent of the tunnels is still unknown and various leaders, including Perón, added to them in case they needed to flee the nearby Casa Rosada in the event of unexpected coups (which he did, escaping to Paraguay). *Ratearse*, the Argentine slang for playing hooky that literally means "to become a rat," comes from the tunnels, as this is where students from the Colegio hid when they didn't want to go to class. In addition to weekend tours, the Comisión Nacional de la Manzana de las Luces organizes a variety of cultural activities, including folkloric dance lessons, open-air theater performances, art expositions, and music concerts.

Calle Perú 272 (at Moreno). 🕻 **11/4342-6973** or 11/4343-3260 for tours, or 11/4331-9534 or 11/4342-3964 for cultural events. www.manzanadelasluces.gov.ar. Metro: Bolívar.

Catedral Metropolitana ★★
Juan de Garay allotted land for the main church of Buenos Aires in 1580, and various church structures have existed here and been incorporated into others over time. The current Metropolitan Cathedral was built over a period of decades in the early 1700s. It was given a new facade with carvings telling the story of Jacob and his son Joseph in the early 1800s and was designated a cathedral in 1836. The look was changed from a traditional Spanish colonial to Greek revival, with a pediment and colonnade in front, though the sides, back, and exterior dome remain similar to the original. Inside lies an ornate mausoleum containing the remains of General José de San Martín, the South American liberator regarded as the "Father of the Nation." (San Martín fought successfully for freedom in Argentina, Peru, and Chile alongside the better-known Simón Bolívar.) His body was moved here in 1880 to become a rallying symbol of Argentina's unification and rise to greatness when Buenos Aires became the capital of Argentina at the end of a long civil war. The tomb of the unknown soldier of Argentine independence is also here, and an eternal flame burns in remembrance on the church's facade. The church also contains a memorial to Jews who died in the Holocaust as well as in the 1990s in Buenos Aires at the **Israeli Embassy** (p. 110) and **AMIA** (p. 118) bombings. Among the chapels of note is the one with a statue of Jesus with the notation, "Santo Cristo del Gran Amor," or the Holy Christ of Great Love. It was donated in 1978 by an Argentine soccer player whose family had disappeared. He swore he would donate a statue to the church if they were ever found, and they were. While Argentina is a strongly Catholic nation, it is not very big on ritual. However, the most important midnight Mass in Argentina occurs in this church. Called the "Noche Buena," it is held every December 24, at 10pm, presided over by current Archbishop Cardinal Jorge Mario Bergoglio.

San Martín 27 (at Rivadavia, overlooking Plaza de Mayo). 🕻 **11/4331-2845.** www.catedralbuenosaires. org.ar. Metro: Bolívar, Catedral, or Plaza de Mayo.

6 MEN IN uniform: THE CHANGING OF THE GUARD

Watching the changing of the guard at various historical sites throughout Buenos Aires is part of the fun of visiting. Many tourists take particular delight in photographing these men in early-19th-century military clothing parading through Plaza de Mayo. But did you know there is more than one kind of guard? Granaderos guard national monuments such as the San Martín Mausoleum and the Casa Rosada. Patricios guard city-owned buildings, such as the Municipal Palace and the Cabildo. Both dress in costumes dating from the Napoleonic era. The Patricios represent the oldest branch of the military and were formed before the country's independence, in response to British attacks on Buenos Aires. The Granaderos were formed after independence. You can also tell the difference between the guards by the pants they wear: white for Patricios, and blue for Granaderos. The Islas Malvinas–Falkland Islands War Memorial in Plaza San Martín is guarded by the three branches of the military, the navy, air force, and the army. Each branch rotates, holding the honor for a 2-week cycle.

Plaza de Mayo ★★ ☺ Juan de Garay founded the historic core of Buenos Aires, the Plaza de Mayo, upon the city's second founding in 1580. The plaza's prominent buildings create an architectural timeline: the Cabildo, or Old City Hall, and Metropolitan Cathedral are vestiges of the colonial period (18th and early 19th c.), while the Pirámide de Mayo (Pyramid of May) and the buildings of the national and local government and union offices reflect the styles of the late 19th and early to mid–20th centuries, including some that typify the severe Fascist style popular in South America at the time, with smooth surfaces and enormous Roman-style metal doors. In the center of the plaza, you'll find palm trees, fountains, and benches. Though many of these facilities are in need of an upgrade, the plaza is still full of local people at lunchtime, chatting and eating takeout food.

Plaza de Mayo remains the political heart of Buenos Aires, serving as a forum for protests with many camping out here overnight, including a group of Islas Malvinas veterans denied combat pay who have been living in a tent since 2008. The mothers of the *desaparecidos*, victims of the military dictatorship's campaign against leftists, known as the Dirty War, have demonstrated here since 1977. An absolute must-see for understanding Argentina's recent history, you can watch them march, speak, and set up information booths every Thursday afternoon at 3:30pm (p. 130).

Mass demonstrations are very common here, and most protests begin in front of the Casa Rosada (now separated from the crowds by permanent barricades) and proceed up Avenida de Mayo toward Congreso. For the most part, these demonstrations are peaceful, usually led by people who have suffered the economic consequences of the peso crisis, known as *piqueteros*. However, at times, protests have broken into violence, so be aware when demonstrations are occurring and leave immediately if things seem to be getting out of hand. The presence of a group of protestors with covered faces carrying metal sticks is a definite sign to leave.

Plaza de Mayo begins at the eastern terminus of Av. de Mayo and is surrounded by calles Yrigoyen, San Martín, Rivadavia, and Balcarce. Metro: Bolívar, Catedral, or Plaza de Mayo.

Monserrat, San Telmo & La Boca

Austro-Hungarian Empire Embassy ★   Construction of the Austro-Hungarian Embassy, which remains today one of the city's most imposing buildings, was started just before World War I. By the time the war was finished so was the empire. Massive and masculine, the granite building is decorated with eagles and severe sculptures of semi-nude male warriors, topped by a double domed mansard roof. It is filthy and neglected, now used merely as an office building, but as it was built with a lookout point, there are talks of some day opening it to the public.

Belgrano 600 (at Perú). Metro: Moreno.

Instituto Nacional de Musicología Carlos Vega ★   This sumptuous building belies its location on a quiet, almost run-down block of San Telmo. Its main exhibition hall boasts an intricate stained-glass ceiling within a cast-iron dome, held up by four oversized and graceful female goddesses and other angel-like figures. The Institute, named for founder and musical conductor Carlos Vega, hosts lectures, art exhibits, and musical recitals during the day. But the turn-of-the-last-century building itself is the true star; this was the original site of the National Library, where Borges was director from 1955 to 1973, before it moved to its current Palermo location in 1992.

México 564 (at Perú). © **11/4300-7374,** 11/4361-6520, or 11/4361-6013. www.inmuvega.gov.ar. Tickets sometimes free, or up to $5 for exhibitions. Mon–Fri 10am–5pm; additional hours and admission vary based on exhibition. Metro: Independencia.

Plaza Dorrego ★★   Originally the site of a Bethlehemite monastery, this plaza, the second-oldest square in the city, is where Argentines met to reconfirm their declaration of independence from Spain. On Sunday from 10am to 5pm, the city's best **antiques fair** ★★★ takes over. You can buy leather, silver, handicrafts, and other products here along with antiques, all while tango dancers perform on the square. The tall, darkly handsome dancer Pedro Benavente, nicknamed El Indio, is the star of the plaza. Sundays here are not to be missed and even locals come to enjoy themselves. The local restaurants also have outside seating here, but whether you're dining or watching the entertainment, keep a very close eye on your personal belongings.

Intersection of Defensa and Humberto I. Metro: Independencia.

San Telmo Market ★★ 📷   Though this is definitely a place to shop, the building is worth seeing on its own. The San Telmo market opened in 1897, and it is a masterpiece not just for its soaring wrought-iron interior, but for the atmosphere you'll find here. Half of the market is made up of things that locals need—butchers, fresh-fruit-and-vegetable grocers, and little kiosks selling sundries and household items. This part looks like the kind of place where your grandmother probably shopped when she was a child. I recommend chatting with the staff in these places, who seem to have all the time in the world. The other half is more touristy, but never overly so, with various antiques and vintage-clothing shops. There are several entrances to this large market; it's almost a block in size and squeezed between several other historical buildings.

Defensa 961 or Bolívar 998 (both at Carlos Calvo). Daily 10am–8pm, but each stand will have individual hours. Metro: Independencia.

The Engineering School/The Eva Perón Foundation   This imposing building takes up an entire block. It was once the headquarters for the Eva Perón Foundation, a foundation Evita established to distribute funds to needy children and families, as well as, some say, to siphon funds for personal use. Today there is little to mark the former use of the building, miraculously saved by the subsequent military regime, which felt it was too important and expensive a building to allow to be demolished as had been the case with other sites associated with Evita. Only a tiny plaque, affixed to a lobby column in 2002, explains the relationship. Nevertheless, this is a grand 1940s classical building, reserved in style, with simple Doric columns fronting Paseo Colón. The floors and walls throughout are decorated with sumptuous multi-colored marble. As an engineering school, it is brimming with students but still maintains a hushed atmosphere of quiet academic pursuits. The dean's office was once Evita's own. It's a public building and anyone can enter it, but the school offers no information or tours based on its former use and discourages random wanderers.

Paseo Colón (btw. Independencia and Estados Unidos). Metro: Independencia.

Caminito This is the main attraction in La Boca, Buenos Aires's original Little Italy. A pedestrianized street a few blocks long with a colorful, kitschy collection of painted houses known as *conventillos* (flimsily built houses that immigrants lived in), it's lined with art displays explaining the history of the area. Untold numbers of tacky T-shirt and souvenir vendors and artists set up stalls here and cater strictly to tourists. To be honest, I find this area repulsive and insulting to visitors to Buenos Aires. The history of La Boca is very important to Buenos Aires and the development of the tango. However, what remains here today has little to do with any of that. Even the touristy name of the street "Caminito" has nothing to do with Buenos Aires at all. It's from a song about a flower-filled remote rural village, not an intensely urban neighborhood where Italian-immigrant gangsters, prostitutes, and sailors once roamed the streets committing crimes and other acts of mayhem. To top it all off, in the summertime, the stench from the polluted port can also be simply overwhelming.

Come to Caminito if you must, and if you're on a tour, you will anyway. However, if you are on a very short stay in Buenos Aires, skip La Boca. For true authenticity and a flavor of old Buenos Aires, visit San Telmo instead.

Btw. Av. Pedro de Mendoza and Gral. Gregorio Aráoz de Lamadrid at Garibaldi. No metro access.

Boca Juniors Stadium & El Museo de la Pasión Boquense ★ This stadium overlooks a desolate garbage-strewn lot at the corner of calles Del Valle Iberlucea and Brandsen. But on game day, when street parties and general debauchery take over the area, it's another story. This is the home of the *fútbol* (soccer) club Boca Juniors, the team of Argentine legend Diego Maradona, who, like his country, went from glory to fiery collapse (and revival) rather quickly. For information on *fútbol* games, see the *Buenos Aires Herald* sports section. Wealthy businessman Mauricio Macri, the former president of the Boca Juniors Fútbol Club, opened the Museo de la Pasión Boquense in the stadium, part of his bid to eventually woo Porteños into electing him the city's mayor, which worked. The museum is full of awards, TV screens showing important events that happened on the field, and more things related to this legendary team. For a map of the stadium and museum, see the "La Boca" map on p. 97.

Brandsen 805 (at Del Valle Iberlucea). ✆ **11/4362-1100**. www.museoboquense.com. Free admission. Daily 10am–6pm. No metro access.

Congreso Area

Congreso ★★ Opened in 1906 after nearly 9 years of construction, and built in a Greco-Roman style with strong Parisian Beaux Arts influences, Congreso is the most imposing building in all of Buenos Aires. One of the main architects was Victor

Meano, who was also involved in designing the **Teatro Colón** (p. 189), but he was murdered before completion of either building. Congreso is constructed of Argentine gray granite, with walls more than 1¾m(5¾ ft.) wide at their base. Congreso is also the best example of the Argentine practice of taking architectural elements from famous buildings around the world. It resembles the U.S. Capitol, with a central dome also reminiscent of St. Peter's spreading over the two wings holding the bicameral legislative chambers. The ornamental bronze roofline also calls to mind Garnier's opera house, and the central pediment is topped by a Quadriga or Triumph carried by four horses that echoes Berlin's Brandenburg Gate. This sculpture was designed in Venice by artist Victor de Pol, took more than 4 years to make, weighs 20 tons, and was cast in Germany.

Tours take visitors through the fantastic chambers, adorned with bronze, statues, German tile floors, Spanish woods, and French marbles and lined with Corinthian columns. The horseshoe-shaped Congressional chamber is the largest, with the Senatorial chamber an almost identical copy but at one-fifth the size. The power of the Catholic Church is also evident in both chambers—the archbishop has his own seat next to the president of either section of Congress and, though he has no voting power, is allowed to preside over all of the sessions. The old seats for representatives and senators have a form of electronic whoopee cushion—simply by sitting down, attendance is taken based on the pressure of a politician's buttocks. The tour also takes you to the very pink Salón Rosado, now called the Salón Eva Perón. She opened this room after women received the right to vote, so that women politicians could sit without men around them to discuss feminist issues. Upon her death, Evita's body was temporarily placed under Congreso's central rotunda so that citizens could view her during the 2-week mourning period in 1952.

The building faces the Plaza Congreso, with its enormous fountain called the Dos Congresos. This multilevel confection of statues, horses, lions, condors, cherubs, and other ornaments has stairs leading to a good spot for photographing the Congreso. Unfortunately, the park became quite run-down over the years, with homeless encampments and graffiti. It was renovated in 2007 as part of the city's refurbishment in anticipation of the 2010 Bicentennial Independence celebrations, with new paving and cleaning and restoration of the fountain and other monuments. The gate surrounding the fountain is usually locked, but ask the guard if you can enter. Near the fountain, on the southeast corner of the intersection of Callao with Rivadavia, is Argentina's **National AIDS Monument,** a tiny concrete stub with a red ribbon.

For more on Congreso, visit the Congressional Library across the street and request the book *El Congreso de la Nación Argentina* by Manrique Zago, which provides rich detail in English and Spanish. Though both English and Spanish tours of Congreso are available, they are often subject to cancellation, depending on functions occurring in the building. Plus, English-speaking tour guides aren't always available, in spite of the schedule. Entrance is usually through the Rivadavia side of the building, but can switch to the Yrigoyen doors, so arrive early and let the guards know that you are there. Guides will not be called down unless they know people are waiting. This is an incredible building and worth the confusion. Its beauty also speaks for itself, even if you have to take the Spanish tour and don't know a word.

Entre Ríos at Rivadavia. © **11/4370-7100** or 11/6310-7100, ext. 3725. Free guided tours in English on Mon–Tues and Thurs–Fri 11am and 4pm. Spanish tours Mon–Tues and Thurs–Fri 11am, and 4 and 5pm. Metro: Congreso.

Asociación Madres de Plaza de Mayo ★★★ 📷   I highly recommend visiting Plaza de Mayo on a Thursday afternoon to see the Madres speak about their missing children in front of the **Casa Rosada** (p. 99). Here at their headquarters, on Plaza Congreso, you can learn even more. This complex contains the office of the Madres, the Universidad Popular Madres de Plaza de Mayo, the Librería de las Madres, the Café Literario Osvaldo Bayer, and the Biblioteca Popular Julio Huasi, among other facilities. At this busy center of activity, you will find the Madres themselves, now mostly very old women, surrounded by young people who come to work and take university classes with a decidedly leftist bent. Many lectures, video conferences, and art exhibitions are held throughout the space. The bookstore has perhaps the largest collection of books anywhere in the world on Che Guevara, a Madres personal hero, though he was killed before their movement began. The large library of reference books on liberal causes is decorated with depictions of events around the world in which people have sought justice from their governments. On Friday, Saturday, and Sunday from 11am to 6pm, the Madres hold a fundraising market with antiques, crafts, food, book vendors, and occasional live music on Plaza Congreso, in front of the building. This is also good for children, because it is next to the part of the park with the merry-go-round and other rides.

Hipólito Yrigoyen 1584 (at Ceballos). ✆ **11/4383-0377** or 11/4383-6340. www.madres.org. Various hours, but building is generally open Mon–Fri 10am–10pm; Sat 10am–9pm. Metro: Congreso.

Palacio Barolo ★★★ 🏛   Among the most impressive buildings in Buenos Aires, and once the tallest in South America, this oddly decorated building with a central tower is a showstopper among all those on Avenida de Mayo. Its eclectic design can be called many things, among them Art Nouveau, neo-Gothic, neo-Romantic, and Asian Indian revival. The design of the building is based on Dante Alighieri's Divine Comedy. Opened in 1923, it was the work of eccentric Italian architect Mario Palanti, who used largely materials imported from his home country. Palanti was part of a movement of architects who believed that Europe would suffer another great apocalypse, and that South America would be the only place where architecture would survive. The building's entrance is supposed to be Hell, and the patterned medallions on the floor here simulate fire. The interior gallery at this level is decorated with grotesque dragons, and if you look closely, you will notice that those on the east side are smaller and female, those on the west are male. Floors 1 through 14 represent Purgatory and 15 to 22 represent Heaven. The interior is significantly less interesting than the exterior and lobby. However, tours take you to the rooftop lighthouse, meant to represent God and Salvation. The views up and down Avenida de Mayo, and especially to Congreso, are unparalleled. The building is also designed so that at 7:45pm on July 9, Argentine Independence Day, the Southern Cross directly lines up over the tower. On the 25th of every month, the lighthouse is turned on and on Friday nights, there is a special tour with wine tasting, called Extraordinary Nights.

Palanti hoped Italy would send Dante's ashes here, and he designed a statue of him with a receptacle for that purpose. Neither the statue nor the ashes ever made it to the building. Palacio Barolo was renovated in 2008, and in 2010 a replica statue, created by Amelia Jorio, was placed in the lobby, but certainly the ashes will never be brought here. Palanti designed a similar version of this building in Montevideo, the Palacio Salvo, as well as the Hotel Castelar a few blocks down Avenida de Mayo. Miqueas Tharigen, the nephew of the building manager, started giving tours in English and Spanish of the building in 2004. He is now joined by his brother Tomas, and

THE madres: A UNION OF A MOTHER'S PAIN

The **Madres de Plaza de Mayo** was formed in 1976, with the concept in mind that even the cruelest man can identify with a mother's pain in trying to find her missing child. The military government that came into power on March 24 that year, after the fall of Perón's third wife Isabel's administration, began what it called a reorganization of society based largely on making up lists of suspected socialist dissidents and making them disappear. Estimates range from 13,000 to 30,000 *desaparecidos,* or disappeared ones, mostly young people who were kidnapped, tortured, and murdered during this era. Many of the bodies were thrown naked into the Atlantic rather than buried so that they could never be found or identified. The children of the dead were given out as gifts to military families who had none of their own. This era of murdering people for their political beliefs was called the *Guerra Sucia* (Dirty War). It did not end until the collapse of the military government upon Argentina's loss of the Islas Malvinas/Falkland Islands War in June of 1982.

It is easy to think of the dead as statistics and the mothers as a curiosity for tourists and history buffs, but this terrible chapter of Argentina's history is far from closed, as families still seek to find out what became of their children and grandchildren. Unfortunately, both young Argentines who have no recollection of this period as well as old Argentines involved in the murders wish the mothers would simply go away. Still, though many of the mothers have died, their work goes on.

Their work was extremely dangerous, and the mothers were themselves threatened. The first gatherings of the Madres in Plaza de Mayo took place on Saturdays in April 1977. However, since there weren't many people around the plaza on weekends, they changed their meeting day to Thursday. It was only then that other citizens started becoming aware of what was going on. Realizing the power the Madres began to wield, the government started arresting them.

Eventually they were told by the government they could march so long as they spoke to no one. This tradition continues today with the silent main march around the Pirámide de Mayo, called "La Marcha de la Resistencia." *Pañuelos* (handkerchiefs) are painted in a circle surrounding the Pirámide, commemorating how the mothers wrote the names of their children on the handkerchiefs and wear them on their heads, hoping someone would know their children's whereabouts and contact them later in a safer setting.

After the military regime fell out of power in 1982, with the loss of the Islas Malvinas/Falkland Islands War with the U.K., little was done to bring the murderers to justice. In fact, during the 1990s under President Ménem, immunity was granted to many and there were few investigations. Still, the Madres never stopped marching. With Néstor Kirchner's winning of the presidency in 2003, the Madres found new hope, and investigations were reopened. He also removed immunity for politicians who tortured and murdered dissidents. This work has continued under Cristina Fernandez de Kirchner's administration, with extensive trials and convictions in 2010. (See p. 115 for the **Instituto Espacio Para la Memoria.**)

There are different schools of thought regarding the mothers. Even they argue about whether economic reparations, monuments, and museums will bring an end to the dispute, or if they should push to continue investigations to ensure that the murderers are finally brought to trial. Yet no matter what each mother's ultimate goal is, the fight goes on for all of them.

they include a visit to the uncle's administrative office, preserved from the 1920s. In addition to the tour, where they explain the secret Masonic symbols, they offer wine tastings, using a special Palacio Barolo wine label, produced in Mendoza. Tours are scheduled as listed below, but if you contact Miqueas, he can make other arrangements or schedule evening tours. Be aware that elevators and passages are tiny in this building, and that what is usually a 40-minute tour will take longer for groups of more than 10 people.

Av. de Mayo 1370 (at San José, Administrative office, 9th floor, desks 249–252). © **11/4383-1065,** 11/4381-1885, or 11/15-5027-9035. www.palaciobarolotours.com.ar. Admission $10 for day tours, $20 for Extraordinary Nights. Tours Mon and Thurs on the hour 2–7pm, or by arrangement. Metro: Sáenz Peña.

Recoleta

Biblioteca Nacional (National Library) ★
Opened in 1992, though begun in the 1970s, this modern architectural oddity stands on the land of the former Presidential Residence where Eva Perón died. (The building was demolished by the new government so that it would not become a holy site to Evita's millions of supporters after her death.) It is a spectacular example of 1970s Brutalist architecture that was popular under the dictatorship. Built almost as a fortress, among its distinctions are its porthole windows at ground level, the raising of the structure off the ground, long approach ramps, moatlike berm landscaping, and the difficulty in determining where the actual entrance is. With its underground levels, the library's 13 floors can store up to 5 million volumes. Among its collection, the library has 21 books printed by one of the earliest printing presses, dating from 1440 to 1500. Visit the reading room—occupying two stories at the top of the building—to enjoy an awe-inspiring view. The library also hosts special events in its exhibition hall and auditorium.

Calle Aguero 2502 (at Libertador). © **11/4808-6000.** www.bn.gov.ar. Free admission. Mon–Fri 9am–9pm; Sat–Sun noon–8pm. No metro access.

The Israeli Embassy Memorial ★
On March 17, 1992, a bomb ripped through the Israeli Embassy in Buenos Aires, located on a peaceful and seemingly out-of-the-way corner of Recoleta at the intersection of calles Suipacha and Arroyo. Twenty-nine people lost their lives in the tragedy, and—as with the 1994 attack on the Jewish community group, the Asociación Mutual Israelita Argentina (p. 118), which killed 85 people—the culprits are still unknown, but they are suspected to have been working with overseas groups. Under former President Néstor Kirschner, investigations related to the bombings were reopened. The site is now a very tranquil place for contemplation, converted into a park graced by 22 trees and seven benches to represent the people who died in the embassy bombing. The outline of the once-elegant building remains on the adjacent structure, like a ghost speaking for the dead. This open-air memorial is the only major Jewish memorial and historical site open to the public not requiring an appointment or identification to visit.

Intersection of Suipacha and Arroyo. Metro: San Martín.

Plazoleta Carlos Pellegrini ★
This is one of the most beautiful of all the small plazas in Buenos Aires—not just for the plaza itself, but for the surroundings too. This is the part of Recoleta most reminiscent of Paris, due in large part to the ornate Belle Epoque French Embassy presiding over it. The Brazilian Embassy, another beautiful building in a former mansion once owned by the Pereda family, also overlooks the plaza. A large statue of President Carlos Pellegrini sits in the center of the plaza. It was created in France by Félix Coutan and dedicated in 1914. A small fountain and

a bench add to the relaxed environment. Nearby are several other mansions, including the Louis XIII–style "La Mansion," part of the Four Seasons, and the Palacio Duhau, which forms the entrance to the new Park Hyatt. The park is the terminus of the Avenida Alvear, the city's most exclusive shopping street, near where it hits Avenida 9 de Julio. The collection of intact buildings here will give you an idea of the beauty that was lost in Buenos Aires with the widening of Avenida 9 de Julio in the 1960s. In fact, the demolition of the French Embassy, which France refused, was originally part of the plan. Thankfully, that, at least, never happened.

Intersection of Av. Alvear and Cerrito (9 de Julio). No metro access.

Recoleta Cemetery ★★★ ☺ 📷 Open daily from 8am to 6pm, this is the final resting place of many of the wealthiest and most important Argentine historical figures. Weather permitting, free English-language tours are held every Tuesday and Thursday at 11am. Ask for information at the small office with the sign reading JUNIN 1790, between the cemetery gate and the church. The door is sometimes closed and locked during office hours, but you can still peek into the windows and talk to the staff, particularly Marta Granja, who speaks English. If you can't take a tour or want to explore on your own, cemetery maps are also for sale at the gate, with proceeds going to the Friends of Recoleta Cemetery, a private group that helps with upkeep.

Once the garden of the adjoining church, the cemetery was created in 1822 and is among the oldest in the city. You can spend hours here wandering the grounds that cover 4 city blocks, full of tombs adorned with works by local and international sculptors. More than 6,400 mausoleums form an architectural free-for-all, including Greek temples and pyramids. The most popular site is the tomb of Eva "Evita" Perón, which is always heaped with flowers and letters from adoring fans. To prevent her body from being stolen, as it had been many times by the various military governments installed after her husband's fall from grace in 1955, she was finally buried in a concrete vault 8.1m (27 ft.) underground in 1976. Many other rich or famous Argentines are buried here as well, including a number of Argentine presidents whose tomb names you'll recognize because they match some of the streets of the city. The newest presidential tomb is that of Raúl Ricardo Alfonsín, who died in 2009 and was the first president elected when the 1976–82 military dictatorship ended.

Most tourists who come here visit only Evita's tomb, but among the many others, two are worth singling out and should not be missed. One is the tomb of the Paz family, who owned the newspaper *La Prensa*, as well as the palatial building on Plaza San Martín now known as the **Círculo Militar** (p. 113). It is an enormous black stone structure covered with white marble angels in turn-of-the-20th-century dress.

 Recoleta's Living Residents

The dead are not the only residents in Recoleta Cemetery. About 84 cats also roam among the tombs. The cats are plumper than most strays because a dedicated group of women from the area comes to feed and provide them with medical attention at 10am and 4pm. Normally, the cats hide away from visitors, but at these times, they gather in anticipation at the women's entrance. This is a good time to bring children who might otherwise be bored in the cemetery. The women, who are not official cemetery workers, pay for these services out of their own pocket and welcome donations of cat food.

The angels seem to soar to the heavens, lifting the spirit of those inside with their massive wings. The sculptures were all made in Paris and shipped here. Masonic symbols such as anchors and pyramid-like shapes adorn this as well as many other Recoleta tombs.

Another tomb I recommend seeing is that of Rufina Cambaceres, a young woman who was buried alive in the early 1900s. She had perhaps suffered a coma, and a few days after her interment, workers heard screams from the tomb. When it was opened, there were scratches on her face and on the coffin from her attempts to escape. Her mother then built this Art Nouveau masterpiece, which has become a symbol of the cemetery. Her coffin is a Carrara marble slab, carved with a rose on top, and it sits behind a glass wall, as if her mother wanted to make up for her mistake in burying her and ensure she could see her coffin if she were ever to come back again. The corner of the tomb is adorned by a young girl carved of marble who turns her head to those watching her; she looks as if she is about to break into tears, and her right hand is on the door of her own tomb. Many locals often place sprigs of flowers into her hand.

Calle Junín 1790 (at Plaza Francesa). Administrative office next door at Calle Junín 1760. ℂ **11/4804-7040** or 11/7803-1594. Free admission. Daily 8am–6pm. Free English-language tours, weather permitting, Thurs 11am. No metro access.

Tribunales

Teatro Colón ★★★ 📷   Buenos Aires's golden age of prosperity gave birth to this luxurious opera house. It's one of the crowning visual delights of Avenida 9 de Julio, though its true entrance faces a park on the opposite side of the building. Over the years, the theater has been graced by the likes of Enrico Caruso, Luciano Pavarotti, Julio Bocca, Maria Callas, Plácido Domingo, Arturo Toscanini, and Igor Stravinsky. Work began in 1889 and took close to 20 years to complete, largely because the first two architects died during the building process, one because of love affair gone wrong in a deadly manner, a drama worthy of an opera itself. The majestic building opened in 1908 and combines a variety of European styles, from the Ionic and Corinthian capitals and stained-glass pieces in the main entrance to the Italian-marble staircase and French furniture, chandeliers, and vases in the Golden Hall. In the main theater, which seats 3,000 in orchestra seats, stalls, boxes, and four rises, an enormous chandelier hangs from the domed ceiling painted by Raúl Soldi in 1966 during a previous renovation. The theater's acoustics are world-renowned. In addition to hosting visiting performers, the Colón has its own Philharmonic orchestra, choir, and ballet company. Opera and symphony seasons last from February to late December. The building was recently renovated, a process that, like its creation, was years behind schedule and full of drama and intrigue, with accusations of theft of historical costumes in storage and corrupt use of renovation funds. Officially, the building reopened on May 24, 2010, though at press time, portions of the building are still unrenovated, which means that tours have not resumed. These were run between 11am and 3pm weekdays, and from 9am to noon Saturday. Call ℂ **11/4378-7130** for more information or check the website www.teatrocolon.org.ar before your visit.

Calle Libertad 621, Calle Toscanini 1180, or Cerrito (9 de Julio) 628 (at Tucumán); enter through carriageway portal in middle of building on Tucumán. ℂ **11/4378-7100.** www.teatrocolon.org.ar. Seating at various prices. Metro: Tribunales.

Escuela Presidente Roca ★   Workers in this building say that people often mistake it for the Teatro Colón, which sits across the street. Opened in 1904 and designed as a Greek temple, it is one of the most impressive buildings on Plaza

Libertad. Though it's not technically open to the public, polite curious visitors will be allowed into the courtyard with its Doric colonnade and may be able to catch a glimpse of its interior. The upstairs areas, which include a theater and activity center for the school's children, have beautiful fresco ceilings with Greek decoration.

Libertad 581 (at Tucumán, overlooking Plaza Libertad next to Teatro Colón). Metro: Tribunales.

Plaza San Martín Area

Círculo Militar ★★★ You're certain to notice this grand marble building overlooking Plaza San Martín. The Círculo Militar is one of the most beautiful buildings in all of Buenos Aires, and it seems to have been plucked out of France's Loire Valley. It was built as the mansion of the Paz family, the owners of the newspaper *La Prensa*, whose original office was on Avenida de Mayo and is now the Casa de Cultura (p. 99). The Paz family was one of the wealthiest and most powerful families in the whole country, and some will still call this building by its two old names—Palacio Paz and Palacio Retiro. But it is now officially called the Círculo Militar, named for the society of retired military officers who bought the building in 1938, when the economics of the Depression made such a building impossible to keep. It was built in stages spanning from 1902 to 1914, under the direction of the French architect Louis H. M. Sortais. The commissioner of the project, family patriarch José Clemente Paz, died in 1912 and never saw its completion. (If you go to **Recoleta Cemetery** [p. 111], don't miss his tomb, among the most impressive.) Marble and other materials throughout the building were imported from all over Europe.

Most rooms are reminiscent of Versailles, especially the bedrooms and the gold-and-white music hall with an ornate parquet floor and windows overlooking the plaza. Other rooms are in the Tudor style, and the Presidential Room, where men would retreat for political conversation, is the most unusual. Very masculine and dark, it is lit by strange chandeliers decorated with naked hermaphrodite characters with beards and breasts, whose faces contort as they are lanced through their private parts. It is unclear why this was chosen as the decorative theme of a room intended for politics. The six elevators are original to the building and the overall height of the building is eight stories, though it actually has only four floors with very tall ceilings. The most impressive room is the round Hall of Honor, which sits under an interior rotunda and even has a balconied second level overlooking a stage. It was a private mini–opera house, covered in multicolored marble and gilded bronze, used now for conferences.

Av. Santa Fe 750 (at Maipú, overlooking Plaza San Martín). © **11/4311-1071.** www.circulomilitar.org. Admission $2. Tours Tues–Fri 11am and 3pm, Sat 11am, English Wed–Thurs 3:30pm. Metro: San Martín.

Islas Malvinas–Falkland Islands War Memorial ★★ Today, the notion of a country like Argentina challenging a major world power like Great Britain seems almost ridiculous—and when it actually happened, it was treated as such by English-language media. Virtually forgotten by most Brits, this short war lasted from April to June 1982, and it remains an extremely touchy and serious subject among Argentines, with the first Monday after April 2, the date of Argentina's taking of the Islands, recognized as a national holiday. Regardless of your personal opinion on the logic of Argentina declaring war on Great Britain, the topic must be treated very delicately in any conversation with locals. The war came during a period of rapid inflation and other troubles when the Argentine military government, under the leadership of General Leopoldo Galtieri, wanted to distract attention from its failed economic

British Names Post–Islas Malvinas

British influence was once visible all over Buenos Aires, but since the Islas Malvinas/Falkland Islands War, the city has made an effort to honor Argentines in places once named for British heroes. The person worst affected by this was George Canning, the British foreign secretary who recognized Argentina's independence from Spain. He once had a major Buenos Aires thoroughfare named after him (the name of which was since changed to Scalabrini Ortiz), but now the only remnant of this epoch is **Salón Canning,** a tango hall on that street. At the subway station Malabia, under many layers of paint, you might find the old signs that once announced it as Station Canning. Worst hit, though, was the statue of Canning that was once part of the **Torre Monumental,** formerly known as the British Clock Tower. An angry mob tore down this statue during an Islas Malvinas/Falkland Islands War anniversary service. British citizens shouldn't be alarmed: It's now in a public park bound by República de Libano, Libertador, and Agote, near the British Ambassador's Residence. And besides, with all that tourism, Argentines speak more English now than they ever did before the war, keeping Canning's legacy alive, at least through his language.

policies. Argentina lost the war and suffered more than 700 casualties, sparking the government collapse that Galtieri was trying to avoid. Democracy returned to Argentina, and the 6-year Dirty War, under which 30,000 political opponents were tortured and murdered, finally ended. The United States tried to remain neutral and serve as a diplomatic channel between the two countries during the war, but it effectively sided with Great Britain, in technical violation of the Monroe Doctrine.

The legal basis of Argentina's claim to the Falkland Islands, known here as Las Islas Malvinas (and you'd better use that term, not the British one, while you're here), is due to their inclusion in the territory of Argentina when it was still ruled by Spain. (There is, however, a conflicting historical argument that they remained in Spanish hands via rule from Montevideo, before Uruguay's independence and therefore never passed to Argentina.) However, as a fledgling nation after independence, Argentina could do little to prevent Great Britain from setting up a fishing colony and base there. This colonization by Britain of the islands, however, spurred Argentina to explore and populate Patagonia to prevent losing more land to the European power. To most Argentines, having lost the war does not mean that they have no rights to the islands, and diplomatic maneuvers continue with the ongoing dispute. The argument is over more than mere sovereignty: Oil reserves have been discovered in the area.

This monument contains Vietnam Memorial–like stark plaques with lists of names of the Argentines who died. An eternal flame burns over a metallic image of the islands, and the three main branches of the military, the army, the navy, and the air force, each guard the monument in 2-week rotations. The location of the monument, at the bottom of a gentle hill under Plaza San Martín, is itself a message. It faces the Torre Monumental, previously known as the British Clock Tower, a gift from British citizens who made a fortune developing the nearby Retiro railroad station complex. Like stalemate in a game of chess, the two sides, Argentina and Great Britain, stand facing each other, representing the dispute that has no end.

Av. Libertador under Plaza San Martín, across from Retiro Station. Metro: San Martín or Retiro.

Torre Monumental (British Clock Tower) ★ This Elizabethan-style clock tower, which some call the Argentine Big Ben, was a gift from the British community of Buenos Aires after building the nearby Retiro railroad station complex. At the turn of the 20th century, Argentina had vast natural resources such as grain and cattle waiting to be exploited, but it was the British Empire that had the investment capability and technology to create Retiro and connect Buenos Aires to its hinterlands to get products to markets overseas. This, however, was always a sore point, and for years, many Argentines felt exploited by Great Britain. The tower was renamed the Torre Monumental, in response to the very common post–Islas Malvinas/Falkland Islands War trend of renaming anything associated with Great Britain, yet nearly all locals still call it the British Clock Tower (see "British Names Post–Islas Malvinas," below). The monument survived the war unscathed, but a few years later, during an anniversary memorial service, an angry mob attacked it. They destroyed portions of the base and also toppled a statue of George Canning, the first British diplomat to recognize the country's independence from Spain. (He has been moved to a public park bound by República de Libano, Libertador and Agote, near the British Ambassador's Residence.) The Islas Malvinas–Falkland Islands War Memorial (p. 113) was purposely placed across the street as a permanent reminder of Britain's battle with Argentina. There is little to see inside the monument itself, save for a small museum of photographs. The main attraction here is the view: A free elevator ride will take you to the top floor with its wraparound view of the port, the trains, and the city of Buenos Aires itself. There is also a small Buenos Aires city tourism information center inside.

Av. Libertador 49 (across from Plaza San Martín, next to Retiro Station). ✆ **11/4311-0186.** www.museos.buenosaires.gov.ar. Free admission. Thurs–Sun 11am–6pm. Metro: Retiro.

Microcentro

Café Tortoni ★★★ 🖸 You cannot come to Buenos Aires and not visit this important Porteño institution. I mention this cafe in the restaurants chapter as well, but it's a must-see whether you plan to dine there or not. This historic cafe has served as the artistic and intellectual heart of Buenos Aires since 1858, with guests such as Jorge Luis Borges, Julio de Caro, Cátulo Castillo, and José Gobello. Wonderfully appointed in woods, stained glass, yellowing marble, and bronzes, the place tells more about its history by simply existing than any of the photos on its walls. This is the perfect place to stop for a coffee or a small snack when wandering along Avenida de Mayo. Twice-nightly tango shows in a cramped side gallery, where the performers often walk through the crowd, are worth seeing. I've recently found that when the cafe is overwhelmed with visitors, they don't allow tourists to come in for a quick peek. If that happens, make a plan to come back either very early in the day or late at night.

Av. de Mayo 825 (at Piedras). ✆ **11/4342-4328.** www.cafetortoni.com.ar. Mon–Thurs 8am–2am; Fri–Sat 8am–3am; Sun 8am–1am. Metro: Av. de Mayo.

Club Atlético ★★★ The **Instituto Espacio Para la Memoria,** Av. Pte. Roque Sáenz Peña 547, 4th floor (✆ 11/4342-6103 or 11/4342-7797; www.institutomemoria.org.ar) is an organization whose work entails documenting the atrocities of the 1976–82 military dictatorship to enable prosecution of those culpable, along with preserving the physical spaces associated with them. This involves tracking documents, recording interviews, locating missing children from among the 30,000 *desaparecidos*, or the disappeared, along with the gruesome task of exhuming bodies and other evidence, some of which continues to be done within the heart of Buenos Aires.

Among the most easily seen torture and detainment sites in Buenos Aires is the Club Atlético, or Athletic Club, which is in the Microcentro, under the 25 de Mayo highway overpass at the juncture of Paseo Colón. (You might pass it many times during your trip without knowing it is there.) The building was demolished in the late 1970s when the highway was constructed, but the underground rooms, used as torture chambers and prison cells, remain. Local area residents have outlined an angel form in the ground above as a folk memorial to those who died here. The area is fenced off while archaeological and evidence-gathering work proceeds, but is visible and periodically open for visits. A monument to the disappeared is across the street from the site. In addition, the Institute has been involved in ESMA (the Escuela Superior de Mecánica de la Armada, or Navy School), located near Newberry airport, though various groups, including the Madres de Plaza de Mayo, maintain portions of the site, allowing access on an appointment basis. This massive complex contained areas where political prisoners were detained and tortured, some of whom were then dumped into the Río de la Plata from airplanes. While these sites are not always easy to visit beyond looking through fences, they are important for understanding Argentina, and are a visceral depiction of the wide reach of the military dictatorship in its ability to terrorize the local population.

Under Av.. 25 de Mayo at Paseo Colón. www.exccdytclubatletico.com.ar. Metro: San Juan.

Obelisco   The Obelisco is the defining monument of Buenos Aires. It was inaugurated in 1936 to celebrate the 400th anniversary of the first, but unsuccessful, founding of the city by Pedro de Mendoza. (The city was later reestablished in 1580.) It sits at the intersection of Corrientes and Avenida 9 de Julio, the heart of the Theater District and the focal point of the vista from Plaza de Mayo through Diagonal Norte and along 9 de Julio. The monument sits in the oval Plaza de la República, once the site of Iglesia de San Nicolás, where the Argentine flag was first displayed on August 23, 1812, shortly after independence from Spain. This church was demolished, but an inscription on the north side of the Obelisco honors its noble sacrifice. Like the Eiffel Tower in Paris, the project was criticized by many when it was first built but has since been embraced by the city as its main symbol.

When Argentines have something to celebrate, the Obelisco is where they head. If you're in town when Argentina wins an international event, you can be sure that hundreds of people will gather around the Obelisco with flags in their hands, waving them at the cars that honk in celebration as they head past. The edges of the plaza have plaques that celebrate the various provinces that make up the country. Unfortunately, many had to be replaced with replicas when the plaza was renovated in 2007, since the originals were stolen for the value of their copper in the years following the 2001 peso crisis. The view from the Obelisco would undoubtedly be fantastic, but the structure was not built for this purpose. As the city's preeminent phallic symbol, it has occasionally been graced with a very large condom on December 1, International AIDS Awareness Day. Though this has not been done in years, postcards of this event are available at kiosks.

Av. 9 de Julio at Corrientes. Metro: Carlos Pellegrini, Diagonal Norte, or 9 de Julio.

Paseo Obelisco   This shopping complex and underground pedestrian causeway (which you may have to pass through at some point on your trip anyway) is itself worth a short trip. Paris, New York, London, and virtually every major city with a subway once had similar underground complexes, but this area under the Obelisco, where three subway lines converge, seems to have remained unchanged since the

1960s. The shops are nothing special—several barbershops, shoe-repair spots, and stores selling cheap clothing and other goods make up the bulk of them. Yet together, with their cohesive old signs, fixtures, and furnishings, they look like a movie set.

Subway entrances surrounding the Obelisco, along Av. 9 de Julio. Metro: Carlos Pellegrini, Diagonal Norte, or 9 de Julio.

Galería Güemes ★★ 🏢 This sumptuous 1915 building, mixing retail and office, was one of the city's tallest at 85m (279 ft.) when it opened. The ugly modern Calle Florida entrance, rebuilt in 1971 after a fire, makes it easy to overlook. Its back entrance on San Martín hints at its original glory. The shopping gallery has a mix of stores without distinction, but look around at the walls and decorations. The architecture is a mix of Art Nouveau, Gothic, Byzantine, and neoclassical—all heavily ornamented—and was the creation of the architect Francesco Gianotti who designed the now-closed Café del Molino next door to Congreso. Make sure to look at the ornate elevator banks. Much of the exquisite material came from Italy, having had to be created twice as the original shipment was destroyed on a boat fire. The building also houses the Piazzolla tango show (p. 201). The Art Nouveau theater in which it sits was closed for nearly 40 years and was restored in the early 2000s, and it is the most beautiful of all the tango show palaces in Buenos Aires. *Little Prince* author Antoine de Saint-Exupéry lived in this building too. A gallery on the second level has photos from the early days of the building.

Calle Florida 165 (at Perón). 🕾 **11/4331-3041.** www.galeriaguemes.com.ar. Metro: Florida.

Centro Cultural de Borges ★★ You can shop all you want in Galerías Pacífico, but if it's culture you're after, you can find it there too. Inside of the shopping mall is this arts center named for Jorge Luis Borges, Argentina's most important literary figure. You'll find art galleries, lecture halls with various events, an art cinema, and art bookstore. There's also the **Escuela Argentina de Tango** (🕾 **11/4312-4990;** www.eatango.org), which offers a schedule of lessons tourists can take with ease, and the ballet star Julio Bocca's **Ballet Argentino** performance space and training school (🕾 **11/4394-5521;** www.juliobocca.com), full of young ballet stars and their not-to-be-missed performances, though he himself has since retired from public performances.

Enter through Galerías Pacífico or at the corner of Viamonte and San Martín (the back of the Galerías Pacífico Mall). 🕾 **11/5555-5359.** www.ccborges.org.ar. Various hours and fees. Metro: San Martín.

Puerto Madero

Bridge of Woman ★★ Looking for a romantic spot to share a kiss at sunset in Puerto Madero? This is the place. The Bridge of Woman (or Puente de La Mujer) is a white, sinewy structure resembling a plane taking flight, which was designed by Santiago Calatrava, the Spanish architect famed for his unusual approach to public architecture. It was opened in 2001 and crosses Dique 3, or Port Area 3. Calatrava is said to have listened to tango music while designing the bridge and to have intended it to be an abstraction of a couple dancing. The name of the bridge also refers to the naming pattern of the district of Puerto Madero, where all the streets are named for important women—the only major city in the world with such a neighborhood. A sign between docks 2 and 3 gives biographies of the women.

Dique 3 (btw. Villafor and Güemes, connecting Dealissi with Alicia Moreau de Justo), Puerto Madero. Metro: Alem.

Ecological Reserve ★★ The Ecological Reserve is an unusual and unexpected consequence of highway construction throughout Buenos Aires during the mid–20th century. Construction debris and the rubble of demolished buildings were unceremoniously dumped into the Río de la Plata. Over time, sand and sediment began to build up, and then grass and trees began to grow. The birds followed, and now the area is a preserve. Various companies offer biking and bird-watching tours of the area. Ask your travel agent about it or see our list of tour companies (p. 24). Since there are few genuine beaches in the Buenos Aires area, some people come here to sunbathe, sometimes in the nude. Whatever you do, don't go into the water, since it is heavily polluted and still full of rough construction debris in some parts. The Costanera walkway, extending from Puerto Madero, has been improved since 2007, with ice-cream kiosks and other services for the increasing amount of spillover wanderers from the port. In spite of its being a preserve, development is slowly encroaching as the Puerto Madero area grows. Though the police do have a patrol station here, some homeless people also camp out here, meaning you should be cautious.

Along the Costanera near Puerto Madero. ✆ **11/4893-1588.** Metro: N. Alem.

Palermo Soho

Plaza Serrano ★★ 📷 This is the bohemian heart of Palermo Soho. During the day, not much goes on here, but at night the plaza comes alive with young people gathering to drink, celebrate, sing, dance, play guitar, and just generally enjoy being alive. Many of the kids are dreadlocked Rastafarians, some selling funky jewelry and other crafts, and it's easy to join them and start up a conversation. The plaza is surrounded by numerous restaurants and bars (see chapters 5 and 9). On Saturday and Sunday from 11am to 6pm, and later in the summer, there is an official but not-to-be-missed fair here with even more funky jewelry and arts and crafts. The true name of this plaza is Plazoleta Julio Cortázar, but few people will call it that. The plaza is at the intersection of Calle Serrano and Calle Honduras, but Calle Serrano is also named Calle Borges on some maps.

Intersection of Serrano (Jorge Luis Borges) and Honduras. www.palermoviejo.com. No metro access.

Once

For a map of this neighborhood, see the "Abasto & Once" map on p. 95.

AMIA (Asociación Mutual Israelita Argentina) ★★ The Asociación Mutual Israelita Argentina, better known as AMIA, is located in Once in the heart of Buenos Aires's historical Jewish district. The organization is most famous for a very sad part of its history—the still unsolved bombing on July 18, 1994, which left 85 people dead and was the largest attack on Jews since World War II. A new structure was created over the ruins, set from the street and protected by a wall that is covered by the names of those who died in the tragedy. AMIA remains an important center for the Jewish community, with education, employment, and cultural and arts programming as well as programs for children and an online TV program featuring Jewish-Argentine journalist Diego Melamed. It is possible to visit AMIA on your own or by visiting with Jewish tour guides and groups (see p. 25). One of the most striking elements in the inner courtyard is the Monument to the Memory of the Victims of the Terrorist Attack on AMIA by Israeli artist Yaacov Agam, which is a Star of David dynamically designed to change patterns as visitors move around it. AMIA has also helped visitors locate Jewish relatives who have immigrated to Argentina.

Pasteur 633 (btw. Tucumán and Viamonte). ✆ **11/4959-8800** or 11/4959-8863. www.amia.org.ar. Metro: Pasteur.

Greater Buenos Aires

Quinta San Vicente & Juan Perón Mausoleum ★★★   *Quinta* is an Argentine word meaning country home. This is where Juan and Evita lived on weekends, escaping the routine of their work in Buenos Aires. It is the only one of their homes that you can visit today, located about 45 miles from the center of Buenos Aires, beyond Ezeiza Airport. The home dates from the 1940s, but the majority of furnishings are from the early 1970s, when Perón returned to power and shared this house with his third wife, Isabelita. The complex is also called the **Museo de 17 de Octubre,** named in honor of the date that Peronism began. The house is tiny, and the complex also contains a museum explaining the history of Peronism, which was curated by Gabriel Miremont, who also designed the **Museo Evita** (p. 122). Interesting items on display include a cross given by the city of Santiago, Spain, to Evita during the famous Rainbow Tour of 1947. In addition, the colossal marble statues of Juan, Evita, and a *descamisado* (worker), originally intended for the never-built Evita memorial planned for Avenida Libertador in front of the former Presidential Palace, are also in the gardens. The statues of Juan and Evita are headless now, damaged in the 1955 revolution that deposed Juan Perón. According to speculation, the heads are in the Río Riachuelo running through La Boca. (So as not to offend the workers, the head of the *descamisado* was spared the same fate.)

An imposing mausoleum on the grounds now holds the remains of Juan Perón, moved here from Chacarita Cemetery in a chaotic and violent parade on October 17, 2006. A space exists for Evita, but her family will not allow her to be moved from Recoleta Cemetery. The stark setting is ornamented with a mosaic produced by Lilian Lucía Luciano and the Azzurro group of artisans and is inspired by "The Embrace," or El Abrazo, a famous photo of Evita and Juan taken by Pinelides Fusco on October 17, 1951, at her last speech as she was dying of cancer. (You'll recognize its reenactment in Madonna's *Evita* movie.) The museum complex costs $1 to enter, but it is only open weekends and you should call to verify closing time. Because it is hard to get to, it is best to take a taxi from Buenos Aires, which costs about $60 each way.

Intersection of Lavalle and Av. Eva Perón, off Hwy. 58 in San Vicente. ℰ **222/548-2260.** www.ic.gba. gov.ar. Sat–Sun and holidays only 10am–4:30pm fall and winter, until 7:30pm spring and summer, but call ahead to verify the hours.

MUSEUMS

Beatles Museum and Cavern Club ★   Opened in December 2010, the Beatles Museum is based on the personal collection of Argentine native Rodolfo Vazquez, who holds the Guinness World Record for the largest Beatles memorabilia collection in the world with over 8,500 objects. This museum holds about 2,000 of them in a small, cluttered room. It is only the third Beatles museum in the world, and the only not in Europe. It's adjacent to Buenos Aires's Cavern Club which Vazquez owns, named for the famous Liverpool club where the Beatles performed. It's a real joy for Beatles enthusiasts, and unusual in that it's open only in the evening, in order to encourage visitors to stay and enjoy a night out in the Cavern Club.

Corrientes 1660 (btw. Rodríguez Peña and Montevideo in the Paseo la Plaza nightlife and shopping complex). ℰ **11/6320-5361.** www.thecavernclub.com.ar. Admission $5. Daily 5pm–midnight. Metro: Callao.

ESPECIALLY FOR kids

Argentines pamper their children in every way possible, and you'll see this in the multitude of kid-friendly activities in Buenos Aires. A handful of restaurants, such as **Garbis** (p. 90), have indoor playgrounds, and several museums have been created just for kids. If you're traveling with children, don't miss the following attractions:

- **Museo de Los Niños** (p. 121)
- **Museo Participativo de Ciencias** (p. 122)
- **Zoological Gardens** (p. 133)

- **The Water Palace & The Museo del Patrimonio** (p. 124)
- **Museo de las Armas de la Nación** (p. 121)

In addition, kids will delight in the numerous outdoor playgrounds scattered across the city. One of them, where you'll often see parents and their kids even after midnight, is in **Plaza San Martín.** There are swing sets and a merry-go-round in **Plaza Congreso,** across from the headquarters of the Madres de Plaza de Mayo. You'll also find playgrounds in the **Botanical Gardens** (p. 133).

Casa Nacional del Bicentenario ★★   The Casa Nacional del Bicentenario is a new permanent museum meant to examine themes related to Argentina's revolution against Spain and the development of the nation into modern times. A recent exhibition focused on the women of Argentina, using Evita as a well-known symbol and looking at the overall role of women in film and in politics, two aspects of her life. Permanent exhibitions look at immigration, industrialization, war, and other themes.

Riobamba 985 (btw. Alvear and Paraguay). © **11/4813-0301.** www.casadelbicentenario.gob.ar. Admission $4. Tues–Sun noon–9pm. Metro: Alem.

Fundación PROA ★   Looking almost out of place in La Boca, the Fundación PROA is built into an historical structure painted a gleaming white with a modern structure attached to it. PROA simply means "prow" of a boat, symbolizing the museum's cultural direction and the area's harbor and maritime history. The museum explores themes related to Argentine history and has an excellent film and lecture series, often held after normal closing hours. There is an excellent art book shop and a cafe attached to a rooftop patio with a fantastic harbor view. For a map of this museum, see the "La Boca" map on p. 97.

Av. Pedro de Mendoza 1929 (at Caminito on the La Boca waterfront). © **11/4104-1000.** www.proa.org. Admission $5. Tues–Thurs 11am–7pm. No metro access.

Museo Amalia Lacroze de Fortabat ★   This gleaming low-rise structure in Puerto Madero houses the private collection of Amalia Lacroze de Fortabat. Opened in 2008, this airy museum can be seen as a female version of the MALBA, which was started by a male real-estate mogul; in this case it was a grande dame, Amalia Lacroze de Fortabat, something of an Argentine Brooke Astor. The museum contains an enormous collection of Argentine artists, as well as works by Warhol, Dalí, Chagall, the Breugels, and other well-known painters, as well as a collection of ancient art. Many of the paintings are of Amalia when she was a young, stunning beauty.

Olga Cossettini 141 (at Sanchez de Thompson). © **11/4310-6600.** www.coleccionfortabat.org.ar. Admission $4. Tues–Sun noon–9pm. Metro: Alem.

Museo Che Guevara Run by Eladio González, an eccentric character with an amazing depth of knowledge about Che, along with Irene Perpiñal, this space is a hardware store–museum combination. It was created when the original stand-alone museum ran into financial problems around the 40th anniversary of Che's death and Eladio moved the exhibits into his store. You'll find Che's clothes and other items from his life and signs from the original museum. The rest of the place is an odd hodgepodge of used electrical parts, Evita sculptures, old dishes, and Halloween masks. English-fluent Eladio will beguile you with stories about Argentine-born Che, his place in the world, and how he continues to impact generations, along with his own visits to Cuba. It's a strange place, but definitely worth a visit.

Rojas 129 (at Yerbal). © **11/4903-3285.** www.museochegevaraargentina.blogspot.com. Free admission. Mon–Fri 9am–7pm. Metro: San Martín.

Museo de las Armas de la Nación ★ ☺ This small museum in the impressive Círculo Militar overlooking Plaza San Martín will give you a better understanding of the Argentine side of the Islas Malvinas/Falkland Islands War. In Argentina that war is called the Guerra de las Islas Malvinas, using the name of the island chain from when it was part of the Spanish Empire, which is the basis for Argentina's dispute with Great Britain. Despite losing the war, Argentina still claims the islands to be part of their territory. Calling them by their English name is likely to stoke an argument with even the most polite Argentine. The curator of the museum is Isidro Abel Vides, a veteran of the war. Among items of note related to the war is a display about the sinking of the *General Belgrano,* where 323 Argentines perished—the greatest individual loss of life in a single event of the war. Other displays show uniforms of the time period. Children will like the collection of toy soldiers showing the history of military costume in Argentina and other countries up to the 1940s. There are also models of Argentine frontier forts.

Av. Santa Fe 702 (at Maipú overlooking Plaza San Martín). © **11/4311-1071.** www.circulomilitar.org. Admission $4. Museum and library Mon–Fri 1–6pm. Metro: San Martín.

Museum of the Federal Administration of Public Revenue (Tax Museum) Numismatists, accountants, and others interested in the history of money and taxes will enjoy this small and unique museum, one of only three of its type in the world. Photographs, tax-record books, and other documents here tell the history of Customs and other forms of tax collection in Argentina. One room has also been set up as a re-creation of 1930s tax offices, complete with period machines. Though it has nothing to do with taxes, a highlight of the museum's collection is a desk used by Manuel Belgrano, the man who designed the Argentine flag.

Hipólito Yrigoyen 370 (at Defensa). © **11/4347-2396.** www.afip.gov.ar. Free admission. Mon–Fri 11am–5pm. Metro: Bolívar, Catedral, or Plaza de Mayo.

Museo de Los Niños ★★★ ☺ This museum, really a play center, located in the Abasto Shopping Center, is a fun way for kids to learn about different careers and about Buenos Aires too, since many of the displays relate to the city. You'll find miniature versions of the Casa Rosada, Congreso, and a street layout to demonstrate how traffic flows, so it's a great way to orient your kids to Buenos Aires. Various careers can be explored here through a miniature dentist's office, doctor's office, TV station with working cameras, gas station and refinery, working radio station, and newspaper office. Even more fun is a giant toilet where kids learn what happens in the sewer system after they use the bathroom. Intellectual kids can also seek some solitude in the library, and budding dramatists can play dress-up in a little theater complete with costumes and a stage. A patio has rides for small children. Don't worry if the kids wear you out—there are couches where weary parents can rest. This is a great stop for large groups and an excellent venue for birthday parties. While the museum claims to target kids 15 and under, however, I think that kids over the age of 12 will be bored here. For a map of this museum, see the "Abasto & Once" map on p. 95.

Abasto Shopping Center Food Court, Av. Corrientes 3247. ⒞ **11/4861-2325**. www.museoabasto.org.ar. AE, DC, MC, V. Admission $7; family/group discounts available; free for seniors, the disabled, and kids 1 and under. Tues–Sun and holidays 1–8pm. Metro: Gardel.

Museo Participativo de Ciencias ★★ ☺   Okay, so you came to the Centro Cultural Recoleta, adjacent to the Recoleta Cemetery, to see art and be sophisticated. Well, here's the place to bring the kids afterward, or let them wander in on their own. In this museum, unlike so many others, *not* touching is prohibited! There are two floors full of science displays where kids can touch, play, and see how electricity, gravity, and many other things work—all designed with fun in mind. Communications rooms, mechanical rooms, and wave and sound rooms all have various interactive stands that are aimed at kids of all ages. Sure, it's a noisy place, but if you can find a way to make learning fun, that's not such a bad side effect.

Junín 1930 (inside the Centro Cultural Recoleta, adjacent to the Recoleta Cemetery). ⒞ **11/4807-3260** or 11/4806-3456. www.mpc.org.ar. Admission $5. Mon–Fri 10am–5pm; Sat–Sun 3:30–7:30pm. No metro access.

Museo de Casa Gardel ★   Carlos Gardel, the preeminent Argentine tango singer whose portraits you see all over the city and who is nicknamed Carlitos, bought this house in 1927 for his mother, with whom he lived when he was not traveling. The house dates from 1917 and, in keeping with tango's sordid history, it was once home to a brothel. It served various functions after his mother's death in 1943—from a tailor shop to a tango parlor—until it reopened as a museum in his honor on June 24, 2003, the 68th anniversary of his death in a plane crash in Colombia. Visitors will find articles about him from the time, original musical notes, contracts, portraits of his singing partner José Razzano, records and sheet music from the period, as well as some of his clothing, including his signature fedora. His kitchen, bathroom, and ironing room remain almost untouched from the time he lived here. Most tours are in Spanish, but there are some in English. This small, out-of-the-way museum is a must-see not only for tango lovers, but for anyone wishing to understand this important man in Argentine history, whose work brought tango to the world. A favorite phrase in Buenos Aires is that Carlos sings better every day, meaning that as time passes, his music, the most Porteño thing of all, becomes more and more important to Argentines. For a map of this museum, see the "Abasto & Once" map on p. 95.

Jean Jaures 735 (at Tucumán). ⒞ **11/4964-2071** or 11/4964-2015. www.museos.buenosaires.gov.ar. Admission 1 peso, about 25¢. Mon and Wed–Fri 11am–6pm; Sat–Sun and holidays 10am–7pm. Metro: Carlos Gardel.

Museo Evita ★★★   It is almost impossible for non-Argentines to fathom that it wasn't until 50 years after her death that Evita, the world's most famous Argentine, was finally granted a museum. The Museo Evita opened on July 26, 2002, the 50th anniversary of her death, in a mansion where her charity, the Eva Perón Foundation, once housed single mothers with children. The placement of the house here had been meant as a direct affront to the wealthy neighbors who hated Evita.

While the museum treats her history fairly, looking at both the good and the bad, it is quickly obvious to the visitor that each presentation has a little bit of love for Evita behind it, and indeed, members of the family are involved in the museum. Evita's grandniece, the Buenos Aires Senator Cristina Alvarez Rodríguez, is president of the Evita Perón Historical Research Foundation, the group that runs the museum, and she is often in the building meeting with the staff. Gabriel Miremont, the museum's curator, is Argentina's preeminent expert on Evita history; he became personally interested in Evita as a child, when he was punished by his father for listening to lyrics from the Evita play. (It was technically illegal to do so during this period of military rule, following the collapse of Perón's second government in 1976.) Thus, while historically accurate, the museum has a close personal touch that sets it apart from most museums.

The museum displays divide Evita's life into several parts, looking at her childhood, her arrival in Buenos Aires with hopes of becoming an actress, her ascension to First Lady and unofficial saint to millions, and her death and legacy. You can view her clothes, remarkably preserved by the military government that took power after Perón's fall in 1955, along with photos of her wearing them. Other artifacts of her life include her female voter card, marked #1, the first issue. It was through Evita's work that Argentine women gained the right to vote in 1947. There are also toys and schoolbooks adorned with her image, given to children to indoctrinate them into the Peronist movement. The most touching artifact of all, though, is a smashed statue of Evita, hidden for decades by a farmer in his barn, despite the threat of being jailed for saving it. Whether you hate, love, or are indifferent to Evita, this is a museum that no visitor to Argentina should miss. Digesting the exhibits here will help you understand why she remains such a controversial figure within the Argentine psyche. The museum also houses a cafe and restaurant (open daily 9am–12:30am; ✆ 11/4800-1599), praised for its atmosphere and Italian food, that has become popular among locals and fashionistas in particular and is worth a trip all on its own.

Calle Lafinur 2988 (at Gutierrez). ✆ **11/4807-9433.** www.museoevita.org and www.evitaperon.org. Admission $4–$6. Tues–Sun 11am–7pm. Metro: Plaza Italia.

Museo Judio (Jewish History Museum) & Templo Libertad ★★ This impressive Byzantine-style temple is the home of the CIRA (Congregación Israelita de la República de Argentina). Sitting a block from the Teatro Colón, it is one of the stars of Plaza Libertad. The small building housing the temple's administrative office also contains the Jewish History Museum, known also as the Museo Kibrick after its founder. You'll find material related to the Jewish community in Buenos Aires, with both Sephardic and Ashkenazi items from their original homelands. Menorahs, altar cloths, spice holders, and various pieces of religious art make up much of the collection. Special exhibits relate to the history of Jewish agricultural colonies in rural Argentina. Admission is generally open to the public with proper passport identification. However, the guards sometimes refuse entry or claim the Museum's posted hours are incorrect. If you are denied entry, call and speak to Museum manager Laura Szames.

Libertad 769 (btw. Córdoba and Viamonte, overlooking Plaza Libertad). ✆ **11/4123-0832** (ext. 101 for Temple, 105 for Museum). www.judaica.org.ar. Admission $8. Tues and Thurs 3–5:30pm; other hours by appointment. Metro: Tribunales.

Museo Nacional de Arte Decorativo (National Museum of Decorative Arts) ★ French architect René Sergent, who designed some of the grandest mansions in Buenos Aires, also designed the mansion housing this museum. The building is itself a work of art, and it will give you an idea of the incredible mansions that once lined this avenue, overlooking the extensive Palermo park system, before high-rise construction was their demise. The building's 18th-century French design provides a classical setting for the diverse decorative styles represented within. Breathtaking sculptures, paintings, and furnishings make up the collection, and themed shows rotate seasonally. The **Museo de Arte Oriental (Museum of Eastern Art)** displays art, pottery, and engravings on the first floor of this building.

Av. del Libertador 1902 (at Lucena). © **11/4801-8248.** www.mnad.org. Admission $1.25. Tues–Sun 2–7pm. No metro access.

Museo Nacional de Bellas Artes (National Museum of Fine Arts) ★★
This building, which formerly pumped the city's water supply, metamorphosed into Buenos Aires's most important art museum in 1930. It houses the world's largest collection of Argentine sculptures and paintings, along with European art dating from the medieval period to today, including works by Picasso, Renoir, Monet, Rodin, Toulouse-Lautrec, and van Gogh, many collected in Argentina's golden period. Concentrate on the Argentine paintings to better understand the country's history. Among them is *La Hora Del Almuerzo* (*The Lunch Break*, 1903), by Pío Collivadino, depicting Italian immigrant construction workers, one with a Garibaldi cap; another staring directly at you as he bites into a sandwich, his features reminiscent of young Argentine men today. At the turn of the last century, when Buenos Aires was rapidly reconstructing itself, such scenes were live, everywhere. Angel Della Valli's 1892 *La Vuelta del Malon* (*The Return of the Indian*) is a panoramic and emotional work, propaganda for General Julio A. Roca's Campaign of the Desert, when he slaughtered untold numbers of Indians in the Pampas. In the painting, horseriding Indians have captured a white woman, carried bare-breasted, a small cross in her cleavage, her complexion contrasted against the dark skin of her native captors who hold in triumph suitcases, skulls, crosses, and other signs of a sacked church. Don't miss the Manuel Jose de Guerrico Hall. He was one of the city's earliest collectors of medieval and Renaissance art and other decorative objects, including silver *maté* sets. Other works of distinction include the 15 sumptuous panels of gold and mother of pearl inlays Tablas de La Conquista de Mexico, from the workshop of Miguel Gonzalez.

Av. del Libertador 1473 (at Pueyrredón). © **11/4803-0802** or 11/5288-9900. www.mnba.org.ar. Free admission. Tues–Fri 12:30–8:30pm; Sat–Sun 9:30am–8:30pm. No metro access.

The Water Palace & The Museo del Patrimonio ★ ☺   Many people pass by this massive, high Victorian structure on Avenida Córdoba in Barrio Norte and stop in wonder. This is Buenos Aires's Water Palace, a fantastic structure of more than 300,000 lustrous, multicolored faience bricks made by Royal Doulton and shipped from Britain. Its original interior engineering components were made in various countries, largely Belgium. Originally, the Water Palace was meant to be a humble building, constructed in response to the yellow fever epidemic that hit San Telmo and other areas of Buenos Aires in 1877. In the days before plumbing, drinking water was held in collecting pools in individual homes, which spread the disease. Alarmed, the city began looking for a spot to construct new, sanitary facilities to prevent another outbreak. This was the highest point in the city, meaning water stored here could flow through pipes to the city's residences using only the force of gravity.

However, two events changed the plans, resulting in the 1887 building seen here now. First, Buenos Aires was made the capital of Argentina in 1880, and the city planners felt the building must not only serve a purpose but also reflect the glory of the new nation. (Still, Argentina did not have the technology, hence the need for foreign help.) In addition, the yellow fever epidemic itself meant that the area surrounding this location was filling up with new mansions of wealthy families fleeing San Telmo. The water purification building not only had to fit into its surroundings, it had to outshine them.

The engineering works have been removed, and the building is now the headquarters of the water company Aguas Argentinas. It also contains one of the most unusual museums in the whole city, one kids will get a kick out of. Explaining the history of water sanitation, this museum is home to hundreds of toilets spanning the decades. Faucets and giant sewer pipes are also on display.

Av. Córdoba 1750 (at Riobamba). Entrance at Riobamba 750 (1st floor). © **11/6319-1882** or 11/6319-1104. Admission $3. Mon–Fri 9am–1pm; guided tours in Spanish Mon, Wed, Fri at 11am. Metro: Facultad de Medicina.

Museo de la Ciudad   Like a huge common attic for Buenos Aires, the Museo de la Ciudad is a kitschy collection of everything and anything related to the history of this city. It's built into an old pharmacy in Monserrat dating from 1894. As disorganized as the place feels, this museum gives you a glimpse into the pride Porteños have for the everyday aspects of their lives in the city, from tango to Little Italy to bicycles to a personal doll collection. Be sure to also take a look at the working pharmacy in the building's ground level with its turn-of-the-last-century interior and exquisite ceiling paintings.

Defensa 219 (at Alsina). © **11/4331-9855.** Admission 25¢. Daily 11am–7pm. Metro: Bolívar.

El Museo Histórico Nacional (National History Museum) ★★   Argentine history from the 16th through the 19th centuries comes to life in the former Lezama family home. The expansive Italian-style mansion houses 30 rooms with items saved from Jesuit missions, paintings illustrating clashes between the Spaniards and the Indians, and relics from the War of Independence against Spain. The focal point of the museum's collection is artist Cándido López's series of captivating scenes of the war against Paraguay in the 1870s. The museum was renovated for the 2010 Bicentennial celebration, its exhibit spaces reorganized and expanded. It also includes an interesting collection of art objects related to African slaves in Argentina and their emancipation. Once close to a majority in Buenos Aires, the Afro-Argentine population has largely disappeared due to the Paraguay War in the 1860s, yellow fever, and other unfortunate historical events, but their influence remains in tango and Carnaval. For a map of this museum, see the "La Boca" map on p. 97.

Calle Defensa 1600 (in Parque Lezama). © **11/4307-1182.** Free admission. Wed–Sun noon–6pm. Closed Jan. Metro: Constitución.

MALBA (Museo de Arte Latinoamericano de Buenos Aires Colección Costantini) ★★★   The airy and luminescent MALBA houses the private art collection of Eduardo Costantini, a wealthy Argentine real estate developer. Opened in late 2001, it is among the most impressive collections of Latin American art anywhere, and includes art by Antonio Berni, Pedro Figari, Frida Kahlo, Marta Minujín, Cândido Portinari, Diego Rivera, and Antonio Siguí. Many of the works confront social issues and explore questions of national identity. Even the benches are modern pieces of art. Ask about the schedule for films and lectures.

Av. Figueroa Alcorta 3415 (at San Martín). © **11/4808-6500.** www.malba.org.ar. Admission $5. Free admission on Wed. Wed–Mon noon–8pm. No metro access.

NEIGHBORHOODS WORTH A VISIT

La Boca

La Boca, on the banks of the Río Riachuelo, originally developed as a trading center and shipyard. It was the city's first Little Italy, the main point of entry for Italians at the end of the 19th and beginning of the 20th centuries, giving the neighborhood the distinct flavor it still maintains. Literally, *La Boca* means "the mouth," taking its name from a natural harbor formed by a twist in the Río Riachuelo, a tributary that feeds into the Río de la Plata. La Boca is most famous for giving birth to tango in the bordellos, known as *quilombos*, that once served this largely male population.

The focus of La Boca is the **Caminito** (p. 106), a pedestrian walkway, named ironically after a tango song about a rural village. The walkway is lined with humorously sculpted statues and murals explaining its history. Surrounding the cobblestone street are corrugated metal houses painted a hodgepodge of colors, recalling a time when the poor locals decorated with whatever paint was left over from ship maintenance in the harbor. Today, many artists live or set up their studios in these houses. Along the Caminito, art and souvenir vendors work side by side with tango performers. This Caminito "Fine Arts Fair" is open daily from 10am to 6pm.

La Boca is, however, a victim of its own success, and it has become an obscene tourist trap. While the area is historically important, most of what you will find along the Caminito is overpriced souvenir and T-shirt shops and constant harassment from people trying to hand you fliers for mediocre restaurants. In summer, the smell from the heavily polluted river becomes almost unbearable. Come to this area because you have to, but if you are short on time, don't let the visit take up too much of your day. What remains authentic in the area is off the beaten path—art galleries and theaters catering both to locals and to tourists, and the world-famous **Estadio de Boca Juniors** (**Boca Juniors Stadium and Museum;** p. 106). Use caution if you stray far from the Caminito, however, as the less-patrolled surrounding areas can be unsafe. It's best to avoid the entire neighborhood at night, even the Caminito. The police are here to protect the tourists, not the locals, and when the shopkeepers go home, so do they. For a map of this neighborhood, see the "La Boca" map on p. 97.

San Telmo

One of Buenos Aires's oldest neighborhoods, San Telmo was originally home to the city's elite. But when yellow fever struck in the 1870s, the aristocrats moved north. Poor immigrants soon filled this neighborhood, and the houses were converted to tenements, called *conventillos*. In 1970, the city passed regulations to restore some of San Telmo's architectural landmarks. Still, gentrification has been a slow process, and the neighborhood maintains a gently decayed, authentic atmosphere, reminiscent of Cuba's old Havana. It's a bohemian enclave, attracting tourists, locals, and performers 7 days a week. A victim of its own success in many ways, the area is home to a large number of English-speaking expats, and sometimes you'll wonder if you're actually in South America when you sit at a cafe and realize many tables are engaged in conversations you can fully understand. The collapse of the peso has also meant that a glut of antiques, sold for ready cash, are available for purchase, though most of the best bargains are long gone. The best shops and markets in San Telmo line **Calle Defensa.** After Plaza de Mayo, **Plaza Dorrego** is the second-oldest square in the city.

San Telmo is full of tango clubs; one of the most notable is **El Viejo Almacén,** at Independencia and Balcarce. An example of colonial architecture, it was built in 1798 and was a general store and hospital before its reincarnation as the quintessential Argentine tango club. Make sure to come here at night for a show (p. 200). If you get the urge to take a beginner or refresher tango course while you're in San Telmo, look for signs advertising lessons in the windows of bars and restaurants.

Barracas

Barracas is an up-and-coming neighborhood in the south of Buenos Aires, bordering La Boca and San Telmo. It's not fully on the radar yet, though for years, tourists have been coming to its most famous destination, the tango show palace **Señor Tango** (p. 201), all while being told by their tour guides not to wander off, an indication of the neighborhood's rough reputation. As housing prices in adjacent neighborhoods rise, many artists and young people have begun to move here, gentrifying it. The neighborhood takes its name from the *barracas,* the warehouses and barracks that served as storage areas for the nearby port at La Boca. Long since abandoned, many are being converted into luxury apartments and art centers.

The district's main street is **Avenida Montes de Oca.** While the neighborhood has working-class roots, **Avenida Caseros** was lined with beautiful housing for British railroad engineers. Here, you'll find several restaurants, including **Caseros** (p. 96) and **Club Social** (see p. 97), which seems a step back in time. The most colorful street is **Pasaje Lanín,** where, starting in 2000, the local artist Marino Santa María painted each house, beginning with his own gallery at number 33 (www.marino-santamaria.com.ar), covering them with colorful mosaics. From July through December, the street hosts a weekend arts festival. For now, few tourists visit the area, and many businesses claim to actually be in San Telmo. Overnighting options include **Garden Buenos Aires,** Piedras 1677 (© **11/4300-3455;** www.gardenbuenosaires. com), opened in 2008 by American Pamela Murphy; and apartment hotel **Casa Bolívar,** Bolívar 1701 (© **54-11-4300-3619;** www.casabolivar.com), opened in 2007. For a map of these hotels, see the "La Boca" map on p. 97.

Palermo

Palermo ★★★ is a nebulous catchall for a large chunk of northern Buenos Aires. It encompasses **Palermo** proper, sometimes called **Alto Palermo,** with its park system extending on Avenida Libertador and Avenida Santa Fe; **Palermo Chico; Palermo Viejo,** which is further divided into **Palermo Soho** and **Palermo Hollywood;** and **Las Cañitas,** which is just to the side of the city's world-famous polo field.

PALERMO NEIGHBORHOODS

Palermo proper is a neighborhood of parks filled with magnolias, pines, palms, and willows, where families picnic on weekends and couples stroll at sunset. Designed by French architect Charles Thays, the parks take their inspiration from London's Hyde Park and Paris's Bois de Boulogne. Take the metro to Plaza Italia, which lets you out next to the Jardín Botánico or **Botanical Gardens ★★** (© **11/4831-2951;** p. 133) and the **Zoological Gardens ★★★** (© **11/4011-9900;** p. 133), open dawn to dusk, both good spots for kids. Stone paths wind their way through the Botanical Gardens. Flora from throughout South America fills the garden, with more than 8,000 plant species from around the world represented. It is famous for its population of abandoned cats, tended by little old ladies from the neighborhood, another delight for kids to watch. Next-door, the city zoo features an impressive variety of animals.

There are many sections of this complex park system. **Parque Tres de Febrero ★★,** a paradise of trees, lakes, and walking trails, begins just past the Rose Garden off Avenida Sarmiento. In summer, paddleboats are rented by the hour. Nearby, small streams and lakes meander through the **Japanese Gardens ★** (*©* 11/4804-4922; daily 10am–6pm; admission $2; p. 136), where children can feed the fish (*alimento para peces* means "fish food") and watch the ducks. Small wood bridges connect classical Japanese gardens surrounding the artificial lake. A simple restaurant serves tea, pastries, sandwiches, and a few Japanese dishes such as sushi and teriyaki chicken. You'll also find listings for various Asian events throughout the city. Within the **Plaza Naciones Unidas,** or United Nations Plaza, off Avenida Figueroa Alcorta between Quiroga and Bibiloni is the **Floralis Genérica,** a 2002 sculpture by the Argentine architect Eduardo Catalano. One of the city's most recognizable symbols, it's a shiny metal flower opening and closing on a hydraulic system near the University of Buenos Aires Law School building.

Previous visitors to the Palermo parks will notice security changes that affect your visit here. As a result of vandalism and theft, driven both by increased poverty and the high value of metals, many statues and fountains are now surrounded by gates, and sections of the park are locked at night. You can still look at the statues, of course, but many are impossible to get close to. Many of the statues and other monuments have been cleaned as part of this, and are freer of graffiti than in the past.

Part of Palermo proper, **Palermo Chico** is an exclusive neighborhood of elegant mansions off of Figueroa Alcorta, an offshoot of Libertador. Other than the beauty of the homes and a few embassy buildings, this small set of streets tucked behind the MALBA museum has little of interest to tourists.

Palermo Viejo, once a run-down neighborhood of warehouses, factories, and tiny decaying stucco homes in which few people cared to live as recently as 15 years ago, has been transformed into the city's chicest destination. Once you wander through the area and begin to absorb its charms—cobblestone streets, enormous oak-tree canopies, and low-rise buildings giving a clear view of the open skies on a sunny day—you'll wonder why it had been overlooked for so many years. Palermo Viejo is further divided into **Palermo Soho** in the south and **Palermo Hollywood** (sometimes also written as **Palermo Holywood**) in the north, with railroad tracks and Avenida Juan B. Justo serving as the dividing line. The center of Palermo Soho is Plazaleto Jorge Cortazar, better known by its informal name, Plaza Serrano, a small oval park at the intersection of calles Serrano (also called Calle Borges) and Honduras. Young people gather here late at night for impromptu singing and guitar sessions, sometimes fueled by drinks from the myriad of funky bars and restaurants that surround the plaza. On weekends, there is a crafts festival, but someone is always selling bohemian jewelry and leather goods here no matter the day. Palermo Soho is well known for boutiques owned by local designers, with fancy restaurants and hotels mixed in. Palermo Hollywood is considerably quieter and less gentrified than Palermo Soho, which, in some ways, has become a victim of its own success, populated during the day by lost tourists with maps and guidebooks in hand. Palermo Hollywood gained its name because many Argentine film studios were initially attracted to its once-cheap warehouse spaces and easy parking. There was an attempt to further relabel areas of Palermo Viejo as Palermo Queens, but this has largely failed.

evita perón: WOMAN, WIFE, ICON

Maria Eva Duarte de Perón, known the world over as Evita, captured the imagination of millions of Argentines because of her social and economic programs for the working classes. An illegitimate child of a wealthy businessman, she was born in Los Toldos, deep in the province of Buenos Aires. At 15, she moved to the capital to pursue her dreams of becoming an actress. She quickly achieved success, but was known more for her striking beauty than for talent. In 1944, she met Colonel Juan Perón, a rising figure in the Argentine government during a volatile period in the country's history. They married in 1945 and Evita became an important part of his presidential campaign. After he took office, she created the Eva Perón Foundation, which redirected funds traditionally controlled by Argentina's elite to programs benefiting hospitals, schools, homes for the elderly, and various charities. In addition, she raised wages for union workers, leading to the eventual growth of

the Argentine middle class, and she succeeded in realizing women's right to vote in 1947. When Evita died of cancer on July 26, 1952, the working classes tried (unsuccessfully) to have her canonized. She is buried in **Recoleta Cemetery** (p. 111) in her father's family's tomb. She is one of only a few nonaristocratic figures in this most elite of final resting places.

You will find that even today there is considerable disagreement among Argentines over Evita's legacy. Members of the middle and lower classes tend to see her as a national hero, while many of the country's upper classes believe she stole money from the wealthy and used it to embellish her own popularity. Since the 50th anniversary of her death, the establishment of the **Museo Evita** (p. 122), and the return of the Peronist party to power, her role in the country's history has been revisited far less emotionally.

Las Cañitas was a favored neighborhood of the military powers during the dictatorship period of 1976 to 1982, and the area remains among the safest of all central Buenos Aires neighborhoods. A military training base, hospital, high school, and various family housing units encircle the neighborhood, creating an islandlike sense of safety on the area's streets. Today, the area is far better known among the hip, trendy, and nouveau riche as the place to dine out, have a drink, party, and be seen in the fashionable establishments built into converted low-rise former houses on Calle Báez. Before Palermo Viejo became popular, this was the trendiest part of the city, and its density of restaurants, bars, and design shops, often overlooked by tourists, is still truly unrivaled. The polo field where the International Championships take place is also in the neighborhood and is technically part of the military bases. The polo field's presence makes the neighborhood bars and restaurants great places for enthusiasts to catch polo stars celebrating their victories in season. I group Las Cañitas with Palermo in this guidebook, though some refer to the area as a section of Belgrano or a location independent of any other neighborhood.

Recoleta

The city's most exclusive neighborhood, La Recoleta has a distinctly European feel, and locals call it a piece of Paris transplanted. Here, tree-lined avenues lead past fashionable restaurants, cafes, boutiques, and galleries. Much of the activity takes place along the pedestrian walkway Roberto M. Ortiz and in front of the cultural center and Recoleta Cemetery. This is a neighborhood of plazas and parks, a place where tourists and wealthy Argentines spend their leisure time outside. Weekends bring street performances, art exhibits, fairs, and sports.

The **Recoleta Cemetery ★★★** (p. 111), open daily from 8am to 6pm, pays tribute to some of Argentina's historical figures, most famously Evita. Weather permitting, free English guided tours take place every Thursday at 11am from the cemetery's Doric-columned entrance at Calle Junín 1790.

Adjacent to the cemetery, the **Centro Cultural Recoleta ★★** (p. 188) holds art exhibits and theatrical and musical performances, and includes the **Museo Participativo de Ciencias** (p. 122). Next-door, the **Buenos Aires Design Recoleta** (p. 168) features shops specializing in home decor. On the other side of Avenida 9 de Julio, the **Asociación Argentina de Cultura Inglesa (British Arts Centre;** p. 188) offers film, theater, culture, and art programs.

One word of caution about Recoleta: If you're a tourist staying in the area or visiting, there's an assumption that you're extremely wealthy and possibly naive. It's more likely here than in any part of the city that you might be given the runaround by taxi drivers who can't seem to find the location you've requested. They assume that if you can afford Recoleta, you can afford a fraudulent fare, so be extra vigilant and know where you're going.

Plaza de Mayo

Juan de Garay founded the historic core of Buenos Aires, the **Plaza de Mayo** (p. 104), in 1580. The plaza is the political heart of the city, serving as a forum for protests.

The mothers of the *desaparecidos,* victims of the military dictatorship's war against leftists, have demonstrated here since 1977. You can see them march, speak, and set up information booths Thursday afternoons at 3:30pm. The circle of headscarves, known as *panuelos,* on the ground surrounding the Pirámide de Mayo marks their demonstration route. The use of the headscarves as a symbol dates from a time when the military finally granted the mothers the right to march in protest, but forbid them from speaking to anyone. They wrote the names of missing children on the scarves, hoping someone would see and later, in a safer space, tell them what had happened to their children.

The Argentine president goes to work at the **Casa Rosada ★★★** (p. 99). It was from a balcony of this mansion that Eva Perón addressed adoring crowds of Argentine workers. You can watch the changing of the guard in front of the palace every hour on the hour, and around back is the **Presidential Museum** (p. 99) with information on the building's history and items owned by presidents over the centuries.

The original structure of the **Metropolitan Cathedral ★★** (p. 103) was built in 1745 and given a new facade and designated a cathedral in 1836. The **Cabildo ★★★** (p. 99), the original seat of city government established by the Spaniards, was completed in 1751 and restored in 1939, with another restoration in 2010. The **Legislatura de la Ciudad (City Legislature Building;** p. 102) features a striking neoclassical facade and houses exhibitions in several of its halls; ask about tours. Farther down Calle Perú are the **Manzanas de las Luces (Blocks of Enlightenment) ★★** (p. 102), which served as the intellectual center of the city in the 17th and 18th centuries. **San Ignacio,** the city's oldest church, stands at the corner of calles Bolívar and Alsina, and has a beautiful altar currently under renovation. Also located here is the **Colegio Nacional de Buenos Aires (National High School of Buenos Aires),** where Argentina's best-known intellectuals have gathered and studied (p. 102). In addition to weekend tours, the Comisión Nacional de la Manzanas de las Luces (© **11/4331-9534;** www.manzanadelasluces.gov.ar) organizes cultural activities during the week.

Puerto Madero

Puerto Madero became Buenos Aires's second major gateway to trade with Europe when it was built in 1880, replacing La Boca's port in terms of importance. But by 1910, the city had already outgrown it. The Puerto Nuevo (New Port) was established to the north to accommodate growing commercial activity, and Madero was abandoned for almost a century. Urban renewal saved the original port in the 1990s with the construction of a riverfront promenade, apartments, and offices. Sterile and businesslike during the day, the area attracts a fashionable crowd at night. It's lined with restaurants serving Argentine steaks and fresh seafood specialties, and there is a popular cinema showing Argentine and Hollywood films, as well as dance clubs such as **Asia de Cuba** (p. 192). The entire area is rapidly expanding, with high-rise luxury residences, making this a newly fashionable, if somewhat isolated and artificial, neighborhood. All the streets in Puerto Madero are named for important Argentine women. Look for the Buenos Aires City Tourism brochure *Women of Buenos Aires* to learn more about some of them. A sign between docks 2 and 3 explains these spectacular women. At sunset, take a walk along the eastern, modern part of the port, and watch the water shimmer in brilliant reds with the city as a backdrop.

As you walk out from the port, you'll also come across the **Ecological Reserve ★★** (p. 118). This area is an anomaly for a modern city and proof nature can regenerate from an ecological disaster. In the 1960s and 1970s, demolished buildings and debris were dumped into the Río de la Plata after the construction of the *autopista* (highway system). Over time, sand and sediment built up, plants and grasses grew, and birds now use this space as a breeding ground. Ask travel agents about bird-watching tours. In the summer, adventurous Porteños use it as a beach, but the water is too polluted to swim in and you must be careful of jagged debris and the homeless who set up camp here. In spite of limited protection, Puerto Madero development is slowly creeping onto the preserve. While the Ecological Reserve is a lung for the city, the height of Puerto Madero buildings has been blamed for blocking Río de la Plata winds, decreasing air quality in downtown Buenos Aires. The focal point for the Puerto Madero area is Santiago Calatrava's **Bridge of Woman,** opened in 2001 (p. 117).

Plaza San Martín & the Surrounding Microcentro and Retiro Area

Plaza San Martín ★★★, a beautiful park at the base of Calle Florida in the Retiro neighborhood, is the nucleus of the Microcentro district. In summer months, Argentine businesspeople flock here during their lunch hours, loosening their ties, taking off some layers, and sunning themselves amid the plaza's flowering jacaranda trees. A monument to General José de San Martín towers over the scene. The park is busy at all hours, and the playground is often teeming with kids and their parents well after midnight. Plaza San Martín was once the location of choice for the most elite Porteño families at the beginning of the 20th century. The San Martín Palace, now used by the Argentine Ministry of Foreign Affairs; the Círculo Militar, once the home of the

Paz family who own the *La Prensa* newspaper; and the elegant Plaza Hotel testify to this former grandeur. The shift from private residences to apartments and commercial structures began in the 1930s with the Depression, when many residents were forced to sell their mansions. In 1936, the Art Deco Kavanagh Building opened, then the tallest building in South America, and it still dominates the plaza. Temporary art exhibits, usually with a social purpose, often occur within the plaza.

Plaza San Martín cascades gently down a hill, at the base of which is the **Islas Malvinas–Falkland Islands War Memorial** (p. 113). The memorial directly faces the Elizabethan-style **British Clock Tower,** renamed the **Torre Monumental** (p. 115), though most locals use the old name. It was a gift from the British who built and ran the nearby Retiro train station complex. It remained unscathed during the war, but was attacked years later by a mob that also toppled an accompanying statue of George Canning, the British foreign secretary who recognized Argentina's independence from Spain. The tower is open to the public and provides a view of the city and river.

Calle Florida ★★★, Buenos Aires's main pedestrian thoroughfare, is lined with boutiques, restaurants, record stores, and the upscale shopping mall **Galerías Pacífico** (p. 168). The busiest section is between Plaza San Martín and Avenida Corrientes, but the street extends all the way south to Avenida de Mayo, where it turns into Calle Perú. Occasionally, you'll find street performers along the route. Be very careful of pickpockets when watching any of these shows. Calle Florida intersects **Calle Lavalle,** a smaller version of itself that has even more stores, most of lesser quality, and some inexpensive *parrillas* worth visiting. The street is also home to numerous arcades, so it's a good place for teenagers to hang out while you shop around—though beware that seedy characters and prostitutes also hang around the area. **Calle Reconquista,** east of and parallel to Florida, was pedestrianized in 2009, along with small adjacent streets, and is full of bars and restaurants. The area is a focus of St. Patrick's Day celebrations. In 2010, **Calle Suipacha,** parallel and west of Florida, was pedestrianized and given a bicycle lane. The city is planning more bike lanes and pedestrian streets downtown.

Avenida Corrientes ★ is a living diary of Buenos Aires's cultural development. Until the 1930s, Avenida Corrientes was the favored hangout of tango legends. When the avenue was widened in the mid-1930s, it made its debut as the Argentine Broadway. Today Corrientes, lined with Art Deco cinemas and theaters, pulses with cultural and commercial activity day and night. It is also home to many bookstores, from the chains that sell bestsellers and English-language guidebooks, to independent bargain outlets and rare booksellers. The **Obelisco,** opened in 1936 as Buenos Aires's defining monument to mark the 400th anniversary of the first (unsuccessful) founding of the city, marks the intersection of Corrientes with **Avenida 9 de Julio.** Whenever locals have something to celebrate, they gather here. It's exciting to come here when Argentina wins an international soccer match.

THE PALERMO GARDENS COMPLEX & ZOO

More than just a neighborhood with a park in it, Palermo has the feel of a park where some people happen to live. This wide, miles-long expanse of green open space along the waterfront was an estate until the mid-1800s. While you'd need a long time to really see the entire complex fully, I have listed some must-see highlights below.

The park contains the Rose Gardens, the Planetarium, the Patio, several museums, jogging trails, and too many monuments to count. The area expands out beyond Jorge Newberry, the domestic airport, into the neighboring district Belgrano. Though it's easy to get lost here, you'll never get stuck, as cabs cruise the boulevards cutting through the park.

Jardín Botánico (Botanical Gardens) ★★ ☺ The Botanical Gardens are a true delight, with a myriad of tree-lined walkways. A central greenhouse is often the location of rotating art shows, with young artists standing and sweating next to their artwork. Plants from all over the world are here, including many from Argentina and other parts of South America. They're labeled with their local and Latin names, making for a fun lesson for kids as you walk along. Not all the paths are well maintained, however, so watch your step. If you're here as a couple without kids, the gardens are also a romantic spot. Bring a picnic basket and share some quality time, as you'll see many locals doing.

Like the Recoleta Cemetery, this is another cat lover's dream, and you'll find plenty of women from the neighborhood coming to take care of these strays. The cats are also more playful and friendly here, and like to come up to visitors to be petted. Sit on a bench, and you'll very likely find one cuddling up next to you.

Av. Las Heras at Plaza Italia, across from the subway entrance. ✆ **11/4831-2951.** Free admission. Daily 8am–6pm. Metro: Plaza Italia.

Jardín Zoológico (Zoological Gardens) ★★★ ☺ The Buenos Aires city zoo features an impressive array of animals, including rare white tigers, indigenous birds and monkeys, giant turtles, llamas, elephants, polar bears, and brown bears. The eclectic and kitschy buildings housing the animals, some designed as exotic temples, are as much of a delight as the inhabitants. A giant lake near the entrance is filled with pink flamingos hanging out near mock Byzantine ruins in the center of the lake. Overlooking the water is a building that resembles a Russian church, which contains monkey cages. Camels are surrounded by Moroccan-style architecture, and the kangaroo holding pens are painted with aboriginal designs. The lions, the kings of the jungle, are in a castle complex with its own moat. The most stunning building, however, is the Elephant House. Built to look like an Indian temple, it is overgrown with vines to make you feel as if you are a jungle explorer who has come across an elephant sanctuary. There are three elephants: Two are African and one is Asian.

The Asian elephant, named Mara, was rescued by the zoo after years of abuse as a circus animal. Having been caged too tightly, she suffers from an emotional illness, standing in one place while she shakes her head back and forth. The other elephants, named Pupy and Kuki, seem to take care of her, and try to prod her along at feeding time and massage their heads against her. It is sad and yet interesting to watch the social behavior of these magnificent creatures. I recommend making time to see them.

Don't miss the polar bears, whose habitat comes with an underwater viewing area. All the caretakers throughout the zoo are great with kids, but here especially they take the time to teach kids about the bears, though sometimes in Spanish only. They also feed the bears, and kids can watch them retrieve food from the water. In the back of the zoo is an enclosed jungle habitat full of various plant species, which even has a waterfall with a rope bridge that a caretaker will lead you through. Giant bugs are also in display cases here. It's hot and steamy inside, just like a real jungle, and the interior is a labyrinth surrounded by plants, so keep an eye on kids as they can easily get lost.

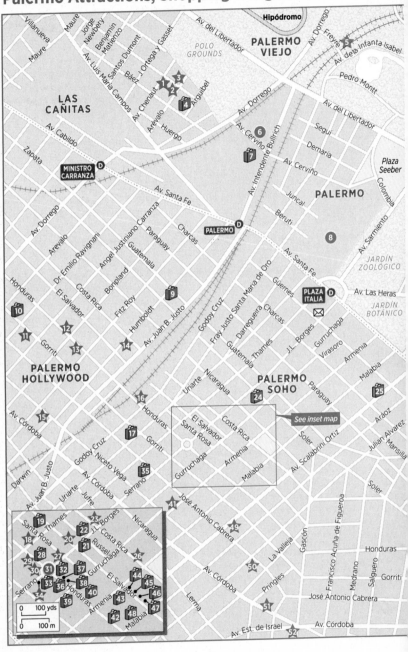

SHOPPING 🛍

Akiabara **40**
Alto Palermo **61**
Bakú **4**
Bien Fifí **35**
Bio **9**
Bokura **45**
Bolivia **39**
Calma Chicha **38**
Capital Diseño & Objetos **36**
Casa Barbie **57**
Diseño Arg **28**
Florentina Muraña **22**
Galería Mar Dulce **17**
Jumbo Palermo
   Commercial Center **7**
Librería Otras Letras **24**
Lupe **42**
Mancini **19**
Maria Cher **43**
Mishka Shoes **44**
Palermitana & Escaparate
   Designer Complex **33**
Papelera Palermo **37**
Pasión Argentina/
   Diseños Etnicos **25**
Planeta Bs As **32**
Prototype **47**
Rapsodia **46**
Rodrigo Reyes **48**
Tienda Puro Diseño **10**
Ufficio **21**

ATTRACTIONS ●

Centro Cultural Islámico Rey Fahd
   (King Fahd Islamic Cultural Center) **6**
La Rural & Opera Pampa **8**
MALBA (Museo de Arte
   Latinoamericano de Buenos
   Aires Colección Costantini) **58**
Museo Evita **56**
Museo Nacional de Arte Decorativo
   (National Museum
   of Decorative Arts) **59**
Museo Nacional de Bellas Artes
   (National Museum of Fine Arts) **60**
Plaza Serrano **31**

NIGHTLIFE ★

Acá Bar **12**
Amerika **52**
Bach Bar **50**
Bar Isabel **18**
Crobar **5**
Crónico Bar **27**
Human **55**
Jackie O. **2**
Kika **16**
La Viruta **41**
Macondo Bar **23**
Niceto Club **15**
Olsen **11**
OMM Bar **13**
Pachá **53**
Pride Resto-Bar/Pride Hollywood **14**
República de Acá **34**
Salón Canning **49**
Sitges **51**
Soul Café and SuperSoul **1**
Sugar **26**
Sullivan's Drink House **20**
Tazz **30**
Tequila **54**
Utopia Bar **29**
Van Koning **3**

✉ Post office
◖D◗ Subway

Peacocks and some of the small animals are allowed to roam free, and feeding them is allowed, with special food for sale at kiosks. Animals on the loose will flock to your kids, and many cages have feeding chutes where the animals line up. Boats can also be rented on the zoo's artificial lake. The zoo is a must for anyone, but especially families with kids. I recommend at least half a day to explore and a full day if you have kids.

Av. Las Heras at Plaza Italia across from the subway entrance. ✆ **11/4011-9900.** www.zoobuenosaires. com.ar. Admission $8, additional charges for boats, jungle habitat, and other extras; multi-amenity and family passes also available for purchase. V. Hours change throughout the year but are generally Tues-Sun 10am–8pm. Metro: Plaza Italia.

Jardín Japonés (Japanese Gardens & Cultural Center) ★ ☺ 🎒   Tucked in the midst of all the other Palermo gardens is this tiny gem opened in 1969 in honor of an official visit by one of the Japanese princes. Special landscaping, rock islands, and small red bowed bridges give you the feeling of being in Japan as soon as you step through the gates here. Carp swim in the large central lake, a delight for children as well as adults. Beyond the lake lies the Cultural Center, with a small museum and various art exhibitions. Kids can also learn origami folding and many other Asian crafts. Asian fairs are held throughout the year in both the center and the park, so pick up one of the calendars while visiting, or check out the website below for more details.

Av. Figueroa Alcorta at Av. Casares. ✆ **11/4804-4922.** www.jardinjapones.com.ar. Admission $2. Daily 10am–6pm, though hours vary with exhibitions and fairs. Metro: Plaza Italia.

La Rural & Opera Pampa ★   The grand Belle Epoque stadium known as La Rural was built at the turn of the 20th century on Plaza Italia as the parade ground for the Sociedad Rural Argentina, an association of wealthy landowners founded in 1866. During their annual meetings in Buenos Aires, they would parade their most prized animals, along with their gaucho workers, and compete for awards. This event is still held every July, and is the most important agricultural exposition in the country. Interesting artisanal gourmet food purveyors also take part in the event. It was through this association's promotion of Argentina's agricultural resources that Argentina was able to become an important world economic force by the end of the 1800s. Their headquarters remain in Buenos Aires on the 400 block of Calle Florida. A modern exhibition hall has been added and is often the site of international expos, conferences, and other exhibitions. The United States Embassy is located behind this complex.

To get an idea of what the experience was like in the society's heyday, tourists should book a night at **Opera Pampa,** an event held in the old stadium. The show covers the at-times-violent history of Argentina, beginning with the Spanish conquest, 1810 Independence, and Roca's slaughter of thousands of Indians in Buenos Aires province, through European immigration at the beginning of the 20th century. The scenes related to Indian history are exceedingly violent and sad, and include the song "Fuera Fuera" ("Away, Away") as the Indians are forced to leave and one Indian remains behind, begging a soldier to let him stay. The most dramatic scenes are those relating to San Martín and the revolution, full of charging horses and simulated cannon fights. Cheerier portions include gaucho gatherings in *pulperías,* country bars where they would sing and dance after working on the *estancias* (farms). The *Zamba,* the national dance performed with white handkerchiefs, is featured in these scenes. (The tango, in spite of its association with Argentina, is not the national dance.) The show is brilliantly choreographed and exciting to watch. Afterward, patrons can stay for an *asado* (Argentine barbecue) in the stadium's dining hall. An evening here will help you understand Argentina's history. Parents with young children will have to make a decision about whether the violence outweighs the educational value.

La Rural Stadium and Exhibition Hall on Av. Las Heras at the intersection of Av. Santa Fe overlooking Plaza Italia. Opera Pampa office and information is at Av. Sarmiento at Calle Paso. ℭ **11/4777-5557.** www.operapampa.com.ar. Sociedad Rural Argentina www.sra.org.ar. Tickets are $42 show only, $100 show and dinner. Showtimes Thurs–Sat 8pm, dinner following. Metro: Plaza Italia for La Rural Stadium; Pueyrredón for Opera Pampa office.

ARCHITECTURAL HIGHLIGHTS
Must-Sees for Architecture Buffs

Buenos Aires is full of architectural highlights. Here are some particularly impressive standouts, some of which are closed to the public but are still worth checking out from the street. See also the walking tours in chapter 7.

Centro Naval ★★ Inaugurated in 1914 and designed by the Swiss architect Jacques Dunant, this building is an incredible combination of Italian rococo elements and rustication, all executed in a high Beaux Arts style. The building is made of cast stone and is extremely well maintained. The ornate bronze doors feature shields, arrows, and other symbols of war, overseen by a nude bronze sea god in a Spanish galleon announcing triumph through a conch shell. Other bronze boats line the balustrades on the upper floors. The building is not open to the public, but at times people are allowed in the small lobby. There are also various events and functions held here, including weddings, so if you hear of any, find a way to get yourself invited.

Calle Florida 801 (at Córdoba, across from the Galerías Pacífico). Not usually open to the public. Metro: San Martín.

Confitería del Molino ★★ Unfortunately, not only will you not be able to enter this incredible masterpiece, but it is also rapidly crumbling away. Across the street from Congreso, this was once among the city's most important cafes, where politicians would mingle with well-to-do citizens and dignitaries from around the world. The cafe closed in 1997, and the building is now only rarely open to the public for events designed to raise consciousness of the need to restore the building before it disappears forever. (So bad is its condition that plants and moss are growing on the facade.) Primarily Art Nouveau, stained glass and ornate tile work were once part of the ornamentation here, and its main feature is the tower imitating a windmill. (*Molino* is Spanish for windmill.) The architect was Francesco Gianotti, an Italian who also designed Galería Güemes and its theater housing the Piazzolla tango show. These are open to the public if you want to get an idea of Molino's fabulous interior (p. 201).

Callao 10 (at Rivadavia, next to Congreso). Not open to the public. Metro: Congreso.

Teatro Nacional Cervantes ★★ One of the country's most important theaters, the architecture here is a show all its own. Built in Spanish Habsburg Imperial style, it overlooks Plaza Lavalle, 2 blocks from the more famous Teatro Colón. The building was a gift from two Spanish actors who opened the theater in 1921. Within a few years, it went bankrupt and was taken over by the Argentine government. The interior is decorated with materials from Spain, including tapestries from Madrid and tiles from Valencia and Tarragona. The theater was renovated in 2009. It's open to the public for tours and has productions throughout the year, so ask about upcoming shows.

Av. Córdoba 1155 (at Libertad, overlooking Plaza Lavalle). ✆ **11/4815-8883.** www.teatrocervantes.gov. ar. Guided tours Tues 2pm. Metro: Tribunales.

Religious Buildings

Iglesia San Nicolás de Bari ★★ ☺ This is an exceedingly beautiful and impressive church built for a local Italian Roman Catholic community. Its interior is reminiscent of a mini–St. Peter's, with Corinthian columns and white marble with colored accents. The block that surrounds it also has an array of exceptionally interesting buildings of various styles from the beginning of the 20th century, with a beauty not usually seen on most of Avenida Santa Fe.

Santa Fe 1364 (at Uruguay). ✆ **11/4813-3028.** Metro: Callao.

Centro Cultural Islámico Rey Fahd (King Fahd Islamic Cultural Center) ★
With its broad expanses, well-tended lawn, minarets, and palm trees, the Centro Cultural Islámico brings a little bit of the Middle East to Buenos Aires. Overlooking the polo grounds, this enormous structure, which becomes simply radiant in strong sunlight, is the largest Islamic center and mosque in all of Latin America. At night, the lit-up minarets are a striking contrast with the surrounding apartment complexes. The project began under former President Carlos Ménem, who is of Syrian Muslim descent but converted to Catholicism because of restrictions on non-Catholics becoming president. Construction began in 1998, and the center was opened in 2000. The center is open for free tours in Spanish and sometimes in English, Tuesday and Thursday at noon. Lasting 45 minutes, they include the gardens, interior courtyard, library, and other spaces. Institutions can make special requests for tours at other times. The Centro offers classes on the Koran and Arabic language, and has a library open to the public daily from 10am to 5pm. Though the Centro is closed to the public on Muslim holidays, Muslim visitors to Buenos Aires are welcome to visit for services. Estimates place the Islamic and Arabic population in Argentina at about 750,000. Many Argentines call anyone of Arabic or Muslim descent "Turcos," or Turks, regardless of their country of origin, based on the fact that the majority are from areas once controlled by the Ottoman Empire, the capital of which was in modern-day Turkey.

Av. Bullrich 55 (at Libertador). ✆ **11/4899-1144.** www.ccislamicoreyfahd.org.ar. Free tours Tues and Thurs at noon. Metro: Palermo.

Centro Cultural SGI (The Soka Gakkai International Buddhist Center) This Buddhist temple and cultural center sits in two modern buildings spanning 1 block in the Belgrano neighborhood, close to Chinatown. There are several meeting and chanting spaces and a bookstore. The building is open to the public and provides a peaceful respite from the bustle of the city. Various cultural and musical events related to Buddhism and other Asian philosophies are also held here.

Donado 2150 (at Juramento). ✆ **11/4545-6000.** www.sgiar.org.ar. Daily 9:30am–7:30pm; hours may differ based on events. Metro: Juramento.

Claustros del Pilar (Basílica Nuestra Señora del Pilar) ★★ This imposing white Spanish colonial church overlooks Recoleta Cemetery. While many step inside to see the worship area, few take the time to explore the religious art museum within the former convent area, full of gorgeous pieces from Buenos Aires's early years. A step back in time, the convent retains the original flooring, stairs, walls, and other components from its 1732 construction. Most interesting are the windows with special panes, made from agate so that light could come into the structure, but the nuns would be hidden. Other highlights include the ecclesiastical wardrobes on display.

Junín 1904 (next to Recoleta Cemetery). ☏ **11/4803-6793.** www.iglesiadelpilar.com.ar. Admission $1. Tues–Sat 10:30am–6:15pm; Sun 2:30–6:15pm. No metro access.

Basílica y Convento de San Francisco (San Francis's Church & Convent) ★
The San Roque parish to which this church belongs is one of the oldest in the city. A Jesuit architect designed the building in 1730, but a final reconstruction in the early 20th century added a German baroque facade, along with statues of Saint Francis of Assisi, Dante Alighieri, and Christopher Columbus. Inside, you'll find a tapestry by Argentine artist Horacio Butler and an extensive library.

Adolfo Alsina 380 (at Defensa). ☏ **11/4331-0625.** Free admission. Hours vary. Metro: Plaza de Mayo.

SPORTS

There's no shortage of sporting events in Buenos Aires, from the highbrow International Polo championships where locals hobnob with European royalty, to rowdy, immensely popular soccer events. Check the papers for events, especially the English-language *Buenos Aires Herald*. If you want to have your experience planned for you (and to be escorted to and from the game), see "Sports Tours," p. 27.

GOLF Argentina has more than 200 golf courses. The closest to downtown Buenos Aires is **Cancha de Golf de la Ciudad de Buenos Aires,** Av. Torquist 1426, at Olleros (☏ **11/4772-7261**), 10 minutes from downtown and with great scenery and a par-71 course. Prices start at $10 during the week and $15 on weekends, with additional fees for caddies and other services. **Jockey Club Argentino,** Av. Márquez 1700 (☏ **11/4743-1001**), is in San Isidro, about 30 minutes from downtown. It has two courses (par 71 and 72). The entrance fee ranges from $40 to $60, but be prepared for extra fees for caddies and other services.

HORSE RACING Over much of the 20th century, Argentina was famous for its thoroughbreds. It continues to send prize horses to competitions around the world, and you can watch some of the best right here in Buenos Aires. Races happen at **Hipódromo Argentino de Palermo,** Av. del Libertador 4205, at Dorrego (☏ **11/4778-2839**), in Palermo, a classically designed track with modern additions, open all year. Entry is free and race times run from late afternoon until past midnight. In the suburbs, a few miles from Buenos Aires, is also the **Hipódromo de San Isidro,** Av. Márquez 504, at Fleming in San Isidro (☏ **11/4743-4010**). This modern location is open year-round. Most races begin in the early afternoon and run through early evening, and entry prices range from $1 to $10, depending on your seating area.

POLO Argentina has won more international polo tournaments than any other country, and the **Argentine Open Championship,** held late November through early December, is the world's most important polo event. There are two seasons for polo: March through May and September through December, and competitions are held at the **Campo Argentino de Polo,** Avenida del Libertador and Avenida Dorrego (☏ **11/4576-5600**). Tickets can be purchased at the gate for about $25 per person. This is one of the most important polo stadiums in the world, and visits by European royalty are not uncommon. Contact the **Asociación Argentina de Polo,** Hipólito

Yrigoyen 636 (✆ **11/4331-4646** or 11/4342-8321), for information on polo schools and events.

SOCCER   One cannot discuss soccer (called *fútbol* here) in Argentina without paying homage to Diego Armando Maradona, Argentina's most revered player and one of the sport's great (if fallen) players. Passion for soccer in Argentina could not be more intense. Any sense of national unity dissolves when Argentines watch their favorite clubs—River Plate, Boca Juniors, Racing Club, Independiente, and San Lorenzo—battle on Sunday in season, which runs from February until November. There is also a summer season when teams travel, so essentially soccer never really stops in Buenos Aires. Try to catch a game at the **Estadio Boca Juniors,** Brandsen 805 (✆ **11/4309-4700**), in San Telmo, followed by raucous street parties. Ticket prices start at $4 and can be purchased in advance or at the gate.

CITY STROLLS

Buenos Aires is a great walking city. No matter where you start out, you'll find beautiful architecture and tree-lined streets. If you get lost, friendly Porteños will help you, as well as offer advice on their favorite sights. The tours below are just a few suggested routes for those who wish to explore the city on foot. Many of the buildings on these tours were recently renovated for the 2010 Bicentennial celebrations.

WALKING TOUR 1: HISTORICAL CALLE FLORIDA

GETTING THERE: **Take the metro to San Martín.**

START: **Corner of Avenida Córdoba and Calle Florida.**

FINISH: **Calle Florida at Diagonal Norte.**

TIME: **2 hours, not including eating or shopping stops.**

BEST TIMES: **Daylight hours in the midafternoon, when you can see the buildings most clearly and most are open (some interiors not visible after 8pm).**

Pedestrianized Calle Florida mostly has a reputation as a shop-till-you-drop and people-watching destination. However, there are a number of points of historical and architectural interest here as well. I highlight the most beautiful features of the street here, and I recommend that you keep your head up as you walk along (trying, of course, not to bump into anyone or step in Buenos Aires's infamous dog doo-doo.) While many of the buildings on this street have been modernized at storefront level, the original facades higher up are often preserved. The last portion of this trip along Calle Florida takes you into Buenos Aires's banking center, nicknamed "La City" after London's financial district. This tour is an easy walk and is also wheelchair accessible in most cases.

To start the tour, begin at the northeastern corner of Calle Florida, where it hits Avenida Córdoba. You will be in front of Córdoba 810, which is the:

1 Centro Naval

This is one of the city's most exquisite buildings, a masterpiece of cast stone architecture. A nude sea god in a Spanish galleon, announcing triumph through a conch shell, oversees its corner doorway. Naval themes continue along the upper balustrades. The building was opened in 1914 and was designed by Swiss architect Jacques Dunant. It's not generally open to the public, but sometimes visitors

The **Buenos Aires City Tourism** kiosks scattered throughout the city have maps that can be used for self-guided tours. The **Golden Map**, available at almost all hotels, also has some self-guided walks for various neighborhoods in the city. One pamphlet that the city provides contains information about a special cellphone tour, in which participants punch in codes at various destinations and hear explanations in English, Spanish, and other languages, including recordings of historical events at the various locations. Ask for this specific brochure, but know that the phone system does not always work well. Other themed tours include "Women of Buenos Aires" or focus on such important historical figures as Evita, Lorca, Borges, or Gardel, with addresses and descriptions of the places you will see. Be aware that some of these tours cover large distances that cannot realistically be traversed solely on foot. See "Free Buenos Aires City Tourism Office Tours," p. 26.

are allowed to pop into the circular lobby. If you ever get invited to an event here, be sure to go.

Cross Avenida Córdoba heading south and stop just after crossing the street, at the:

2 Galerías Pacífico

The most famous shopping mall in Buenos Aires, Galerías Pacífico was opened in 1891. The building was designed to recall the Galleria Vittorio Emanuele II in Milan, with its long halls, glass ceilings, and several tiers of shops. An economic crisis shortly after its opening, however, meant that it was converted into office space for the Pacífico Railroad Company. In 1992, everything old became new again, and the building was converted back into a shopping center. Enter the building and see the central staircase where all the halls meet. In 1945, while it was still an office building, paintings about the history of mankind by Antonio Berni and other artists were installed under the main dome, and the shopping center has daily information sessions explaining their history.

Take a Break 🍴

If you're hungry, make a pit stop in the food court at the Galerías Pacífico. Try a fast-food *asado* (Argentine grill), and finish your meal with a Patagonian chocolate treat—you won't be sorry!

When you're finished shopping here, head back out the door facing Calle Florida and turn left, walking south on Calle Florida until you get to Lavalle, another pedestrianized street. No need to look out for cars at this intersection, which is crowded with pedestrians and sometimes street performers as well. (Take a break here and watch if one catches your attention.) After crossing Lavalle, stop midblock and turn to face the building at Calle Florida 460 on your right, or west, side. It's the:

3 Sociedad Rural Argentina

Surrounded by modern storefronts, this small, ornate French rococo building seems out of place among its neighbors. The people working inside almost undoubtedly feel the same way, for this is the headquarters of the Sociedad Rural Argentina, an organization created in the mid-1800s by the country's wealthiest oligarchs. This society was integral to the creation of Argentina's great

Walking Tour 1: Historical Calle Florida

Legend:
- ⓘ Information
- ⊠ Post office
- Ⓐ Subway
- Ⓓ—Ⓔ Subway transfer

1 Centro Naval
2 Galerías Pacífico ☕
3 Sociedad Rural Argentina
4 Ana Díaz Historical Homestead
5 Galería Mitre/Falabella
6 Banco Francés/Optician Store
7 HSBC Building
8 Gath & Chaves
9 Galería Güemes
10 Standard Bank
11 Roque Sáenz Peña Monument

agricultural wealth. The door to this important institution is almost always closed, but if you find it open, take a chance and wander in to see the Belle Epoque interior. Visitors are not officially allowed in the building, however, and you'll likely be sent quickly out the door.

Continue walking south on Calle Florida until you get to Avenida Corrientes. Cross the street and stop in front of Burger King, which was once the site of the:

4 Ana Díaz Historical Homestead

Women's history buffs take note: While men usually get all the credit for founding cities, Spanish explorer Juan de Garay's 1580 expedition, which permanently founded Buenos Aires, was not without a lady's touch. Ana Díaz, whose house was located on the property where Burger King now sits, came along with him. The first time that the Spanish tried to settle the city of Buenos Aires in 1536, it was an all-male group of explorers and the settlement failed. Who knows how many times it might have taken to settle Buenos Aires if a woman hadn't been around to take care of things the second time around? Still, it's unclear historically what her exact role was in the founding. Was she a Spanish conquistadora, a woman with Indian blood who served as a guide, or a lover of one of the men? Ana Díaz's original home is long gone, but it was located on this corner. A stunning turn-of-the-20th-century home was later built here and was intact until Burger King got its hands on it. Still, enter the hamburger joint and take a walk up the staircase to your left. Try not to gasp in awe as you head upstairs to the colonnaded rotunda, stained-glass ceilings, and various rooms with their ornamental plaster ceilings. Imagine what the ground floor looked like before "ground meat" took over. This is one of the most stunning hidden gems of Calle Florida in terms of both beauty and historical value. On the Corrientes side of the building, you can read plaques that explain more about Ana Díaz and her often-overlooked importance to the founding of Buenos Aires.

Upon leaving Burger King, turn right and continue south on Calle Florida. Don't stop until you're midblock between Corrientes and Sarmiento. Then look to the east side of the street (your left) to see the:

5 Galería Mitre/Falabella

This is one of the most visually impressive and unusual buildings on Calle Florida. It was designed in a robust Spanish colonial style, imitating the Argentine missions along the Paraguayan border. The most unique feature is the ornamentation around the doorway and the frieze above it, with men in 16th-century Spanish clothing, depicted in a rustic style. This design mimics art created by Indian slaves for their Spanish masters in that region of Argentina during the early colonial period in the late 1500s and early 1600s. The building had been closed for many years and is now home to a branch of Chilean department store Falabella.

Continue in the same direction on Calle Florida, crossing Sarmiento. Stop midblock before Perón, this time facing the west side of the street (your right), so that you're looking at the:

6 Banco Francés/Optician Store

At street level, you'll wonder why you've stopped here. But look up and you'll see a beautiful 1920s-era building that was once an optician's headquarters. Notice the bronze eyeglasses adorning the windows and beautiful maidens surrounding them. Four-eyed nerds can only dream to have it so good.

Continue down Calle Florida to Perón, but don't cross it yet. Instead, turn left, or east, for a glimpse of the:

7 HSBC Building

This ornate Spanish Gothic building, one of my favorites, is faced with travertine marble and the corner entrance is covered with heavy bronze doors. It, however, is very often covered with graffiti.

Continue down Calle Florida in the same direction, stopping just as you hit Calle Perón, and look to the corner opposite (the southwest corner), to see:

8 Gath & Chaves

You'll notice the BANCO MERIDIEN sign under a glass-and-wrought-iron doorway simulating old Parisian subway entrances. Look above and you will still see the old name of this one-time British department store on the corner tower—Gath & Chaves. Like Harrods, it shows the former influence of British culture on Argentina. Inside, only hints of its former beauty remain, in the bank lobby.

Cross Perón and walk half a block on Calle Florida, stopping on the east side in front of Calle Florida 165, the:

9 Galería Güemes

The Calle Florida entrance of this shopping gallery, opened in 1915, is nothing special, having been reconstructed in a modern style after a 1971 fire. The most interesting thing is the sign for **Piazzolla Tango** show (p. 201), held in the basement theater. However, step through the threshold and you'll find one of the city's most exquisite buildings. It was designed by Italian architect Francesco Gianotti, who also designed the now closed Confitería del Molino. Much of the material used in the decoration was brought over from Italy. Don't miss the ornamental elevator bays with their bronze details. A second-level art gallery has old photos of the building. *Little Prince* author Antoine de Saint-Exupéry once lived here.

Continue south on Calle Florida and cross Calle Bartolomé Mitre. Stop immediately, facing the wedge-shaped building on your left, or east, side at Calle Florida 99. This is the:

10 Standard Bank

Formerly known as Bank of Boston, this is another ornate Spanish colonial building, even more impressive than the HSBC bank, full of beautiful details on its facade and within the interior. Much of the limestone and structural steel necessary to construct this building came from the United States. The 4-ton bronze doors, now missing, were made in England. Since the peso crisis, the building has often been a flashpoint for anti-American sentiments and, at times, is covered with "Yankee go home" graffiti. If the building is open, enter its spacious lobby, with slender columns supporting a gilded and coffered ceiling. The building is topped by an enormous, ornate cupola, part of the row that lines Diagonal Norte, marking each intersection with the connecting streets. (This pattern begins at Plaza de Mayo and continues up Diagonal Norte, where it intersects with Av. 9 de Julio, forming the vista point for the Obelisco.)

When leaving the building, face the plaza and look at the:

11 Roque Sáenz Peña Monument

Inaugurated in 1936, this Art Deco monument commemorates Roque Sáenz Peña, president of Argentina from 1910 to 1914, who died while in office. It overlooks Diagonal Norte, which is also sometimes known as Avenida Roque Sáenz Peña. The construction of Diagonal Norte was part of a plan to rebuild Buenos Aires with vista points along the lines of Haussmann's redesign of Paris. Diagonal Norte was completed in the mid-1930s.

This statue marks the end of this walking tour. During the day you can head across the street to the Buenos Aires City Tourism kiosk, the modern metal structure with a winged cover, if you need any kind of information or help. Behind it, if you need travel assistance, you'll find the main customer service center for Aerolíneas Argentinas. If you just want to head home after the tour, the D line Catedral subway station is here, or you can walk a little toward Plaza de Mayo for more subway line access (lines A and E).

WALKING TOUR 2: PLAZA SAN MARTIN & RETIRO

GETTING THERE: **Take the metro to San Martín.**

START: **The east side of Plaza San Martín, facing the Kavanagh Building.**

FINISH: **Retiro Station.**

TIME: **1½ hours if you're just walking; 3 to 4 hours if you go inside all buildings mentioned.**

BEST TIMES: **Monday through Saturday between 11am and 4pm (not at night when things are closed).**

At the turn of the 20th century, some of Buenos Aires's most fabulous mansions were built overlooking Plaza San Martín, and quite a few remain. The enormous plaza, with its overgrown trees and lazy atmosphere, might call to mind the squares of Savannah, Georgia. The Retiro area spreads down a gentle hill from the plaza and encompasses the train station complex built by the British, once the main entrance to this grand city. This tour has a moderate walking level, but steps and a hill overlooking San Martín, as well as the expanse of Retiro, can be a slight challenge.

Start in the plaza itself, looking toward the east at the:

1 Kavanagh Building

At the time of its construction in 1936, this was the tallest building in South America, standing at about 120m (394 ft.) with over 30 stories, and designed as a residential structure. However, it took more than 16 years to sell the apartments in this Art Deco building. Since its construction, many buildings have risen higher throughout the city, but this structure still dominates the Plaza.

Turn to your right and walk a few meters along the park (you'll be making a circle around the plaza) until you see the:

2 Marriott Plaza Hotel

The grande dame of Buenos Aires's hotels, the Marriott Plaza Hotel (p. 39), opened in 1908, is among the city's most traditional hotels. When it opened, it

Walking Tour 2: Plaza San Martín & Retiro

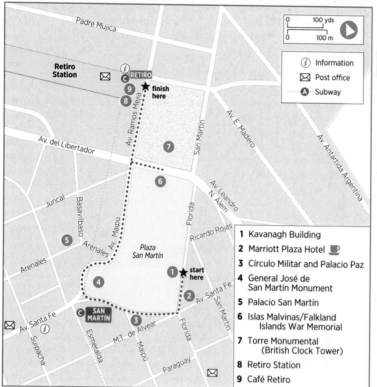

1	Kavanagh Building
2	Marriott Plaza Hotel ☕
3	Círculo Militar and Palacio Paz
4	General José de San Martín Monument
5	Palacio San Martín
6	Islas Malvinas/Falkland Islands War Memorial
7	Torre Monumental (British Clock Tower)
8	Retiro Station
9	Café Retiro

was considered so far from the main hotel district (along Av. de Mayo) that many assumed it would fail. History, of course, has proven that sentiment wrong, as numerous famous guests and royalty have stayed here. The facade of the hotel was renovated for its 100th anniversary.

Take a Break ☕

If you have the time, check out Marriott's Plaza Grill (p. 69) to get an idea of the old-style dining once common throughout the city. This spot has been a center of elite dining and socializing in Buenos Aires for nearly a century. Stop in for lunch or dinner, depending on when you are exploring. This is a full-service restaurant, so expect the meal to take longer than if you were running in for just a snack. Or grab a brandy on the rocks at the adjacent Plaza Bar, where local businesspeople often have strategy meetings.

Continue in the same direction around the plaza. Soon after Avenida Santa Fe hits the park, you'll see:

3 Círculo Militar & Palacio Paz

Perhaps the most beautiful of the Beaux Arts mansions in Buenos Aires, the Círculo Militar looks plucked from the Loire Valley. It was the home of the Paz family and took almost 12 years to build; the patriarch who commissioned it died before it was finished. The family owned the *La Prensa* newspaper. The Palacio Paz is now home to the Círculo Militar, an elite organization for retired military officers, which bought the building in 1938 when the Depression made keeping such a home a burden. The Museo de las Armas, which sheds light on the Islas Malvinas/Falkland Islands conflict, is also in the building.

Continue walking around the plaza to your right. Stop at the:

4 General José de San Martín Monument

This fantastic monument celebrates General José de San Martín, who battled against Spain in the wars of independence and is known as the founder of the Argentine nation. Though the monument was originally designed in 1862, it was expanded in 1900 into the over-the-top spectacle here. You'll see San Martín atop his horse in the middle on a raised platform, surrounded by soldiers and their women seeing them off before battle. The statue is a favorite hangout spot for the young, and it's where visiting dignitaries from other countries usually leave a ceremonial wreath. The best time to see this statue is in October and November, when the jacaranda trees are in full bloom. Unfortunately, many of the bronze plaques and wreaths were stolen when the price of copper skyrocketed in recent years. You can see some of their outlines in the granite base.

Turn around so that the statue of San Martín is to your back and cross the very wide Calle Maipú, being careful of traffic in this chaotic intersection. Walk up Calle Arenales, toward the grand marble building slightly to your right, which is known as the:

5 Palacio San Martín

Another of the grand mansions that line Plaza San Martín, this was the home of the powerful Anchorenas family whose prestige dated to colonial times in Argentina, and for whom the Avenida Anchorena is named. In 1936, the Ministry of Foreign Affairs took over the building, again largely as a result of Depression-era costs of running such a large home. From the street, you'll mostly be able to see its enormous French gates, although these do have intricate grillwork, which you can look through and see the large circular courtyard. The building is open periodically for free tours.

Retrace your steps from here, and head back to the Plaza San Martín, in front of the San Martín monument. Once you reach the plaza, turn to your left and continue walking forward through the expanse of the plaza, following the balustrade, until you come across a large set of stairs cascading down a hill. This is one of the favorite city tanning spots in warm weather. Try not to gawk too much at the bathing-suit-clad locals—you have other things to do! At the bottom of the stairs, to your right side, you'll come across the:

6 Islas Malvinas–Falkland Islands War Memorial

This monument honors the 700-plus Argentines who died in the brief war with Great Britain over the Islas Malvinas/Falkland Islands chain in early 1982. The war was treated as almost silly by most English-speaking countries, all of which sided with Great Britain, including the United States. Argentina lost the war, but became a democracy once again in the process. The war and sovereignty over the islands still remain sore points among Argentines, and it is best to treat these topics delicately in discussions. The three branches of the military, the army, navy, and air force, take turns guarding the monument and its eternal flame, and the changing of the guard is worth seeing.

Turn your back to the Islas Malvinas–Falkland Islands War Memorial and head to the crosswalk across Avenida Libertador. Carefully cross this very wide street and head to the middle of the plaza, to the:

7 Torre Monumental (British Clock Tower)

This 1916 gift from the British community in Buenos Aires, along with all other things British, was renamed in response to the Islas Malvinas/Falkland Islands War and is called the Argentine Big Ben by some. Decorated with British royal imperial symbols, the base was partly destroyed by an angry mob during an Islas Malvinas/Falkland Islands memorial service. Inside the tower, you'll find a small Buenos Aires City Tourism Information Office, as well as an elevator you can ride to the top for an excellent view of the city. The tower was placed here to celebrate the completion of the nearby Retiro Station, which was built with British technology.

Walk out of the Torre Monumental and walk to your left in the direction of the:

8 Retiro Station

The Retiro Station was opened in 1915 and built with the assistance of Great Britain. Four British architects designed it, and the steel structure was made in Liverpool and shipped to Argentina to be assembled there. For years, before the advent of the airplane, the station was the main entry point into Buenos Aires. It's still very busy, a hub for trains to the suburbs and the resort area of Tigre. The mint-green circular ticketing area is particularly distinctive, among the many interesting details in this station. The central hallway is enormous, and while some of the interior ornamentation has disappeared, you'll still see some bronze lighting fixtures adorning the walls.

A few other train stations are in this complex—Bartolomé Mitre and Manuel Belgrano among them, as well as the modern Retiro Station Bus Depot.

Enter the station and its main hall. Turn to the left and continue to the end of the hall. Look for signs to the left for the:

9 Café Retiro

This cafe opened in 1915 along with the station. For years, it sat empty, until it was reopened in 2003. Its interior is historically listed as one of the *cafés notables* protected by law in the city of Buenos Aires. The ornamentation includes massive bronze chandeliers, stained glass, and gilded columns. The kitchen is a branch of the chain Café Café, and the menu consists of simple, Argentine cafe fare, including coffee and pastries. Now is the time to take a break and celebrate completing this walk.

When you want to leave, the subway Retiro Station is just outside the door.

WALKING TOUR 3: PLAZA LAVALLE & THE TRIBUNALES AREA

GETTING THERE:	**Take the metro to Tribunales.**
START:	**Teatro Cervantes, overlooking Plaza Lavalle.**
FINISH:	**Obelisco.**
TIME:	**1½ hours; 3 to 4 hours if you go inside all buildings mentioned.**
BEST TIMES:	**Monday through Saturday between 11am and 4pm (not at night when things are closed).**

After languishing for years in a state of disrepair, the Plaza Lavalle area received a face-lift for the 2010 Bicentennial celebrations. The area represents the heart of the country's judicial system, taking its name from the Supreme Court, or Tribunales Building, which is the focus of the plaza. This was also one of the city's main theater districts before the widening of Avenida Corrientes in the 1930s. The majestic Teatro Cervantes and the world-famous Teatro Colón are a testament to the area's thespian grandeur. This tour is an easy walk and sidewalks are wheelchair accessible.

Start at the northeast corner of Libertad, where it hits Córdoba, at the:

1 Teatro Nacional Cervantes

This theater (p. 137), which opened in the 1920s, was the project of Spanish actors working in Buenos Aires. It went bankrupt, was bought by the government, and has since become a national theater. It is designed in a Spanish Imperial style with the Habsburg double eagles decorating the outside of the building. The sumptuous interior uses materials from Spain, such as imported carved-wood ornamentation and colorful Seville tiles, on many of the walls and surfaces.

Standing on Córdoba with the Teatro Cervantes behind you, cross Córdoba and walk along Libertad, stopping one building in at Libertad 785, site of the:

2 Templo Libertad & Jewish History Museum

This Byzantine-style temple was constructed in 1897 by CIRA (Congregación Israelita de la República de Argentina). Next door, you'll find the Jewish Museum, also known as the Kibrick Museum, which contains religious and historical items related to Buenos Aires's Jewish community. For more information on the temple and museum, see p. 123.

Continue to walk south along Libertad and cross Calle Viamonte. Stop at Libertad 621, between Viamonte and Tucumán, to see the:

3 Teatro Colón

The Teatro Colón first opened in 1908. It had taken more than 18 years to build, largely because of the dramatic tragedies that befell its various architects, especially Víctor Meano, who was murdered in a love triangle. Materials for the theater came from all over Europe, and the building functioned as Buenos Aires's overture to the world, proving that it was a city of culture to be reckoned with. Unfortunately, in a modern tragedy worthy of its own stage production, the much-touted multimillion-dollar renovation of the theater, intended to show it off for its 100th anniversary, fell years behind schedule. The theater finally reopened on May 24, 2010, but was still not technically complete. Even as of this writing, tours, a highlight of any visit to Buenos Aires, are not yet scheduled and ongoing union disputes have disrupted programming schedules. But if you're on this walk and the building is open, don't hesitate to go inside. Tours, if they resume, will allow you to see marble from all over the world lining the lobby and making up the grand staircase; the wooden and bronze seating area, which soars five levels to an immense chandelier; and the underground storage and practice areas where ballerinas rehearse.

Continue walking along Libertador and cross Calle Tucumán, stopping at the building on the corner, at Calle Libertad 581, site of the:

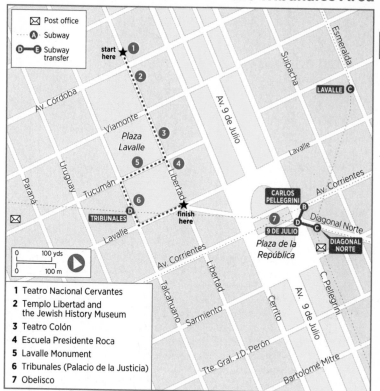

Key
- ⊠ Post office
- Ⓐ Subway
- Ⓓ—Ⓔ Subway transfer

1 Teatro Nacional Cervantes
2 Templo Libertad and the Jewish History Museum
3 Teatro Colón
4 Escuela Presidente Roca
5 Lavalle Monument
6 Tribunales (Palacio de la Justicia)
7 Obelisco

4 Escuela Presidente Roca

The employees of this beautiful 1904 Greek revival structure (p. 112) note that people often wander in thinking it's the Teatro Colón, and it's no wonder, given its Doric colonnade and ornamental statues along the central pediment. This is actually a local school, however. Technically, it's not open to the public, but polite people will be allowed in the courtyard and maybe even upstairs to see the beautiful ceiling with painted acanthus leaves.

Turn around so that the Escuela Presidente Roca is to your back, and face Plaza Libertad. Head to the column in the center of the plaza, the:

5 Lavalle Monument

As a very young man, Juan Lavalle fought along with San Martín in the wars for Argentine independence. He continued on in the Argentine military, rising to the rank of general. His statue, on a slender column, is the central focus of this plaza. Wander around the plaza, though, and take a look at the various other monuments. Be aware that an underground parking garage was built under the plaza, so you have to watch out for cars, especially at the corner of Libertad and Tucumán, where the entry ramp is located. Periodically, the Plaza is the site of protests.

Turn and walk to the southwest corner of the plaza to look at the enormous Supreme Court Building, also known as:

6 Tribunales (Palacio de la Justicia)

The Tribunales neighborhood takes its name from this building: the Supreme Court, or Tribunales building (also called the Palacio de la Justicia). It is immense and hulking, with obvious Greek architectural elements. The facade was cleaned and restored in 2008, though the sides of the building were somehow overlooked in the process. If you are here during the day, try to enter. The building used to be fully open to the public, but since the peso crisis and numerous protests, police barricades have often surrounded it; try to look like you have a reason to enter the building and you'll have a better chance of getting in. Inside, the central courtyard is lined with columns and pilasters. Ornamentation on the walls and between the columns includes symbols imitating the smiling sun from the center of the Argentine flag.

Turn your back to the Supreme Court building and walk east along the edge of the plaza. At the plaza's eastern end, look to your right toward the pedestrianized section of Diagonal Norte, also known as Avenida Roque Sáenz Peña, with a vista to Avenida 9 de Julio and the:

7 Obelisco

The Obelisco (p. 116) was inaugurated in 1936 in honor of the 400th anniversary of the first (unsuccessful) founding of the city by Pedro de Mendoza. (The second, permanent, founding was in 1580.) This towering 68m (223-ft.) structure marks the intersection of Avenida 9 de Julio and Corrientes. Diagonal Norte stretches behind the Obelisco, linking the Plaza de Mayo, at its southeast terminus, and the Tribunales, at its northwest terminus. The Obelisco sits in the oval Plaza de la República, once the site of Iglesia de San Nicolás, where the Argentine flag was first displayed on August 23, 1812, shortly after independence from Spain. This church, of course, was demolished to create the city's most iconic symbol, but an inscription on the north side of the Obelisco honors its noble sacrifice.

This pedestrianized area of Diagonal Norte is lined with cafes and little restaurants, so take a break here if you like. Otherwise, walk up toward the Obelisco itself. If Argentina has won an international event, join the flag-waving crowds here and cheer on the country. Underneath the Obelisco, you have access to three subway lines (B, C, and D), so it is easy to get back to hotels in many parts of the city from here.

WALKING TOUR 4: **AVENIDA DE MAYO TO CONGRESO**

GETTING THERE: **Take the metro to Bolívar, Perú, Catedral, or Plaza de Mayo.**

START: **Casa de Cultura, at Av. de Mayo 575.**

FINISH: **Plaza Congreso.**

TIME: **2 hours, 5 if buildings and museums are entered.**

BEST TIMES: **Monday through Saturday between 11am and 4pm (not at night when things are closed).**

Avenida de Mayo opened in 1894 and was meant to be the Gran Via or Champs-Elysées of Buenos Aires, full of lively cafes, theaters, and hotels. The design of the

Walking Tour 4: Avenida de Mayo to Congreso

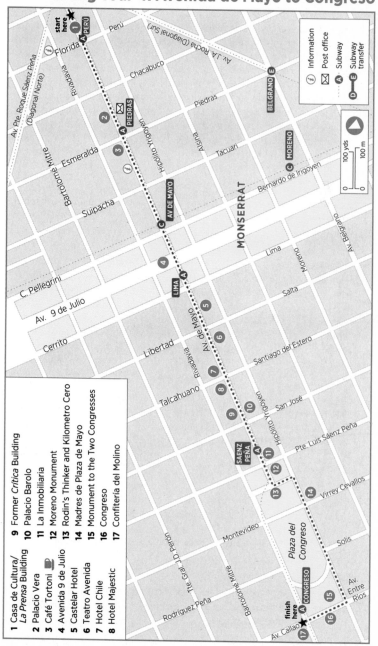

Legend:
- *i* Information
- ⊠ Post office
- Ⓐ Subway
- Ⓓ–Ⓔ Subway transfer

0 100 yds
0 100 m

MONSERRAT

1 Casa de Cultura/
La Prensa Building
2 Palacio Vera
3 Café Tortoni
4 Avenida 9 de Julio
5 Castelar Hotel
6 Teatro Avenida
7 Hotel Chile
8 Hotel Majestic
9 Former *Crítica* Building
10 Palacio Barolo
11 La Inmobiliaria
12 Moreno Monument
13 Rodin's Thinker and Kilometro Cero
14 Madres de Plaza de Mayo
15 Monument to the Two Congresses
16 Congreso
17 Confitería del Molino

start here

finish here

Plaza del Congreso

street was just one early part of an even grander plan to rebuild Buenos Aires in preparation for the 1910 Independence Centennial and to declare to the world that Buenos Aires was a city to be reckoned with. Some of the greatest concentrations of Beaux Arts and Art Nouveau buildings in the city are along this route, which connects Plaza de Mayo in the east to Congreso in the west. This is the historical processional route both for grand parades and for when people have something to protest to the president and to Congress. While many buildings along this route are badly in need of repair, others have recently been renovated as the tourism boom brought more attention to this area. It is not hard to imagine how glorious this street must have been in its heyday at the beginning of the 20th century. With the emphasis on Palermo Soho in most travel articles, many tourists are now ignoring this area, but it should not be overlooked on a visit to Buenos Aires.

This tour is an easy walk, but long distances (about 2.4km/1½ miles) are covered. Most sidewalks are wheelchair accessible, but pavement is broken in places. Also, note that you'll be crossing the wide Avenida 9 de Julio, which can take two to three traffic-light cycles for pedestrians to cross; be extra careful with children.

Start just in from the northeastern corner of Avenida de Mayo and San Martín, at Av. de Mayo 575, site of the:

1 Casa de Cultura/La Prensa Building

Once the home of the newspaper *La Prensa,* owned by the very wealthy and powerful Paz family, this building is simply sumptuous, with carved granite, bronze ornamentation, and sinuous lanterns among its most striking features. Now home to the Casa de Cultura (the Office of Culture for the City of Buenos Aires; p. 99), it is open for tours on the weekend. The tour is a must-do if you have the time. If you don't, at least enter the building and take a peek at the lobby to get an idea of its splendor.

With the Casa de Cultura to your back, turn right and continue moving along Avenida de Mayo in a western direction. Cross Calle Perú and Calle Maipú and stop at Av. de Mayo 769, location of the:

2 Palacio Vera

One of the best examples of Art Nouveau along Avenida de Mayo, the details along its balconies are the most interesting part of the Palacio Vera facade. Now made up of businesses and apartments, it was designed as the home for the Díaz Vélez family, who gained prominence at the beginning of the 1800s, just before independence. If the El Ventanal bookstore is open, pop in for its unique collection of antique books and historical front pages for important Argentine events.

Continue walking along Avenida de Mayo, cross Calle Esmeralda, and stop when you've reached Av. de Mayo 825, home of the:

3 Café Tortoni

As the city's most famous cafe (p. 198), this establishment has been graced by numerous political, intellectual, and historic figures from Argentina and around the world. There are tango shows here, but the real treat is the ornate interior of the building itself. Above the cafe is the office of the National Tango Academy, which also offers lessons. I have found recently that with the enormous surge of tourists to Buenos Aires, the door attendant will sometimes limit or refuse entry to foreigners who just want a peek inside the building. If you have a hard time getting in, come back at a less busy time, such as early morning or in the late evening, or better yet, come in for real, sit down, and enjoy a cup of coffee here.

Take a Break 🍵

As long as you're here, you might as well sample the atmosphere and have a bite to eat. Don't expect excellent service, as the waiters seem to ignore the customers. Still, the food is inexpensive, and a tea or coffee with croissants, known here as *medialunas,* makes an excellent snack and will rejuvenate you for the second half of your walk.

Continue walking along Avenida de Mayo to the world's widest boulevard:

4 Avenida 9 de Julio

It will probably take you a few traffic-light cycles to cross this massive street. Construction on 9 de Julio began in the 1930s, and it was officially completed in 1937. Expansion, however, continued for decades, up through the 1960s. Unfortunately, during the construction of this boulevard, much of the city's beautiful turn-of-the-20th-century architectural heritage was lost. The avenue got a makeover in 2006, when new flowers, plants, sidewalks, brighter lighting, and street furniture were added. Spend some time wandering this stretch of the avenida; be sure to see the fountains and the Don Quixote monument inaugurated by Queen Sofía of Spain.

Cross Avenida 9 de Julio completely, and continue on to Av. de Mayo 1152, location of the:

5 Castelar Hotel

One of the jewels of Avenida de Mayo, this hotel opened in 1929. One of its most notable features is its extensive Turkish bath on its basement level; it's worth stopping in to get a treatment or just to view the space. The Castelar (p. 45) has a strong association with Spanish literary giant Federico García Lorca, who lived here for many months. His room has been converted into a miniature museum. The eccentric Italian architect Mario Palanti, who also designed the nearby **Palacio Barolo** (p. 108), designed the Castelar.

Continue walking along Avenida de Mayo and cross Calle Salta to Av. de Mayo 1222, site of the:

6 Teatro Avenida

This theater, opened in 1908, is largely dedicated to Spanish productions. It presented material by Lorca when he was living in the Castelar down the street in the 1930s. Many other artists from Spain also had work presented here at the time, and the theater was an integral part of making Buenos Aires the center of Spanish-language culture while Spain was engaged in civil war. After a fire in the 1970s, it was partially rebuilt.

Cross Avenida de Mayo and head to the corner of Santiago del Estero, to the:

7 Hotel Chile

This is a very unique Art Nouveau hotel with Middle Eastern elements. Take special note of the windows, with their round tops and faience ornamental tiling. The hotel was designed by the French architect Louis Dubois and opened in 1907. Like many other hotels on Avenida de Mayo, Hotel Chile was once luxurious and the utmost in style, but has since become rather dilapidated, with its facade the only hint of its former glory.

Cross Santiago del Estero, staying on Avenida de Mayo, and stop immediately on the corner of the next block to see the:

8 Hotel Majestic

Opened in 1910 in time for the Centennial celebrations, this is one of the city's most renowned hotels, though it no longer operates as one. Most Porteños point to it with extreme pride as the place where Infanta Isabel stayed to represent Spain at the celebrations. It was also where the Russian ballet star Vaclav Nijinsky spent his wedding night after getting married in Buenos Aires in 1913. The lobby is sumptuous but extremely dark and badly in need of repair. As one of the most prominent buildings on Avenida de Mayo, it is currently undergoing a long-delayed renovation. Technically, it is no longer open to the public, but if you ask politely, you might be allowed to peek at the lobby.

Continue walking along Avenida de Mayo and stop at the next building, no. 1333, home of the:

9 Former Crítica Building

Ornate Art Deco buildings are a rarity in Buenos Aires, which did not take to the style in the same way as New York, Los Angeles, and Paris. The Crítica Building, however, is one of the best that you'll find in the city. Take note of the windows, with their faceted frames, and the statues adorning the facade. The building was originally opened in 1926 for the *Crítica* newspaper, for which Argentine literary giant Jorge Luis Borges had worked. The building is not generally open to the public. Until very recently it served as the police headquarters, and it is now an office building.

Stay on this block but walk across the street to Av. de Mayo 1370 to reach the:

10 Palacio Barolo

This, in my opinion, is the most unusual building in all of Buenos Aires (p. 108). Designed by the eccentric Italian architect Mario Palanti, who also designed the nearby Hotel Castelar, this building is meant to recall Dante's *Inferno*. The lobby symbolizes Hell, with its bronze medallions representing fire and male and female dragons lining the walls. The scale of the 1923 building is massive; in fact, it was once the tallest building in South America, though Palanti later designed a similar, taller structure in Montevideo. A statue of Dante, meant to hold his ashes, was created for the lobby, but was never delivered. It was re-created by artist Amelia Jorio and placed in the lobby in 2010. (It will never hold the ashes as Italy will not send them.) The facade was restored in 2007. Guided tours take you through the building to the lighthouse tower representing God and Salvation, from where you'll get an excellent view up and down Avenida de Mayo and to other parts of the city (p. 22).

Continue walking along Avenida de Mayo and cross Calle San José. Stay on this block (btw. San José and Luis Sáenz Peña) and take in:

11 La Inmobiliaria

Taking up this entire block, La Inmobiliaria was designed as the office for a real estate and apartment agency. Today, it houses apartments and offices, but the tiled Art Nouveau sign indicating its former use still remains along the top of the facade. The building's most distinctive features are the matching corner towers, which form a kind of endpoint to Avenida de Mayo before it flows into Plaza Congreso.

Continue walking along Avenida de Mayo, crossing into Plaza Congreso, to see the:

12 Moreno Monument

This statue, in a part of Plaza Congreso that's overgrown with large trees, is of Mariano Moreno, the secretary of the First Government Assembly following independence from Spain. He was also an important journalist who founded both the Argentine National Library and the *Buenos Aires Gazette*. Moreno is memorialized elsewhere in the city, with a street and subway stop.

Turn around and with Moreno behind you, walk forward to the central walk in the middle of the plaza. Then turn to the left and walk to the next statue:

13 Rodin's The Thinker & Kilometro Cero

This is a copy of Rodin's famous statue *The Thinker,* and it's a favorite play area for children. Just next to it is a block marking Kilometro Cero, the point at which all distances from Buenos Aires are marked.

Continue walking through the plaza, but veer toward your left. Cross Calle Yrigoyen and head to Yrigoyen 1584, near the corner of Ceballos, home base of the:

14 Madres de Plaza de Mayo

The Madres de Plaza de Mayo (p. 108), who march every Thursday at 3:30pm in the Plaza de Mayo in honor of their missing children, have their main headquarters here. They also run a university, library, a very left-wing bookstore with many books on Che Guevara, and a small cafe on the premises. It's worth taking the time to enter and linger here, and maybe have a coffee or a snack. You might also get a chance to talk with one of the by now very old Madres about this heart-wrenching period in Argentina's history, when nearly 30,000 young people were tortured and killed by the military government.

Cross the street and head back into Plaza Congreso, heading toward the enormous no-longer-functional fountain in front of Congreso itself, to view the:

15 Monument to the Two Congresses

Quite a confection of marble and bronze, this enormous monument celebrates the two congresses that were held in the aftermath of independence from Spain to lay out the foundations for the new nation of Argentina. This multilevel structure has stairs that lead to a fantastic view of Congreso, where you can snap pictures of the building or pose with it behind you. The fountain underwent an extensive renovation in 2007. A fence now surrounds the fountain to protect it from vandals, which is only intermittently opened. Ask the guard politely if it is locked. As it is an area where many homeless live, it is not advisable to wander the park and fountain area at night.

Leave the Two Congresses monument and walk toward the Congreso building. Cross the street, being very careful at this extremely busy intersection, and head to the:

16 Congreso

The most imposing building in all of Buenos Aires (p. 106), this structure opened in 1906. It combines influences from some of the world's most famous structures, from the U.S. Capitol to Berlin's Brandenburg Gate. Made of massive blocks of granite, the walls are over 1.8m (6 ft.) thick at their base. Tours will take you through both chambers of the bicameral legislature and are available if you ask at the Rivadavia entrance.

With Congreso at your back, turn left (north) and continue up Callao. Cross Calle Rivadavia and stop on the corner to view the:

17 Confitería del Molino

This fantastic structure (p. 137), now in a terrible state of disrepair and closed to the public, was the creation of Francesco Gianotti, an Italian who also designed Galería Güemes and its theater housing the Piazzolla tango show. Once the informal meeting place of politicians from the nearby Congreso, the cafe closed in 1997, though for years there have been plans to renovate and reopen it. Primarily an Art Nouveau structure, stained glass and ornate tile work were once part of the ornamentation here, but these have been covered by tarps to prevent rain damage and further deterioration of the facade. The main visible feature from the street is the windmill top (*molino* means "windmill" in Spanish).

Congratulations, you have finished this walking tour! I recommend you keep walking north along Avenida Callao, which was rebuilt in an almost imperial style after the opening of Congreso. Congreso has a subway stop for the A line, and the C and D lines have nearby stops along Callao.

WALKING TOUR 5: **AVENIDA ALVEAR**

GETTING THERE: **There are no real public transportation options, so a taxi is best.**

START: **The Alvear Palace Hotel.**

FINISH: **The Four Seasons Mansion.**

TIME: **1 hour, provided you don't get caught up shopping.**

BEST TIMES: **Monday through Saturday between 11am and 8pm (not at night when things are closed).**

You may have to be wealthy to do your shopping on Avenida Alvear, but you don't need a penny to walk on it. In this tour, I'll touch on the architectural highlights of this exclusive area and only briefly on the shopping. I'll leave that up to you for later. Unlike most walks where the numbers go up, you'll be proceeding down in the numbering system as you follow this tour along Avenida Alvear. This tour is an easy walk and a short distance. However, not all the streets have cutouts for wheelchairs, and there are also some gently sloping hills.

Begin at Av. Alvear 1891, at the intersection of Ayacucho, site of the:

1 Alvear Palace Hotel

This is the most famous hotel in Buenos Aires (p. 48), and certainly its most elegant. Opened in 1928 and built in a French neoclassical style, the lobby is a gilded marble confection, and the central dining area, known as L'Orangerie, resembles the Palm Court in New York's Plaza Hotel. I highly suggest taking the time for the hotel's brunch buffet. While expensive by Argentine standards ($41–$71 per person), it is a relative bargain compared to a similar setting in Europe or North America. Attached to the hotel is a shopping gallery full of exclusive art and bridal shops.

Walking Tour 5: Avenida Alvear

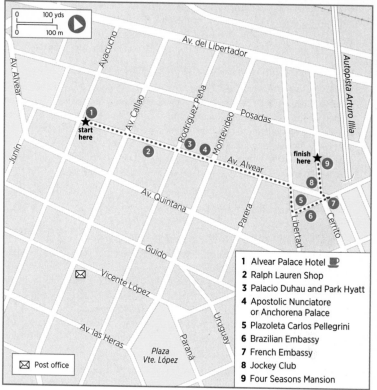

1 Alvear Palace Hotel ☕
2 Ralph Lauren Shop
3 Palacio Duhau and Park Hyatt
4 Apostolic Nunciatore
   or Anchorena Palace
5 Plazoleta Carlos Pellegrini
6 Brazilian Embassy
7 French Embassy
8 Jockey Club
9 Four Seasons Mansion

☒ Post office

Walk out of the Alvear Palace Hotel and with the hotel to your back, cross Avenida Alvear, turn to your left, and then cross Calle Callao before heading to Av. Alvear 1750, home to the:

2 Polo Ralph Lauren Shop

Shop here if you want, but I recommend taking a look at the building of this Polo Ralph Lauren store, one of the most exquisite of all the shops on this street. It was once a small Art Nouveau mansion. Within the interior, much of the ornate and heavy wood decoration remains, with a stained-glass skylight over the central staircase.

Cross to the opposite side of Avenida Alvear and continue along it in the same direction. Cross Calle Peña and stop at Av. Alvear 1661, location of the:

3 Palacio Duhau and Park Hyatt

The Palacio Duhau was the spectacular home of the Duhau family, built at the beginning of the 20th century. It is now part of the Park Hyatt Buenos Aires, which maintains an entrance through this building as well as in the new tower built behind on Calle Posadas. The family was involved in the Ministry of Agriculture, and many of the decorations of the building use agricultural elements such as wheat, corn, and cow heads. The Hyatt has worked well in restoring these elements, along with adding modern materials. Be sure to walk inside and take a look at the Piano Nobile or library room off the lobby, with its decorations mimicking Versailles, or the Oak Bar, with its paneling taken from a medieval French castle. The back garden leads to the new building and is a place for tea for the ladies-who-lunch crowd as well as business executives.

Continue walking down Avenida Alvear until you get to no. 1637, the:

4 Apostolic Nunciatore, or Anchorena Palace

Though originally built for the wealthy Anchorena family, they never lived in this magnificent French-style mansion with its distinctive circular front. The next owner wanted to give the building to the Vatican, but the local representative felt it was too ostentatious and refused to live in it at the time. The papal insignia, a papal tiara over a pair of keys, is on the building. It remains owned by the Catholic Church.

Continue walking for 2 more blocks until you reach a widening of the street and a small plaza with a statue and fountain, the:

5 Plazoleta Carlos Pellegrini

I think this is one of the most beautiful of all the small plazas in Buenos Aires, not just for the plaza itself, but also for the buildings that surround it. A large, recently restored statue of Carlos Pellegrini, a famous intellectual and industrialist and president of Argentina in the early 1900s, sits in the center of this plaza. The statue was created in France by Félix Coutan and dedicated in 1914. A small fountain and a bench add to the relaxed environment. This plaza is the most Parisian-appearing part of Recoleta, and it gives an idea of all that was lost when Buenos Aires decided to widen Avenida 9 de Julio in the 1960s, destroying other little corners of the city that were similar to this one.

With the plaza to your back, turn to your right and cross Calle Arroyo, heading to Arroyo 1130, site of the:

6 Brazilian Embassy

First, a note about the name of this street. *Arroyo* means "stream" in Spanish and one once flowed here until it was filled in as the city developed. The Brazilian Embassy, one of the city's most beautiful embassies, is one of the two most impressive structures overlooking this plaza. Known also as the Palacio Pereda, in honor of its original owner Doctor Celedonio Pereda, it took almost 20 years to build and has details borrowed from the Palais Fontainebleau in France. It was originally designed by the French architect Louis Martin and finished by the Belgian architect Julio Dormal.

With the Brazilian Embassy behind you, turn to your right, cross Calle Cerrito, and stop once you reach the other side. Be aware that this odd intersection has a confusing traffic pattern, so be careful when crossing to see the:

7 French Embassy

It's hard to believe when you see this beautiful structure, but the plans for the expansion of Avenida 9 de Julio originally included demolition of this building. Fortunately, the French government refused to give up the building, and it now serves as the vista point for the northern terminus of Avenida 9 de Julio. Created by the French architect Pablo Pater, it became the French Embassy in 1939.

The building is a beautiful example of Beaux Arts, and you should take note of the main dome and the grillwork on the surrounding fence. You'll notice *trompe l'oeil* mansard roofs and windows on some of the surfaces of the surrounding modern buildings, an attempt to give an impression of the once surrounding Belle Epoque buildings that were demolished to make way for the expansion of Avenida 9 de Julio.

With the Obelisco on Avenida 9 de Julio to your back, cross Arroyo and Cerrito, stopping at the corner, where you'll find the:

8 Jockey Club

Carlos Pellegrini, whose statue sits across the street in the plaza out front, started the Jockey Club in 1882 along with other like-minded equestrians. The Jockey Club became a major part of the social networking scene for the wealthy and powerful of Argentina. The Jockey Club's original Calle Florida headquarters were burned to the ground on April 15, 1953, after a Perón-provoked riot against this elite institution. Perón seized the assets of the organization, but it was able to regroup in 1958 a few years after he had been thrown out of power. This current building was once the mansion of the Uzué de Casares family, and the organization moved here in 1966. It is not open to the public, but its interior is full of tapestries, works of art, and a library.

Walk back across Cerrito, walking only for a few feet toward the immense tower a block down, and stop when you get to Calle Cerrito 1455, site of the:

9 Four Seasons Mansion

The official name of this Louis XIII–style redbrick palace with heavy quoins is Mansión Alzaga Unzue. It was built in 1919 and was given three facades, anticipating the eventual construction of Avenida 9 de Julio to the east of the building. It was designed with an extensive garden complex in front of its northern facade. The mansion is now part of the Four Seasons Hotel, and it is attached to the main tower through a garden courtyard. The tower sits on what were once the mansion's gardens. Some Porteños can still recall the tragic day when the trees here were cut down to make way for the tower. The tower and the mansion were formerly the Park Hyatt until the Four Seasons purchased the property. (A new Park Hyatt has reopened close by.) Renting the entire mansion is the ultimate in luxury, and it's often here where stars party in Buenos Aires. When Madonna filmed the movie *Evita*, she used the mansion's balcony to practice her "Don't Cry for Me, Argentina" scenes as mobs gathered on the street out front trying to catch a glimpse.

Congratulations, you've finished another tour. There are no nearby metro stations, but there are plenty of cabs in the area that can get you wherever you want to go next.

SHOPPING

Throughout South America, Buenos Aires is famous for its shopping. You'll find it in glitzy malls, along major shopping thoroughfares, and in small boutiques and little out-of-the-way stores. Buenos Aires is most famous for its high-quality leather goods, which, since Argentina is a beef-loving country, should come as no surprise. You won't find as many native crafts here, however, as you will in other South American capitals.

Argentina's peso crisis spawned an interesting trend: With Argentina's inability to import designer fashion items, demand for locally made items increased, and creative-minded local boutiques were able to expand and flourish. In particular, you'll find a wealth of young designers catering to the young-women's market, offering unique, feminine, and funky fashions. While not the bargain they once were, most items are still reasonably priced compared to their European and North American counterparts. Antique shops, especially in San Telmo, are also a famous part of the Buenos Aires shopping scene.

Many Buenos Aires stores, particularly those catering to tourists, also allow for tax-free shopping. You'll know them by the blue-and-white logo on the door; ask if you don't see one. Leather-goods stores are exceptionally well versed in the process, and it is part of the sales spiel. For more details on this process, see the "Hours, Shipping & Taxes" box below. You can save even more money by looking for the Groupon offers that are posted on some of the websites of stores we list.

Look for the **Mapas de Buenos Aires** shopping map series (www.mapasbsas.com) as well as the **GO Palermo** (www.gopalermo.com.ar) shopping booklet at your hotel and tourism kiosks. **DeDios** has an excellent laminated shopping map, available at Buenos Aires bookstores and online at **www.dediosonline.com** and **www.amazon.com**. To help you make sense of it all, a number of tour guides specialize in shopping tours, like Argentine native **Julieta Caracoche** who runs **Al Tuntunno Tours** (✆ **11/15-4197-238** [cell]; www.altuntunno.com). Look also for fashion articles in the English-language publications *Buenos Aires Herald* (www.buenosairesherald.com), or *The Argentina Independent* (www.argentinaindependent.com).

THE SHOPPING SCENE
Major Shopping Areas

Buenos Aires has many shopping areas, but the following places are where you'll find most of the action.

MICROCENTRO   Calle Florida, the Microcentro's main pedestrian thoroughfare, is home to wall-to-wall shops from Plaza San Martín all the way past Avenida Corrientes. As you approach Plaza San Martín from Calle Florida, you'll find a number of well-regarded shoe stores, jewelers, and shops selling leather goods. Most stores here are decidedly middle class, and some clearly cater to locals and carry things you'd never buy. However, if you're looking for basic items such as converters and extension cords, you'll find what you need here. Calle Lavalle is also pedestrianized. The **Galerías Pacífico** mall is the epicenter of shopping in this area (p. 168).

AVENIDA CORDOBA   Looking for off-season bargains? Then the 3000 block of Avenida Córdoba, in the area bordering Barrio Norte and Palermo, is the place to head. Best of all, off season in Argentina is usually the right season in the Northern Hemisphere, so you can wear your purchases as soon as you get back home.

AVENIDA SANTA FE   Popular with local shoppers, Avenida Santa Fe has a wide selection of clothing stores with down-to-earth prices typical of stores catering to the local middle class. You will also find bookstores, cafes, ice-cream shops, and cinemas here. The **Alto Palermo Shopping Center,** Av. Santa Fe 3253 at Bulnes (© **11/5777-8000;** www.altopalermo.com.ar), is another excellent shopping center, with 155 stores open daily from 10am to 10pm.

PALERMO VIEJO   Everything old is new again in Palermo Viejo, further divided into Palermo Hollywood and Palermo Soho. Lots of young designers have opened boutiques in this area, or they combine forces on weekends around Plaza Serrano, when restaurants fold up tables and the area is filled with clothing racks. As a rule, shopping here is best for women, but men's fashion is definitely catching up.

RECOLETA   Avenida Alvear is an elegant, Parisian-like strip of European boutiques and cafes. Start your walk from Plaza Francia across from Recoleta Cemetery and continue past the Alvear Palace Hotel, along to the French Embassy at Cerrito (Av. 9 de Julio) for one exclusive shop after another, many in French-style mansions. Avenida Quintana provides a similar atmosphere. Nearby, **Patio Bullrich,** Av. del Libertador 750, between Montevideo and Libertad (also entered at Posadas 1245; © **11/4814-7400;** www.shoppingbullrich.com.ar), is one of the city's most famous and upscale malls. Its 68 shops are open daily from 10am to 9pm. It has an excellent food court, too, and is a good place to stop for a snack.

SAN TELMO & LA BOCA   These neighborhoods have excellent antiques as well as artists' studios and arts and crafts that celebrate tango. Street performers and artists are omnipresent, especially on weekends. La Boca should be avoided at night, however.

Outdoor Markets

One of the pleasures of Buenos Aires is its open-air markets (called *mercados*) or fairs (*ferias*), many of which combine shopping with entertainment. The bargains you'll find are often accompanied by the wonderful, romantic sights and sounds of tango. I've listed below just a few of the many open-air markets you can find all over the city.

The **San Telmo Antiques Fair ★★,** which takes place every Sunday from 10am to 5pm, and later in summer, at Plaza Dorrego and spilling onto Calle Defensa, is a vibrant, colorful experience that will delight even the most jaded traveler, and has also become a place among locals to meet, befriend, and flirt with tourists. As street vendors sell their heirlooms, singers and dancers move amid the crowd to tango music. Among the hundreds of vendor stands, you'll find antique silversmith objects, porcelain, crystal, and other antiques. The fair is especially famous for tango performances

Buenos Aires Shopping

Altel **31**
Aristocracia **8**
Ashanti Leather Factory **37**
Asunto Impreso **56**
Buenos Aires Design Recoleta **1**
Cabildo Patio Feria **49**
Casa López **26**
C-Disueria **23**
Chabeli **53**
Clara Ibarguren **15**
Clásica y Moderna **20**
Cosentino **43**
Cousiño Jewels **24**
Distal Libros **40**
El Ateneo (Grand Splendid) **18**
El Boyero **30**
El Nochero **10**
Ermenegildo Zegna **3**
Escada **11**
Estación Sur **33**
Falabella (Department Store) **45**

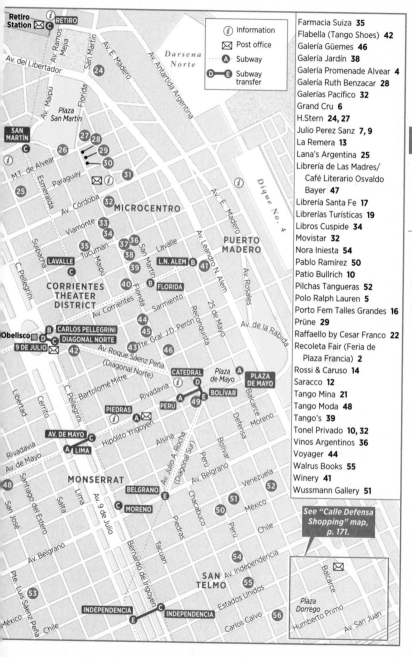

Farmacia Suiza **35**
Flabella (Tango Shoes) **42**
Galería Güemes **46**
Galería Jardín **38**
Galería Promenade Alvear **4**
Galería Ruth Benzacar **28**
Galerías Pacífico **32**
Grand Cru **6**
H.Stern **24, 27**
Julio Perez Sanz **7, 9**
La Remera **13**
Lana's Argentina **25**
Librería de Las Madres/
  Café Literario Osvaldo
  Bayer **47**
Librería Santa Fe **17**
Librerías Turísticas **19**
Libros Cuspide **34**
Movistar **32**
Nora Iniesta **54**
Pablo Ramírez **50**
Patio Bullrich **10**
Pilchas Tangueras **52**
Polo Ralph Lauren **5**
Porto Fem Talles Grandes **16**
Prüne **29**
Raffaello by Cesar Franco **22**
Recoleta Fair (Feria de
  Plaza Francia) **2**
Rossi & Caruso **14**
Saracco **12**
Tango Mina **21**
Tango Moda **48**
Tango's **39**
Tonel Privado **10, 32**
Vinos Argentinos **36**
Voyager **44**
Walrus Books **55**
Winery **41**
Wussmann Gallery **51**

*See "Calle Defensa
Shopping" map,
p. 171.*

SHOPPING tips: HOURS, SHIPPING & TAXES

Most stores are open on weekdays from 9am to 8pm and Saturday from 9am until midnight, some closing for a few hours in the afternoon. You might find some shops open on Sunday along Avenida Santa Fe, but few will be open on Calle Florida. Shopping centers are open daily from 10am to 10pm.

Certain art and antiques dealers will crate and ship bulky objects for an additional fee; others will tell you it's no problem to take that new sculpture directly on the plane. If you don't want to take any chances, contact UPS at ☏ **800/222-2877** or Federal Express at ☏ **810/333-3339.**

Various stores participate in a tax-refund program for purchases costing more than 70 pesos. Ask for a special receipt, which can entitle you to a refund of the hefty 21% tax (IVA) when you leave the country. Most of these stores have blue-and-white TAX FREE signs, but always ask when making a purchase. The process is this: The store

will provide you with a special Global Refund check form that indicates the value of what you will get back when you leave the country. You must have this special form, which participating stores will create for purchases costing more than 70 pesos, to get a refund. Some restrictions do apply, however. The item has to have been made in Argentina and purchased with the intention of taking it out of the country (so food does not qualify). The system is used mostly for clothing and leather goods, but you should ask about it whenever making a purchase, even if you do not see the sign. Upon leaving the country, have all of these checks ready and look for the Global Refund desk. At Ezeiza airport, it is located in the immigrations area just before you have your passport stamped to leave the country. For more information, check the website **www.global-blue. com**, and choose Argentina under the selection of countries.

that can go on into the late evening, even if most of the vendors themselves close up at 5pm. The star of the show is Pedro Benavente, the tall, dark, handsome dancer known as "El Indio," and you'll see his photos on sale throughout the city. This fair alone is worth scheduling a Sunday in San Telmo. More information can be found at **www.feriadesantelmo.com**.

Head to **Cabildo Patio Feria** when sightseeing in the Plaza de Mayo area. This fair is held on Thursday and Friday from 11am to 6pm in the small garden patio behind the Cabildo, or old city hall. You'll find lots of locally made crafts here, especially pottery, stained glass, and jewelry.

Considered the most authentic of the outdoor *ferias* in Buenos Aires, the **Feria de Mataderos** (☏ **11/4342-9629** or 11/4687-5602; www.feriademataderos.com.ar), also known as the Traditions and Artisans Fair, takes place April to December every Sunday from 11am to 8pm, and January to March Saturdays 6pm to 1am on the streets surrounding the intersection of Avenida de los Corales and Avenida Lisandro De La Torre. *Mataderos*, the name of the Buenos Aires neighborhood where it's held, literally means "slaughterhouses." This area still houses many of them, adding a genuine gaucho feel. The fair is full of music, dancing, and crafts.

Friday to Sunday from 11am to 6pm, the Madres (p. 108) hold the **Feria de Madres de Plaza de Mayo** in front of their headquarters overlooking Plaza Congreso. Children will also enjoy coming here, as it is next to the park's merry-go-round and other rides. The fair has antiques, crafts, food, and book vendors. Sometimes there is also live music. This is among the most casual and least touristy of all of the fairs, so it provides a chance to chat with locals while supporting a good cause.

The **La Boca Fair** is open every day from 10am to 6pm or sundown on the Caminito, the pedestrianized and art-filled thoroughfare in the heart of this neighborhood. It's the most touristy of all the fairs, and most of the items are terribly overpriced. Still, if you need tacky souvenirs in a hurry, you'll quickly get it done here. Tango singers and other street performers will keep your mind off the inflated prices. Safety has improved in La Boca, but tourists should leave the area at night when the police leave and the shops have closed.

Plaza Serrano Fair ★★ is at the small plaza at the intersection of Calle Serrano and Honduras, which forms the heart of Palermo Hollywood. Bohemian arts and crafts are sold here while dreadlocked locals sing and play guitars. Officially, the fair is held Saturday and Sunday from 10am to 6pm, but impromptu vendors will also set up at night when the restaurants are crowded. Those very same restaurants will fold up their tables in the afternoon and fill the spaces with clothing racks for young designers who cannot afford their own boutiques. It's definitely worth a visit. Plaza Serrano is also sometimes called by its official name, **Plazaleto Jorge Cortazar.**

Recoleta Fair (Feria de Plaza Francia) ★★, which takes place Saturday and Sunday in front of Recoleta Cemetery from 10am until sunset, offers every imaginable souvenir and type of craft, in addition to food. This has become one of the city's largest fairs, completely taking over all the walkways and then some in the area, and even the Iglesia Pilar, Recoleta Cemetery's church, gets involved by setting up tables of postcards and religious souvenirs in its courtyard. Live bands sometimes play on whatever part of the hill is left vacant by vendors.

Major Shopping Malls & Department Stores

Here are some of the city's best indoor shopping centers. Some, like Galerías Pacífico, are tourist sites in their own right because of their architectural beauty. Even if shopping's not your bag, **Galerías Pacífico** is not to be missed. The **Abasto Shopping Center** is a great place to bring the kids, with its **Museo de los Niños** in the food court. Until recently, something that made the shopping experience here very different from North America and Europe was a lack of department stores. However, **Falabella,** the Chilean chain, opened up in 2006 in Buenos Aires with a large store on Calle Florida. Still, most shopping centers are a collection of smaller stores and chains, some uniquely Argentine, others South American—and some that you won't find anywhere else in the world. Most shopping malls are open daily from 10am to 10pm, with exceptions noted below.

Abasto Shopping Center ★★ ☺   The Abasto Shopping Center is one of the largest in Buenos Aires. The 1934 structure was built over the original 1893 market, a place famous for where tango crooner Carlos Gardel got his start, singing as a child to the fruit and meat vendors. They would give him a few centavos to entertain them, and from this humble beginning, his fame spread. Only a classical stone arch outside of the main market is left from the earlier structure. The Art Deco building was converted into a mall in 1998 with several levels of shopping, aimed at the middle and upper-middle class. It's a great place to bring kids, with its extensive food court, enormous arcades with video games, and especially the very fun **Museo de Los Niños,** located in the food court (p. 121). As Abasto was one of Buenos Aires's main Jewish neighborhoods, you'll also find the only kosher McDonald's in the world outside of Israel (p. 94). There is also a large cinema complex here. The food court and cinemas here are open later than 10pm. For a map of this shopping center, see the

"Abasto & Once" map on p. 95. Av. Corrientes 3247 (at Agüero). *11/4959-3400.* www.abasto-shopping.com.ar. Metro: Gardel.

Alto Palermo   Located on Santa Fe in the Barrio Norte shopping area, Alto Palermo has several floors of shopping, with about 155 stores and services. This mall is significantly less touristy than the Galerías Pacífico. The mall's design is not very straightforward and the connections between levels can be confusing. If you're shopping with children, this is a place where they can easily get lost. Av. Santa Fe 3253 and Coronel Díaz. *11/5777-8000.* www.altopalermo.com.ar. Metro: Agüero.

Buenos Aires Design Recoleta ★★   This is one of my favorite malls in Buenos Aires, and home-design connoisseurs should head here immediately. Small, elegant, and set behind the Recoleta Cemetery, it houses several home-design stores selling high-quality, high-design items, almost all produced in Argentina. Ironically, the peso crisis created more opportunities for local designers, as importing goods from overseas became too expensive. The mall is both indoors and outdoors, with the outdoor section called "La Terrazza," though some call it "Los Arcos" because of the archways lining this area. It's a pleasant place to relax and have a coffee after seeing the nearby cemetery. There are often changing sculpture exhibits in the gardens. Hours are Monday through Saturday from 10am to 9pm, Sunday and holidays from noon to 9pm. Av. Pueyrredón 2501 (at Libertador). *11/5777-6000.* www.designrecoleta.com.ar. No metro access.

Falabella   This Chilean department store chain opened its most visible Buenos Aires location in 2006 at Calle Florida 202 at the intersection of Perón. It also now has a home goods branch at Calle Florida 343 in the former Galería Mitre, and another store at Calle Florida 665. Between the three stores, you'll find everything you would find in any department store—cosmetics; jewelry; clothing for men, women, and children; home goods; luxury goods; furniture; and even cellular phones. It's open Monday to Saturday 9am to 9pm, and Sundays noon to 9pm. Calle Florida 202 (at Perón). *11/5950-5000* or 0810/555-3252. www.falabella.com. Metro: Florida.

Galerías Pacífico ★★★   Located on Calle Florida, the pedestrian walking street in the Microcentro, the Galerías Pacífico is probably the most famous mall in Buenos Aires. Architecturally, it is stunning, designed to recall the Galleria Vittorio Emanuele II in Milan, with its long halls, glass cupola, and several tiers of shops. First opened in 1891, in 1945 its main dome was covered with stunning frescoes painted by local artists. There are more than 180 shops here, and they offer a free service whereby all your purchases can be sent to your hotel, so you can shop without having to schlep. But Galerías Pacífico is more than shopping: The building also houses the Centro Cultural Borges, where you can see shows, check out art displays, take tango lessons, and see performances by Julio Bocca's Ballet Argentino. Calle Florida 750 (at Av. Córdoba). *11/5555-5110.* Metro: San Martín.

Jumbo Palermo Commercial Center   This mall is near the polo grounds, but is of interest mostly if you plan on staying long-term in Buenos Aires and renting an apartment. Most of the stores are home-related, with a few clothing stores in the mix. The anchors of the mall are **Easy,** an IKEA-like store full of inexpensive furniture, construction material, and other things for settling in, and **Jumbo,** an enormous grocery store with a large selection of imported and luxury foods. Av. Bullrich 345 (at Cerviño). *11/4778-8000.* Metro: Palermo.

Patio Bullrich   This is considered one of the most exclusive shopping malls in Buenos Aires, but most stores cater to the middle and upper-middle classes rather than the truly wealthy. If you're looking for truly exclusive shopping, you'd do better checking out the boutiques on nearby Alvear. There is, however, an excellent food court here, full of ladies-who-lunch and local businesspeople talking deals. The mall is located in a historic building originally meant for auctioning cattle, and it's worthwhile to take a look at the facade. Hours are Monday through Saturday from 10am to 9pm, Sunday and holidays noon to 9pm. Posadas 1245 (at Libertad, with the historic facade facing Libertador). ✆ **11/4814-7400.** www.shoppingbullrich.com.ar. No metro access.

Other Shopping Centers & Highlights

Hours will vary as each store within these centers sets its own, but most will be open weekdays from 10am to 5pm.

Galería Güemes ★★ 👜 This sumptuous 1915 building, mixing retail and office, was one of the city's tallest at 85m (279 ft.) when it opened. The ugly modern Calle Florida entrance, rebuilt in 1971 after a fire, makes it easy to overlook. Its back entrance on San Martín hints at its original glory. This is a shopping gallery with a mix of stores without distinction and several kiosks that obscure the views, but look around at the walls and decorations. See my writeup in chapter 6 for more details (p. 117). Calle Florida 165 (at Perón). Metro: Florida.

Galería Promenade Alvear Naturally, any place attached to the Alvear Palace Hotel is going to be exclusive. Here you'll find wedding shops, jewelry stores, antiques, and art boutiques, as well as a few clothing stores. Store hours vary tremendously, with some shops only open on weekdays and some closing during lunch hours. Others are by appointment only. Each store has a phone number in its window, so if a place is closed, write down the number and call, or ask the Alvear's concierge for more information. The back of L'Orangerie, the Alvear's lobby restaurant, opens into the central courtyard of the shopping area, making for a pleasant place to grab a coffee. Av. Alvear 1883 (at Ayacucho; attached to the Alvear Hotel). No metro access.

Palermitana & Escaparate Designer Complex ★★ 👜 This complex overlooks Plaza Serrano and is actually two connected designer boutique incubators. Here you'll find a variety of small designer boutiques. The complex allows struggling designers to have a space in Palermo to show their wares but at a significantly reduced overhead cost, similar to the **Diseño Arg and Planeta Bs As** complex (p. 176), also on Plaza Serrano, started years earlier. Among the stores featured within the complex is **Tienda de Diseño** (www.tiendadedisenio.com.ar), a collaborative effort by Elianara Lapola, German Iglesias, and other designers, previously in its own free-standing store. Hours vary but are generally Wednesday to Friday 3 to 8pm and Saturday and Sunday 2 to 8pm, sometimes later. Serrano 1555 and 1557 (overlooking Plaza Serrano at Honduras). ✆ **11/4833-5053 or** 11/15-6285-6120 (cell); http://palermitana.blogspot.com for Palermitana. ✆ 11/483-0742 for Escaparate. No metro access.

San Telmo Market ★★ 📷 Though definitely a place to shop, this building is itself worth a visit. The San Telmo Market opened in 1897 and is a masterpiece not just for its soaring wrought-iron interior, but also for the atmosphere reminiscent of a market decades ago. Half the market is geared toward locals, with butchers, fresh-fruit-and-vegetable grocers, and little kiosks selling sundries and household items. This part looks like the kind of place your grandmother probably shopped in when she was a child. I recommend chatting with the staff at these places—they seem to have all the time in the world. The other half is more touristy (but never overly so), with random antiques (for example, old matchboxes) and vintage-clothing shops. The market is almost a block in size, but squeezed between several other historic buildings, and there are several entrances. It's open daily from 10am to 8pm, but each stand has individual hours. 961 Defensa or Bolívar 998 (both at Carlos Calvo). Metro: Independencia.

SHOPPING A TO Z

Antiques

You'll find the city's best antiques shops in San Telmo. Don't miss the antiques fair that takes place all day Sunday at Plaza Dorrego (see "Outdoor Markets," above). There are also a number of fine antiques stores along Avenida Alvear and Suipacha in Recoleta, including a collection of boutique shops at **Galería Alvear,** Av. Alvear 1777. Note that many of the stores listed under "Artists, Art Stores & Galleries," below, also sell antiques. Antiques and art stores along Calle Arroyo and much of the surrounding area (near the Israeli Embassy Monument in Recoleta) participate in **Gallery Night.** This event is held on the last Friday of every month (though not always in Jan–Feb), and antiques and art stores stay open late and frequently have tea and coffee for patrons. The streets are closed to traffic, creating a comfortable environment for walking and exploring. If you're here as a couple, it can be a romantic shopping experience. Keep in mind that most of the museums in Buenos Aires have high-quality art and replica shops, so you might find interesting gifts there as well.

Calle Antigua ★★   This store sells religious art, chandeliers, furniture, and other decorative objects. The owner, José Manuel Piñeyro, opened the shop more than 20 years ago. He now has two storefronts, both on the same block of Calle Defensa. The stores accept cash and foreign checks, but no credit cards. Both stores are open daily from 10am to 7pm. Calle Defensa 914 and Calle Defensa 974 (at Estados Unidos). ✆ **11/4300-8782** or 11/15-4472-4158 (cell). Metro: Independencia.

Galería El Solar de French   Built in the early 20th century in a Spanish colonial style, this is where Argentine patriot Domingo French lived. Today, it's a gallery, with antiques shops and photography stores depicting the San Telmo of yesteryear. Most of the shops here are open Monday to Friday from 10am to 7pm. Calle Defensa 1066 (at Carlos Calvo). Metro: Independencia.

Jorge Gudiño Antigüedades   Jorge Gudiño, who has more than 20 years of experience selling antiques, opened this store in 1991. The store has beautiful pieces of antique high-end furniture, which are displayed in interesting ways. This makes the store more visually appealing than many others on the street, as well as providing shoppers with original decorating ideas. Only cash and overseas checks are accepted. The store is open Sunday through Friday from 10:30am to 7pm. Calle Defensa 1002 (at Carlos Calvo). ✆ **11/4362-0156.** Metro: Independencia.

Buying Antiques in Buenos Aires

Most antiques stores will come down 10% to 20% from the prices they list if you bargain. It is almost impossible to pay for antiques with credit cards in Buenos Aires; virtually no store will accept them, largely because of Customs and tax issues. However, international checks, once verified, are accepted by almost all San Telmo stores. Cold cash, of course, is never an issue, whether pesos, dollars, or euros (though British pounds are not generally accepted).

Calle Defensa Shopping

Calle Antigua **3**
Cándido Silva **7**
Galería El Solar de French **7**
Jorge Gudiño Antigüedades **4**
L'ago **1**
Marcelo Toledo Gallery **8**
Pallarols **5**
San Telmo Antiques Fair **6**
San Telmo Market **2**

⊠ Post office

Pallarols ★   Located in San Telmo, Pallarols sells an exquisite collection of Argentine silver and other antiques. The Pallarols family represents six generations of silversmithing. Their work is featured in various museums in Buenos Aires, and family members will sometimes conduct silversmith workshops at museum stores. The shop is open Monday to Friday from 10am to 7pm, Saturday 10am to noon. Calle Defensa 1015 (at Carlos Calvo). ✆ **11/4362-5438.** www.pallarols.com.ar. Metro: Independencia.

Artists, Art Stores & Galleries

Buddha BA Asian Art Gallery   In Belgrano's small but delightful Chinatown, this Asian art gallery sells high-quality Asian art and antiques and connects to a Chinese teahouse. It's open Monday to Friday noon to 8pm. Arripeña 2288 (at Mendoza). ✆ **11/4706-2382.** www.buddhaba.com.ar/galeria_art.html. Metro: Juramento.

Cándido Silva ★★★   Filled with antiques and religious objects, this store is the standout in the Galería El Solar de French. Objects come in a range of materials—from wood to marble to silver. Many items are centuries-old antiques. Others are tasteful and exquisite reproductions, including a wide selection of canvases painted by indigenous people from throughout South America: Renaissance portraiture comes together with Frida Kahlo's magical realism, in representations of saints, angels, Christ, and numerous renditions of the Virgin Mary. Rural silver and gaucho items are also part of the display. Don't worry about fitting it all on the plane—they ship around the world. The store is open Tuesday to Sunday from 10:30am to 7pm. Calle Defensa 1066 (at Carlos Calvo in Galería El Solar de French). ✆ **11/4361-5053 or** 11/15-5733-0696 (cell). www.candidosilva.com.ar. Metro: Independencia.

Dominique Bernard   Dominique Bernard works in brilliant colors and in abstract themes, and is represented by various galleries. In addition to selling her own artwork, she also teaches art and offers guided art gallery tours. Call for an appointment at her studio in the suburbs. ✆ **11/4743-6508.** www.domartviajero.blogspot.com.

Fernando Donati   Displayed at several art galleries in Buenos Aires, Fernando Donati's art has also been exhibited in various countries. Contact him for more details. ✆ **11/4623-5955 or** 11/15-4479-2962. www.fernandodonati.com.

Galería Mar Dulce You'll find fresh, interesting modern art in this Palermo Soho gallery, including artists like Luciana Betesh, Marcelo Bordese, Ral Veroni, María Guerrieri, Pablo Mattioli, and others who have exhibited internationally. It's directed by British-born Linda Neilson and open Monday to Friday from 3pm to 8pm, Saturdays 11am to 2pm and 3pm to 8pm. Uriarte 1490 (at Gorriti). ✆ **11/15-5319-3597** (cell). www.galeriamardulce.blogspot.com. No metro access.

Galería Ruth Benzacar This avant-garde gallery, in a hidden underground space at the start of Calle Florida next to Plaza San Martín, hosts exhibitions of local and national interest. Among the best-known Argentines who have appeared here are Alfredo Prior, Miguel Angel Ríos, Daniel García, Graciela Hasper, and Pablo Siguier. It's open Monday to Friday from 11:30am to 8pm. Calle Florida 1000, overlooking Plaza San Martín. ✆ **11/4313-8480.** www.ruthbenzacar.com. Metro: San Martín.

Luis Formaiano Psychologist and artist Luis Formaiano has exhibited throughout South America and in Europe and creates paintings with explosive, carnival-like color. Many are abstract depictions of male nudes. Contact him to schedule a visit to his home studio in the Villa Crespo neighborhood. ✆ **11/4854-7735** or 11/15-6748-1849. luisformaiano@gmail.com; www.absolutearts.com/portfolios/f/formaiano.

Museo Casa/Taller de Celia Chevalier ★★ I don't get excited about much in La Boca, but I highly recommend this place, a boutique and house museum of an artist located just 2 blocks from El Caminito. Celia Chevalier grew up in Buenos Aires and creates whimsical paintings based on her childhood memories. She is charming and open, though she speaks Spanish only. The house is a restored *conventillo,* the type that Italian immigrants moved into when they came to Buenos Aires before the turn of the 20th century. The house dates from 1885 and was made into her studio museum in 1998. Credit cards are not accepted for art purchases. There is a nominal 5-peso entry fee (just over a dollar). It's open weekends and holidays from 2 to 7pm; call for an appointment on weekdays. Irala 1162 (at Calle Olavarria). ✆ **11/4302-2337.** celia_chevalier@yahoo.com.ar. No metro access.

Nora Iniesta ★ Nora made herself famous within Buenos Aires for her kitschy art, incorporating symbols of Argentina such as tango dancers and gauchos. With the combination of the tourist boom and the return of the Peronist political movement to power, Evita-inspired themes dominate her art. Beyond that, modern shadow boxes, collages, and montages of detritus, dolls, souvenirs, and buttons make up the bulk of her work. Some is sold at Museo Evita, or you can come see the much larger selection here. Nora is sometimes in her San Telmo studio during the week from noon to 6pm, but it is best to call her for an appointment. Perú 715, Ste. #2 (btw. Independencia and Chile). ✆ **11/4331-5459** or 11/15-5319-1119 (cell). www.norainiesta.com. Metro: Independencia.

Wussmann Gallery This is a beautiful gallery with fantastic works of art, concentrating on contemporary work. Among the artists represented is Ral Veroni, a native Argentine who has lived around the world. It's open Monday to Saturday 10am to 6pm. Venezuela 574 (btw. Bolivar and Perú). ✆ **11/4343-4707.** www.wussmann.com. Metro: Belgrano.

Bookstores & Stationery

Asunto Impreso ★★ This bookstore, part of a small chain, makes a great intellectual pit stop in San Telmo. Its tag line, "bookstore for the imagination," is quite apt: You'll find educational and art books of the highest quality here, many of specific interest to the tourist looking to delve a little deeper into the history and culture of Buenos Aires. Open Tuesday through Sunday 1 to 9pm. Perú 1064 (at Humberto I). ✆ **11/4361-8210.** www.asuntoimpreso.com. Metro: Independencia.

Clásica y Moderna ★★ This important bookstore saved itself from extinction by opening a restaurant inside to increase traffic. The bookstore opened in this location in 1938, though the company dates from 1918. Emilio Robert Díaz was the original owner, and now his grandchildren run it. In 1988, books were relegated to the back to make way for diners, but it is still one of the best bookstores for English-speaking tourists in the city. You'll find Buenos Aires photo and history books, as well as Argentine short-story collections, all translated into English. Events of all kinds are held here too, from literary readings to plays, dance shows, and art exhibitions. It's open Monday through Saturday 9am to 1am and Sunday from 5pm to 1am. Callao 892 (at Córdoba). © **11/4812-8707** or 11/4811-3670. www.clasicaymoderna.com. Metro: Callao.

Distal Libros Distal is one of Buenos Aires's largest chain bookstores, with branches throughout the city, including several on the pedestrianized Calle Florida. It has a large selection of English-language books (including Frommer's books). It's open Monday through Friday from 8am to 10pm, Saturday 10am to 10pm, and Sunday 10am to 9pm. Calle Florida 436 (at Lavalle; many other locations on Calle Florida and throughout the city). © **11/5218-4372.** www.distalnet.com. Metro: Lavalle.

El Ateneo (Grand Splendid) ★★ 🖸 This is one of Buenos Aires's most magnificent bookstores, in terms of selection as well as location. It's built into a former turn-of-the-last-century theater, maintaining its ornamentation, its stage, and even its theater boxes, which now serve as reading cubbyholes. Among the largest bookstores in South America, it certainly qualifies as one of the most beautiful. Open Monday through Saturday from 10am to 10pm, and Sunday from 10am to 9pm. Av. Santa Fe 1860 (at Callao). © **11/4813-6052.** www.tematika.com. Metro: Callao.

Eterna Cadencia ★★ 🖸 One of Buenos Aires's most charming smaller spaces dedicated to books, this is both a store and an editorial house. Full of wood, shelves, tables, and comfy chairs in which to sit and peruse books, this is the place to experience Palermo's intellectual side. Open Monday through Saturday from 10am to 9pm, and Saturday and Sunday from 11:30am to 8pm. Honduras 5574 (btw. Fitzroy and Humboldt). © **11/4774-4100.** www.eternacadencia.com. Metro: Palermo.

Librería de Las Madres/Café Literario Osvaldo Bayer ★★ This combination bookstore and cafe offers what few places in Buenos Aires can—the opportunity to speak with people whose family members disappeared during Argentina's military dictatorship. You'll also find young students who come here to study and continue to seek justice in this cause. The Madres bookstore is just to the side of the cafe, and it's full of books and newspapers on liberal causes from throughout Latin America. It also has one of the largest collections of books on Che Guevara anywhere in the world. An Argentine native, he is a personal hero for many of the Madres, and his image adorns walls throughout the building. In addition to books, there are posters, pamphlets, and other items here, all with a very socialist slant. It's open Monday through Friday from 10am to 10pm, Saturday from 10am to 8pm. Hipólito Yrigoyen 1584 (at Ceballos). © **11/4382-3261.** Metro: Congreso.

Librería Otras Letras ★ This is the first gay bookstore in Buenos Aires, carrying a large selection of Spanish-language gay books, as well as some in translation. If you're seeking to better understand Argentina's unique gay history, pick up a copy here of *Historia de la Homosexualidad en la Argentina* by Osvaldo Bazan. The store is a de facto community house; it's a good place to come for information about gay events, and the owners can often be found dispensing advice to tourists. Open daily noon to 8pm. Soler 4796 (at Jorge Luis Borges). © **11/4831-5129.** www.libreriaotrasletras.com. Metro: Plaza Italia.

Librería Santa Fe This store, part of a chain, has a large selection of books on Argentina, travel guides, and English-language bestsellers. It's open Monday to Saturday from 10am to 8pm. Av. Santa Fe 2582 (at Pueyrredón). © **11/4827-0100** or 11/5254-2376. www.lsf.com.ar. Metro: Pueyrredón.

Librería Sigal Close to the Abasto Shopping Center, this Jewish bookstore and Judaica shop has been in business for more than 70 years, in an area that was once a major Jewish immigration center. Books are mostly in Hebrew and Spanish. They also sell menorahs, yarmulkes, and other items of Jewish interest. Only cash is accepted. It's open Monday through Thursday from 10am to 1pm and 3 to 7:30pm, Friday from 10am to 4:30pm, sometimes later in summer. For a map of this bookstore, see the "Abasto & Once" map on p. 95. Av. Corrientes 2854 (at Ecuador). © **11/4861-9501** or 11/4865-7208. www.libreria-sigal.com. Metro: Gardel.

Librerías Turísticas Every and any kind of tourism book on Argentina and other parts of the world can be found in this store. The company is itself a publisher and seller of books. Open Monday through Friday from 9am to 7pm, Saturday from 9am to 1pm. Paraguay 2457 (at Pueyrredón). © **11/4963-2866** or 11/4962-5547. www.libreriaturistica.com.ar. Metro: Pueyrredón.

Libros Cuspide This is one of the biggest chains in Buenos Aires, and you won't have any trouble finding its branches in the city's neighborhoods and in other cities of Argentina. I list here the Calle Florida one—it has a large selection of books that will be of interest to tourists seeking to learn more about Argentina. It's open Monday to Saturday 9am to 9pm, Sunday noon to 8pm. Calle Florida 628 (at Tucumán). © **11/4328-0575.** www.cuspide.com. Metro: San Martín.

Papelera Palermo ★ 📖 If you're looking for an unusual "only in Argentina" gift, and beautiful paper to wrap it in, this is the place. You'll find small notebooks, bound in leather or with a handcrafted Evita or Che Guevara cover, to write down your thoughts on Buenos Aires. Artistic photo books and other unique leather office goods are also for sale, along with a large selection of colorful specialty papers and notecards. Open Monday to Saturday 10am to 8pm, Sunday 2 to 8pm. Honduras 4945 (at Serrano). © **11/4833-3081.** www.papelerapalermo.com.ar. No metro access.

Walrus Books ★ This unique English-language bookstore was opened by Geoffrey Hickman, an American who moved to Buenos Aires after falling in love and marrying Josefina, his Argentine wife. They stock thousands of used English-language books, translations of historical South American texts and literature, and new books and travel guides. If you're looking for something literary in English to read on the *subte* or the plane ride home, this is the place to find it. Open Tuesday to Sunday noon to 8pm. Estados Unidos 617 (at Perú). © **11/4300-7135.** www.walrus-books.com.ar. Metro: Moreno.

Cameras & Accessories

Cosentino If you need something for your camera, are looking for a new one, or want to develop film, Cosentino offers it all. They also do repairs. Open Monday through Friday 9am to 7pm, Saturday 9am to 12:30pm. Av. Roque Sáenz Peña (Diagonal Norte) 738 (at Perón). © **11/4328-9120.** www.opticacosentino.com.ar. Metro: Catedral.

Cellphones

Altel This is a cellphone-rental company aimed at tourists. It offers free delivery and rental; you pay only for calls. Be aware, however, that while a tremendous convenience, cellphone rentals are expensive, and you should always read the fine print no matter what company you choose or how good the offer seems to be. Av. Córdoba 417, 1st floor (at Reconquista). 🕻 **11/4311-5000.** www.altelphonerental.com. Metro: San Martín.

Movistar   Through this carrier, tourists can buy inexpensive cellular phones along with a SIM card for use in Buenos Aires. There's a shop on Lavalle (open Mon–Fri 9:30am–7pm), and a booth in Galerías Pacífico (open daily 10am–9pm). Lavalle 567 (at Florida). 🕻 11/4328-5624. Booth in Galerías Pacífico (2nd level), Calle Florida 750 (at Av. Córdoba). 🕻 **11/5555-5287.** Metro: San Martín.

Electronics & Computers

Galería Jardín   Ugly but useful, this multilevel electronics and computer outlet center has dozens of tiny shops for computers, computer accessories, and other electronics needs. Be forewarned that these items are much more expensive in Argentina than in Europe or North America. Each store has its own phone number, payment policy, and hours, but in general the gallery is open Monday to Saturday from 10am to 6pm. Florida 561 in Torre Florida (btw. Tucumán and Lavalle). Metro: Florida.

Eyeglasses & Contact Lenses

Saracco   This store offers fast, high-quality vision services. The eye exam is included in the price of eyeglasses. Eyeglasses and contact lenses cost about a third of what they do in North America, though some designer frames will have similar prices. The company has several branches surrounding Plaza San Martín. Interestingly, perhaps because of the large number of descendants of Italian immigrants in Buenos Aires, you'll find the Zyloware Sophia Loren collection is especially popular and featured in this and many other eyeglass stores. Juncal 821 (near Plaza San Martín). 🕻 **11/4393-1000.** Metro: San Martín.

Fashion & Apparel

Akiabara   This store is a chain, with very pretty, feminine creations, many made in Argentina. It is moderate- to high-end for Buenos Aires. It's open daily from 10am to 9pm. Honduras 4865 (btw. Gurruchaga and Armenia). 🕻 **11/4831-9420.** www.akiabara.com. Metro: Plaza Italia.

Aristocracia ★★   An elegant store that's been in Recoleta for over 17 years, Aristocracia contains the work of many designers, including dresses by Lucrecia Gamundi and Marcelo Señra and accessories by Gloria Lópes Sauqué. The store also imports clothes from France, England, Italy, and other countries. Managed by Ana Frigerio, this store has excellent service, and some of the staff also speaks English. It's open Monday through Saturday from 10am to 9pm. Rodriguez Pena 2023 (at Posadas). 🕻 **11/4812-3795.** No metro access.

Bakú ★★ 🖉   All the designs in Bakú are the brainchild of Liliana Basili, who opened her own store in 2003 in the Las Cañitas neighborhood of Palermo. She produces unique pocketbooks, leather accessories, belts and belt buckles, and various jewelry items. All items are produced in Argentina. Though her shop is in an expensive part of the city, everything here is priced very reasonably. The shop is open Monday from 1 to 10pm and Tuesday through Saturday from 10am to 10pm. Av. Arguibel 2890 (at Arce). 🕻 **11/4775-5570.** Metro: Carranza.

Bokura ★ 🖉   The amazing decor of this men's store almost detracts attention from the clothes. Built into a soaring former warehouse, the two-level shop is painted black, with Chinese dragons and other Asian decorations throughout. The store concentrates on jeans, designer T-shirts, and other clothing for young men, all produced in Argentina and perfect if you're looking for something to wear to go clubbing. The shop is open Monday through Saturday from 11am to 8:30pm and Sunday from 2 to 8:30pm. El Salvador 4677 (btw. Armenia and Malabia). ℰ **11/4833-3975.** www.bokura.com.ar. No metro access.

Bolivia ★ One of the city's best casual men's stores, this place sells everything from sportswear and jeans to fashion underwear. The shop is open Monday through Saturday from 11am to 8:30pm. Gurruchaga 1581 (at Honduras). ℰ **11/4832-6284.** www.bolivia paratodos.com.ar. No metro access.

Clara Ibarguren ★ Though she's not related, Argentina history buffs will recognize the last name of this designer as Evita's true but hidden maiden name. Clara offers young, fresh designs in this Barrio Norte shop, with other locations throughout Buenos Aires. The shop is open Monday through Saturday from 10am to 8pm, and Saturday 10am to 7pm. Santa Fe 1338 (btw. Uruguay and Talcahuano). ℰ **11/4811-6413.** www. claraibarguren.com. Metro: Facultad de Medicina.

Diseño Arg and Planeta Bs As ★★ More a collection of stores than one store, Diseño Arg was started by fashion journalist Claudia Jara. Just before the 2001 peso crisis, as Argentina's economy was stagnating, the young designers she interviewed started asking her how they could show their designs when they had no money to open a boutique. Claudia answered their questions by opening this space, which became even more relevant after the crisis ensued. You'll find dozens of designers here selling their clothes and explaining how they created them. The shop is primarily for women, with a few men's items thrown in too. In 2004, Claudia also opened the nearby Planeta Bs As, Jorge Luis Borges 1627, just off Plaza Serrano (ℰ **11/4832-2006**). Planeta Bs As is open Tuesday through Sunday from 11am to 8pm. Diseño Arg is open Tuesday to Friday 2 to 8pm, and Saturday and Sunday noon to 8pm. Honduras 5033 (off Plaza Serrano). ℰ **11/4832-2006.** www.disenioargshopping.com.ar and www. mujermilenio.com.ar. No metro access.

Ermenegildo Zegna This famous Italian chain sells outstanding suits and jackets made of light, cool fabrics. If you've landed in Buenos Aires without your suit and find that you need one, this is among your best options. The shop is open Monday to Friday from 10am to 8pm, Saturday from 10am to 2pm. Av. Alvear 1920 (at Ayacucho). ℰ **11/4804-1908.** No metro access.

Escada This boutique shop sells casual and elegant selections of women's clothing. Clothing from this international brand is slightly less expensive here than in North America and Europe. Av. Alvear 1444 (btw. Parera and Libertad). ℰ **11/4814-0292.** No metro access.

Florentina Muraña ★★ 👔 This wonderful little store in Palermo Soho takes its name from a character in a Borges story that takes place in Palermo. You'll find very pretty, feminine clothing made of interesting materials here. Some examples of the offerings include popcorn shag sweaters, handmade in Argentina from Italian wool, crystal jewelry, and an extensive collection of leather clothing and accessories. The owner is Gabriela Sivori; she works in the shop and designs some of the items for sale, all of which are made solely in Argentina. Open daily from 11:30am to 8pm, though hours fluctuate in the summer. Jorge Luis Borges 1760 (at Pasaje Russel). ℰ **11/4833-4137.** www. florentinamurania.com.ar. No metro access.

La Remera ★★ One of the newest designer shops in Buenos Aires, opened in November 2010, La Remera is the creation of Ariel Estanga, an Argentine who had also worked in Spain for Zara and Mango. *Remera* means T-shirt, and the clothes are simple and chic, utilitarian, and multifunctional. Ariel calls his clothes "simple and basic pieces you always need, something to use for the day and into the night"—perfect for travelers. Most designs are for women, some are unisex, and a few are for men. Open Monday to Friday 10:30am to 7pm, Saturday 11am to 2pm. Arenales 1239, the Rue des Artisans Passageway, 1N (btw. Libertad and Talcahuano). ✆ **11/4519-8074.** www.laremera. com. Metro: Callao.

Lupe ★★ 👜 Designer Guadalupe Villar opened this white, airy, and always busy store in 2004. Her designs are young and feminine, with an emphasis on casual sportswear at reasonable prices. Open Monday to Saturday from 11am to 8pm and Sunday 3 to 7pm, though hours will vary in summer. El Salvador 4657 (btw. Armenia and Malabia). ✆ **11/4833-9205.** www.lupeba.com.ar. No metro access.

Mancini ★★ 👜 While women can shop 'til they drop with the mind-boggling number of choices in Buenos Aires, most clothing stores in Argentina tend to have a limited selection of interesting men's clothing. Mancini, a chain with men's and women's clothing, is an exception to the rule. This branch, in Palermo Viejo, offers chic clothing, with an emphasis on black. Either because they are unfriendly or simply jaded, the staff generally leaves shoppers in this store on their own, not following them around as in other stores in the city. Open Monday to Saturday from 10am to 8:30pm, Sunday 11am to 7pm. Honduras 5140 (btw. Uriarte and Thames). ✆ **11/4832-7570.** No metro access.

Maria Cher ★ This boutique is a work of art in itself, with its glass-and-steel construction and its own interior bamboo garden. Maria Chernajovky's store has an emphasis on dresses and leather coats and other leather clothing. It's a perfect spot for a woman looking for mature, fashionable clothing with a more sophisticated air. Open Monday to Saturday from 10am to 9pm, and Sunday 2 to 7:30pm, though hours will vary in summer. El Salvador 4724 (at Armenia). ✆ **11/4832-3336.** www.maria-cher.com. ar. No metro access.

Mishka Shoes ★★ 👜 If you're a woman with a shoe fetish, head to this small boutique in Palermo Soho. It's not cheap by any means—prices range up to $500 for Swarovski Crystal beaded sandals and other unique handmade footwear—but it's definitely a place to splurge. All the shoes are made in Argentina, and custom-made sizes and details can also be arranged if you find combinations and colors you think might work for your wardrobe. If your travel companions get bored, make them wait on the long white settee, while you drool over the selection. Open Monday to Saturday from 11am to 8:30pm. El Salvador 4673 (at Armenia). ✆ **11/4833-6566.** www.mishkashoes. com. No metro access.

Pablo Ramírez ★★ 👜 This elegant boutique, which seems out of place in the San Telmo and Monserrat area, is the main showroom for designer Pablo Ramirez, whose designs have been featured in shops in New York and other major cities. His lines are sleek and simple, monochrome, and have a touch of *Breakfast at Tiffany's* nostalgia to them. It's open Sunday through Friday from noon to 1am, Saturday noon to 2am. Perú 587 (btw. México and Venezuela). ✆ **11/4342-7154.** www.pabloramirez.com.ar. Metro: Moreno.

Polo Ralph Lauren This is the Buenos Aires branch of the famous American luxury retailer. You will find slightly lower prices here than in North America or Europe. The building, an old turn-of-the-20th-century Art Nouveau mansion, is also a reason to come shopping here: The ornate wooden trim and balustrades remain,

Chic, trendy Palermo is a burgeoning shopping district, with creative boutiques springing up around Plaza Serrano in Palermo Soho in particular. For a map of shops in this area, see the "Palermo Attractions, Shopping & Nightlife" map on p. 134.

and a stained-glass skylight oversees the whole shop. Open Monday to Saturday 10am to 8pm. Av. Alvear 1780 (at Callao). © **11/4812-3400.** No metro access.

Porto Fem Talles Grandes   Who says big girls can't be fashionable? While most of the clothes in Buenos Aires seem aimed at the extremely thin, this store has the same styles in plus sizes. Be aware that a law passed in 2006 states that all stores are supposed to carry large sizes, but in anorexic Argentina, few stores do. This shop is open Monday through Friday from 10am to 8pm, Saturday from 10am to 2pm. Av. Santa Fe 1129 (btw. Libertad and Cerrito). © **11/4813-6219.** www.portofem.com. Metro: San Martín.

Prototype ★   This store features sleek, well-designed men's clothing that ranges from office wear to outfits for a night on the town. Most clothes are Argentine-made, and there is also a great selection of shoes and small leather accessories. Part of a chain, the store has locations throughout Buenos Aires. Some of the stores have furniture sections, with an eye to modern male tastes, concentrating on dark leathers, functional lamps, and black-glass knickknacks and other household goods. It's open Monday through Saturday from noon to 9pm. Malabia 1720 (btw. El Salvador and Costa Rica). © **11/4832-8540.** www.prototypeweb.com. Metro: Carranza.

Rapsodia   Clothing in this chain store ranges from items made of exotic fabrics in fantastic color combinations to the feminine, frilly, and romantic. Most of the clothing is made in Argentina. Several of the boutiques exist throughout Buenos Aires. This shop is open daily from 10am to 9pm. El Salvador 4757 (btw. Gurruchaga and Armenia). © **11/4832-5363.** www.rapsodia.com.ar. No nearby Metro.

Rodrigo Reyes   If you're looking for a great selection of well-made, sporty shoes for both men and women, this is a great place. It specializes in sneakers in an array of funky styles and colors. All products are made in Argentina. The shop is open daily from 11am to 8pm, though summer hours fluctuate. Malabia 1682 (at El Salvador). © **11/4834-6093.** www.rodrigoreyes.com.ar. No metro access.

Gaucho Clothing & Accessories

El Boyero   Here you'll find high-quality, classic-style polo and other clothing inspired by the gaucho (Argentine cowboy) lifestyle. There's a large selection of beautiful leather products made in Argentina. Fine silver gaucho jewelry, knives, and other accessories are also available. The store has two branches, one in Galerías Pacífico (p. 168) and the one listed here on Calle Florida. It's open Monday through Saturday from 9am to 8pm (sometimes on Sun). Calle Florida 953 (at Plaza San Martín). © **11/4312-3564.** www.elboyero.com. Metro: San Martín.

Estación Sur   This small store packs in a lot of merchandise, from gaucho ponchos and knives to leather horse harnesses. You'll also find a mixed variety of kitsch and elegant *mate* holders and other items for gift giving. Monday through Saturday from 10am to 8pm. Calle Florida 680 (at Viamonte). © **11/4328-7189.** www.estacion-sur.com. Metro: San Martín.

Home Design

Calma Chicha ★   You'll find a wide range of well-designed items here, from throw pillows to rugs made from checkerboard-patterned cowskin, all easily brought home as a souvenir of your trip. Best known for home design, Calma Chicha also has clothing and small accessories. It's open Monday to Friday 10:30am to 8:30pm, Saturdays 11am to 8pm, and Sundays 2pm to 8pm. Honduras 4909 (btw. Serrano and Gurruchaga). ✆ 11/4831-1818. www.calmachicha.com. Metro: Palermo.

Capital Diseño & Objetos   This is one of the most interesting home-design stores in Palermo Viejo, and you'll find all kinds of well-designed, kitschy, and funky things here. There's also a large selection of items for children. Among my favorite things are the decorative key holders and coat hangers designed by Fernando Poggio. There is also a lot of leather. It's open Monday to Saturday from 10am to 10pm. Honduras 4958 (btw. Serrano and Gurruchaga). ✆ 11/4834-6555. www.capitalpalermo.com.ar. Metro: Palermo.

L'ago   Located along San Telmo's antiques row, this store has creative and modern designs and vintage mid-20th-century items. The main focus is lamps, but there's also an extensive collection of items that can be used for children's rooms or for those with whimsical, young-at-heart tastes. Virtually all of the new items are made in Argentina. The store is open daily from 10am to 8pm. Defensa 970 (at Estados Unidos). ✆ 11/4362-4702. www.lagosantelmo.com. Metro: Independencia.

Tienda Puro Diseño Argentino ★★★ 🛍   This is one of my favorite stores in Buenos Aires. It features high-quality, high-design items created by more than 120 Argentine designers, with only Argentine materials, in Argentina, all at good value. The idea came from a design expo of the same name, which in spite of the country's economic crisis was successful enough to spawn a stand-alone store. The concentration is on home design, but products also include jewelry, clothing fashions, leather accessories, and children's products. Many of the household items have an updated frontier feeling, leather playing a significant role. It's open from Monday through Saturday from 10am to 8pm. Gorriti 5953 (btw. Arévalo and Ravignani). ✆ 11/4776-8037. www.purodiseno.com.ar. No metro access.

Jewelry

The city's finest jewelry stores are located in Recoleta and inside many five-star hotels. You can find bargains on gold along Calle Libertad, near Avenida Corrientes. Also, see "Fashion & Apparel," above. Many of the small women's boutiques detailed there also carry handmade jewelry produced locally.

Chabeli   This store offers an interesting selection of handmade Argentine jewelry from crystals and semiprecious stones, in addition to leather accessories. Open Monday through Friday from 10am to 6pm, Saturdays 10am to 3pm. Calle Venezuela 1454 (btw. San Jose and Sáenz Peña). ✆ 11/4384-0958. Metro: Sáenz Peña.

Cousiño Jewels   Located along the Sheraton hotel's shopping arcade, this Argentine jeweler features a brilliant collection of art made of the national stone, the rhodochrosite, or Inca Rose. In the Sheraton Buenos Aires Hotel, Av. San Martín 1225. ✆ 11/4318-9000. Metro: Retiro.

H.Stern   This upscale Brazilian jeweler, with branches in major cities around the world, sells South American stones, including emeralds and the unique imperial topaz. It's the top jeweler in Latin America. Branches in the Marriott Plaza (✆ 11/4318-3083) and the Sheraton (✆ 11/4312-6762). Metro: San Martín or Retiro.

Julio Perez Sanz Julio Perez Sanz designs unique pieces of jewelry, some inspired by native patterns. His shops in Recoleta show jewelry, small accessories, and amazing designs for the home. His Christmas tree ornament collections are often featured for sale in hotel boutiques throughout Buenos Aires. Monday to Friday 10am to 8pm, Saturday 10am to 7pm. Posadas 1477 (at Callao; *©* **11/4815-9190**) and Posadas 1377 (at Callao; *©* 11/4812-1417). perezsanz.com.ar. No metro access.

Marcelo Toledo Gallery ★★★ The jewelry and silver objects made in Marcelo Toledo's gallery are exquisite, and represent some Argentina's finest traditional craftsmanship. Famous clients include U.S. President Bill Clinton and various royal heads of state. In 2007, he launched a special collection called Evita, based on artifacts of the time of Maria Eva Duarte de Perón, available in his own and various hotel gallery shops throughout Buenos Aires and in Museo Evita. The store is open Sundays to Fridays, 10:30am to 5:30pm. Humberto I no. 462 (btw. Bolívar and Defensa). *©* **11/4362-0841.** www.marcelotoledo.net. Metro: San Juan.

Kosher Grocers

For a map of these grocers, see the "Abasto & Once" map on p. 95.

Autoservicio Ki Tob This large kosher grocery store also has a kosher meat section. You'll find everything kosher here, from basic staples to junk food. Only cash is accepted. It's open Monday through Thursday from 8am to 2:30pm and 4pm to 9pm, Friday from 8am until 2 hours before sunset, Saturdays 1 hour after sunset to 11pm, and Sunday from 3 to 8pm. Tucumán 2783 (at Boulogne Sur Mer). *©* **11/4964-5909.** Metro: Pueyrredón.

Heluini This small, friendly kosher store concentrates on Sephardic kosher foods, known locally as Oriental kosher. You'll find spices and other items with a decidedly Middle Eastern flavor here. They also carry peanut butter, a very difficult item to find in Argentina, so if you or the kids have a craving, this is the place to head. The store has been open since 1937. It's open Monday through Thursday from 9am to 9pm, Friday from 9am until 2 hours before sunset. Tucumán 2755 (at Boulogne Sur Mer). *©* **11/4966-1007.** Metro: Pueyrredón.

Leather

With all that beef in its restaurants, Argentina could not be anything but one of the world's best leather centers. If you're looking for high-quality, interestingly designed

---

The Calle Murillo Leather District

Looking to compare prices and selection in a hurry? Then head to the **Calle Murillo** leather warehouse district in the **Villa Crespo** neighborhood. I've listed several places in this section, including the large **Murillo 666** (p.182), one of the street's main stores. Items are often made above the storefront, or in a factory nearby. Don't be afraid to bargain, or ask if custom items can be made if you don't find exactly what you like.

The highest density of leather stores is at Murillo between Malabia and Acevedo, but you'll find about 50 stores total, with everything from leather jackets to purses, luggage, furniture, and more. Many of the smaller stores are owned by Orthodox Jews, and so will be closed on Friday evenings, Saturdays, and certain holidays, so keep that in mind when scheduling your shopping time.

leather goods, especially women's shoes, accessories, and handbags, few places beat Buenos Aires's selection. Many leather stores will also custom-make jackets and other items for interested customers, so do ask if you see something you like in the wrong size or want to combine features from different pieces. While most shops can do this in a day or two, to avoid disappointment, you should start checking out stores and prices early. If something is complicated to make, it might take more time than usual—and some stores can take as long as a week.

Ashanti Leather Factory ★   This small store on Calle Florida offers a wide selection of leather goods, from men's and women's jackets to funky and interesting women's pocketbooks. Their factory is in the basement of the shop, so they can easily custom-make almost anything for you. Ask them for a tour, through which you can meet the craftspeople Roberto, Victor, and Oscar, who sit surrounded by sewing machines and colorful bolts of leather. Open daily from 10am to 10pm. Calle Florida 585 (at Lavalle). **🕾 11/4394-1310.** Metro: San Martín.

Beith Cuer   You'll find an excellent selection of women's coats and accessories in this store, from hats to purses to items such as fur gloves and hats. For men, you'll find coats, hats, wallets, and belts, too. The staff is very attentive. It's open Monday to Saturday from 9am to 7pm; closed Sunday. Murillo 525 (btw. Malabia and Acevedo in Villa Crespo). **🕾 11/4854-8580.** Metro: Malabia.

Casa López ★★   Widely considered among the best *marroquinerías* (leather-goods shops) in Buenos Aires, Casa López sells an extensive range of Argentine leather products. Open Monday to Friday 9am to 9pm, and Saturdays and Sundays 10am to 6:30pm. Marcelo T. de Alvear 640 (at Maipú, near Plaza San Martín). **🕾 11/4311-3044.** www.casalopez.com.ar. Metro: San Martín.

Chabeli   This store has a wide selection of women's shoes and pocketbooks at reasonable prices along with interesting handmade Argentine jewelry from crystals and semiprecious stones. Designs fall into two main categories: native Argentine, with indigenous and gaucho patterns; and pretty and feminine, with pink and other pastel materials. They also have another branch in the Patagonian resort town of Bariloche. Open Monday through Friday from 10am to 6pm, Saturdays 10am to 3pm. Calle Venezuela 1454 (btw. San Jose and Sáenz Peña). **🕾 11/4384-0958.** Metro: Sáenz Peña.

El Nochero   All the products sold at El Nochero are made with first-rate Argentine leather and manufactured by local workers. Shoes and boots, leather goods and clothes, and decorative silverware (including *matés*, for holding the special herbal tea Argentines love) fill the store. Open Monday through Saturday from 10am to 9pm, Sunday and holidays noon to 9pm. Posadas 1245 (in the Patio Bullrich Mall). **🕾 11/4815-3629.** www.elnochero.com. No metro access.

Hard Leather ★   The name might make you wonder if you walked into a Buenos Aires S&M shop, but the selection is anything but. Plus, there's nothing hard about the leather (all of it soft and supple), but the owners missed the double entendre when they looked for a word meaning "durable" to replace *dura,* the Spanish word for "hard." While there are coats for men, women will find a much larger selection. The shop is open Monday to Saturday from 10am to 8pm. Murillo 627 (btw. Malabia and Acevedo, in Villa Crespo). **🕾 11/4856-8920.** Metro: Malabia.

Louis Vuitton   The famous Parisian boutique sells an elite line of luggage, purses, and travel bags here. It's located alongside Recoleta's most exclusive shops. It's open Monday through Friday from 10am to 8pm, Saturday from 11am to 6pm. Av. Alvear 1901 (at Ayacucho). **🕾 11/4802-0809.** No metro access.

Murillo 666 ★★   This store is the main outlet in the Calle Murillo leather district in the Villa Crespo neighborhood. They have a large selection of women's coats and accessories, and one of the largest assortments of men's jackets, which they will custom-make. They also have the largest furniture showroom in the district. Officially, unlike many stores around here, they offer the same prices for cash or for credit, but sometimes you can still bargain a price down slightly if you're paying with cash. Open daily 9:30am to 8pm. Murillo 666 (btw. Malabia and Acevedo in Villa Crespo). ✆ **11/4856-4501.** www.murillo666.com.ar. Metro: Malabia.

Outlet ★   The name says it all for this store just off Murillo: This is definitely a place to bargain, and shopping with friends might save you even more money, because they offer group discounts. In addition to large selections of jackets, handbags, gloves, and other items, this store also carries a small selection of shoes. Those couches you're sitting on as your friends try everything on? You can buy those in various colors as well. There is also a small selection of women's fur coats here. Open Monday to Friday 10am to 7:30pm, and Saturday 10am to 2pm. Scalabrini Ortiz 5 (at Murillo, in Villa Crespo). ✆ **11/4857-1009.** Metro: Malabia.

Outlet de Cuero   Smaller than some of the other stores, this shop still provides great service, though the selection is better for women than men. Items range from jackets to handbags. If you can't find what you want, this is a perfect place to ask about what can be made from their various leather swatches on hand. Open Monday to Saturday 9am to 7pm. Murillo 643 (btw. Malabia and Acevedo, in Villa Crespo). ✆ **11/4854-8436.** Metro: Malabia.

Paseo del Cuero ★   Along with coats and the usual items for men and women, this factory outlet in the Murillo district also has a great selection of men's and women's small luggage carry-ons and gym bags. Feel free to bargain, as the staff often gives you a slightly lower price if you hesitate or offer to pay in cash. Looking for cowhide throw rugs? They're here too! They do take American Express, Diners Club, MasterCard, and Visa. The outlet is open Monday to Saturday from 9:30am to 7:30pm. Murillo 624 (btw. Malabia and Acevedo, in Villa Crespo). ✆ **11/4855-9094.** www.paseodelcuero.com.ar. Metro: Malabia.

Pasión Argentina/Diseños Etnicos ★★   Owner Amadeo Bozzi concentrates on leather goods primarily for women, accessories for men and women, and home goods. All produced in Argentina, they are well designed and well made. Some combine leather with other native materials made by members of the Wichi tribe, a native group in the Chaco region. I highly recommend visiting this store, which is technically by appointment only, from Monday through Friday from 10am to 6pm, and at other times. Scalabrini Ortiz 2330 (btw. Charcas and Güemes). ✆ **11/4832-7993.** www.pasion-argentina.com.ar. Metro: Scalabrini Ortiz.

Prüne ★★   This is a chain with additional stores in Alto Palermo, Patio Bullrich, and many other locations in town and throughout Argentina, but the Calle Florida store is among the largest. It's great for women's accessories and small leather goods, and carries some of the best purses in all of Buenos Aires. The store has a light, airy feel and even a back patio. Most items are Argentine, but a few are Chinese-made. It's open daily from 10am to 8pm. Calle Florida 963 (at Plaza San Martín). ✆ **11/4893-2634.** Metro: San Martín.

Raffaello by Cesar Franco ★★   Cesar Franco got his start designing for theater and tango shows, and his background comes through in the flair of his clothing designs. His shop has everything from sportswear to wedding dresses, and exquisite leather coats for both men and women, many made by combining leather strips with rich fabrics, in designs that recall the Renaissance. The shop is open Monday to Friday from 10am to 6pm, Saturday 10am to 2pm, and by appointment. Rivadavia 2206, 1st floor, Ste. A (at Uriburu). ☏ 11/4952-5277. www.raffaellobuenosaires.com. Metro: Congreso.

Rossi & Caruso　Offering some of the best leather products in the city since 1868, this store is the choice for visiting celebrities—the king and queen of Spain and Prince Philip of England among them. Products include luggage, saddles, and accessories as well as leather and chamois clothes, purses, wallets, and belts. There is another branch in the Galerías Pacífico mall (p. 168). Open daily 9:30am to 8:30pm. Av. Santa Fe 1377 (at Uruguay). ☏ 11/4814-4774. www.rossicaruso.com. Metro: Bulnes.

626 Cueros　The blasting disco music here tells you you're in a place with a little edge compared to some of the other leather stores in the Murillo district. Here you'll find interestingly designed men's and women's coats. You'll also pay less if you pay in cash. Open Monday to Saturday 10am to 6pm. Murillo 626 (btw. Malabia and Acevedo, in Villa Crespo). ☏ 11/4857-6972. Metro: Malabia.

Luggage

Voyager　If you've been shopping too much and need a way to get it all home, heading here might be a good idea. The combination of price, selection, service, and location makes it a great place to purchase a new suitcase or other luggage items. Airplane pillows and electric converters are also sold. It's open Monday through Saturday from 10am to 8pm. Florida 250 (btw. Sarmiento and Perón). ☏ 11/5032-2578 or 11/5032-2579. Metro: Florida.

Music

C-Disueria　This music store has a variety of CDs and tapes covering all musical genres. The store has a vast selection of tango music at reasonable prices—you can buy a few CDs to listen to at home to bring back memories of your trip. Monday to Friday 10am to 9pm, Saturday 11am to midnight, Sunday 6pm to 11pm. Corrientes 1274 (at Talcahuano). ☏ 11/4381-0754. Metro: Tribunales.

Tango's　You can't miss hearing this store, blasting sensual tango music from speakers at its door. Inside, you'll find a huge collection of tango CDs and other Argentine music. The shop is open Monday through Friday from 9am to 8pm, Saturday 9:30am to 9pm, and Sunday 10am to 8pm. Lavalle 582 (at Florida). ☏ 11/4326-8125. Metro: Florida.

Organic & Vegetarian Food

Bio　This is an organic restaurant with a large selection of items that can be bought separately. It's a great place for veg-heads to go shopping for snacks to bring back to their hotel. All the ingredients are organic, and all are strictly grown or produced in Argentina. Only cash is accepted. It's open Monday from 8pm to 1am, and Tuesday through Sunday from noon to 3:30pm and 8pm to 1am, often later on weekends. Humboldt 2199 (at Guatemala). ☏ 11/4774-3880. www.biorestaurant.com.ar. No metro access.

Pet Accessories

Bien Fifí　Looking for something special for your pet back home? Head to this store run by Silvana Faldani for unique, Argentine-made collars, leashes, pet carriers, and other pet-related items. Only cash is accepted. It's open Monday through Saturday from 11am to 8pm, and Sunday 2 to 8pm. Cabrera 5050 (btw. Thames and Uriarte). © **11/4899-1924.** www.bienfifi.com.ar. No metro access.

Pharmacy

Farmacia Suiza   You won't have a problem finding places to buy medicine in Buenos Aires, but I recommend this place for its atmosphere. It's an old apothecary, tucked into the Microcentro area. The shelves are adorned with wooden carvings and lined with old jars and flasks from the turn of the 20th century. The medicine and services, however, are fully up to date. It's open Monday to Friday from 8am to 8pm. Calle Tucumán 701 (at Maipú). © **11/4313-8480**. Metro: San Martín.

Tango Clothing, Shoes & Accessories

Abasto Plaza Hotel Tango Shop   Whether you're staying at the Abasto Plaza Hotel or not, it's worth taking a look at this store in the lobby for its tango clothing selection, especially the sexy dresses. Tango music and other items are also sold here. It's open Monday through Friday from 10am to 7pm, but closes for the month of January. For a map of this shop, see the "Abasto & Once" map on p. 95. Av. Corrientes 3190 (at Anchorena, near the Abasto Shopping Center). © **11/6311-4466.** www.abastoplaza.com. Metro: Carlos Gardel.

Carlos Custom Shoes   This is not a shoe store, but a custom crafter of excellent, high-quality tango shoes. If you call, Carlos Farroni can come to your hotel to take measurements and then handcraft your shoes, or you can visit his home studio in Mataderos. His work takes longer than most stores with their own factory, up to 10 days or 2 weeks, but it is worth it, so make sure to contact him early during your trip. © **11/4687-6026** or 11/15-6756-3043 (cell).

Flabella   This is an extremely busy store, selling mostly shoes and other items for tango dancers. The best items are women's shoes, but there's also a variety of men's shoes. Many shoes are in stock for immediate purchase, but many styles have to be custom-made. This can take up to a week, so plan around this during your trip. Shoe prices begin at about $60 a pair. Eduardo is one of the most talented shoe technicians in the city, and he can also offer tips on the tango scene. The store is surrounded by several similar ones, so check out the whole block for a wider selection. This store is open Monday through Friday from 10am to 10pm and Saturday 10am to 6pm. Suipacha 263 (at Diagonal Norte). © **11/4322-6036.** www.flabella.com. Metro: Carlos Pellegrini.

La Vikinga Tango Fashions ★★   Already famous in Buenos Aires from when she ran her now closed *milonga* Mano a Mano, Helen Halldórsdóttir, nicknamed La Vikinga because she's Icelandic, has started a private tango clothing and shoe boutique. Contact her directly to view her designs, which range from tango dresses and other apparel to tango shoes and even tango sneakers. © **11/4383-6229** or 11/15-5865-8279 (cell). www.lavikinga.eu.

Pilchas Tangueras ★   Opened by tango dancer Mariela Piotti, formerly of Tango Moda, in late 2010, Pilchas Tangueras has tango clothes and accessories for men and women. The store also offers tango lessons and other tango services including helping arrange tango tours. The shop is open Monday through Saturday from noon to 7pm, Sunday 10:30am to 8pm. Defensa 566, Station 3 (btw. México and Venezuela). © **11/15-5658-1167** (cell). www.marielapiotti.com.ar. Metro: Moreno.

Tango Mina ★   If you've been seduced by Argentine tango, you'll want to spend an afternoon dressing for the part. Anne Midón (a devotee of tango herself) sells cutting-edge women's tango clothing and handmade shoes, inspired by the culture of tango. The styles span classic and traditional to hip and modern. The shop is open Monday through Friday from 2 to 7pm, Saturday noon to 3pm. Riobamba 486, 10th floor (at Lavalle). ✆ **11/4952-3262** or 11/15-5960-8195 (cell). www.tangomina.com.ar. Metro: Callao.

Tango Moda ★★★   There is no more stunningly situated store in Buenos Aires than this tango clothing store on the roof of the Palacio Barolo. An array of women's and men's tango clothes, accessories, and shoes await you, but it's the view—from the 16th floor of one of the city's most prominent buildings—that will take you away. About once a month (and more in summer), owner Jorge Arias throws sunset tango parties on the store's gargantuan terrace. Sip wine as you watch couples tango, with the Congreso as the backdrop. You're not dreaming, you're in Buenos Aires. Jorge is also the father of America TV news anchor Luciana Arias, whose early modeling pictures can be seen around the store. The store is open Monday to Friday from 2 to 9pm. This store might move to a new location in late 2011; call or check the website for details. Av. de Mayo 1370, 16th floor (at San José in Palacio Barolo). ✆ **11/4381-4049** or 11/15-4033-6746 (cell). www.tangomoda.com.ar. Metro: Sáenz Peña.

Toys & Children's Items

Casa Barbie ★★ ☺   Forget about a little pink plastic house. In Buenos Aires, Barbie gets a three-story mansion, the world's first free-standing store of its kind. Little girls and their moms can dream at Barbie wedding displays, or sit at the Barbie tearoom. There is also a beauty salon for a Barbie beauty makeover to impress your own Ken. The shop is open Monday to Saturday from 10am to 8:30pm, Sunday 1 to 8pm. Scalabrini Ortiz 3170 (btw. Cerviño and Cabello). ✆ **0810/4444-BARBIE** (4444-227243). www.barbie-stores.com. Metro: Scalabrini Ortiz.

Ufficio ★★   Most of the products in this store are handmade in Argentina and are solid wood, but they also have a few Chinese imports. Products include lamps, wooden rocking horses, dolls, jigsaw puzzles, guitars, baby bibs, and a few other clothing items. Many of the items are good gifts for kids as an alternative to video games and the usual. The store is open daily from 11am to 8pm. Jorge Luis Borges 1733 (at Pasaje Russel). ✆ **11/4831-5008.** No metro access.

Wine

Stores selling Argentine wines abound throughout Buenos Aires. Among the best are **Grand Cru,** Rodríguez Peña 1886 at Avenida Alvear (✆ **11/4816-3975;** www.grandcru.com.ar); **Tonel Privado,** in the Patio Bullrich Shopping Mall at Av. del Libertador 750 (✆ **11/4814-7526;** www.tonelprivado.com), with a second location in Galerías Pacífico at Calle Florida 750 (✆ **11/5555-5147**), both open daily 10am to 9pm; **Winery,** which has several branches including one at Av. Corrientes 300 at Avenida 25 de Mayo (✆ **11/4394-2200;** www.winery.com.ar), open Monday to Friday 9am to 8pm and Saturday 9am to 2pm; **Vinos Argentinos,** Tucumán 565 just off Calle Florida (✆ **11/4312-4841**); and **Lo De Joaquin Alberdi,** Jorge Luis Borges 1772 at Costa Rica, Palermo Viejo (✆ **11/4832-5329;** www.lodejoaquinalberdi.com.ar). If you're in a rush and don't mind overspending, you can easily buy good Argentine wine at most hotel bars and restaurants.

Wool & Sweaters

Lana's Argentina   The word *lana* is Spanish for "wool." At Lana's Argentina, you'll find a fine selection of Argentine wool sweaters made from fibers of Patagonian sheep and lambs. The shop also carries leather goods and accessories to complement your purchase. The store is open Monday to Friday from 9am to 8pm, Saturday 9am to 6pm. Suipacha 984 (at Paraguay). © **11/4328-8798.** Metro: San Martín.

BUENOS AIRES AFTER DARK

While other cities sleep, darkness makes Buenos Aires come alive. One thing you'll notice immediately in this city is that nightlife is a huge part of the Porteño experience. From Avenida Corrientes theaters to tango salons to big techno clubs, Buenos Aires offers an exceptional night out.

For Porteños, the evening usually begins with a play or movie around 8pm, followed by a late and long dinner. Then, after 11pm or midnight, it'll be time to visit a bar or two, before heading to clubs around 2am. On Thursday, Friday, and Saturday, Porteños stay out really late, heading to big dance clubs and bars in neighborhoods like Recoleta, Palermo, and the Costanera. By the time they head home, the sun is rising. Summertime nightlife is quieter because many flee to the coast, moving their nocturnal activities to places such as Mar del Plata and Punta del Este.

But nightlife is not just about clubbing. There are numerous cultural activities for visitors and residents alike. Professional theaters (many located along Av. Corrientes, btw. Av. 9 de Julio and Callao and in the San Telmo and Abasto neighborhoods) show Broadway- and off-Broadway-style hits, Argentine plays, and music revues, though most are in Spanish. Buy tickets for most productions at the box office or through **Ticketmaster** (© 11/4321-9700). **Tickets Buenos Aires** (www.ticketsbuenosaires. com.ar) is a reduced-price ticket office at the intersections of Corrientes, Cerritos (9 de Julio), and Diagonal Norte, open Wednesday to Sunday 11am to 8pm. The **British Arts Centre,** Suipacha 1333 (© 11/4393-2004), offers entertainment in English, ranging from lectures to standup comedy to Shakespeare.

For current information on after-dark activities, consult the English-language **Buenos Aires Herald** (www.buenosairesherald.com), which lists events held in English and Spanish and often features events by Irish, British, Australian, and North American expats. **The Argentine Independent** (www.argentinaindependent.com), produced by Brit Kristie Robinson, has similar listings and intelligent cultural articles. **Clarín, La Nación, Página 12** and many of the major local publications also list events, but in Spanish only. **QuickGuide Buenos Aires,** available in the city's tourism kiosks and in various hotels, has information on shows, theaters, and nightclubs. **Ciudad Abierta** (www.ciudadabiertatv.gov.ar) is a free weekly published by the city government and lists cultural events all over the city. Also check out their cable-access channel (by the same name), which highlights cultural and tourist interests around the city. *Llegas a Buenos Aires* (www.revistallegas.com.ar) lists cultural, arts, tango, and other events. This free newspaper is published weekly and distributed at locations across the city. Its website is an excellent planning resource for your trip. The websites **www.bainsomnio.com** and **www.whatsupbuenosaires.com** also list entertainment of all kinds in this city that never sleeps. Additionally, you can ask the Buenos Aires City Tourism offices for the "Funny Night Map," which lists bars and clubs throughout Buenos Aires (www.funnymaps.com.ar).

THE PERFORMING ARTS

Cultural Centers

Asociación Argentina de Cultura Inglesa (British Arts Centre) ★★★ This multifunction facility was established over 77 years ago by a British ambassador who wanted to do more to promote British culture within Argentina. Today the AACI teaches English to tens of thousands of students a year; runs several film, theater, culture, and art programs; and provides a welcoming environment for homesick English speakers. The center has a limited summer schedule from January to March and at press time British austerity measures are likely to also have an impact on programming. Pick up brochures at the center, or look up listings in the English-language *Buenos Aires Herald*. Suipacha 1333 (at Arroyo). ✆ **11/4393-2004.** www.aaci.org.ar and www.british artscentre.org.ar. Metro: San Martín.

Centro Cultural de Borges ★★ Not only can you shop all you want in Galerías Pacífico, but, if it's culture you're after, you can find that there too. The shopping mall houses this arts center named for Jorge Luis Borges, Argentina's most important literary figure. You'll find art galleries; lecture halls with various events; an art cinema; an art bookstore; the **Escuela Argentina de Tango,** which offers a schedule of lessons tourists can take with ease (✆ **11/4312-4990;** www.eatango.org); and the ballet star Julio Bocca's **Ballet Argentino** performance space and training school, full of young ballet stars (see below). Enter through Galerías Pacífico or at the corner of Viamonte and San Martín. ✆ **11/5555-5359.** www.ccborges.org.ar. Ticket prices vary. Metro: San Martín.

Centro Cultural Recoleta (Recoleta Cultural Center) ★★ To the side of the famous cemetery, this distinctive building—originally designed as a Franciscan convent—hosts Argentine and international art exhibits, experimental theater works, occasional music concerts, and an interactive science museum for children called Museo de Ciencias Participativas, where children are encouraged to touch and play with the displays. Some events within the Centro require tickets, but many exhibitions are free. The Hard Rock Cafe is behind the Cultural Center in the Recoleta Design Shopping Center. Junín 1930 (next-door to the Recoleta Cemetery). ✆ **11/4803-1040.** www.centroculturalrecoleta.org. Tickets $2–$15, many events free. Mon–Fri 2–8pm; Sat–Sun 10am–9pm. No metro access.

Dance, Classical Music & Opera

Julio Bocca and Ballet Argentino ★★★ Julio Bocca is Argentina's greatest ballet and dance star. Many of his performances combine tango movements with classical dance, creating a style uniquely his own, and uniquely Argentine. He runs a studio in the Centro Cultural de Borges for classical dance and ballet performances, as well as another performance space in Teatro Maipo on Calle Esmeralda, offering a range of events from dance to comedy plays. Mr. Bocca himself has officially retired, but even without him on stage, his Ballet Argentino troupe is a must-see for lovers of ballet and dance, especially the performances featuring Claudia Figaredo and Hernan Piquin. Ballet Argentino at the Centro Cultural Borges, in Galerías Pacífico at the corner of Viamonte and San Martín. ✆ **11/5555-5359.** www.juliobocca.com. Metro: San Martín. Teatro Maipo spaces at Teatro Maipo at Esmeralda 449 (at Corrientes). ✆ **11/4394-5521.** Metro: Lavalle.

Luna Park   Once the home of international boxing matches, Luna Park is the largest indoor stadium in Argentina, hosting shows and concerts, including those of the National Symphonic Orchestra. Numerous international stars have played here, and seeing them in Argentina costs significantly less than in North America and Europe. Though they had actually met previously, legend states that it was here, at a 1944 fundraiser for the victims of the San Juan earthquake, that Juan Perón first met the young actress Eva Duarte, changing Argentine history forever. The song "On This Night of a Thousand Stars" in the musical commemorates this event. Av. Madero 420 (btw. Corrientes and Lavalle). ✆ **11/4311-1990.** www.lunapark.com.ar. Metro: L. N. Alem.

Teatro Colón ★★★ ◙   For a more detailed description of this venue, see p. 112. The building itself is a major tourist stop, in addition to being a performance space. This magnificent structure, home to the country's finest opera, classical music, and theater performances, recently underwent an extensive renovation that was more than 2 years behind schedule. If you're in Buenos Aires, don't miss this venue: The memory of an opera or musical in the Teatro Colón will last a lifetime. Calle Libertad 621 (at Tucumán). ✆ **11/4378-7100.** www.teatrocolon.org.ar. Metro: Tribunales.

Theaters and Theater Companies

Grupo de Teatro Catalinas Sur   This theater company presents outdoor weekend performances in different areas of La Boca, as well as in their own theater in a converted warehouse. It's in Spanish, but it's mostly comedy, and both adults and children are likely to enjoy the productions. Av. Benito Pérez Galdós 93 (at Caboto). ✆ **11/4300-5707.** www.catalinasur.com.ar. Tickets $3–$10. No metro access.

KONEX   This sprawling complex, built into a former warehouse, holds theater and concert events as well as other cultural programs. Among the most popular local musicians who has played here is the Argentine-American rock star Kevin Johansen and his band the Nada. For a map of this venue, see the "Abasto & Once" map on p. 95. Sarmiento 3131 (btw. Anchorena and Jean Jaures). ✆ **11/4864-3200.** www.GrupoKonex.com. Metro: Carlos Gardel.

Proyecto 34S   This theater company, started by South African Nikki Froneman, is one of the most interesting in Buenos Aires. It organizes festivals and theater events connecting peoples and cultures of Africa and Latin America. Though small, the Afro-Argentine community has recently been experiencing a cultural revival. Visit the website for specific venues. ✆ **11/4775 6023** or 11/15-6938-4281 (cell). www.proyecto34s.com.

Teatro Gran Rex   Within this sleek, imposing, Art Deco theater, you'll be able to see many national and foreign music concerts. Av. Corrientes 857 (at Suipacha). ✆ **11/4322-8000.** Metro: Carlos Pellegrini.

Teatro Municipal General San Martín   This entertainment complex has three theaters staging drama, comedy, ballet, music, and children's plays. The lobby itself, which often hosts exhibitions of photography and art, is worth a special visit during the daytime. Lobby exhibitions are usually free. Corrientes 1530 (at Paraná). ✆ **0800/333-5254.** www.teatrosanmartin.com.ar. Metro: Uruguay.

Buenos Aires After Dark

Teatro Nacional Cervantes   Some of the city's best theater takes place here, in this production house originally built by a group of Spanish actors as a thank you to Buenos Aires. The building is sumptuous, in an ornate Spanish Imperial style, using materials brought from Spain. Thanks to a restoration program in 2008 and 2009, the detailed facade gleams anew. Av. Córdoba 1155 (at Libertad). ℭ **11/4815-8883.** www.teatro cervantes.gov.ar. Metro: Tribunales.

Teatro Opera Citi ★   This futuristic, Art Deco theater has been adapted for Broadway-style shows. The building is itself a rare example of Art Deco in Buenos Aires. The facade has undergone a renovation, revealing the lightning-bolt glass panels once hidden by advertising signs. Citibank is now the official sponsor of the theater. Many locals complained when Citibank removed the neon Opera sign, replacing it with its own. Since then, a compromise has been reached: The neon sign now reads Opera Citi. Av. Corrientes 860 (at Suipacha). ℭ **11/4326-1335.** Metro: Carlos Pellegrini.

Teatro Presidente Alvear   Tango, classical, and other music performances take place at this theater. Av. Corrientes 1659 (at Montevideo). ℭ **11/4374-6076.** Metro: Callao.

DANCE CLUBS

Dancing in Buenos Aires is not just about tango; in fact, much of the younger generation prefers salsa and European techno. The biggest nights out are Thursday, Friday, and Saturday. Generally, clubs, called *boliches*, open around midnight, get busy around 2 or 3am, and close around 7am. The websites **www.adondevamos.com** and **www.bsasinsomnio.com** are great resources for Buenos Aires nightlife. Club entry will generally run from $10 to $15, but getting yourself on a website or Facebook guest list can reduce or eliminate this cost. Young women should take note that young Argentine men can be very aggressive in their approach techniques in bars and nightclubs. Most of the advances are harmless, however, even if they may be annoying. Take note that while smoking is officially banned in all indoor spaces in Buenos Aires, most venues take a laissez-faire attitude toward folks lighting up.

Asia de Cuba ★   Come early for a meal at this supper club, and then enjoy sophisticated drinking and dancing under the golden Buddha. It's also a place where women are less likely to be harassed by men on the prowl. Pierina Dealessi 750 (at Güemes, on Dique 3). ℭ **11/4894-1328** or 11/4894-1329. www.asiadecuba.com.ar. No cover. No metro access.

Crobar   One of Buenos Aires's most popular mega clubs, holding up to 3,000 people, it's located under the train arches in the Bosques de Palermo park. Various DJs from around the world have played here, including Dutch sensation Armin van Buuren. Don't even think of heading here until 2am for dancing, but during the early evening, various concerts are also held here. Marcelo Freyre at Paseo de la Infanta. ℭ**11/4778-1500.** www.crobar.com.ar. Metro: Palermo.

Kika   This club, tucked away in what was once a railroad warehouse, attracts a young, fun Palermo Soho crowd dancing to rock and techno. Honduras 5339 (at Juan B. Justo). ℭ**11/4137-5311.** www.kikaclub.com.ar. Metro: Federico Lacroze.

Niceto Club ★   You'll find live music performances and DJ dancing in this popular Palermo Hollywood club, which takes its name from the street on which it is located. Niceto Vega 5510 (btw. Humboldt and Fitzroy). ℭ **11/4779-9396.** www.nicetoclub.com. Various covers and charges. Metro: Palermo.

Pachá ★   This club is inside the Costa Salguero riverfront industrial complex, near Palermo, but far enough away to prevent waking up the neighbors. It's modeled in music and style after the iconic Ibiza nightclub. Call or check Facebook for VIP tables. Av. Rafaela Obligada 6151 (at Pampa). © **11/4788-4280.** www.pachabuenosaires.com. Cover 50 pesos. No metro access.

Tequila   This mega club has a great mix of Latin music and techno. Be aware that the club closes from December to March in Buenos Aires, and opens a temporary summer venue in La Barra, outside of Punta del Este in Uruguay. Av. Costanera Norte and La Pampa. © **11/4781-6555.** Cover 40 pesos. No metro access.

THE BAR SCENE

There is no shortage of popular bars in Buenos Aires, and Porteños need little excuse to party. While dancing isn't the main draw at most bars the way it is at clubs, some do have DJs or live performers. You'll really be in luck if you catch a bachelor or bachelorette party out on the town; they'll be happy to have you come along to help embarrass the soon-to-be wedded. Most smoking now takes place outside, though you'll still find plenty of people breaking the ban indoors. For a special section on gay and lesbian bars and dance clubs, see p. 206.

Acá Bar ★   This is a crowded, fun bar, and also a restaurant. Opened in 1996, it's decorated in funky colors reminiscent of La Boca with an array of hodgepodge ornaments hanging from the walls, and famous for its inexpensive food, high-quality fruit drinks, and table games. The place is huge, seating over 500, and the name of the bar is a double-entendre. *Acá bar* means "here is the bar," but *acabar* has a sexual connotation. Ask a Spanish-speaking friend for the other meaning, or perhaps a friendly person at the bar will explain it to you. Honduras 5733 (btw. Bonpland and Carranza). © **11/4772-0845** or 11/15-5248-5253 (cell). www.acabarnet.com.ar. Metro: Carranza.

Bar Isabel ★   When this bar opened in Palermo Soho, next to Casa Cruz, it took the city by storm, becoming famous as a place to spot models. One of the most famous models of the Dotto Modeling Agency, Florencia Gomez Cordoba, once worked here, giving you an idea of its glamorous pull. It's hit-or-miss, though, and usually Tuesdays are when the models flock here. The bar was opened by Juan Santa Cruz, the original force behind Casa Cruz. Drinks are expensive, and are purchased with *Isabelitas,* which are 25-peso poker chips that you buy when entering the club. You'll need one for water or soft drinks, two for mixed drinks, meaning that the latter go for about $13 each, a very high price in Buenos Aires. The club is a mix of mod funk and classics—with veneered 1940s style nightclub tables, edged with S&M studs, lit from above by orange-glowing mushroom lights. Outside, the fireplace patio is a great place to smoke and chat, whether or not your companion has graced the cover of *Vogue.* Owner Juan Santa Cruz recommends tourists wanting to see a glamorous edge to Buenos Aires

Palermo Nightlife

Hip, lively bars and innovative restaurants cluster around Plaza Serrano in Palermo Soho and spread throughout the neighboring districts of Palermo Hollywood and Palermo Viejo, so come for dinner and stay for drinks. For a map of nightlife in this neighborhood, see the "Palermo Attractions, Shopping & Nightlife" map on p. 134.

BUENOS AIRES AFTER DARK

The Bar Scene

come to Bar Isabel because "it's where they are going to have the most fun, the most beautiful place, the best music, you can dance, and anything goes." Uriarte 1664 (at Honduras). ℂ **11/4834-6969.** www.barisabel.com. Metro: Plaza Italia.

Crónico Bar The bar has overlooked Plaza Serrano for nearly 25 years, and the movie posters outside are probably the first thing you'll notice. Inside, it's a busy place where people sit at tables painted with nude women in the style of Picasso. The menu includes typical bar food such as sandwiches and hamburgers, but with a larger selection than most of the surrounding bars. There's occasionally live rock music. It's also open 24/7, so it's a great place for an after-hours snack, or a morning drink. Borges 1646 (at Plaza Serrano). ℂ **11/4833-0708.** www.cronicobar.com. Metro: Plaza Italia.

El Alamo/Shoeless Joe's No matter what time of day it is, you'll find something going on at this American-owned 24/7 bar. The bar was originally simply called Shoeless Joe's, but when Texas-born owner Pete found Argentines could not pronounce it, he added an homage to his home state in the name. It's a great place to gather and watch football games and other American sports events, but locals come here too. The interior is full of wood, with a "Cheers"-type feel. Beer of all kinds is sold by the bottle or in huge pitchers from the tap, and there's a food menu as well, with most entrees costing about $4 to $12. The breakfast specials are a treat after a night of clubbing, and there's free pizza during the happy hour from 8 to 10pm during the week. Ask about student discounts. Uruguay 1175 and 1177 (btw. Santa Fe and Arenales). ℂ **11/4813-7324.** www.elalamobar.com. Metro: Callao.

Gran Bar Danzon A small, intimate bar, Danzon attracts a fashionable crowd with its small selection of international food and smart, relaxing lounge music. An excellent barman serves exquisite cocktails and a variety of liquors and wines. Libertad 1161 (at Santa Fe). ℂ **11/4811-1108.** www.granbardanzon.com.ar. Metro: San Martín.

Jackie O. ★ It might be named for America's favorite First Lady, but this bar seems more English in style than American, with its wood-paneled interior and classic paned windows. Always crowded, even on a Monday, it's an important and very busy fixture on the Las Cañitas bar scene. With three levels, including a covered rooftop patio, it's also one of the largest. A simple menu of Argentine and American food is served, and many patrons come early to eat and then linger over drinks with the rowdy crowd. Báez 334 (btw. Chenaut and Arévalo). ℂ **11/4774-4844.** Metro: Carranza.

The Kilkenny This trendy cafe/bar is more like a rock house than an Irish pub, although you will still be able to order Guinness, Kilkenny, and Harp draft beers. It's packed with locals and foreigners, and you're as likely to find people in suits as in jeans and T-shirts. The Kilkenny offers happy hour from 6 to 8pm and live bands every night after midnight; it stays open until 5am. Marcelo T. de Alvear 399 (at Reconquista). ℂ **11/4312-9179** or 11/4312-7291, www.thekilkenny.com.ar. Metro: San Martín.

Come for Dinner, Stay for Drinks

The Palermo restaurants **Olsen ★★** (p. 86) and **Sullivan's** (p. 88) are open late and each have a full bar, so you can stick around after dinner or stop by just for drinks. The restaurant and bookstore **Clásica y Moderna ★★** (p. 79), in Barrio Norte, often has evening literary readings, plays, and dance shows. See chapter 5.

La Divina Observing the purple-silhouetted naked woman who adorns the entry, you might wonder if this is a strip joint or trannie bar. Instead, you'll come across a bit of Miami, Palermo, and London thrown together. La Divina, with a nod to Dante, is a resto-bar upstairs, with a blue color scheme representing heaven, and a dance club downstairs, decorated in red for hell, where DJs spin on a crowded dance floor and comedians try to get a laugh. It's an unusually modern space in retro San Telmo. Defensa 683 (at Chile). ✆ **11/4781-3358.** Metro: Moreno.

Macondo Bar ★★ Macondo Bar is one of the stars of Plaza Serrano, with sidewalk seating and lots of levels overlooking the action. Inside, the low-ceilinged restaurant twists around several staircases. There's a food menu that consists of typical bar food, including sandwiches, pizzas, salads, and *picadas* (masa tartlets). DJs blast music of all kinds throughout the bar, from folkloric to techno to electronica. Technically there's no live music, but sometimes people come around and play on the street in front of the bar. It's a loud and busy place for sure, but the setup adds a certain sense of intimacy. Borges 1810 (at Costa Rica). ✆ **11/4831-4174.** Metro: Plaza Italia.

Milion ★★ A bar and a restaurant, this place really comes alive at night, especially on weekends. It's one of the most stunningly set venues in Buenos Aires, inside a turn-of-the-last-century mansion in Barrio Norte. On the ground floor is the restaurant, but head upstairs to the bar, where a glamorous set of locals is invariably ordering drinks and getting to know each other. The activity spreads up the French wrought-iron staircase throughout the building's various levels, where rooms are strewn with chairs, couches, and ottomans. There's also an outdoor patio, and drinking and socializing flows down the marble staircase leading into the garden. Paraná 1048 (at Santa Fe). ✆ **11/4815-9925.** www.milionargentina.com.ar. Metro: Callao.

OMM Bar ★ OMM moved and expanded since our last edition, adding a glamorous touch to its funky vibe, and with an expanded drinks and food menu. Still, it's all about the music in this dance bar. Honduras 5656 (btw. Bonpland and Fitzroy). ✆ **11/4774-4224.** www.ommbuenosaires.com.ar. Metro: Carranza.

Plaza Bar Nearly every Argentine president and his or her cabinet have come here, in addition to visiting celebs such as the queen of Spain, the emperor of Japan, Luciano Pavarotti, and David Copperfield. A mix of Art Deco and English country, the bar features mahogany furniture and velvet upholstery, where guests sip martinis and other classy drinks. Tuxedo-clad waiters recommend a fine selection of whiskeys and brandies. In 2005, *Forbes* magazine declared this among the world's top nine hotel bars, based on several factors—the clientele, beverage selection, and the way the staff makes everyone feel welcome, even if they're not regular customers. This was the city's most famous cigar bar, but the 2006 anti-smoking law put an end to that decades-long tradition. Inside the Marriott Plaza Hotel, Calle Florida 1005 (at Santa Fe, overlooking Plaza San Martín). ✆ **11/4318-3000.** Metro: San Martín.

República de Acá ★★ Charcoal drawings of Hollywood actors and other stars decorate the walls of this fun comedy club and karaoke bar overlooking Plaza Serrano. Drinks are the main event here, but food includes pizzas, *picadas* (plates of cut cheese and meat that you "pick at"), salads, and other easy-to-make small items. Drinks come with free use of the Internet, and the menu tells how many minutes of Internet use are included with each drink. About half of this club is taken up by computers. Drink prices rise by about 10% after 11pm. At night, the shows begin, and there is entertainment of all kinds. On weekends, live music shows begin at 10pm, followed by comedy routines at 12:30am, karaoke at 3am, and then dancing until way past sunrise. There is a $5 entrance fee after 10pm on weekends, which includes one drink. After 2am, this drops to a little over $3 to enter and still includes one drink. Many mixed drinks are made with ice cream, an adult interpretation of soda floats. TVs wrap around the whole space, so there is always something to watch. Serrano 1549 (at Plaza Serrano). © **11/4581-0278.** www.republicadeaca.com.ar. Metro: Plaza Italia.

Rey Castro ★　A giant statue of Castro greets you as you enter this club and restaurant. They have an excellent Caribbean menu, and salsa and Latin dancing on two levels. Monday to Thursday, come for the happy hour from 6 to 9:30pm, with an emphasis on mojitos and Cuba Libres. Perú 342 (at Moreno). © **11/4342-9998.** www.rey castro.com. Metro: Moreno.

The Shamrock　The city's best-known Irish pub is more likely to play hot Latin rhythms than Gaelic music. It's popular with Argentines and foreign visitors alike and a great spot to begin the night. A game room with pool tables and other attractions is in the basement. Rodríguez Peña 1220 (at Juncal). © **11/4812-3584.** Metro: Callao.

Soul Café and SuperSoul ★★　This retro, funky 1970s-style bar complex is the centerpiece of the Las Cañitas bar scene. There are two bars in the complex; you'll find one side might be more happening than the other, depending on the night. Deep inside the space is a small lounge area with live music. There's a velvet rope, but don't get the glamour worries—it's just for show. Still, most of the action takes place in the front bar, and if you're looking to maybe get lucky Buenos Aires style, this might be the place to check out on your trip. Báez 352 (at Chenaut). © **11/4778-3115.** Metro: Carranza.

Sugar ★★　Owned by Irishman Keith Lang and Americans Marty Hanna and Martin Frankel, this Palermo Soho spot has become trendy with English-speaking expats who have decided to make Buenos Aires their home and Argentines who like to meet them. When major news or sports events happen of interest to the English-speaking world, this is where people gather to watch them. They have a bar menu, focused on inexpensive comfort food ranging from $5 to $10. Come for their daily $2-a-drink happy hour, from 7pm to midnight, and DJ-accompanied mingling. Costa Rica 4619 (btw. Armenia and Gurruchaga). © **11/4831-3276.** www.sugarbuenosaires.com. No metro access.

Tazz ★　Mexican snack food is the highlight of this place, with its blue spaceship-themed interior. The sidewalk space overlooking Plaza Serrano is one of the largest, so this is a great place to come in the summer or in warm weather. The crowd here is very young. Serrano 1556 (at Plaza Serrano). © **11/4833-5164.** www.tazzbars.com. Metro: Plaza Italia.

Utopia Bar　This is an excellent place to grab a drink and a bite to eat in this trendy area. Yellow walls and soothing rustic wood tables add a sense of calm, though the live music, scheduled on an irregular basis, can be loud at times. Flavored coffees are one of the specialties here. The upstairs, open-air terrace on the roof of the bar is one of the best spots to sit, but its small size, with just a few tables, makes it hard to claim a spot. Because Utopia is open 24 hours, this is your go-to spot for a drink at any time of the night or day. Serrano 1590 (at Plaza Serrano). © **11/4831-8572.** Metro: Plaza Italia.

Van Koning　With a model of van Gogh and its Dutch beers on tap, this is where you go to party Netherlands style, making sure to toast Princess Maxima, the Argentine beauty who will one day be a Dutch queen. Anyone is welcome to come here, of course, but the first Wednesday of every month around 11pm is when local Dutch expats gather for a communal bash. Báez 325 (at Arévalo). © **11/4772-9909.** www.vankoning. com. Metro: Carranza.

Historical Bars & Bares Notables

Buenos Aires is blessed with a large collection of historical bars, cafes, pubs, and restaurants. Most of these are concentrated in San Telmo, Monserrat, the Microcentro, and other older areas of the city. I highly recommend checking them out all over the city, and I have listed some of them in various sections of this book, including chapter 5. Below are just a few highlights. You should ask for the *Bares y Cafés Notables* map from the Buenos Aires tourism kiosks to see a longer list of these remarkable spaces, which I hope will continue to be preserved.

Bar El Federal ★★ This bar and restaurant, on a quiet corner in San Telmo, represents a graceful step back in time. It has been in business since 1864, and fortunately, as another *café notable*, it will continue to be preserved. The first thing that will strike you is the massive, carved-wood and stained-glass ornamental stand over the bar area, which originally came from an old pastry shop. Local patrons sit at the old tables whiling away their time looking out onto the streets, chatting, or sitting with a book and drinking tea or espresso. The original tile floor remains, and old signs, portraits, and small antique adding machines decorate the space. Bar El Federal is among the most Porteño of places in San Telmo, a neighborhood that has more *bares* and *cafés notables* than any other. Some staff have proudly worked here for decades. Carlos Calvo 599 (at Perú). ✆ **11/4300-4313.** Metro: Independencia.

La Coruña ★ This extremely authentic old cafe and restaurant bar, another of the *cafés notables* protected by law, is the kind of place where you'd expect your grandfather to have eaten when he was a teenager. Young and old alike come to this bar, which is a very neighborhoody spot, with people catching *fútbol* games on television or quietly chatting away as they order beer, small snacks, and sandwiches. The TV seems the only modern thing in here. Music plays from a wooden table-top radio that must be from the 1950s, and two wooden refrigerators dating from who knows when are still in use. The old couple that owns the place, José Moreira and Manuela Lopéz, subscribe to the view that if it ain't broke, there's no reason for a new one. Bolívar 994 (at Carlos Calvo). ✆ **11/4362-7637.** Metro: Independencia.

Plaza Dorrego Bar ★ Representative of a typical Porteño bar from the 19th century, Plaza Dorrego displays portraits of Carlos Gardel, antique liquor bottles in cases along the walls, and anonymous writings engraved in the wood. One of the specially protected *bares* and *cafés notables*, it's a good place to stop by on Sunday, when the crowd spills onto the street and you can catch the San Telmo antiques market on the plaza out front. Calle Defensa 1098 (at Humberto I, overlooking Plaza Dorrego). ✆ **11/4361-0141.** Metro: Constitución.

TANGO SHOW PALACES

Tango is an essential part of the Buenos Aires experience. Numerous show palaces, from the simple **Café Tortoni** (p. 115) to the over-the-top, special-effects-laden **Señor Tango** (p. 201), compete for your tourist dollar. Many shows are excellent, and each is surprisingly unique. Here, I've listed some of the top show palaces, but new ones seem to open up all the time. Many show palaces include dinner, or you can arrive just in time for the show only. Prices vary tremendously, depending on the venue and how you have booked; the price for a show only is around $75 to $125, with dinner and show about $125 to $400 for VIP seating. Seeing a variety of tango palaces is important, as each show has its own style. Smaller spaces lead to a greater intimacy and more interaction between the dancers and the audience. Sometimes the dancers even grab a few people, so watch out if you're close to the stage! Most shows have bus services that pick you up at your hotel. Book directly, or ask your hotel for help and bus transfer times, which can be up to an hour before the show. Many local bars also have informal tango shows, where locals come to see decades-old favorites singing.

BocaTango   This show palace celebrates tango in one of the neighborhoods associated with its early development. The enormous hall is highlighted by a stage set mimicking the colorful La Boca streets outside. Watch as dancers recount the history and excitement of Buenos Aires's Little Italy from the windows and balconies of their *conventillos*, a form of slum housing that is characteristic of the area. Your meal is served in an Italian bistro setting, and the food is good enough to make you wonder if Mamma is back there somewhere in the kitchen. Transportation is provided from your hotel. Brandsen 923 (at Practico Poliza). ✆ **11/4302-0808**. www.bocatango.com.ar. No metro access.

Café Tortoni ★★   Four times each day, high-quality yet inexpensive tango shows are held in the back room of the Café Tortoni. The price of the shows does not include dinner, but you can order what you want from the cafe's menu and pay for it separately. The tight space here is not for the claustrophobic. Visit their cumbersome website, look under the heading "cartalera," and click on a day of the week for more information and a description of all the upcoming shows including tango, jazz, children's theater, and more. Av. de Mayo 829 (at Piedras). ✆ **11/4342-4328**. www.cafetortoni.com.ar. Tickets $23. Metro: Piedras.

Complejo Tango ★★   This show palace offers the full tango experience to its patrons. It begins with an optional tango lesson at 7:30pm, then dinner at 9pm, followed by the show at 10pm. The main hall is in an old converted house with a platform in the middle and a retro interior that looks a bit like a stage set for old New Orleans. There are three singers, three pairs of dancers, and a four-person orchestra providing the music for the show, which consists of international-style dancing, a little bit of folklore, and a humorous presentation. Transportation is provided to and

The Disappearing Bandoneón

With just two dancers and a bandoneón, an accordion-like instrument introduced into Argentina in the mid-1800's by German immigrants, a tango performance can be held. Tourists have so come to love these instruments that thousands of them are leaving the country as souvenirs, fueling a black market in stolen bandoneóns. Only a few dozen of these instruments are built every year, and like Stradivarious violins, new ones never match the tone of those that are decades old. American TV journalist Luciana Arias recently covered the issue, releasing a special video on You Tube. The rapid dwindling of the instruments has reached such a crisis point that in 2010 the Argentine government proposed a law registering every bandoneón and forbidding the exportation of those that were above a certain age or that had been used by famous tango musicians. If you're thinking about purchasing one to bring home with you, reflect on how you might be slowly silencing the music that made Buenos Aires famous around the world.

TANGO: LESSONS IN THE dance OF SEDUCTION & DESPAIR

It seems impossible to imagine Argentina without thinking of tango, its greatest export to the world. Tango originated with a guitar and violin toward the end of the 19th century and was first danced by working-class men in La Boca, San Telmo, and the port area. Combining African rhythms with the *habañera* and *candombe,* it was not the sophisticated dance you know today—rather, the tango originated in brothels, known locally as *quilombos.* At that time the dance was considered too obscene for women, and men would dance it with each other in the brothel lounges.

Increasing waves of immigrants added Italian elements to the tango and helped bring the dance to Europe, where it was embraced in Paris. Spurred by European approval, Argentine middle and upper classes began to accept the newly refined dance as part of their cultural identity, and the form blossomed with the extraordinary voice of Carlos Gardel, who brought tango to Broadway and Hollywood and is nothing short of legendary among Argentines. Astor Piazzolla further internationalized the tango, elevating it to a more complex form incorporating classical elements.

Tango music can range from two musicians to a complete orchestra, but a piano and *bandoneón*—an instrument akin to an accordion—are usually included. Lyrics often come from Argentina's great poets, such as Jorge Luis Borges, Homero Manzi, and Horacio Ferrer. Common themes tend to be a downtrodden life or a woman's betrayal, making this style akin to American jazz and blues, which developed at the same time. The dance itself is improvised rather than standardized, consisting of a series of long walks and intertwined movements, usually in eight-step. In the tango, the man and woman glide across the floor as an exquisitely orchestrated duo with early flirtatious movements giving way to dramatic leads and heartfelt turns, with the man always leading the way. These movements, such as the kicks that simulate knife movements, or the sliding, shuffled feet that mimic the walk of a gangster sidling up to someone to stab them, echo the dance's rough roots as the favored dance of La Boca gangsters in spite of its glamorous beauty as performed nowadays.

Learning to dance the tango is an excellent way for a visitor to get a sense of what makes the music—and the dance—so alluring. Entering a tango salon—called a *salón de baile* or *milonga*—can be intimidating for the novice. The style of tango danced in salons is more subdued than "show tango." Most respectable dancers would not show up before midnight, giving you the perfect opportunity to sneak in for a group lesson, offered at most of the salons starting around 7 to 9pm. These usually cost between $10 and $14 for an hour; you can request private instruction for between $25 and $50 per hour, depending on the instructor. In summer, the city of Buenos Aires promotes tango by offering free classes in many locations. Visit the nearest tourist information center for updated information. Before you head to Argentina, free tango lessons are also provided by select Argentine consulates in the United States.

For additional advice on places to dance and learn tango, get a copy of *B.A. Tango* or *El Tangauta,* the city's dedicated tango magazines. Ongoing evening lessons are also offered at the **Academia Nacional de Tango,** located above Café Tortoni, at Av. de Mayo 833 (✆ **11/4345-6968**), which is an institute rather than a tango salon.

from hotels. Prices range from $60 to $160. For a map of this venue, see the "Abasto & Once" map on p. 95. Av. Belgrano 2608 (at Saavedra). ✆ **11/4941-1119** or 11/4308-3242. www.complejotango.com.ar. Metro: Miserere.

El Querandí   El Querandí offers the best historically based tango show in the city, tracing the tradition from its early roots in bordellos, when only men danced it, to its current leggy, sexy style. A great slab of beef and glass of wine are included in your ticket. Open Monday through Saturday; dinner begins at 8:30pm, followed by the show at 10:15pm. Perú 302 (at Moreno). ✆ **11/5199-1770.** www.querandi.com.ar. Tickets $80–$100. Metro: Moreno or Bolívar.

El Viejo Almacén   The most famous of the city's tango salons, the Almacén offers what some consider the city's most authentic performance. Shows involve traditional Argentine-style tango (many other shows feature international-style tango). Sunday through Thursday shows are at 10pm; Friday and Saturday shows are at 9:30 and 11:45pm. Dinner is served each night before the show starts, in the three-story restaurant across the street. Guests may opt for dinner and the show or show only, with standard pricing and VIP pricing for seats closer to the stage. Some hotels offer transportation. Independencia and Balcarce. ✆ **11/4307-6689.** www.viejo-almacen.com.ar. Tickets $60–$137. Metro: Independencia.

Esquina Carlos Gardel ★   In my opinion, this is one of the most elegant tango shows. It's at the former site of the Chanta Cuatro—a restaurant where Carlos Gardel used to dine with his friends—though the building is new. The luxurious old-time-style dining room features high-tech acoustics and superb dancers, creating a wonderful environment for this excellent performance. Doors open at 8pm, and there's standard pricing as well as VIP pricing for seats closer to the stage. For a map of this venue, see the "Abasto & Once" map on p. 95. Carlos Gardel 3200 (at Anchorena, across from the Abasto Shopping Center). ✆ **11/4867-6363.** www.esquinacarlosgardel.com.ar. Tickets $105–$210. Metro: Carlos Gardel.

Evita Vive ★★   One has to wonder why it took so long to develop a show that combines the history of Evita's impact on Argentina with tango. Opened in December 2010, in the Hotel Moreno theater, Evita Vive uses tango, disco, and even essences of rap and hip-hop, taking viewers from Evita's birth in Los Toldos to her death in the Presidential Palace, under the direction of Peter Macfarlane. There's excellent dancing, singing, and live music as performers move through the audience of this intimate 120-seat theatre. Moreno 364 in the Hotel Moreno (btw. Defensa and Balcarce). ✆ **11/6091-2092.** www.evitavive.com. Tickets $84–$200. Metro: Plaza de Mayo.

La Ventana   This show is held in the atmospheric brick-lined cellar of an old building in San Telmo. Performances are a mix of tango, folkloric, and other Argentine styles of dance and music. One of the highlights of the night is a schmaltzy rendition of "Don't Cry for Me, Argentina," complete with a movable balcony and rather glamorous *descamisados* (shirtless ones) holding Argentine flags. Balcarce 431 (at Venezuela). ✆ **11/4331-1314.** www.la-ventana.com.ar. Metro: Belgrano.

Madero Tango   Madero Tango prides itself not just on what you see onstage but what you see outside its terraces. Located in the Puerto Madero area, this building extends along the waterfront of San Telmo, overlooking the port and boats in the water. It's a more modern, chic, and spacious setting than most of the tango shows in Buenos Aires, and the shows are a bit splashy, too. E. Rawson de Dellepiane 150, Dock 1; alternate address is Moreau de Justo 2060 (at Puerto Madero's southern end near highway underpass at waterfront). ✆ **11/5239-3009.** www.maderotango.com.ar. No metro access.

Piazzolla Tango   This tango show spectacular is held in a stunning theater, an Art Nouveau masterpiece created by the architect who designed the now-closed Confitería del Molino, next door to Congreso. This theater had been closed for nearly 40 years and was only recently restored. Of all the tango show palaces in Buenos Aires, this is the most beautiful, which adds even more excitement to the well-choreographed show. Calle Florida 165 in Galería Güemes (at Perón). ℂ **11/4344-8201.** www.piazzollatango. com. Metro: Florida.

Señor Tango ★★   This enormous theater is more akin to a Broadway production hall than a traditional tango salon, but the dancers are fantastic. The owner, who clearly loves to perform, is also a good singer. Walls are covered with photos of what appears to be every celebrity who's ever visited Buenos Aires—and all seem to have made it to Señor Tango. Diners choose among steak, chicken, or fish for dinner. Despite the huge crowd, the food quality is commendable. Have dinner or come only for the show. Dinner is at 8:30pm; shows start at 10pm. There's standard pricing and VIP pricing for seats closer to the stage or private alcoves. Vieytes 1655 (at Domingo). ℂ **11/4303-0231.** www.senortango.com.ar. Tickets $47–$213. No metro access.

Tango Porteño ★★   There's no way you can miss the location of this tango show, with its pulsating light display overlooking 9 de Julio next door to Teatro Colón. This fantastic show, opened in 2008 in a space connected to the NH Tango hotel, brings the "golden decade" of the 1920s to life, with a skilled live orchestra and beautifully choreographed dancing in a mock Art Deco theater. Minimal stage settings and intense lighting keep the focus on the dancing. (Dinner is at 8:30pm; shows start at 10:15pm). Cerrito (9 de Julio) 570 (at Tucumán). ℂ **11/4124-9400.** www.tangoporteno.com.ar. Tickets $80–$225. Metro: Tribunales.

MILONGAS (TANGO SALONS & DANCE HALLS)

While the show palaces and their dance shows are wonderful must-sees, there is nothing like the allure of Buenos Aires's *milongas* (tango salons and the events that take place at these venues). As with the show palaces, there are more now than ever before. Rather than destroy tango, the 2001 peso crisis created a greater awareness of the dance along with all things traditionally Argentine. In the same way that the ancestors of today's Porteños turned to tango more than 100 years ago to alleviate their pain, isolation, and worries, so too did Porteños in the wake of the peso crisis, resulting in an unprecedented flourishing of *milongas.* This recent history, coupled with the increase in tourism and an influx of expats from Europe and North America who have embraced the dance and the culture surrounding it, means that there are more tango opportunities than ever before. This scene is not without its rules and obstacles, however, especially surrounding interactions with dancers of the opposite sex. Be sure to read "Some Tango Rules" (below) for tips on *milonga* etiquette before heading out. (Note also that most *milongas* charge an entry fee of $5–$8.)

You should also pick up the ***Tango Map,*** which has a comprehensive list of *milongas* in all regions of the city. Find it at the tourism kiosks, the various tango-associated venues listed in this book, and also in select locations in San Telmo. Be aware that the same location may have different events by different names, so keeping track of the address of the venue is important. Also, check the listings in ***B.A. Tango, El Tangauta,*** and ***La Milonga,*** the city's main tango magazines. Also look for ***Punto***

Tango, a pocket-size guide with similar information. The numbers that are listed in this section and in the magazines or maps are not necessarily those of the venues, but may be the numbers of the various dance organizations or individual promoters that hold events in the specific dance venue on any given night. See also "Gay & Lesbian Dance Clubs, Resto-Bars & Tango Salons," later in this chapter.

El Arranque 🏙 This dance venue looks like a Knights of Columbus hall, but it's one of the most authentic *milonga* venues; it's also one of the few places that hosts afternoon dancing. Tango's late-night schedule could drive even a vampire crazy, but here you can dance and still get a real night's sleep afterward. No matter how old and pot-bellied a man is, he can dance with any woman in the crowd as long as he dances well. Even older women, however, tend to keep up appearances here, dressing beautifully and stylishly. Older crowds will be very comfortable here. Be forewarned that traditional tango rules separating the sexes are strictly enforced; couples might not even be allowed to sit together. Dancing begins most afternoons at 3pm. Closed Monday. Bartolomé Mitre 1759 (at Callao). ✆ **11/4371-6767.** Admission $5. Metro: Congreso.

El Beso Nightclub 🏙 This club can be a bit difficult to find. It's unmarked, so the street address is your only indication that you're in the right spot. Walk upstairs, pay your fee, and squeeze past the crowded bar blocking your view. The small space beyond maintains the air of a 1940s nightclub, updated somewhat with brilliant reds and modern abstractions painted on some of its walls. Ceiling lamps made from car air filters cast a golden glow on the dancers. Some of the best performers drag their egos with them to the floor, so if you're not so good on your feet, just watch; the last thing you want is to bump into someone. The divisions between the *milongueras* and *milongueros* are not so strong, and the sexes tend to mix informally. Reserve a table ahead of time if you can. Different *milongas* take place on different nights. Check their calendar in advance for details. Snacks, wine, and beer are sold. Riobamba 416 (at Corrientes). ✆ **11/4953-2794** or 11/15-4938-8108 (cell). Admission $5. Metro: Callao.

El Niño Bien ★★ 🏙 If you want to travel back in time to an era when tango ruled Buenos Aires, few places will do you better. The beautiful main dance hall here is straight from the Belle Epoque; you'll half-expect Carlos Gardel himself to show up behind the mic. Dressed in black, men and women tango while patrons at side tables respectfully study their techniques. Don't look too closely at anyone, however, unless you know what you're doing: *Milonga* eyes—staring from across a room, presumably to lure a partner onto the dance floor—are taken seriously. Food is served, but don't bother unless you're famished; it's only so-so. Unfortunately, Niño Bien is becoming a victim of its own success, and many tour groups are starting to unload here. If you're looking to find a tango teacher, one will probably find you first at this venue; many instructors come here seeking students for private lessons. Centro Región Leonesa, Humberto I no. 1462 (at San José). ✆ **11/4483-2588.** Admission $5–$6. Metro: Constitución.

La Viruta 🏙 This is one of the most interesting *milongas*. It has an authentic vibe, but it attracts a very young crowd of Porteños and expats who have come from all over the world to dance their lives away in Buenos Aires. Many nights it is just a *milonga*. Other nights host shows and competitions, many involving tango and folkloric and modern dance. La Viruta is in the cellar of the Armenian Community Center. When decorated with balloons for some events, it looks a little like a high school prom from the 1970s. There is an admission fee, but it is usually free here after 3am, when a throng arrives from other *milongas*. Armenia 1366 (at Cabrera). ✆ **11/4774-6357.** Admission $8. No metro access.

SOME TANGO rules

Certainly the seductive sound of the tango is one of the reasons you came to Buenos Aires in the first place. Maybe you just want to see those fancy kicks and moves performed onstage. Maybe you'd like to learn some of the steps yourself. Or maybe you're nearly an expert and want your own turn on the wooden dance floors where Buenos Aires's best have danced for decades.

The only places most tourists see tango in Buenos Aires are in the big, and expensive, show palace–restaurants, which feature dancers onstage as patrons enjoy meals in which steak is usually the centerpiece. While aimed at tourists, these shows are beautifully and artistically executed, and even jaded Porteños cannot help but be impressed. In spite of the quantity of these stage spectaculars, each has its own personality and focus. Some concentrate on the dance's history, others on the intimacy of the performers with the audience; some throw in other dance forms, especially folkloric, or seem to forget tango all together in an ode to Broadway.

However, I think every tourist should also venture beyond the show palaces. If you can, head to a *milonga*, a place where regulars and novices alike come to dance the tango, usually following a strict protocol of interactions between the sexes. A key concept in these places is *milonga* eyes—perhaps you've heard stories about two sets of eyes meeting across the room and their owners then finding their way to each other on the dance floor. In some *milongas*, men and women sit on opposite sides of the room, couples only mingling in certain spots. Men and women will try to catch each other's eyes, flirting from a distance with nods, smiles, and hand movements. The man finally approaches the woman, offering to dance. Often, not a word passes between the two until they take the floor.

This ritual means that tourists need to be aware of a few things. Firstly, never, ever block anyone's view, especially a woman who is sitting by herself. Be aware of divisions between the sexes in seating (which might be enforced by the management anyway), and follow the rules. Avoid eye contact with members of the opposite sex if you have no idea what you're doing. If a woman wants to dance with new men in order to practice the tango, she should not be seen entering the salon with a male friend, because most of the other men will assume she is already taken. If couples want to practice dancing with new people, they should enter the room separately. If you are coming in a group, divide yourselves up by sex for the same reason.

Each *milonga*, however, maintains its own grip on these rules: Some are very strict, others abide only by some. Some of the stricter *milongas* may tell you that they have no seats if they realize you're a foreigner; if this happens, tell them you're meeting a friend who arrived earlier. It's also best not to go to these places in large groups, and rather with a few people at a time or as a couple. The sudden entrance of a large group of noisy curious foreigners who don't know the place can instantly change the overall atmosphere. And most importantly, show respect for the venue in terms of your appearance. While you needn't dress to the nines, a baseball cap and sneakers can mar the atmosphere of the place (if you're even allowed in).

Find a copy of the *Tango Map*, which lists almost all of the city's *milongas* as well as specific events by date. It is, incidentally, among the best maps of Buenos Aires, and it even includes neighborhoods generally off the beaten tourist path.

Lo de Celia 👥 Don't let the modern setup of this place fool you: This is a very traditional *milonga* where rules are strictly applied. Men and women sit on opposite sides of the dance floor, with couples mingling only at the corners. Music is provided by a DJ. The floors are made of terrazzo, which can make dancing harder on the feet than at other tango venues. The crowd here is generally mature and dancers are very experienced. The strict enforcement of separation by gender means women will be treated like ladies in this place. Contests are often held close to the end of the night, which are fun to watch and bring levity to the tense atmosphere that accompanies the late-night tango egoists. Humberto I no. 1783 (at Solis). ✆ **11/4184-4244.** Cover $6. No metro access.

Plaza Bohemia 👥 In what seems like an isolated part of the Microcentro, you'll notice this place for its open door late at night. Inside, the interior is plain, highlighted by mirrors and a DJ booth. It's all about the dancing here, though, with various events on different nights, including the Wednesday-night gay tango **La Marshall** (p. 208). Admission fees will vary, and check local listings for various nightly events, including special tango presentations. Maipú 444 (at Corrientes). ✆ **11/4328-0465** or 11/15-6657-9867 (cell). www.plazabohemia.net. Admission $5–$8. Metro: Florida or Lavalle.

Salón Canning ★★ 👥 This is among the most authentic of all of the *milongas*. At the end of a long hallway, spectators crowd around the main dance floor to watch couples make their way around it. Salón Canning is known for its smooth, high-quality wooden parquet floor, considered one of the best for dancing in all of Buenos Aires. This tango hall is among the few things left in Buenos Aires that still bear the name of George Canning—a British diplomat who opened relations between Argentina and Great Britain after independence from Spain. Many events are run by the group ParaKultural (**www.parakultural.com.ar**) and you may hear locals referring to Salón Canning with this name. Some nights incorporate a mix of tango dancing and special guest dancers who are often old tango stars, along with live orchestras. It is a place that should not be missed. Friday is one of the best nights to come here, as it's packed with young, fashionable tango enthusiasts, many of whom reside in Palermo. Saturday is more traditional. Scalabrini Ortiz 1331 (at Gorriti). ✆ **11/4832-6753.** Admission $8. No metro access.

Tango Tours

There are literally hundreds of tango tours here in Buenos Aires, the city where it all began. Here are just a few. All of these individuals and groups also offer lessons. I've also listed additional instructors below (p. 205).

ABC Tango Tours Gabriel Aspe, who is one of the co-owners of this company, also manages one of the tango shows at the Café Tortoni and is a native of Argentina. The company offers several tango show palace event tours, as well as tours to traditional tango salons. ✆ **11/15-5697-2551** (cell). www.abctango.com.

Buenos Aires Tango Off This company offers several tango-themed tours, including its unusual "Dos Pasiones Argentinas," which takes the "Land of Evita and Tango" phrase to heart by combining tango lessons with a visit to the Museo Evita (though she was known to hate the dance, ironically). ✆ **11/4829-1417** or 11/15-4991-2477 (cell). www.bsastangooff.com.ar.

Narrative Tango Tours Two young American women in love with tango and Buenos Aires, Elizabeth Cooke and Cyrena Drusine, started this company, along with two native Argentines, Ivan Inofrez and Flavio Romanelli. They offer various services related to tango, including classes, historic tango tours, outings to *milongas*, and classes on the history of tango music with a professional guitarist. ℭ**11/15-5906-8262** or 11/15-6918-7651 (cell). www.narrativetangotours.com.

Tango with Judy Judy and Jon are an American tango-loving and -dancing couple who live in both Buenos Aires and Arizona. They both know the scene well and offer highly specialized and individual tango tours, some of which can be combined with lessons. They give four weekly classes and also private lessons anytime. Their work has been featured in tango magazines as well as *Caras,* a Buenos Aires celebrity gossip magazine. ℭ**520/907-2050** or 213/536-4900 in U.S., 11/4863-5889 or 11/15-6161-1838 (cell) in Buenos Aires. www.tangowithjudy.com.

Tango Taxi Dancers Eduardo Amarillo has tangoed since he was 3 years old, having learned the dance from his grandparents. Now he and Tango Taxi Dancers offer individual tours and private lessons, and will provide male or female partners to go to *milongas* with you to practice. The company offers lessons in their studio near Obelisco, or in your hotel or apartment. ℭ**11/4382-5947** or 11/15-5753-9131 (cell). www.tango taxidancers.com.

Tango Teachers

All of the above tour groups offer tango lessons, either in a group or individually. Alternatively, you can try the professional tango teachers I've listed here. Check out the magazines **B.A. Tango, Tangauta,** and **La Milonga** for more listings. Also consider group and individual lessons through **Escuela Argentina de Tango,** inside Galerías Pacífico (ℭ **11/4312-4990;** www.eatango.org).

○ **Estudio Zarasa Tango,** Av. Independencia 2845 at Pichincha (ℭ **11/3527-7840,** or 11/15-4405-6464 and 11/15-5528-9826 [cells]; www.julioycorina.com. ar), is run by Julio Balmaceda and Corina DeLaRosa, one of the most accomplished tango couples in Buenos Aires. They have toured the world with their shows, including performing in New York's Carnegie Hall, and now impart their incredible talent to their students.

○ **Julietta Lotti** (ℭ **11/4328-9842** or 11/15-5750-2008; julietalotti@hotmail. com) has taught and danced tango for years. She is a member of the Las Fulanas troupe of dance professionals. She does not speak much English, however.

○ **Julio Corazza** (ℭ **11/4752-0213** or 11/15-6058-6189; www.tango-milonga-tour.9f.com) has taught tango for more than 20 years, and can work with individuals and groups, as well as arrange tango tours for experts and beginners.

○ **Helen Halldórsdóttir** (ℭ **11/4383-6229** or 11/15-5865-8279 [cell]; www. lavikinga.eu), a striking blonde who resembles the actress Brigitte Nielson, is nicknamed La Vikinga because she is from Iceland. She ran the now-closed *milonga* Mano a Mano and teaches tango lessons in Argentina, Europe, and North America. Her spectacular home near Congreso is a beautiful setting for tango lessons. She also sells tango clothing at her home and via her website.

○ **Pedro Sánchez** (ℭ **11/4923-2774** or 11/15-6295-1015 [cell]; pedromilonguero@ yahoo.com.ar) has been dancing tango for more than 50 years, and many women I know swear by his instruction methods. He speaks little English, but always makes himself understood. He will give private lessons, and also has Monday evening sessions for small groups, which might be a good way to get to know him and see his techniques.

9

BUENOS AIRES AFTER DARK

Milongas (Tango Salons & Dance Halls)

o **Patricia Herrera** (**Yuyu;** ✆ **11/4805-1457** or 11/15-6716-5351; yuyutango@ yahoo.com.ar; www.yuyutango.blogspot.com), an excellent and patient teacher who goes by the nickname Yuyu, teaches from her home in Recoleta or will visit people at their home or hotel.

GAY & LESBIAN DANCE CLUBS, RESTO-BARS & TANGO SALONS

Buenos Aires has a thriving gay and lesbian scene that's the most impressive in South America. Though there's no official gay neighborhood, much of the action is in Barrio Norte, Palermo, and San Telmo, whose gentrification has been accompanied by an influx of gay men and is the site of the city's main gay hotels, **El Lugar Gay** (p. 47) and **Axel** (p. 46). Gay nightlife begins late, with nightclubs opening around midnight, picking up between 2 and 3am, and closing around 7am. Bars might open as early as 8pm. Pick up a free copy of *GMap* (www.gmaps360.com) or the city's own gay map at tourism kiosks and other venues, or buy *La Otra Guía* (www.laotraguiaweb.com. ar) or *Imperio* magazine (www.revista-imperio.com) at newsstands. Gay welcome center **Pink Point,** Lavalle 669, Luxor Galería shop 24 (✆ **11/4322-1343;** www. pinkpointbuenosaires.com), provides information and offers nightlife tours.

Dance Clubs & Bars

Amerika   This is one of the city's most popular gay clubs, and even straight people come for the great music. In general, straights hang out on the uppermost level of the club near the glassed-in area that resembles a spaceship pod, while gays, lesbians, and others mingle throughout the many other levels of this enormous venue. Open Thursday through Sunday only. Gascón 1040 (at Córdoba). ✆ **11/4865-4416.** www.ameri-k.com. ar. Cover $12. Metro: Angel Gallardo.

Bach Bar   This is one of the most popular bars for lesbians in Buenos Aires. It's a lively place built into a former house, with lots of individual social spaces. Cabrera 4390 (at Julian Alvarez). ✆ **11/15-5184-0137** (cell), www.bach-bar.com.ar. Metro: Scalabrini Ortiz.

Contramano   Popular with a mature crowd, this was the first gay bar or dance club opened in Buenos Aires, just after the fall of the last military government in the early 1980s. The dance floor area is closed for now, though it may eventually reopen. Rodríguez Peña 1082 (at Santa Fe). No phone. Cover $4. No metro access.

Human   This Saturdays-only spot has become the most popular gay club in Buenos Aires. It's a large space with a main dance floor and a covered outdoor patio overlooking the Río de la Plata. Av. Costanera Norte Rafael Obligado at Av. Sarmiento. www.humanclub. com.ar. Cover $12. No metro access.

KM Zero   Those who have been to Buenos Aires before will remember that this was formerly the Titanic Bar. It's the same space, with different themed parties, and open for drinking and dancing 7 nights a week. It sometimes attracts a rougher crowd than you'll find in the more glamorous bars. Av. Santa Fe 2516 (at Pueyrredón). ✆ **11/4822-7530.** Cover $6 Fri–Sat and special nights. Metro: Pueyrredón.

Sitges   One of the city's largest and most popular gay bars, this venue has a stage that sometimes features very silly acts. Av. Córdoba 4119 (btw. Palestina and Pringles). ✆ **11/4861-3763.** No cover. Metro: Angel Gallardo.

BUENOS AIRES: LATIN AMERICA'S gay tourism CAPITAL

For the past few years, Buenos Aires has reigned as Latin America's preeminent gay travel destination. Gays and lesbians are estimated at 15% to 20% of international tourists, and many mainstream venues stress their gay friendliness. Legal advances on the national level have helped: In 2003, Argentina legalized same-sex civil unions, and in July 2010 it became the only country in Latin America and one of the few worldwide to legalize same-sex marriage. The bill was signed in the Casa Rosada by President Cristina Fernandez de Kirchner, who expressed at the event her hopes that other Latin American countries would soon follow Argentina's example. She also commented to this writer that the new law might influence Americans to move to Argentina seeking a freedom unavailable in the United States. While discrimination against the transgendered remains a serious problem, in 2010, Florencia de la V, a transgendered celebrity and event promoter, became the first to have her identity card changed to match her new gender, representing a major leap for transgendered rights.

With its enormous collection of bars, dance clubs, restaurants, and tango halls catering to the gay and lesbian community, Buenos Aires is rivaled by no other Latin American city in terms of its offerings for visiting gays and lesbians. The Buenos Aires Tourism Office, the **Ronda** (www.theronda.com.ar), and **G-Maps** (www.gmaps360.com) all publish maps detailing the gay scene. Check out *La* *Otra Guía* (www.laotraguiaweb.com.ar) or *Imperio* magazine (www.revista-imperio.com) at newsstands, or the websites **www.gayinbuenosaires.com.ar** and **www.sentidog.com.ar**, for more listings and news. The **Comunidad Homosexual de Argentina** (**CHA**; ✆ 11/4361-6382; www.cha.org.ar) and the **Argentine Federation of Lesbians, Gays, Bisexuals and Transsexuals** (www.lgbt.org.ar) are additional resources; together, they also organize the annual Gay Pride March, known as **Marcha del Orgullo Gay,** always held the first Saturday in November.

A number of international resources for LGBT travelers also provide information on travel in Buenos Aires, including the **International Gay and Lesbian Travel Association (IGLTA;** ✆ 800/448-8550 or 954/776-2626; www.iglta.org) and the websites **www.PlanetOut.com** and **www.Outtraveler.com**. *Spartacus International Gay Guide* (Bruno Gmünder Verlag; www.spartacusworld.com/gay guide) and *Odysseus* (Odysseus Enterprises Ltd.) are annual English-language guidebooks targeting a gay male audience, with some information for lesbians. Look for them at gay and lesbian bookstores or order them from **Giovanni's Room,** 1145 Pine St., Philadelphia, PA 19107 (✆ 215/923-2960; www.giovannisroom.com). In Buenos Aires, visit the gay bookstore **Otras Letras** (p. 173) and purchase *Historia de la Homosexualidad en Argentina,* by Osvaldo Bazan, for a better historical understanding of gay Argentina.

Resto-Bars

A resto-bar is a restaurant-bar combination. You can come for a meal or for drinks only. In general, the bar portions of resto-bars don't get busy until after 11pm. These are more relaxed than traditional bars and it's easier to chat with locals.

Inside Resto-Bar ★★   The waitstaff and owner Diego provide great, attitude-free service in this resto-bar. It's a good place to go just for drinks at their small bar, where many locals gather for conversation. There are male strippers daily and tango shows on weekends. Bartolomé Mitre 1571 (at Montevideo). ✆ **11/4372-5439.** Metro: Congreso.

Pride Resto-Bar   There are two Pride Resto-Bars—Pride Café in San Telmo and Pride Hollywood in Palermo Hollywood. Both have a casual, social atmosphere and offer sandwiches, snacks, salads, and a variety of alcoholic and non-alcoholic drinks. The Pride Café in San Telmo is especially popular on Sundays during the San Telmo Antiques Fair. Pride Café San Telmo, Balcarce 869 (at Pasaje Giuffra). ✆ **11/4300-6435.** Metro: San Juan. Pride Hollywood, Humboldt 1897 (at Costa Rica). ✆ **11/4776-6197.** www.pridehollywood.com.ar. Metro: Palermo.

Tango Salons & Lessons

Tango was originally danced by men together, because the form was at first considered too obscene for women to dance with men. In the modern era, gay Porteños take this step further, with three gay tango salons bringing back old-fashioned, same-sex tango.

Bayres Folk   These events combine same-sex tango dancing with folkloric and other traditional dances, including the gaucho-esque Zamba on Monday nights, with lessons beginning at 8pm and *milonga* a few hours later. Cochabamba 360 (at Defensa). ✆ **11/4300-2364** or 11/15-5654-1658 (cell). http://www.tango-club.com/bayresfolk. Metro: Constitution.

La Marshall   The originator of the gay tango spots in Buenos Aires, La Marshall has moved around over the years. It begins with a group lesson at 10pm then on to a show and *milonga.* The event is held on Wednesdays at Maipu 444 and Saturdays at Rivadavia 1392. La Marshall also runs gay tango lessons on Sunday evenings at the San Telmo gay hotel **El Lugar Gay** (p. 47) at 7pm. Wed at Maipu 444 (at Corrientes); Sat at Rivadavia 1392 (at Uruguay). ✆ **11/4300-3487** or 11/15-5458-3423 (cell). www.lamarshall.com.ar. Metro: Florida, Lavalle, or Congreso.

Tango Queer ★★   Run by Mariana Docampo and a group of women friends, but aimed at both sexes, Tango Queer is an event and an organization. There are shows, classes, and individual lessons and *milonga* for gays, lesbians, and others every Tuesday starting at 8:30pm at the Buenos Aires Club. Double-check their website for other events and locations. Perú 571 (at México). ✆ **11/15-3252-6894** (cell). www.tangoqueer.com. Metro: Belgrano.

FILM

Buenos Aires has over 250 movie theaters showing Argentine and international films. There are cinemas at two shopping malls: **Alto Palermo,** Av. Santa Fe 3251, at Agüero (✆ **11/4827-8000**), and **Galerías Pacífico,** at Calle Florida 753 and Córdoba (✆ **11/4319-5357**). Other convenient Microcentro locations include the six-screen **Atlas Lavalle,** Lavalle 869, at Esmeralda (✆ **11/5032-8527;** www.atlascines.com.ar), and the four-screen **Monumental Lavalle,** Lavalle 739, at Maipú (✆ **11/4322-1515**). Most films are American and shown in English with Spanish subtitles; however, some are Argentine films, which are not subtitled. The average movie ticket price is 20 pesos. Check the *Buenos Aires Herald* for film listings. Every April, Buenos Aires hosts an international film festival (http://www.bafici.gov.ar). The MALBA also has a film program (p. 125).

CASINOS, ARCADES & BINGO HALLS

Calle Lavalle, with its bright lights and big-city tackiness, is the perfect place for adults and teenagers alike to test their luck. This can often be done together with a movie viewing, since many of the city's cinemas are here as well.

Bingo Lavalle   If you think bingo is just for seniors living out their retirement days, think again. Porteños of all ages love bingo, and here is where you'll find some of the most competitive. I recommend spending some time checking out this interesting venue with its cross section of locals. Alcoholic drinks and bar snacks are served. You must be at least 18 to enter. It's open Monday to Thursday from 9am to 3am, Friday 9am to 6am, Saturday noon to 6am, and Sunday noon to 3am. Lavalle 842 (at Esmeralda). **11/4322-1114.** Metro: Lavalle.

Casino Puerto Madero   Feel like trying to win some money to upgrade your hotel accommodations? This 24-hour casino is the place. It's housed in a Mississippi river-boat parked on the Buenos Aires docks. There are over 117 gaming tables, hundreds of slot machines, and other ways to win (or lose). Parking is nearby and there are restaurants onboard. It's open 24 hours daily. Elvira Rawson de Dellepina, Darsena Sur Puerto de Buenos Aires (Southern Port beyond Puerto Madero). **11/4363-3100.** No metro access.

Magic Play ☺   This is a great place for the kids during the day, and teenagers later at night. Slots, racing cars, pool, and video games keep them entertained. It's open daily from 9am to 1am. Lavalle 672 (at Maipú). **11/4322-5702.** Metro: Lavalle.

SIDE TRIPS FROM BUENOS AIRES

I f you're spending more than 4 or 5 days in Buenos Aires, you might want to consider taking a side trip—especially if you're visiting in summer, when many Porteños have already fled town.

Just over the river in Uruguay is the day-tripper's paradise of **Colonia,** a UNESCO Heritage City, less than an hour from Buenos Aires by boat. And if you want to see more of Uruguay, visit the glamorous beach resort of Punta del Este, or the capital, **Montevideo**.

During the summer months, Porteños hit the beach resorts. **Mar del Plata** is Argentina's most popular resort area. So many people head here from Buenos Aires during this season that the capital can feel like a ghost town in certain neighborhoods. Calling Mar del Plata crowded is an understatement; more than eight million people visit this city over the course of the summer.

Beyond Buenos Aires's suburbs is the **Tigre Delta,** a beautiful complex of islands and marshland full of small bed-and-breakfasts, resorts, and adventure trails. You can take a day trip here on mass transit from Buenos Aires or make it an overnight stay. An easy train ride from Buenos Aires, it's perfect for a day trip or an overnight getaway.

The Pampas are the fertile plains surrounding Buenos Aires, and this is where you should go to find gaucho culture. The main town at the center of it all is **San Antonio de Areco,** about 1½ hours north of the capital. Some visitors stay in town, while other stay at surrounding *estancias* (ranches), several of which are listed here.

COLONIA DEL SACRAMENTO, URUGUAY

140km (87 miles) W of Buenos Aires

The tiny gem of Colonia del Sacramento, declared a World Heritage Site by UNESCO, appears untouched by time. Dating from 1680, when it was established by Manuel Lobo as a Portuguese buffer colony against the Spanish, the old city boasts beautifully preserved colonial artistry down its quiet, bougainvillea-draped, cobblestone streets. A leisurely stroll into the **Barrio Histórico (Historic Neighborhood)** leads you under flower-laden windowsills to churches dating from the 1680s, past simple single-story homes—from Colonia's days as a colonial settlement—and on to local museums detailing the riches of the town's past. The Barrio Histórico contains brilliant examples of colonial architecture and many of Uruguay's oldest structures. A mix of lovely shops, tiny *posadas*, and charming cafes and restaurants makes the town more than just a history lesson.

The majority of visitors take day trips to Colonia from Buenos Aires. However, it's worth it to spend an extra day or more exploring the region. Colonia is surrounded by wineries, *estancias* (ranches), and some of Uruguay's most beautiful landscapes, as well as spa resorts. Only recently touched by international tourism, many of these places have a more authentic atmosphere than their Argentine counterparts. Overnighting in Colonia allows you to have the town to yourself, small as it is, to wander its cobblestone streets unencumbered after day-trippers have left. Photography buffs in particular will find this delightful. For couples, the small town is serenely romantic; watch a sunset together and then head to candlelit restaurants serving steaks, locally caught fish, and wines from the surrounding vineyards.

Planning

GETTING THERE

The easiest way to reach Colonia from Buenos Aires is by ferry. **Seacat Colonia,** formerly known as **FerryLíneas** (② **02/915-0202** in Uruguay or 11/4314-5100 in Argentina; www.seacatcolonia.com) runs a fast boat that takes 45 minutes. **Buquebús** (② **02/916-1910** in Montevideo or 11/4316-6500 in Buenos Aires; **www.buquebus.com**) also offers two classes of service, costing from $30 to $95 each way. **Colonia Express** (② **54/11-4317-4100** in Buenos Aires or 02/901-9597 in Montevideo; www.coloniaexpress.com) has similar prices but runs less frequently.

Colonia is a good stopping-off point if you're traveling between Buenos Aires and Montevideo. **COT** (② **02/409-4949** in Montevideo; www.cot.com.uy) offers bus service from Montevideo and from Punta del Este.

VISITOR INFORMATION

The main **Oficina de Turismo,** General Flores and Rivera (② **0452/26141**) is open daily from 9am to 8pm. Just outside the gates of the Barrio Histórico, open daily 9am to 6:30pm, is a smaller **Oficina de Turismo,** Calle Manuel Lobo 224, between Ituzaingó and Paseo San Miguel (② **0452/28506**). Speak with someone at one of the tourism offices to arrange a guided tour of the town, or contact the **Asociacion de Guías Profesionales de° Turismo del Departamento de Colonia** (② **0452/22309;** asociacionguiascolonia@gmail.com, www.asociacionguiascolonia. blogspot.com). Visit **www.colonia.gub.uy** or **www.uruguaynatural.com** for information about Colonia and the surrounding region. The website **www.guiacolonia. com.uy** has useful information, and keep an eye out for the bimonthly booklet *Güear* (www.guear.com), which has shopping, restaurant, hotel, and nightlife listings as well as profiles of local chefs. A PDF of the booklet can be downloaded from the website.

At the end of 2010, Colonia's area code changed from 052 to 0452, but both numbers can still be used for the time being; you will see this reflected in literature and on websites. Try both numbers if you're having trouble calling. When you're calling from overseas and thus adding Uruguay's country code of 598, remember to drop the 0 at the beginning of the area code. See "Planning Your Trip to Uruguay: Visas, Currency & Phone Numbers," below, for additional information.

What to See & Do
A WALK THROUGH COLONIA'S BARRIO HISTORICO

Your visit to Colonia will be concentrated in the **Barrio Histórico (Old Neighborhood),** located on the coast at the far southwestern corner of town. The sites, which are all within a few blocks of each other, can easily be visited on foot within a few hours. Museums and tourist sites are open Thursday through Monday from 11:15am to 4:45pm. For about $3, you can buy a pass at the Portuguese or municipal museums, which will get you into most museums and buildings. Many locations in Colonia don't have real addresses; often an intersection of two streets is used for directions. Individual museums don't have phone numbers either, so be sure to get a map at the tourist office. While the town is small and convenient for walking, almost nothing in the center of Colonia is handicap accessible. This is a difficult place to visit for anyone in a wheelchair.

Start your tour at **Plaza Mayor,** the principal square that served as the center of the colonial establishment. To explore Colonia's Portuguese history, cross the Calle Manuel Lobo on the southeastern side of the plaza and enter the **Museo Portugués (Portuguese Museum),** which exhibits European customs and traditions that influenced the town's beginnings. The most important item displayed here is the final Portuguese royal medallion to grace the city walls before the city finally fell into Spanish hands. Leading behind the Museo Municipal is the **Street of Sighs,** or the **Calle de Los Suspiros,** so called because it was where the prostitutes conducted their trade in olden days, when the military barracks were just off the Plaza Mayor. It remains the most intact colonial street in the city, with its angled cobblestone drain leading to the waterfront. You also see the differences between Portuguese and Spanish colonial construction here, as these buildings are often juxtaposed. If the roof of a building is flat, it is Spanish. If the roof is angled with tiles, it is Portuguese. Nearby are the **Ruinas Convento San Francisco (San Francisco convent ruins).** Dating from 1696, the San Francisco convent was once inhabited by Jesuit and Franciscan monks, two brotherhoods dedicated to preaching the gospel to indigenous people. You can crawl over the ruins, or climb the adjacent 100-foot-high **Faro (Lighthouse)** after paying the $1 fee. The wind is strong at the top, but there's a view all the way to Buenos Aires on clear days. The lighthouse is open daily from 10am to 8pm and is overseen by the Uruguayan navy, which has a small base just off Plaza Mayor.

Around the corner is the **Casa de Brown (Brown House),** which houses the **Museo Municipal (Municipal Museum).** Here, you will find an impressive collection of colonial documents and artifacts, a must-see for history buffs. For those with a more artistic bent, make sure to check out the **Museo del Azulejo (Tile Museum),** a unique museum of 19th-century European and Uruguayan tiles housed in a gorgeous 300-year-old country house, close to the waterfront on Calle Misiones de los Tapes at Paseo de San Gabriel. Upon exiting the museum, turn right for a walk along the water and then make a right onto Calle de la Playa, enjoying the shops and cafes along the way, heading up to the **Iglesia Matriz,** originally dating from 1680. Fighting meant the church was reconstructed several times, and today's building is a mix of colonial and neoclassical styles. To the side of the church is **Plaza de Lobo,** with its excavated **Ruinas Casa del Gobernador (House of the Viceroy Ruins),** built by the Portuguese and destroyed in 1777 by the Spanish. The House of the Viceroy captures something of the city's 17th- and 18th-century magistrates, when the port was used for imports, exports, and smuggling. Complete your walk by heading back toward the Plaza Mayor. To the left, you'll see the **Portón de Campo (City Gate)** and what remains of the ramparts that once served to protect the city. Climbing them and looking out to the Río de la Plata and the world beyond, you'll begin to understand that, in spite of its tiny size, Colonia played a pivotal role in the global struggle between two European empires to dominate a continent an ocean away.

Where to Stay

COLONIA

Hotel La Misión This hotel overlooking the Plaza Mayor was partly renovated in 2008, adding new bathrooms and rooms that are a mix of the modern and the traditional. An antiques-filled lobby leads to a small courtyard filled with bougainvillea. The original building dates from 1762.

Misiones de los Tapes 171, CP 70000, Colonia. www.lamisionhotel.com. © **0452/26767.** 11 units. From $120 double. Rates include buffet breakfast. AE, MC, V. **Amenities:** Restaurant; concierge; room service. *In room:* A/C, TV, Wi-Fi, minibar.

Posada Plaza Mayor Among the most charming accommodations in Colonia's center, this hotel has several rooms that wrap around a tranquil central courtyard with a fountain. Rooms are a mix of modern and rustic, and the breakfast room has a spectacular view over the Río de la Plata.

Colonia del Sacramento, Uruguay

Calle de Comercio 111, CP 70000, Colonia. www.posadaplazamayor.com. © **0452/23193.** 15 units. From $110 double. Rates include buffet breakfast. AE, MC, V. **Amenities:** Restaurant; concierge; room service. *In room:* A/C, TV, Wi-Fi, minibar.

OUTSIDE COLONIA

Four Seasons Carmelo ★★ One of the most luxurious and award-winning resorts in South America, the Four Seasons Carmelo is about 90km (54 miles) from the center of Colonia, set on the Río de la Plata. The enormous rooms and suites, about 90 to 120 sq. m (1,000–1,300 sq. ft.) and with fireplaces and cathedral ceilings, are set in individual bungalows in a landscaped garden surrounding the pool, making for a romantic getaway or honeymoon spot. The spa offers extensive treatments in a calming Asian-inspired setting. There are also a golf course, polo grounds, and other amenities as well as special children's programs. It takes about an hour to drive here from Colonia, and the hotel also runs a shuttle service from Colonia's port, $90 one-way and $132 to $410 round-trip, per person.

Ruta 21, Km 262, CP 70000, Carmelo. www.fourseasons.com. © **0542/9000.** Fax 0542/9999. 44 units with 24 dual-level suites. From $430 double; $465 suite. Rates include buffet breakfast. AE, DC, MC, V. Valet parking. **Amenities:** Restaurant; bar; babysitting; concierge; golf course; deluxe health club w/ fitness center; massage; polo grounds; indoor pool; outdoor pool; room service; sauna; spa. *In room:* A/C, TV, minibar.

Sheraton Colonia ★★ Opened in 2005, the Sheraton Colonia is a 10-minute cab ride from the center of town. Built on a golf course, with a view to the Río de la Plata, it's a family-friendly, resort-style option if you want to spend more time in the area. The pool cascades over several levels in a landscaped garden, and is spectacular at sunset. A lobby restaurant serves breakfast, lunch, and dinner, and dinner is also available at the golf clubhouse, set in the gardens. The gym and health club area is large, with enormous glass windows overlooking the river. The large spa has 18 treatment rooms, and offers a romantic champagne whirlpool treatment for couples, among many other options. Some suites have kitchens.

Continuación de la Rambla de Las Américas s/n, CP 70000, Carmelo. www.sheraton.com. © **0452/29000.** Fax 0452/29001. 92 units. From $204 double; from $385 suite. Rates include buffet breakfast. AE, DC, MC, V. **Amenities:** Restaurant; bar; babysitting; concierge; golf course; deluxe health club w/fitness center; massage; indoor pool; outdoor pool; room service; sauna; spa. *In room:* A/C, TV, kitchen (in some suites), minibar.

Where to Eat

El Drugstore ★ URUGUAYAN/JAPANESE/SEAFOOD This restaurant is across from Iglesia Matriz and owned by Argentine Guillermo Azulay, who says, "I want to do something that makes people happy." It has a colorful, kitschy interior with posters, bric-a-brac, and polka dot tablecloths. Its most unusual feature is an antique car parked outside, converted into a dining area, which is often used in Colonia photo shoots. Traditional *chivitos* (beef sandwiches), fish, steak, pastas, and Japanese food are on the menu. Live music, an Executive Menu for $17, and an open kitchen make this a great place to dine.

Vasconcellos 179 (at Portugal, across from Iglesia Matriz). © **0452/25241.** Main courses $4–$14. No credit cards. Daily noon–midnight.

Gibellini ★★★ URUGUAYAN/ITALIAN If there is any reason to wander off the beaten path and dine outside of Colonia's Old City, this is it. Run by Alejandro Gibellini and his family, this charming restaurant offers home-cooked Italian meals,

Uruguayan specialties, and other wonderful menu items like crepes and fish. Stop by, even just for a coffee, and peruse his unusual antique collection that adorns the space.

Rivadavia 249 (at Ituzaingo, a block from General Flores). © **0452/29161** or 099-164166 (cell). Main courses $7–$20. No credit cards. Daily 11am–4pm and 7pm–midnight.

Mesón de la Plaza ★ URUGUAYAN   Among the most traditional and elegant spots in Colonia, this location serves fine steaks and Uruguayan cuisine. It's located in a large colonial building with high ceilings, across from Iglesia Matriz.

Vasconcellos 153 (at Portugal). © **052/24807.** Main courses $6–$15. AE, MC, V. Daily noon–midnight.

Pulpería de los Faroles ★ URUGUAYAN   Waiters with vests add formality to this old institution, with ancient brick walls offset by pastel tablecloths. Traditional food includes steak, pasta, and locally caught fish.

Calle Misiones de los Tapes 101 (at Comercio, on the Plaza Mayor). © **052/25399.** Main courses $8–$15. AE, MC, V. Daily noon–midnight.

Colonia After Dark

Believe it or not, there is nightlife in Colonia, whether it's locals partying after work, or tourists staying in the local *posadas* and the surrounding spa-hotels. Bar life begins at 10 or 11pm, but for serious dancing, expect things to get started after 1am. With its white leather lounges and blue-neon backlit bar, **Mar Dulce Resto Pub,** at Virrey Cevallo 232 and General Flores (© **098/500898** [cell]), looks like it was plucked from Miami Beach, and offers live music, DJs, and dancing. **Tresquarto,** Av. Méndez 295 (© **052/29664** or 099/523043 [cell]; www.trescuarto.com), is the town's mega-disco, a four-level venue with three different kinds of music, hence the name. It's open on Fridays and Saturdays only.

MONTEVIDEO, URUGUAY

215km (133 miles) E of Buenos Aires

Montevideo, the southernmost capital on the continent, along with its suburbs, is home to half of Uruguay's total population of 3.5 million people. Located on the banks of the Río de la Plata, Montevideo first existed as a fortress of the Spanish Empire and developed into a major port city in the mid–18th century. European immigrants—including Spanish, Portuguese, French, and British—have influenced the city's architecture. A walk around the capital reveals architectural styles ranging from colonial to Art Deco.

Although Montevideo has few must-see attractions, its charm lies in wait for the observant traveler. A walk along La Rambla, stretching from the Old City to the neighborhood of Carrasco, takes you along the riverfront, past fishermen and their catch, to parks and gardens where children play and elders sip *mate* (a tea-like beverage). Restaurants, cafes, bars, and street performers populate the port area, where you will also discover the flavors of Uruguay at the afternoon and weekend **Mercado del Puerto (Port Market).** Many of the city's historic sites and museums surround or are close to the central **Plaza Independencia** and can be visited within a few hours.

If you're visiting Montevideo as a side trip from Buenos Aires, ignore comments from Porteños that there is nothing here. It's true that Buenos Aires is larger and more vibrant, but Montevideo has its own charms. The relationship between the two cities is representative of the relationship between Uruguay and Argentina. The two countries have similar histories and cultures, but Uruguay has always lived in Argentina's shadow, dominated politically and denigrated culturally. This has resulted in a self-consciousness on the part of Uruguayans upon meeting tourists, who come with little to no knowledge of the country. Knowing you're visiting from a place that likes to throw its weight around, Montevideans will reach out to you and make sure you have a good time in their city, in hopes of disproving whatever Porteños may have told you.

Planning

GETTING THERE

International flights and those from Buenos Aires land at **Carrasco International Airport** (© 02/604-0329; www.aeropuertodecarrasco.com.uy), located 19km (12 miles) from downtown Montevideo. Uruguay's national carrier is **Pluna,** at Colonia and Julio Herrera (© 0800/118-811 or 02/401-5000, or 11/4132-4444 in Buenos Aires; www.pluna.com.uy), which operates several flights daily from Aeroparque. **Aerolíneas Argentinas** (© 02/901-9466 or 000-4054-86527) flies from both Aeroparque and Ezeiza to Montevideo; the flight takes 50 minutes. The fare ranges from $150 to $250 round-trip, depending on how far in advance you make reservations. In 2009, **American Airlines** (© 800/433-7300 in the U.S. and Canada, or 02/916-3929 in Montevideo; www.aa.com) began direct service from Miami to Montevideo—with frequency varying by season—in addition to its already existing flights, which connect to Montevideo with stopovers in Buenos Aires. A taxi or *remis* (private, unmetered taxi) from the airport to downtown is about $17.

BY BOAT OR HYDROFOIL The most popular way to get to Montevideo is by ferry. **Buquebús,** Calle Río Negro 1400 (© 02/916-8801 or 02/916-1910, or 11/4316-6500 in Buenos Aires; www.buquebus.com), operates three to four hydrofoils per day from Buenos Aires; the trip is 3 hours each way and costs about $200 round-trip. Montevideo's port is about 1.5km (1 mile) from downtown. See p. 211 for more ferryboat options in Colonia.

BY BUS **Terminal Omnibus Tres Cruces,** General Artigas 1825 (© 02/409-7399 or 02/401-8998; www.trescruces.com.uy), is Montevideo's long-distance bus terminal, connecting the capital with cities in Uruguay and throughout South America. Buses to Buenos Aires take about 8 hours. **COT** (© 02/409-4949; www.cot.com.uy) offers the best service to Punta del Este, Maldonado, and Colonia.

VISITOR INFORMATION

Uruguay's **Ministerio de Turismo** is at Av. Libertador 1409, corner of Colonia (© 02/1885). It assists travelers with countrywide information and is open daily from 8am to 8pm. There are also branches at Carrasco International Airport (© 02/604-0386); at the Tres Cruces bus station (© 02/409-7399), open daily 8am to 10pm; and at the port, to greet Buquebús and cruise-ship visitors (Rambla 25 de Agosto de 1825 and Yacaré; © 02/916-8434), open Monday to Friday 8am to 6pm, and various hours on weekends, depending on cruise-ship docking schedules. The **Explanada Municipal (Municipal Tourist Office),** inside of the atrium of the **Intendencia (City Hall),** Avenida 18 de Julio and Ejido (© 02/1950-3289), offers city maps and brochures of tourist activities. It's open daily from 10am to 4pm. It also organizes cultural city tours on weekends. Montevideo's **Tourism Office Headquarters,** San Jose 1328 at Ejido (© 02/1950-3171 or 02/1950-2043), is open Monday to Friday from noon to 7pm. It's built into a walkway that is part of the basement of the Sheraton

Montevideo

RESTAURANTS ◆

Arcadia 9
El Fogón 16
El Palenque 3
El Pelegrino 2
Los Leños 14

HOTELS ■

Crystal Palace Hotel 17
Holiday Inn 12
Radisson Montevideo
Victoria Plaza Hotel 11
Sheraton Four Points 18

ATTRACTIONS ●

Catedral 6
El Cabildo 7
Espacio de Arte
Contemporáneo 19
Mercado del Puerto 4
Museo de Arte
Contemporáneo 15
Museo de Artes Decorativas/
Palacio Taranco 5
Museo del Carnaval 1
Plaza Independencia 10
Palacio Salvo 13
Teatro Solís 8

Information

217

Four Points hotel. In the event of an emergency, the **Tourist Police** can be reached at (C) **0800-8226** or 911, and their office is at Colonia 1021. Visit **www.turismo. gub.uy**, **www.uruguaynatural.com.uy**, **www.montevideo.gub.uy**, or **www. presidencia.gub.uy** for more tourism information. The travel magazine *Pasaporte Uruguay* also provides a wealth of information, in English and Spanish, and is available free in some locations, and for sale for about $3 in others. Register for their newsletter at **www.pasaporteuruguay.com.**

Please see "Planning Your Trip to Uruguay: Visas, Currency & Phone Numbers," p. 212, for additional important planning information.

ORIENTATION

Montevideo is surrounded by water on three sides, a reminder of its history as an easily defended fortress for the Spanish Empire. The Old City begins near the western edge of Montevideo, on the skinny portion of a peninsula between the **Rambla Gran Bretaña** and the city's main artery, **Avenida 18 de Julio,** named for the date when the new constitution was adopted. **Plaza Independencia** and **Plaza Constitución** mark the center of the district. Many of the city's museums, theaters, and hotels reside in this historic area, although a trip east on Avenida 18 de Julio reveals the more modern Montevideo, with its own share of hotels, markets, and monuments and the modernist **Intendencia,** or City Hall, with a viewpoint open to the public. Along the city's long southern coastline runs the **Rambla Gran Bretaña,** traveling 21km (13 miles) from the piers of the Old City, past **Parque Rodó,** and on to points south and east, passing fish stalls and street performers along the way.

GETTING AROUND

Navigating central Montevideo on foot or by bus is relatively simple. Safe, convenient buses, costing 15 Uruguayan pesos per ride, crisscross the city, making it easy to venture outside the center. Taxis are safe and relatively inexpensive, but it can be difficult to hail one during rush hour. I recommend calling **Remises Carrasco** ((C) **09/440-5473** or 02/606-2122; www.remisescarrasco.com.uy). You can rent a car through **Thrifty** ((C) **02/204-3373** or 02/682-4495; www.thrifty.com). For roadside emergencies or general information on driving in Uruguay, contact the **Automóvil Club de Uruguay,** Av. Libertador 1532 ((C) **02/902-4792;** www.acu.com.uy), or the **Centro Automovilista del Uruguay,** E. V. Haedo 2378 ((C) **02/903-3344**).

TOUR COMPANIES

In business for nearly 60 years, **Buemes Travel Services,** Colonia 979 ((C) **02/902-1050;** www.buemes.com.uy), is among the largest full-service tour companies in Uruguay. Much of their business involves planning trips and tours for passengers coming into Montevideo by cruise ship. Contact them for day trips or history tours on various themes or to book hotels and airline flights. They also arrange trips to other parts of Uruguay, including Colonia, Punta del Este, and the range of *estancias* near Montevideo that foreigners have only recently discovered. One of the best private tour guides in Montevideo is **Tamara Levinson** ((C) **02/710-3312** or 099/696-518; tamaral@montevideo.com.uy), who conducts individual custom tours of Montevideo and other parts of Uruguay. She works for Buemes, but visitors can hire her, in her spare time, to lead individualized travel tours.

[FastFACTS] MONTEVIDEO

Area Code & Phone Numbers
The country code for Uruguay is **598;** the city code for Montevideo is **02,** and you drop 0 when dialing from overseas. Land line phones have seven digits, but many government offices are now using four-, seven-, or eight-digit systems. Ask for clarification with any phone number that seems unusual. Often, the new four- and eight-digit numbers do not work properly, so ask for alternative numbers or even a contact's cellphone when given them. Cellphone numbers have a three-digit initial code, usually beginning with 09, followed by six digits. These numbers do not require that an area code be added. Drop the 0 when dialing from overseas. Call *C* **122** for information and *C* **0900-2020** for the fee service.

ATMs
ATMs are plentiful; look for the banks

Bancomat and **Redbrou.** Most have access to the Cirrus network. The PLUS system is harder to find. The ATM at the casino in the Radisson takes everything.

Currency Exchange
To exchange money, try **Turisport Limitada** (the local Amex representative), San José 930 (*C* **02/902-0829**); **Gales Servicios Financieros,** Av. 18 de Julio 1046 (*C* **02/902-0229**); or one of the airport exchanges. At press time, the exchange rate is about 20 Uruguayan pesos to the U.S. dollar.

Hospital
The **British Hospital** is located at Av. Italia 2420 (*C* **02/487-1020**) and has emergency-room services.

Internet Access
Internet cafes appear and disappear faster than discos, but you won't walk long before coming across

one in the city center. Reliable cybercafes include **El Cybercafé,** Calle 25 de Mayo 568; **Arroba del Sur,** Guayabo 1858; and **El Cybercafé Softec,** Santiago de Chile 1286. The average price is $2 an hour.

Post Office
The main post office is at Calle Buenos Aires 451 (*C* **0810/444-CORREO** [267736]), open weekdays from 9am to 6pm.

Safety
Although Montevideo remains very safe by big-city standards, street crime has risen in recent years. Travelers should avoid walking alone, particularly at night, in Ciudad Vieja, Avenida 18 de Julio, Plaza Independencia, and the port vicinity. Take a taxi instead. The city has vastly increased the presence of tourism police, particularly in Ciudad Vieja. Look for the men and women in green fluorescent vests.

What to See & Do

Catedral ★   Also known as Iglesia Matriz, the cathedral was the city's first public building. The current structure dates to 1804, but has earlier origins. It houses the remains of some of Uruguay's most important political, religious, and economic figures, and it's distinguished by its domed bell towers.

Calle Sarandí at Ituzaingó, overlooking Plaza Constitución. *C* **02/915-70180.** Free admission. Mon-Fri 8am–8pm.

El Cabildo (Old Town Hall) ★   Uruguay's constitution was signed in the old town hall, which also served as the city's jailhouse in the 19th century. Now a museum, the Cabildo houses the city's historic archives, as well as maps and photos, antiques, costumes, and artwork.

Juan Carlos Gómez 1362 (overlooking Plaza Constitución). *C* **02/915-9685.** Free admission. Tues–Sun 2:30-7pm.

Espacio de Arte Contemporáneo ★★   The newest museum in Montevideo, opened in a former prison in July 2010, the Espacio de Arte Contemporáneo uses prison cells to showcase art. The grounds of the gallery, scattered with crushed bricks, are also used for some parts of various exhibitions.

Arenal Grande 1930 (at Miguelete). ℂ **02/929-2066.** www.eac.gub.uy. Free admission. Tues–Sat 3-9pm; Sun 11am–5pm.

Museo de Arte Contemporáneo (Museum of Contemporary Art) ★   Opened in 1997, this museum is dedicated to contemporary Uruguayan art, and it exhibits the country's biggest names. To promote cultural exchange across the region, a section of the museum is set aside for artists who hail from various South American countries.

Av. 18 de Julio 965 (at Pirovano), 2nd floor. ℂ **02/900-6662.** www.cultura.montevideo.gub.uy. Free admission. Daily noon–8pm.

Museo Municipal de Bellas Artes "Juan Manuel Blanes" (Municipal Museum of Fine Arts) ★   This national art-history museum displays Uruguayan artistic styles from the nation's inception to the present day. Works include oils, engravings, drawings, sculptures, and documents. Among the great Uruguayan artists exhibited are Juan Manuel Blanes, Pedro Figari, Rafael Barradas, José Cúneo, and Carlos Gonzales.

Av. Millán 4015. ℂ **02/336-2248.** www.museoblanes.org.uy. Free admission. Tues–Sun 2-7pm.

Museo de Artes Decorativas (Decorative Arts Museum)/Palacio Taranco ★   Now the Decorative Arts Museum, Taranco Palace was built in the early 20th century and in the French style popular during that period. The museum displays Uruguayan furniture, draperies, clocks, paintings, and other cultural works.

Calle 25 de Mayo 379. ℂ **02/915-6060.** www.cultura.montevideo.gub.uy. Free admission. Tues–Sat 10am–6pm.

Palacio Salvo ★   Often referred to as the symbol of Montevideo, the 26-story Salvo Palace was once the tallest building in South America. It was the work of eccentric Italian architect Mario Palanti, who also designed the very similar structure Palacio Barolo on Buenos Aires's Avenida de Mayo. Though you might expect such an iconic building to be open to the public and have a vista station in its tower, this is not the case here. The lobby to this residential tower is open, however, and periodically has free exhibits related to the structure and other themes. To stay in the building during a Montevideo visit, contact **Carlos Melia Travel** (ℂ **11/15-5760-6959** [cell] in Argentina, and 1-347-944-0026 in the U.S. and Canada; www.carlosmelia. com), which rents out tourist apartments in the structure.

Plaza Independencia and Av. 18 de Julio. www.palaciosalvo.com.

Plaza Independencia ★★   Originally the site of a Spanish citadel, Independence Square marks the beginning of the Old City, and it's a good point from which to begin your tour of Montevideo. Only one gate to the old fortress remains. An enormous statue of Gen. José Gervasio Artigas, father of Uruguay and hero of its independence movement, stands in the center. His ashes are in a mausoleum underground, beneath the monument, free and open daily 8am to 5pm. It's a severe, modern structure, with eerie lighting reminiscent of a horror movie. A changing-of-the-guards ceremony takes place every few hours.

Bordered by Av. 18 de Julio, Florida, and Juncal.

Teatro Solís ★★   Montevideo's main theater and opera house, opened in 1852, underwent an extensive renovation in late 1990. It has hosted Uruguay's most important cultural events over the years. While the structure's historic exterior has been preserved, the interior is a thoroughly modern contrast. Dine at the **Rara Avis** restaurant inside the theater, with its stunning views to Plaza Independencia, before or after a show.

Calle Buenos Aires 652. ⓒ**02/1950-3323** or 02/1950-3325. www.teatrosolis.org.uy. Guided tours are Tues, Thurs–Fri, and Sun 11am, noon and 5pm, and Sat 1pm for about $1 in Spanish and $2 in English and Portuguese. Wed guided tours at 11am, noon, and 5pm are free. Evening cultural productions will vary in price and time. Guided tour schedule will also change season to season. Check website or call for up-to-date schedule.

Montevideo & Carnaval

One of the most delightful times to come to Montevideo is during Carnaval season, usually in late January, February, and early March, corresponding to the period before Ash Wednesday in the Catholic calendar and the 40-day Lent period before Easter, when there are street festivals as well as theatrical competitions. It's at this time that several aspects of Uruguayan culture come to the forefront. The festival seems a mix of Argentine and Brazilian elements, recalling the fact that Uruguay was established as a border colony on the border of the Spanish and Portuguese empires. You'll see *murgas,* or street-dancing bands, similar to those in Argentina, as well as foxy feather-festooned females like those you'd see in Rio. This is also a time when the Afro-Uruguayan population, the descendants of slaves who represent about 7% of the country, become truly visible and celebrated. *Llamadas,* or African drum bands, are part of the festivities. A highlight of Carnaval season is February 2, the day celebrating the sea-goddess *Yemanga,* in some representations resembling a seafaring Virgin Mary, from the *Candomblé* religion, a fusion of African beliefs brought over by slaves and blended with Catholic ideology. (This is the goddess in the Penelope Cruz movie *Woman on Top.*) Thousands head to **Playa Ramirez,** across from Parque Rodó, and other beaches, to listen to music, worship, and leave offerings in the sea. Year-round, the **Museo del Carnaval,** Rambla 25 de Agosto de 1825 no. 218 at Maciel (ⓒ **02/916-5493** or 02/915-0802; www.museodelcarnaval.org), in the port area, provides an excellent perspective on the celebrations.

Where to Stay

Parking is included in the rates of most Uruguay hotels. In 2005, Montevideo repealed its 10% hotel tax for foreigners (though it's still paid by locals).

EXPENSIVE

Belmont House ★★ ♟   A boutique hotel in Montevideo's peaceful Carrasco neighborhood, Belmont House has small, elegant spaces with carefully chosen antiques and wood furnishings that give this hotel the feeling of a wealthy private home. Many rooms have balconies overlooking the courtyard and pool, and two rooms have Jacuzzis. Belmont House is close to the beach, golf, and tennis. Gourmands will find an excellent international restaurant, afternoon tea, and a *parrilla* open weekends next to the pool.

Av. Rivera 6512, 11500 Montevideo. www.belmonthouse.com.uy. ⓒ**02/600-0430.** Fax 02/600-8609. 28 units. $290 double; from $408 suite. Rates include gourmet breakfast. AE, DC, MC, V. **Amenities:** Restaurant; *parrillada;* tearoom; bar; babysitting; discounts for nearby golf and tennis; small fitness center; beautiful outdoor pool; sauna. *In room:* A/C, TV, minibar.

Radisson Montevideo Victoria Plaza Hotel ★★   The Victoria Plaza has long been one of Montevideo's top hotels. Standing in the heart of the financial district, this European-style hotel makes a good base from which to do business or explore the capital. Its convention center and casino also make it the center of the city's business and social scene. Ask for a room in the new tower, which houses spacious guest rooms and executive suites with classic French-style furnishings and panoramic city or river views. The hotel has a large multilingual staff. Inquire about weekend spa packages. The casino has French roulette tables, blackjack, baccarat, slot machines, horse races, and bingo. There are two lobby bars, in addition to the casino bars. **Arcadia** (p. 223), on the 25th floor, is the city's most elegant dining room.

Plaza Independencia 759, 11100 Montevideo. www.radisson.com/montevideouy. ⓒ **02/902-0111.** Fax 02/902-1628. 254 units. $219 double; from $299 suite. Rates include breakfast at rooftop restaurant. AE, DC, MC, V. Parking and valet service. **Amenities:** Restaurant; cafe; 2 bars; concierge; executive floors; excellent health club w/skylit indoor pool; fitness center w/aerobics classes; Internet access; Jacuzzi; massage; room service; sauna; travel agency. *In room:* A/C, TV, minibar, Wi-Fi.

Sheraton Montevideo ★★   When it opened in 1999, the Sheraton Montevideo replaced Victoria Plaza as Montevideo's most luxurious hotel. A walkway connects the hotel to the Punta Carretas Shopping Center, one of the city's best malls. Spacious rooms have imported furniture, king-size beds, sleeper chairs, marble bathrooms, wide panel TVs, and works by Uruguayan artists. Choose views of the Río de la Plata, Uruguay Golf Club, or downtown Montevideo; views from the 20th through 24th floors are the most impressive. Rooms on the top two executive floors feature Jacuzzis and individual sound systems. The main restaurant, Las Carretas, serves Continental cuisine with a Mediterranean flair. Don't miss the dining room's spectacular murals by contemporary Uruguayan artist Carlos Vilaro. Next door, the lobby bar is a popular spot for casual business meetings and afternoon cocktails.

Calle Víctor Soliño 349, 11300 Montevideo. www.sheraton.com. ⓒ **02/710-2121.** Fax 02/712-1262. 207 units. From $225 double; from $325 suite. Rates include buffet breakfast. AE, DC, MC, V. Valet and free parking available. **Amenities:** Restaurant; bar; babysitting; concierge; emergency medical service; executive floors; deluxe health club w/fitness center; massage; indoor pool; room service; sauna. *In room:* A/C, TV, Internet (fee), minibar.

MODERATE

Crystal Palace Hotel ✦   Close to the Intendencia and other sites, this hotel is a good value for its location. Rooms are decorated in neutral tones with splashes of color. A few are on the small side, but all come with free Wi-Fi. The staff is very friendly and helpful. Buffet breakfast is commendable for a hotel in this price range.

Av 18 de Julio 1210 (btw. Michelini and Quijano), 11100 Montevideo. www.crystalpalacehotel.com.uy. ⓒ **02/900 4645.** Fax 02/908-9222. 59 units, including 3 suites. From $105 double; $140 suite. Rates include buffet breakfast. AE, MC, V. **Amenities:** Bar; small health club; room service. *In room:* A/C, TV, minibar, Wi-Fi.

Holiday Inn ★   This colorful Holiday Inn is actually one of the city's best hotels, popular with tourists and business travelers alike. It's in the heart of downtown, next to Montevideo's main square. Bilingual staff members greet you in the marble lobby, which is attached to a decent restaurant and bar. Guest rooms have simple, contemporary furnishings typical of an American chain. Because the hotel doubles as a convention center, it can become very busy.

Colonia 823, 11100 Montevideo. www.holidayinn.com.uy. ⓒ **02/902-0001.** Fax 02/902-1242. 137 units. From $118 double; $168 suite. Rates include buffet breakfast. AE, DC, MC, V. **Amenities:** Restaurant; bar;

fitness center; heated indoor pool; room service; sauna; Wi-Fi in public areas. *In room:* A/C, TV, high-speed Internet, minibar.

Sheraton Four Points Montevideo ★★ The Sheraton Four Points is among the newest of Montevideo's international hotels. It's considered a four-star property, but falls somewhere between a four- and five-star in terms of quality. Whether you're on business or visiting as a tourist, the location across from City Hall is convenient. The lobby is stark and modern, with polished black-granite panels over white walls in the soaring atrium. Many rooms have views to the Río de la Plata. Bathrooms are spacious and suite bathrooms have hydro-massage bathtubs. All rooms have high-speed Internet access, at a charge of $16 a day. While small, the enclosed rooftop gym and spa has an unparalleled view of the city. There is a $5 charge for using these areas. Breakfast is an additional $16 in the lobby restaurant, which is also open for lunch and dinner.

Ejido 1275 (at Soriano, across from the Intendencia [City Hall]), 11000 Montevideo. www.fourpoints. com/montevideo. ℂ **02/901-7000.** Fax 02/903-2247. 135 units, including 18 suites. From $129 double; from $219 suite. AE, DC, MC, V. Free parking. **Amenities:** Restaurant; bar; babysitting; concierge; health club w/fitness center; indoor pool; room service; sauna. *In room:* A/C, TV, high-speed Internet, minibar.

Where to Eat

Restaurants in Montevideo serve steak that rivals anything in Argentina, and they usually include stew and seafood selections as well. You'll find the native barbecue, in which beef and lamb are grilled on the fire, in any of the city's *parrilladas* (the name for *parrillas* in Uruguay). Sales tax on dining in Montevideo is a whopping 23%. There's also usually a table cover charge (*cubierto*) of about $2 per person. Check out the Uruguayan restaurant website **www.saliracomer.com** for more options.

EXPENSIVE

Arcadia ★★ ◙ INTERNATIONAL While the food is great, the wraparound views from this 26th-floor restaurant outshine the menu. Tables are nestled in semi-private nooks with floor-to-ceiling bay windows. The classic dining room is decorated with Italian curtains and crystal chandeliers; each table has a fresh rose and sterling silver place settings. Creative plates, such as terrine of pheasant marinated in cognac, are followed by grilled rack of lamb glazed with mint and garlic, or duck confit served on a thin strudel pastry with red cabbage. We list general main course prices below, but the Uruguayan caviar menu will set you back about $200.

Plaza Independencia 759. ℂ **02/902-0111.** Main courses $6–$25. AE, DC, MC, V. Daily noon–3pm and 7pm–midnight.

MODERATE

El Fogón ★ PARRILLADA/SEAFOOD/URUGUAYAN This brightly lit *parrillada* and seafood restaurant is popular with Montevideo's late-night crowd. The extensive menu includes calamari, salmon, shrimp, and other fish, as well as generous steak and pasta dishes. Food here is priced well and prepared with care. The express lunch menu comes with steak or chicken, dessert, and a glass of wine.

San José 1080 (at Río Negro). ℂ **02/900-0900.** www.elfogon.com.uy. Main courses $7–$15. AE, DC, MC, V. Daily noon–4pm and 7pm–1am.

El Palenque ★ SEAFOOD/PARRILLADA Located in the Mercado del Puerto, this is one of the area's most popular restaurants, crowded with locals and tourists alike. It gets especially crowded when the cruise ships come in. It has been around since 1958. Fish is the highlight, but they also have tapas, pastas, paellas, and lots of grilled meats. A specialty is the Paella Exotica, made with rabbit.

Perez Castellano 1579 (at Rambla 25 de Agosto 400, in the Mercado del Puerto). © **02/917-0190** or 02/915-4704. www.elpalenque.com.uy. Main courses $8–$17. AE, DC, MC, V. Mon–Sat noon–midnight; Sun noon–5pm.

El Peregrino PARRILLADA/SEAFOOD/ITALIAN   This large, charming spot offers atmospheric dining with rustic tables, brick and yellow walls, and old photographs. Also on offer are several fish dishes, Italian dishes, and lots of beef, pork, and chicken.

Calle Pérez Castellano 1553 (at Piedras [at the Mercado del Puerto]). © **02/916-4737.** Main courses $5–$8. AE, DC, MC, V. Daily 11am–midnight.

El Viejo y el Mar ★ SEAFOOD   Resembling an old fishing club, El Viejo y el Mar is on the riverfront near the Sheraton. The bar is made from an abandoned boat, and the dining room is decorated with dock lines, sea lamps, and pictures of 19th-century regattas. The menu includes every kind of fish and pasta imaginable, and the restaurant is equally popular as a place for evening cocktails. An outdoor patio is open most of the year.

Rambla Gandhi 400. © **02/710-5704.** Main courses $5–$10. MC, V. Daily noon–4pm and 8pm–1am.

Los Leños ★★ PARRILLADA/SEAFOOD/URUGUAYAN   This casual *parrillada* resembles one you'd find in Buenos Aires—except it also serves an outstanding range of *mariscos* (seafood dishes), such as the Spanish paella or *lenguado Las Brasas* (a flathead fish) served with prawns, mushrooms, and mashed potatoes. From the *parrilla,* the *filet de lomo* is the best cut—order it with Roquefort, mustard, or black-pepper sauce. The restaurant's fresh produce is displayed in a case near the kitchen. Hillary Clinton once visited, and a picture of her with staff hangs on the wall.

San José 909 (at Convención). © **02/900-2285.** www.parrilla.com.uy. Main courses $2–$17. AE, DC, MC, V. Daily 11:45am–3:30pm and 8pm–midnight.

Shopping in Montevideo

The **Villa Biarritz fair,** at Parque Zorrilla de San Martín-Ellauri, takes place Saturday from 9:30am to 3pm, featuring handicrafts, antiques, books, fruit and vegetable vendors, flowers, and other goodies. The **Mercado del Puerto (Port Market) ★,** open afternoons and weekends at Piedras and Yacaré, lets you sample the flavors of Uruguay, from small empanadas to barbecued meats. Saturday is the best day to visit. There are numerous leather and souvenir stores on Calle Perez Castellano, in the general vicinity of the port. **Tristán Narvaja,** Avenida 18 de Julio in the Cordón neighborhood, is the city's Sunday flea market (6am–3pm), initiated nearly 60 years ago by Italian immigrants. **De la Abundancia/Artesanos** is a food-and-handicrafts market that happens Monday through Saturday from 10am to 8pm at San José 1312. **Tres Cruces Shopping Mall,** Avenida Serra at Acevedo Díaz (© **02/408-8710** or 02/401 8998; www.trescruces.com.uy), is part of the bus terminal complex and has dozens of shops.

Montevideo After Dark

As in Buenos Aires, nightlife in Montevideo means drinks after 10pm and dancing after midnight. For early evening entertainment, ask at your hotel or call the **Teatro Solís,** Calle Buenos Aires 652 (© **02/1950-3323;** www.teatrosolis.org.uy), the city's center for opera, theater, ballets, and symphonies. **SODRE,** Av. 18 de Julio 930 (© 02/901-2850; www.sodre.gub.uy), is the city's "Official Radio Service," which hosts live classical music concerts from May to November and is now overseen by Argentine ballet star Julio Bocca. Gamblers should head to the **Plaza Victoria Casino,** Plaza Independencia (© 02/902-2155; www.casinos.gub.uy), a fashionable venue with French roulette tables, blackjack, baccarat, slot machine, and bingo. It opens at 2pm and remains open for most of the night. **Mariachi,** Gabriel Pereira 2964 (© 02/709-1600), is one of the city's top bars and discos, with live bands or DJ music Wednesday to Sunday after 10pm. **Café Misterio,** Costa Rica 1700 (© 02/600-5999), is another popular bar. **Lotus** (© 2/628-1379; Av Luis Alberto de Herrera 1248 at Lamas in the World Trade Center; www.lotus.com.uy; Thurs–Sat 11pm–6am) is the city's best disco, with tunes by resident DJ Fernando Picon, but it closes in summer. **Cain** (Cerro Largo 1833 at Fernandez Crespo; www.caindance. com) is the main gay disco. Montevideo's best tango clubs are **La Casa de Becho,** Nueva York 1415 (© 02/400-2717 or 094-448-525 [cell]; Fri–Sat after 10:30pm, sometimes closed in summer), where composer Gerardo Mattos Rodríguez wrote the famous "La Cumparsita"; and **Cuareim,** Zelmar Michelini 1079 (no phone; Wed and Fri–Sat after 9pm), which offers both tango and *candombe,* a lively dance indigenous to the area with its roots in early slave culture. The tourist office can give you contact information for Montevideo's other tango salons.

PUNTA DEL ESTE, URUGUAY

320km (198 miles) NE of Buenos Aires

In terms of glamour, few resorts in South America rival Punta del Este. It might be geographically located in Uruguay, but it's where the gliterrati and elite of Buenos Aires make their homes for the summer. As Mar del Plata's reputation downscaled, this Uruguayan resort area became the new place to see and be seen.

Punta is actually a reference to several towns located near each other. The main town of Punta del Este is on a small peninsula where the Río de la Plata meets the Atlantic Ocean. The town is connected to Maldonado, the capital of the Department of Maldonado. Punta del Este and its surrounding towns have over 50km (31 miles) of waterfront, stretching along both coasts. The majority of the city's major hotels are on the calmer river side. The sprawling Conrad Hotel and Casino complex dominates the riverbanks, and serves as a de facto social center even for those who aren't staying at the hotel. Sandy dunes stretch out along the Atlantic side, with rougher waves. The beaches on this side are less crowded. At night, as the tide gets stronger, you'll see many young people carrying surfboards, heading to catch the waves along the coastal highway Ruta 10. As a general rule, the farther you get from the center, the less crowded the beaches become. Little of historical value is left in this former fishing village, now filled with high-rise hotels and condominiums reminiscent of developments in southern Florida. The very heart of the peninsula still has a few historical buildings, such as the Faro (lighthouse), churches, schoolhouses, and a few turn-of-the-20th-century buildings—a reminder of earlier, quieter times, before mass development in the 1950s and 1960s forever changed the way of life here. The port is often jammed with yachts.

Like any place that gets a reputation and becomes a part of package tours, Punta has lost some of its higher-end clients, who have gone elsewhere to look for greater exclusivity. About 10km (6 miles) up from Punta del Este is the small town of **La Barra.** It's an offshoot of Punta del Este that's sprung up on Ruta 10, which serves as its main street, lined with bars, small hotels, clubs, and art galleries. Visitors who have been to California's Laguna Beach will see more than a passing resemblance. Many young beachgoers flock here; at night, in high season, teenagers throw tailgate parties, parking their cars along the road to drink, hang out, dance along the road's shoulders, and blare car stereos. It's never quiet in La Barra during high season.

Farther along Ruta 10 is the very exclusive **José Ignacio,** a small, quiet community that's even more expensive than La Barra. Many celebrities keep second homes here, including international stars such as the supermodel Naomi Campbell. And when the mood strikes and they want to be seen, they head to La Barra.

Most hotels and restaurants in Punta del Este itself are open year-round, regardless of the weather, and Punta maintains a permanent year-round community. In La Barra and José Ignacio, however, many places close up for the winter. Summer season lasts from October to March, but "the Season," as it is known in the area, is a very specific time. From a few days after Christmas through the first 2 weeks of January, the Punta, La Barra, and José Ignacio swell with movie stars and models from all over South America (though mostly from Argentina). Film crews, photographers, and magazine staff follow them and watch their every movement, and parties abound. You may not know who most of them are if you are not from around here, but there are few places in the world with more glamour and beautiful women than Punta during high season. Needless to say, prices at this time are at their highest, so if you plan to see this phenomenon, book in advance and prepare to blow your travel budget.

An ideal time to come to Punta del Este is during the **Punta del Este Food & Wine Festival** held in November. Check **www.puntafoodandwine.com** for venues and ticket prices. For even more natural surroundings, the neighboring department of Rocha has beautiful beaches about an hour and a half from central Punta del Este, from the fishing village of **Punta del Diablo** to tranquil **Cabo Polonio,** where cars are banned. Visit **www.rocha.gub.uy** for more information.

When dialing numbers in Uruguay from overseas, use the country code **598.** You'll also need to drop the "0" in the city codes listed here, **02** for Montevideo and **042** for Punta del Este, when you're dialing from outside the country.

Planning

GETTING THERE

The easiest way to reach Punta del Este from Buenos Aires is by catching a **Buquebús** ferry to either Montevideo or Colonia, and then continuing by bus. **Buquebús's** number is ℂ **02/916-1910** in Montevideo; its fast-service number is ℂ **02/130.** Within Argentina, dial ℂ **54/11/4316-6500.**

COT (ℂ **02/409-4949** in Montevideo, or 042/486810 in Punta del Este; www.cot.com.uy) also offers bus service from Montevideo. **Copsa** (ℂ **02/1975** in Montevideo, or 042/1975 in Punta del Este; www.copsa.com.uy) is another bus company that offers service between Montevideo and Punta del Este. (These unusual numbers cannot be dialed from overseas, but only from within Uruguay.)

You can also fly between Buenos Aires's Jorge Newberry Airport and Punta's **Laguna del Sauce Airport,** about 16km (10 miles) from the city center. Airport information can be obtained by calling ℂ **042/559-777. Aerolíneas Argentinas** services the airports (ℂ **000-4054-86527** in Punta, or 0810/222-86527 in Buenos

Many locations in Punta del Este are not listed with addresses but with *parada* numbers (a reference to the closest traffic light along the coast to their location). Many shops, hotels, and businesses don't seem to know their addresses, only their *paradas*. In other cases, many stores and businesses don't list the number of their building in a street address, referring only to the street they are on and the nearby cross streets (you'll actually perplex them if you press them for a building number). Streets in Punta del Este are also labeled two different ways—as numbers and as names. For instance, Calle 31 is also called Inzaurraga; the main street, Avenida Gorlero, is called Avenida 22. Maps may or may not reflect both names. When in doubt about any address, ask for more information, such as a nearby store or landmark.

Aires; www.aerolineas.com.ar). **Pluna Airlines** is another carrier (© 042/492050 in Punta, or 11/4342-4420 in Buenos Aires; www.pluna.com.uy).

VISITOR INFORMATION

Punta del Este has several tourist information centers. There is a small one with a very helpful staff inside the bus station Terminal Punta Del Este (© 042/494-042). Overlooking the ocean at Parada 1 near Calle 21, the Liga de Fomento also has a tourist information center (© 042/446-519). Another city tourist office is at Plaza Artigas, on Gorlero between calles 25 and 23 (© 042/446-519). The city's offices are open from 10am to 10pm 7 days a week. The government of Uruguay also maintains a tourist information office for the whole country at Gorlero 942 between calles 30 and 29 (© 042/441218). The national office is open 10am to 7pm every day in the summer, and in winter daily from 10am to 5pm. The city government website (www.maldonado.gub.uy) has a section on tourist information; also visit www.uruguaynatural.com. Pick up *Liga News* or *Qué Hacemos Hoy*, two free tourist publications available all over the city with information on events around town.

Please see "Planning Your Trip to Uruguay: Visas, Currency & Phone Numbers," p. 212, for additional important planning information.

GETTING AROUND

If you're staying in Punta del Este itself, most things you need are within walking distance. The hotels generally have great restaurants on-site, and the beaches are just a quick walk over either the **Rambla Claudio Williman** on the Río de la Plata side, or the **Rambla Lorenzo Batlle Pacheco** on the Atlantic side. Although these two *ramblas* have different names, they are part of the same coastal highway, Ruta 10. The city's main shopping street is **Avenida Gorlero,** lined with stores and cafes. Another shopping street is **El Remanso,** 1 block over. Slightly more upscale and with a lot less foot traffic, it's nicknamed "the Little Paris," but you'll be hard-pressed to see why.

Many people hitchhike; you'll see a lot of young folk out there with their thumbs up. It's not considered dangerous at all here. It's best to rent a car, though, if you want to do some exploring or head to La Barra or José Ignacio without the threat of being stranded or ending up sleeping on the beach. Car rental can be expensive, however, starting at $90 a day in high season. **Europcar** has an office at Gorlero and Calle 20 (© 042/495017 or 042/445018; www.europcar.com.uy). **Dollar Rent a Car** is at Gorlero 961 (© 042/443444; www.dollar.com.uy).

Taxis are hard to come by, especially in high season. Keep the following numbers handy: **Shopping** (© 042/484704); **Parada 5** (© 042/490302), and **Aeropuerto** (© 042/559100). The bus company **COT** (© 042/486810) runs a service up and down the coastal routes, connecting the various towns in the area. You may have to wait a long time for one to pass by though. The company **Taller Rego,** Lenzina and Artigas, Parada 2 (© **042/486732**), rents motorcycles and bicycles.

What to See & Do

The main purpose behind a trip to Punta del Este is to spend time on the beach, but if you must do other things besides lie in the sun, work on your tan, and check out other hot bodies, you'll find a few places of interest. The symbol of Punta del Este is **La Mano,** a giant concrete hand sculpture rising out of the sands of the Atlantic across from the bus station. Creepy or playful, depending on your mood, it's a favorite photo-op for tourists and professional fashion shoots alike. The sculpture, by the Chilean artist Mario Irrarazabal, was inaugurated in 1981. On the tip of the peninsula, **Puerto Punta del Este** is pleasant for strolling and watching the boats come in, or, during high season, trying to figure out who's who on the various yachts. A tranquil change of pace from the beach is the church **Nuestra Señora de la Candelaria,** at the corner of Calle 12 (Virazon) and Calle 5 (El Faro), a beautiful sky-blue-and-white Victorian structure. Inside, you'll find high white arches and yellow walls punctuated by simple golden stained-glass crosses in the windows. Across the street is the **Meteorological Station,** Calle 5 (El Faro) and Calle 10 (Calle Dos de Febrero), a modern lookout tower built over a 100-year-old schoolhouse. There's free entry to the museum at its base, which has old pictures of Punta and a collection of weather instruments. The tower is not always open, but it has a great view of the surroundings. Directly across the street is **Faro de Punta del Este,** the city's symbolic lighthouse, dating from 1860, at Calle 5 (El Faro) and Calle 10 (Calle Dos de Febrero). There is a lookout tower with free admission open to the public, but opening hours are sporadic. **Plaza Artigas,** at Gorlero and Arrecifes, has a daily artist market with souvenirs and crafts. Along Ruta 10, just outside of downtown La Barra, is the **Museo del Mar ★★** (© **042/771-817**), an interesting museum with sea shells and other marine items that kids seem to like. It's open in summer from 10am to 10:30pm daily, and in winter from 11am to 6pm daily.

TOUR & EXCURSION COMPANIES IN PUNTA

Various travel companies in Punta del Este provide excursions and city tours. **Novoturismo** (© 042/493154) is in the Terminal de Omnibus and offers city tours. **Alvaro Gimeno Turismo** (© 042/490570; www.alvarogimenoturismo.com) is also located in the Terminal de Omnibus, and offers city tours as well as day trips to nearby cities such as Piriapolis. Call both ahead of time for English-language tours, which are not offered on a daily basis. Both pick up clients at their hotels for city tours, which generally last about 4 hours and cost $20.

Where to Stay

The Awa Hotel ★★   This small, well-designed boutique hotel looks like a 1950s interpretation of alpine architecture, set on a landscaped hill with soaring pine trees. Rooms are a good size, furnished with white linens and stark Italian ebony furniture with simple lines, imparting what co-owner Analia Suarez calls a "Zen" mood. Bathrooms are large and suites have hydro-massage tubs. One of the most amazing things about the hotel is that you can watch DVD movies in its mini-theater rather than just in your room. The lobby restaurant is open for breakfast, lunch, and dinner, with a light international menu and designer sandwiches. Rooms and public areas have Wi-Fi, and the business center has a terminal open 24 hours. The back garden is home to an outdoor heated pool, with a teak-wood deck for suntanning. The hotel is a bit of a walk from the beach, but is surrounded by several restaurants and close to Punta Shopping Mall.

Pedrogosa Sierra and San Ciro, CP 20100, Punta del Este. www.awahotel.com. © **042/499999.** 48 units, including 4 suites and 8 executive corner oversized rooms. Low season from $110 double; from $210 suite; high season from $260 double, from $600 suite. Rates include buffet breakfast. AE, DC, MC, V. Free on-site parking. **Amenities:** Restaurant; concierge; small health club; massage service; mini-theater; heated outdoor pool; room service; spa; Wi-Fi in lobby. *In room:* A/C, TV, minibar, Wi-Fi.

The Conrad Hotel and Casino ★★★

Rooms in this enormous, 14-story blue streamlined structure that dominates the scene within Punta del Este come in a variety of layouts and designs. Some have a California vibe, with casual decor in terra cottas and neutral tones; others are modern or have a tropical playfulness. All rooms facing the Río de la Plata have balconies, and the suites have balconies enormous enough for entertaining several guests. Select suites also have kitchens. There are several restaurants in the lobby and other areas of the hotel, including fine dining at **St. Tropez;** the casual **Las Brisas;** sandwiches, snacks, or just drinks at **Los Veleros;** or **Gaucho's,** by the pool. The pool and spa garden complex is a combination of indoor and outdoor spaces, with a view to the Río de la Plata. A heated indoor pool is also part of the complex, along with a spacious gym, a sauna, and the Children's Complex. The 24-hour casino, which includes a theater, offers shows and modeling events.

Parada 4 on Rambla Claudio Williman (btw. Chivert and Biarritz on Playa Mansa), CP 20100, Punta del Este. www.conrad.com.uy. © **042/491111.** Fax 042/490803. 302 units, including 24 suites. Low season from $180 double, from $400 suite; high season from $340 double, from $500 suite with $7,500 for Conrad suite. Rates can fluctuate drastically within various date ranges. Rates include luxurious buffet breakfast. AE, DC, MC, V. **Amenities:** 5 restaurants; 5 bars; babysitting; 24-hr. casino; concierge; large health club; massage service; indoor and outdoor heated pools; room service; spa; theater and show complex; Wi-Fi in lobby. *In room:* A/C, TV, high-speed Internet access, kitchens in select suites, minibar, Wi-Fi.

Fasano Las Piedras ★★★

Perhaps one of the most stunningly situated hotels in the Punta del Este area, Las Piedras is a part of the luxury Brazilian Fasano chain. The grounds sprawl over rocky hills that spread from the original *estancia* house, and rooms are set in bungalows throughout the property. Their modern weathered concrete exteriors blend into the hills; inside, they're decorated in woods, neutral tones, and creamy whites, and accented with leather and cowhide furnishings. An outdoor pool with its own bar sits on the grounds, and the hotel also maintains a lagoon beachfront a few miles drive away, with jet skis available for rent. There's a large gym and a spa with five massage rooms, including one for couples. A hilltop restaurant is the only part of the complex currently open to the public. Winding paths and the general size of the property mean that virtually nothing is handicap accessible, and golf carts are used to ferry people around. A golf course will be added in 2012.

Cerro Egusguiza y Paso del Barranco, CP 20400 La Barra, Punta del Este. www.laspiedrasfasano.com. © **042/670000.** Fax 042/670707. 32 units, including 10 suites. From $850 double; from $1,300 suite. Rates include luxurious buffet breakfast. AE, DC, MC, V. Free parking. Pets accepted (no fee). **Amenities:** 2 restaurants; 2 bars; babysitting; bikes; concierge; large health club; jet skis; kayaking; massage service; indoor and outdoor heated pools; room service; wet and dry sauna; spa. *In room:* A/C, TV, minibar, Wi-Fi.

Playa Vik and Estancia Vik ★★★ Playa Vik and Estancia Vik are two separate but related properties in the Punta del Este area. Estancia Vik, a luxury *estancia* about an hour from Punta del Este, opened in December 2008. It is a mix of vast, sweeping, beautiful outdoor expanses and art-filled interior spaces. Each room is individually painted—sometimes with provocative images, including nude couples. The Estancia is exceedingly tranquil, offering horseback riding, carriage rides, and polo fields for guests' use. Cows feed on the grass. Playa Vik opened in December 2010 in José Ignacio, half an hour from Punta del Este. It is built directly on the beach, with a combination of stunning art-filled hotel rooms with views to the water, and six small houses, built to look like dunes, and a disappearing edge outdoor pool. Rooms are art-filled also, and both properties have well-equipped spas.

Playa Vik: Calle Los Cisnes, José Ignacio; 9 rooms and 6 houses. Estancia Vik: Camino Eugenio Saiz Martinez, Km 8, José Ignacio. 12 units. www.vikretreats.com, www.estanciavikjoseignacio.com, or www. playavik.com. Reservations: ✆ **094/605212** (cell) or 094/605314 (cell). $500–$1,250. Rates can fluctuate drastically within various date ranges. Rates include luxurious buffet breakfast. AE, MC, V. **Amenities:** Restaurant, babysitting; bikes; concierge; large health club; massage service; polo fields; indoor and outdoor heated pools; room service; wet and dry sauna; spa; tennis courts; Wi-Fi. *In room:* A/C, TV, minibar, Wi-Fi.

Where to Eat

El Viejo Marino ★ SEAFOOD/PARRILLA This charming seafood restaurant and *parrilla* has a sailor theme. The smiling, friendly waitresses all wear dresses inspired by sailor uniforms. The dark interior mimics a ship, with navy-blue walls, dark woods, rope-back chairs, and old marine equipment scattered about. The menu has interesting combinations, such as sole cooked with Roquefort or mozzarella, several varieties of salmon, and catches of the day, much of it from the Río de la Plata. A standout specialty is Paella Viejo Marino—made with a variety of fish and other ingredients. Those who don't want fish can choose from plenty of grill options. A covered outdoor seating area is in front.

Calle 11 at Calle 14. ✆ **042/443565.** Main courses $11–$26. AE, MC, V. Daily noon–3pm and 8pm–2am (in summer, if busy, they will remain open btw. lunch and dinner).

Garzon Restaurant and Finca La Anita ★★ INTERNATIONAL/URUGUAYAN This restaurant is hard to get to; you'll have to hire a car or rent one. Created by Argentine star chef Francis Mallmann, it takes its name from the town it is set in, a sleepy, almost abandoned village an hour inland from Punta del Este. The restaurant overlooks the central plaza. On the menu are Uruguayan basics, like grilled beef and 7[½-hour lamb. The thrill of the restaurant is its remoteness and the difficulty of getting there, along with the country antique–filled setting and pampering staff. Six guest rooms are also available, at $660 a night for a double, which includes all meals and wine.

Plaza de Iglesia, 17km (11 miles) up Sains Martinez Rd., off Uruguay Ruta 9, Garzon, 1 hr. from Punta del Este. ✆ **044/102811** or 44/102809. www.restaurantegarzon.com. Main courses $40–$75. AE, V. Daily 7–10am, 12:30–4pm, and 8–11:30pm.

La Vista Restaurant, Gallery and Disco ★ INTERNATIONAL *La Vista* means "the view," and this restaurant, located on the 24th floor of the building Espacio Torreón, is aptly named indeed. On a clear day, the view extends to almost 40km (25 miles) from Punta del Este. It's simply stunning—but then that's the point. There are only a few items on the menu, but they can be elaborate, with flavors ranging from sweet to salty to tangy. Leonardo, one of the chefs, recommended the Uruguayan lamb cooked with smoked sweet potatoes, followed by a dessert which combines pears and Roquefort cheese, which he calls a "harmonic combination." The restaurant is open for breakfast, lunch, and dinner, with set minimums for each meal: $10 for breakfast; $15 for tea lunch; $20 for afternoon bar; and $50 for dinner, which includes the fee for staying to dance (the restaurant becomes a nightclub until 6am with $15 for admission, or $100 for a VIP table reservation.). The lobby, which provides access to the restaurant via a dedicated elevator, also has an appointment-only art gallery, open 2pm to 2am.

Edificio Torreón on Rambla Claudio Williman at Parada 1. ℂ **042/494949.** www.lavista.com.uy or www.espaciotorreon.com. Set menu prices $50 for dinner. AE, DC, MC, V. Daily 24 hr. Reservations recommended.

Lo de Tere ★ INTERNATIONAL   Overlooking the yacht-filled port, this elegant but casual restaurant is a good choice. The menu includes fish, *parrilla,* pasta, and sandwiches named for celebrities (including the hunky beef sandwich called the Brad Pitt). A very large wine selection complements the food offerings. It's very often busy, with long lines stretching out the door.

Rambla de Puerto at Calle 21. ℂ **042/440492.** www.lodetere.com. Main courses $8–$40. AE, DC, MC, V. Daily noon–4pm and 8pm–1 or 2am.

Shopping in Punta

Shopping can be a major after-beach sport in Punta. The majority of shops are along Avenida Gorlero and Calle 20, also known as El Remanso or the Little Paris. Shop hours vary considerably from winter to summer, and many stores do not open until the evening, after most of their potential customers leave the beach. For leather goods, try **Leather Corner,** Calle 31 at Inzaurraga and Gorlero (ℂ **042/441901**). **Duo,** Calle 20 at Calle 30 (ℂ **042/447709**), is an upscale sportswear store for men and women, with a large selection of Diesel clothes. **100% Uruguayo,** Gorlero 883 at Calle 28 (ℂ **042/446530**), has a large collection of handmade and distinctive locally produced goods; leather is the highlight. **Punta Shopping** is the main mall, with dozens of shops, along the wide pine-tree-lined boulevard Avenida Roosevelt, a few kilometers from the main part of town in the Playa Mansa area (Av. Roosevelt at Parada 7; ℂ **042/489666;** www.puntashopping.com.uy). **Plaza Artigas,** at Gorlero and Arrecifes, has a daily artist market with souvenirs and crafts. The town of La Barra is better known for its art galleries, including the popular **Trench Gallery,** Ruta 10, Km 161, Parada 45 (ℂ **042/771597;** www.trenchgallery.com). Gallery Night is every Friday in the summer in La Barra, when all the galleries have wine tastings.

MAR DEL PLATA

400km (248 miles) S of Buenos Aires

Argentina's most popular beach resort is a sleepy coastal city of about 700,000 long-term residents—until mid-December, when Porteños flock here for their summer vacation. Nearly eight million vacationers will pass through between December and March, the vast majority of them Argentines. Although it's not as luxurious as Uruguay's Punta del Este—the beach favorite of many jet-setting Argentines—Mar del Plata is closer to Buenos Aires and far cheaper. Its long, winding coastline is known for its crowded, tan-bodied beaches and quieter seaside coves, bordered by beautiful landscapes farther

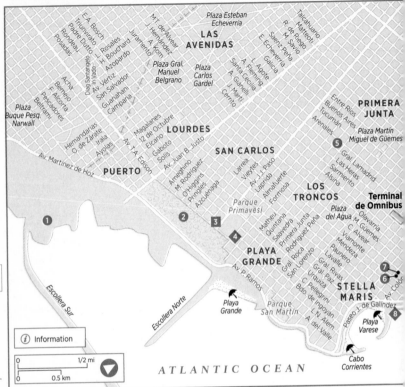

Map of Mar del Plata showing neighborhoods including LAS AVENIDAS, PRIMERA JUNTA, LOURDES, SAN CARLOS, PUERTO, LOS TRONCOS, PLAYA GRANDE, STELLA MARIS, and the ATLANTIC OCEAN.

inland that lead to the edge of the grassy Pampas. The resort was once very exclusive, but in the Perón era, hotels and high-rises were built for labor unions and the middle class, changing the social and physical makeup of the city forever. Some of the magnificent French- and Tudor-style mansions that housed Argentina's elite in the early 20th century have been meticulously preserved as museums.

Mar del Plata offers excellent nightlife in summer, when independent theater companies from Buenos Aires come to town and nightclubs open their doors to passionate Latin partygoers. The months of December, January, and February are the most crowded, wild, and expensive overall. In March, families with children and retired couples make up the bulk of vacationers, taking advantage of a more relaxed atmosphere and the slight reduction in prices. Many hotels and restaurants remain open year-round, so you can visit during other seasons as well, though the weather will be chillier.

Planning
GETTING THERE
You can reach Mar del Plata by plane, car, bus, train, or boat. The airport lies 10 minutes from downtown and is served by **Aerolíneas Argentinas** (☏ **800/333-0276** in

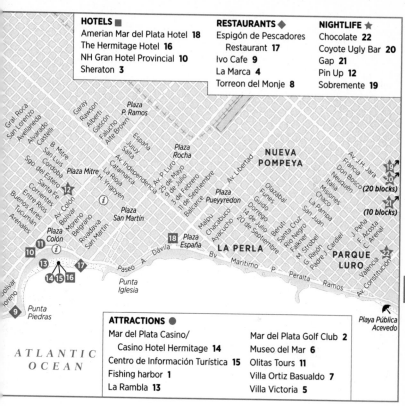

HOTELS ■
Amerian Mar del Plata Hotel **18**
The Hermitage Hotel **16**
NH Gran Hotel Provincial **10**
Sheraton **3**

RESTAURANTS ◆
Espigón de Pescadores
 Restaurant **17**
Ivo Cafe **9**
La Marca **4**
Torreon del Monje **8**

NIGHTLIFE ★
Chocolate **22**
Coyote Ugly Bar **20**
Gap **21**
Pin Up **12**
Sobremente **19**

ATTRACTIONS ●
Mar del Plata Casino/
 Casino Hotel Hermitage **14**
Centro de Información Turística **15**
Fishing harbor **1**
La Rambla **13**

Mar del Plata Golf Club **2**
Museo del Mar **6**
Olitas Tours **11**
Villa Ortiz Basualdo **7**
Villa Victoria **5**

the U.S., or 0810/222-86527 in Argentina; www.aerolineas.com.ar). Flights last just under an hour, and there are about three flights a day. Cabs into the center of town will cost about $15 to $20. The RN 2 is the main highway from Buenos Aires to Mar del Plata; it takes about 4 to 5 hours to drive between these cities. More than 50 bus companies link Mar del Plata with the rest of the country. Buses from Buenos Aires, which arrive at the central bus terminal at Alberti 1602 (© **223/451-5406**), are comfortable and cost under $30. They leave Buenos Aires from the Retiro Bus Station. One bus company serving Mar del Plata is **Chevallier** (© **11/4000-5255** in Buenos Aires or 0223/561-3719 in Mar del Plata; www.nuevachevallier.com). A train run by the company **Ferrobaires** (www.ferrobaires.gba.gov.ar) also connects Mar del Plata with Buenos Aires, and it's only slightly more expensive than the buses. It leaves Buenos Aires from Constitución, in the southern part of the capital, and runs three times a day. In Mar del Plata, purchase tickets at the train station, located at avenidas Luro and Italia (© **223/475-6076** in Mar del Plata, or 11/4304-0028 in Buenos Aires). Bus and train trips take about 4 to 5 hours.

VISITOR INFORMATION

The **Centro de Información Turística,** Bd. Marítimo PP Ramos 2270, at the Casino building (© **223/495-1777;** www.mardelplata.gov.ar or www.turismomardelplata.gov.

ar), has a knowledgeable, helpful staff offering maps and suggested itineraries. It is open daily from 8am to 9pm. There is also a branch at the airport. An additional website for tourism information is **www.mdp.com.ar**.

GETTING AROUND

La Rambla marks the heart of the city, the seaside walk in front of the casino and main city beach. This area itself is walkable, with restaurants and other businesses clustered here and between the nearby bus station and Plaza San Martín. Farther south, the Los Troncos neighborhood houses the city's most prominent residences as well as **Playa Grande** (the main beach), the **Sheraton** hotel (p. 236), and the **Mar del Plata Golf Club.** Mar del Plata has 47km (29 miles) of Atlantic coastline; if you plan to travel between La Rambla and Los Troncos, you'll need to take a taxi or rent a car. **Avis** (✆ **0810/9991-AVIS** (2847); www.avis.com.ar) offers rental cars at the airport.

What to See & Do

The main reason to visit Mar del Plata is the beaches, all of which spread outward from the city's heart at **Plaza Colón.** Here you'll find the **Mar del Plata Casino,** also known as **Casino Hotel Hermitage** (✆ **223/451-9226;** www.loteria.gba.gov. ar). The red brick–and-granite structure guarded by sea lion sculptures is the social center of the city. Walkways and steps lead from here to the beach, with many people posing in front of the giant granite sea lions for their only-in–Mar del Plata photos. In the early evening, as the crowds head home from the beach, you'll often see street performers and musicians here. (Pay attention to your pockets if you stop to watch.) With long, slow breaks, **Waikiki** is the best spot for surfing. This beach is located 7 miles south of the city center and can be accessed by various buses or by taxi. The coastline is nice, but you should not come expecting the mild Caribbean—the Atlantic remains fairly cold, even during summer. Once you've brushed off the sand, visit the **fishing harbor,** where hundreds of red and yellow boats unload their daily catches. The harbor houses a colony of 800 male sea lions that come to bathe on the rocky shores. (Be warned that between the sea lions and the fishing boats, it's an olfactory nightmare.) Next to the colony, there's an ugly but intriguing boat graveyard where rusty boats have been left to rot away.

In the Los Troncos neighborhood, **Villa Victoria,** Matheu 1851 at Arenales (✆ **223/492-0569**), showcases the early-20th-century summerhouse of wealthy Argentine writer Victoria Ocampo, who published the Argentine literary magazine *Sud* and was the first female member of the Argentine Academy of Letters. Some of Argentina's greatest authors, including Jorge Luis Borges, have come here to visit her writing salons. It's open year-round Thursday to Tuesday from 1 to 8pm, with an admission fee of about $4. In summer, musical and theatrical performances are held in the gardens, with various entry prices depending on the event. **Villa Ortiz Basualdo,** Av. Colón 1189 (✆ **223/486-1636**), is an English-style Victorian mansion decorated with exquisite Art Nouveau furniture from Belgium. The building is open daily from 10am to 10pm with an entry charge of just over $1. In the same neighborhood, the **Museo del Mar,** Av. Colón 1114, at Viamonte (✆ **223/451-9779;** www.museo delmar.com), houses a collection of 30,000 seashells. Stop in for a bite at their cafe, surrounded by tanks of sharks staring at you and your meal. This is an ideal spot if you're here with kids, and the rooftop terrace has an amazing view to the ocean a few blocks away. In summer, the museum is open Sunday to Friday 9am to 7pm and Saturday 9am to 10pm. During the winter, it's open daily from 9am to 1pm. Admission is about $3 for the museum, with an additional entry fee for lectures and other events at the adjacent auditorium.

Twenty minutes from the city center, **De Los Padres Lake and Hills** (© **0223/463-0255;** www.sierradelospadres.com.ar) is a picturesque forest with wide parks surrounding a lake, perfect for an afternoon picnic. Visit with a tour group, or on your own using municipal bus 717 along Avenida Luro through Ruta 226. On the grounds of the park is the home of José Hernández, who wrote the epic gaucho poem *Martin Fierro*. Nearby, in the Barrio Sierra de los Padres, is the **Zoo El Paraíso,** Ruta 226, Km 16.5 (© **223/463-0347;** www.zooelparaisoonline.com.ar). The park is open daily from 10am to 7pm, with an entry fee of $8 for adults and $3 for children. It features a wonderful collection of flora and fauna, including plants and trees from all over Argentina as well as lions, pumas, monkeys, llamas, and other animals. For information on surfing, deep-sea fishing, mountain biking, horseback riding, trekking, and other adventure sports, contact the tourism office (above).The tour company **Olitas Tours** also does half-day city tours, as well as a special tour for children on a bus filled with clowns. Visit their kiosk at Plaza Colón, call © **223/500-2816,** or log on to **www.olitas-tours.com.ar**.

Where to Stay

Amerian Mar del Plata Hotel   The Amerian is an Argentine chain hotel, and this branch in Mar del Plata overlooks Plaza España and La Perla Beach. The hotel is surrounded by several nightclubs, so it can be noisy at night. Prices differ based on whether your room has a sea or city view. Rooms are spacious, however, especially for the price category. Junior suites, positioned at angles, all have some form of sea view, even if it's not direct. Suites come with Jacuzzi tubs, and all the bathrooms are on the large side no matter the room category. Parking is free on-site. Wi-Fi is available in the rooms, for a $5 surcharge, and in the lobby, where there's also a small computer station. There is no gym or pool, though staff will help guests arrange to visit one nearby.

Av. Libertad 2936 (at La Rioja and Yrigoyen), 7600 Mar del Plata. www.amerian.com. © **223/491-2000.** Fax 223/491-2300. 58 units (52 doubles, 6 suites). From $102 double; from $123 suite. Rates include buffet breakfast. AE, DC, MC, V. Free parking. **Amenities:** Restaurant; bar; concierge; access to nearby pool and fitness center; limited room service; Internet station; Wi-Fi. *In room:* A/C, TV, minibar, Wi-Fi.

The Hermitage Hotel   This is Mar del Plata's grande dame hotel, opened in 1943, and the place where celebrities often stay. The Louis XV–style lobby has gilded friezes of fishermen, with art and photos of old Mar del Plata. In 2002, the hotel added a second building (on the same property) called **Torre Colón,** at the same time renovating the old building. The new building's rooms are nicer and pricier, with sea or city views. The formal restaurant **Luis Alberto,** where breakfast is served along with lunch and dinner, is in a connecting atrium. The hotel has a private casino and beach with bar and towel service from 8am to 10pm. Casino hours are 3pm to midnight Sunday to Thursday, and until 4am Friday and Saturday. While the hotel faces the ocean, the Torre Colón lobby is the main entrance. There is a small gym and spa, and a rooftop heated pool with a spectacular sea view.

Bd. PP Ramos 2657 and Av. Colón 1643 (overlooking the Casino), 7600 Mar del Plata. www.hermitage hotel.com.ar. © **223/451-9081.** Fax 223/451-7235. 300 units (240 doubles, 60 suites). From $164 double in old building; $200–$215 double in Torre Colón; $300–$350 suite. Rates include buffet breakfast. AE, DC, MC, V. Parking $10. **Amenities:** Restaurant; bar; babysitting; casino; concierge; health club; massage; room service; spa; pool; rooms for those w/limited mobility. *In room:* A/C, TV, high-speed Internet, minibar, Wi-Fi.

NH Gran Hotel Provincial ★★ This is the most iconic hotel in Mar del Plata, renovated and reopened it in 2009. The hotel was designed by Argentine architect Alejandro Bustillo in 1946 as part of a rebuilt Casino and Convention Center, replacing a classical structure destroyed in a fire. The hotel's rooms are spacious, many with wooden floors and windows overlooking either the sea or the city. The lobby is home to both a restaurant and a bar, along with meeting rooms. The hotel also has a restaurant at its pool, and a garden restaurant and beach area.

Av. Peralta Ramos 2502 (at Calle 49), 7600 Mar del Plata. www.nh-hotels.com. ☎ **223/499-5900.** Fax 223/499-5950. 306 units (including 14 suites). $157–$175 double; $569–$762 suite. Rates include buffet breakfast. AE, DC, MC, V. Parking $10. **Amenities:** Restaurant; bar; babysitting; casino; concierge; health club; massage; outdoor heated pool; indoor pool; rooms for those w/limited mobility; spa. *In room:* A/C, TV, minibar, Wi-Fi.

Sheraton ★★ The Sheraton overlooks the golf course and the military port, near Playa Grande. Rooms were renovated in 2007 and include trademark Sheraton Suite Sleeper beds. The hotel has a children's area and a video arcade, making it a great family choice. There are two pools, one indoor and one outdoor. A $15 charge applies for use of the indoor pool, connected to the spa and sauna complex. There are two restaurants in the hotel: the informal **La Pampa,** open for breakfast, lunch, and dinner, with an international menu; and the formal **Las Barcas,** open for dinner only Wednesday to Sunday. The gym received all-new equipment in 2007. With its view to the sea, it's a simply stunning spot for a workout. A garden surrounds the outdoor pool, which can be enjoyed free of charge but is only open in the summer. Rooms are airy and even standards seem oversized; suites have Jacuzzi tubs.

Alem 4221 (overlooking the golf course), 7600 Mar del Plata. www.sheratonmardelplata.com.ar. ☎ **0800/777-7002** or 223/414-0000. Fax 223/499-0009. 191 units (160 doubles, 31 suites). From $236 double with city views; $272 double with ocean views; from $405 suite. Rates include buffet breakfast. AE, DC, MC, V. Parking $15. Pets allowed. **Amenities:** 2 restaurants; bar; babysitting; concierge; golf; large health club; massage; 2 pools (fee for use of indoor pool); room service; rooms for those w/limited mobility. *In room:* A/C, TV, high-speed Internet, minibar, Wi-Fi.

Where to Eat

Espigón de Pescadores Restaurant ★★ SEAFOOD You'll see this restaurant the moment you arrive in Mar del Plata, if only because it's under the enormous neon billboard sign for Quilmes (an Argentine beer) on the pier. This three-level restaurant juts into the ocean and is one of the best seafood restaurants in town. Built into the Fisherman's Club, it's the next best thing to catching the fish yourself. Fish of all kinds is served here, including sole, salmon, calamari, lobster, oysters, and more. Landlubbers will find pasta, salads, and *parrilla* offerings too, and some of the same sauces for fish double as pasta sauces. Naturally, there are a lot of white wines on the menu. I list a high maximum price here, but most main courses cost about $12.

Bd. Marítimo and Av. Luro, in the Club de Pesca, on the city pier. ☎ **223/493-1713.** www.espigonde pescadores.com.ar. Main courses $6–$25. AE, DC, MC, V. Daily noon–3pm and 8pm–midnight.

Ivo Cafe ★★ GREEK/ARGENTINE I can't say enough about this fantastic two-level Greek restaurant at the bottom of a high-rise condo overlooking the ocean with sidewalk seating. The Greek owners serve Greek food along with Argentine *parrilla* options. They have oversized Greek salads, excellent souvlaki, and many other choices. The chic black table is set with olives, bread, and eggplant pastes for dipping. While there is an English-language menu, ask for the Spanish one if you can read it; it has a wider and better range of options. From the plate-glass windows, diners have a view of the sweeping arc of lights on the Mar del Plata shoreline. Come for dinner shows each Thursday, beginning at 9pm, with Greek dancing and a meal totaling about $20 (drinks cost extra). Or come in the wee hours on any day, and you'll find that the staff has a tendency to break into piano playing, singing, and traditional dancing.

Bd. Marítimo 3027 at Güemes. ☎ **223/486-3160.** www.ivocafe.com. Main courses $8–$13. AE, MC, V. Daily 24 hr. in summer; winter Sun–Thurs 8am–3am, Fri–Sat 24 hr.

La Marca ★★ ARGENTINE   This restaurant became famous for serving a whole cow upon special request, for large groups of 50 or more people. It's not often that they do this anymore, but La Marca remains the town's best *parrilla,* serving thick rump steaks, tenderloins, and barbecued ribs of beef, flanks, and other cuts of beef. The tender filet mignon with mushroom sauce is delicious. The menu includes pork chops, sausages, sweetbreads, black pudding, and other delights as well. The salad bar is extensive. Service is polite and unhurried. Try the dulce de leche before you leave.

Almafuerte 253 (at Alem, on Playa Grande near the Sheraton). ☎ **223/451-8072.** www.lamarca restaurant.com.ar. Main courses $8–$12. AE, DC, MC, V. Daily noon–3pm and 8:30pm–1am.

Torreon del Monje ★★ ARGENTINE   It's hard not to notice this restaurant inside a castlelike structure dating from 1904 that overlooks the Atlantic Ocean. Day or night, the plate-glass windows over the sea and opening onto the street offer a fantastic view. Food runs from simple sandwiches to *parrilla* offerings, including steak, chicken, and, of course, locally caught seafood. Almost each night, dinner shows take place while you dine, beginning at 10pm. Some are tango, others flamenco and folkloric. There is no additional charge for the shows. Even if you've dined elsewhere, stop in for drinks at the beautiful oak bar. During the day, many people come for the flavored and alcoholic coffee specials in the Esmeralda lounge.

Paseo Jesús de Galíndez (at the Puente del Monje, on the seafront). ☎ **223/451-9467.** www.torreon delmonje.com. Main courses $6–$15. AE, DC, MC, V. Daily 8am–2am (Fri–Sat until 4am).

Mar Del Plata After Dark

Nightlife follows close behind beaches as Mar del Plata's biggest draw. In summer, theater companies leave Buenos Aires to perform in this coastal resort; ask the tourism office for a schedule of performance times and places. The city's most popular bars are south of Plaza Mitre, off Calle San Luis. The best dance clubs are along Avenida Constitución, 3km (2 miles) from downtown, including **Chocolate,** Av. Constitución 4445 (☎ **223/479-4848;** www.chocolatemdq.com.ar); **Gap,** Av. Constitución 5780 (☎ **223/479-6666**), featuring live rock music; and **Sobremonte,** Av. Constitución 6690 (☎ **223/479-7930**). **Pin Up,** Santiago del Estero 2265 (no phone; www.pinupweb.com), is one of the most popular gay discos. **Coyote Ugly Bar,** Av. Constitución 6690 (☎ **223/479-2600**), is a favorite Mexican restaurant and bar, which breaks into salsa and merengue dancing as the night goes on.

TIGRE & THE DELTA

36km (22 miles) NE of Buenos Aires

The Tigre River Delta is in essence a wild natural suburb of Buenos Aires, but it seems a world apart from the city. The Delta is formed by the confluence of five rivers, where they flow from the Pampas into the Río de la Plata. This marshy complex is full of silt and thousands of tiny islands. Over time, the Delta is continuing to expand down the Río de la Plata; it's grown considerably since the Spanish Conquest.

Tigre & the Delta

ATTRACTIONS ●
Centros de Información Turística **4, 7**
Museo de Arte Tigre **1**
Naval Museum **2**
Parque de la Costa **9**
Puerto de Frutos **10**

RESTAURANTS ◆
Don Emilio Parrilla **5**
El Moño Rojo **8**
La Terraza **3**

HOTELS ■
Casona La Ruchi **6**

In theory, within several hundred years, the Delta will reach the capital. The islands are a mix of grassland, swamp, and true forest, with a variety of animal and plant life. The name Tigre comes from the "tigers" (actually jaguars) that once roamed here.

The development of the Tigre Delta into a resort area owes to two concurrent historical circumstances in Buenos Aires in the 1870s. One was the construction of railroads from Buenos Aires into the rest of the country. The other was the 1877 outbreak of yellow fever, which caused wealthy Porteños to seek out new parts of the city for year-round homes, as well as summer vacation spots. The English were in charge of much of the construction here, so many of the older neo-Gothic and mock-Tudor mansions and bed-and-breakfasts that line the banks of the river passages look like Victorian London buildings transplanted into the wild marshes of the Pampas.

Today, many Porteños come here on weekends to relax, kayak, ride horseback, hike, fish, swim, or do nothing at all. It's also a convenient destination for tourists, since it's easy to come here just for the day, tour the islands by boat, and return to Buenos Aires in time for dinner. There is a year-round population of residents on these car-free inner islands, and they go to school, work, and shop for groceries using a system of boats and docks. The delta fell into decline a number of years ago, but has since been revived. Very wealthy Argentines are beginning to move and vacation here, buying large homes on remote islands, and frequenting the recently developed spa resorts.

Planning

GETTING THERE

The Tigre Delta is best reached by train from Buenos Aires, and then a boat or launch from the train station if you're continuing on to the islands. Trains from Buenos Aires leave from **Estación Retiro** for Estación Tigre, at Avenida Naciones Unidas, every 10 to 20 minutes along the Mitre Line. Tickets cost about $1 round-trip. Call ✆ 11/4317-4445 or 0800-3333-822 for schedules and information, or visit **www.tbanet.com.ar**. **Sturla** (✆ 11/4731-1300 in Tigre or 11/4314-8555 in Buenos Aires; www.sturlaviajes.com.ar); also runs a boat from Puerto Madero in Buenos Aires to Tigre, offering sensational waterfront views. Within Tigre, the **Estación Fluvial Tigre,** where the boats depart to head through the various rivers and islands, is on the next block over from **Estación Tigre,** at Mitre 305. Many companies run launches and services on both banks of the river here; you have to know where you want to go, or simply choose one and go wherever it takes you. Among the many companies are **Catamaranes Interisleña** (✆ 11/4731-0261; www.tigreencatamaran.com.ar), **Líneas Delta** (✆ 11/4749-0537; www.lineasdelta.com.ar), and **Catamaranes Río Tur** (✆ 11/4731-0280; www.rioturcatamaranes.com.ar). To reach **Martín García Island,** one of the most remote parts of the delta, you have to travel with **Cacciola** (✆ 11/4749-0329; www.cacciolaviajes.com). Most of these companies service the various islands but allow you to ride on the boat until the end of the trip and then simply return. Ticket prices vary but start at less than $5. I highly recommend that you find out when the last few boats leave from your destination; toward the end of the day, boats can fill up quickly, leaving some passengers to wait for the next boat. Extra boats are dispatched at peak times, but you still may have to wait a few extra hours at the end of the day, especially on Sunday. Build this time into your plans or you may literally get stuck in the mud. Many tour companies in Buenos Aires also provide excursions to the Tigre Delta; I have included contact information for a handful of these below.

VISITOR INFORMATION

There are two main Centros de Información Turística. One is in Estación Tigre, open daily 9am to 6pm, and another is in Estación Fluvial Tigre, Mitre 305 (✆ 0800/888-TIGRE [84473] or 11/4512-4497; www.tigre.gov.ar and www.vivitigre.gov.ar), open daily 8am to 6pm. This very busy office provides information on the islands, hotels, rentable bungalows, and various activities. You may have to wait for help, but most of the staff speaks English. Other useful tourism sites are **www.laisladelta.com.ar** and **www.puntodelta.com.ar**. Two excellent tour guides for Tigre are Susana Neira (✆ 11/4992-3780; susananeira159@gmail.com) and Mariana Jimenez (✆ 11/4997-7832; mariana.v.jimenez@gmail.com).

GETTING AROUND

Within the town of Tigre itself, where both the train station and the docks are, one can easily walk along both banks. There are restaurants, playgrounds for children, and a few tourist-oriented shops along the waterfront and on the streets heading to the Puerto de Frutos (see below). To get around and see the delta, however, you will need a boat. I have listed the companies that provide these services above, in "Getting There."

What to See & Do

The main thing to see in Tigre is the delta itself and the various islands and resorts that dot the area. Within the town of Tigre, where the train station and boat docks are, there are a few services and various other places of interest. Many people simply stay in this area and dine in the restaurants, sunbathe along the shoreline, or wander the town. Ponies march up and down the eastern shoreline in the city center, near the intersection of calles Lavalle and Fernández; children love riding them. From this area, head along what is called **Paseo Victórica,** a collection of Victorian mansions along the waterfront of Río Lujan, until it intersects Río Conquista. This is one of the prettiest parts of Tigre, and you will find many people sunbathing along the shore here. In the midst of all this Victorian splendor is the **Naval Museum,** Paseo Victorica 602, at Martínez (✆ 11/4749-0608). On the opposite bank is the **Parque de la Costa,** Vivanco, at Montes de Oca (✆ 11/4732-6000; www.parquedelacosta. com.ar), full of rides for kids and grown-ups.

Just outside of the center of Tigre is the famous **Puerto de Frutos,** Calle Sarmiento 160 (✆ 11/4512-4493; www.puertodefrutos-arg.com.ar), along Río Lujan. Fruit farming was integral to the early development of the Tigre Delta, and this market is a leftover from those days. Many tourists rave about their visits to this market, but I have always found it disappointing, with almost no fruit. Besides the traditional basket weavers who create their wares using the reeds that grow in the delta, it's now mostly full of less interesting crafts that can be found in many other places. Still, it's worth a quick visit.

Definitely not to be missed is the **Museo de Arte Tigre,** Paseo Victorica 972 (✆ 11/4512-4528; www.mat.gov.ar), built into what had been the Tigre Casino. The building is among the most impressive Argentine Beaux Arts buildings outside of Buenos Aires and took years to restore. The redesign of the casino as a museum was done by Gabriel Miremont, the curator of the Museo Evita and numerous museums throughout Argentina. The museum is now overseen by Director Diana Saiegh. It has free admission and is open Wednesday to Friday 9am to 7pm, and Saturday and Sunday noon to 7pm. This is a must-see in Tigre, and the collection of art will also help you understand Tigre's history as a destination for wealthy bohemians seeking a refuge from the big city where they could spend their time painting. Another art option is to visit the atelier of **Sebastian Paez Vilaro,** the son of the Uruguayan artist Carlos Paez Vilaro. Visits are by appointment only and can be arranged via the website, **www.sebastianpaezvilaro.com**.

A 3-hour boat ride each way from the center of Tigre will take you to **Martín García Island.** It is famous for its upscale political prison, where various Argentine presidents, including Juan Perón, have been incarcerated, but exploring here will take a full day once you account for the round-trip boat ride.

If you are doing any trekking on the islands, even in hot weather, you will need hiking boots, long pants, and long-sleeved shirts. Saw grass and other sharp plants inhabit the area and will rip into unprotected skin. You should also bring mosquito repellent, though malaria is not a problem in the delta, only painful itching. It's also a good idea to pack binoculars, to view birds and other wildlife. Tigers and jaguars are no longer a concern in Tigre.

EXCURSION COMPANIES SERVING TIGRE DELTA

Various travel companies in Buenos Aires provide day-trip excursions to the Río Tigre Delta or will arrange longer stays in the numerous bed-and-breakfasts, bungalows, and adventure lodges in the area. **Say Hueque Tourism,** with two locations (Viamonte 749, Office 601, 1053 Buenos Aires, ✆ 11/5199-2517; Thames 2062, Buenos Aires, ✆ 11/5258-8740; www.sayhueque.com), is one that I highly recommend, especially for longer trips and adventure excursions to see the natural beauty of the area. **Travel Line** (☎ **11/4393-9000;** www.travelline.com.ar) offers Tigre Delta day tours, among many other excursions. The full-day Tigre tours are Sundays only (ask for an English-speaking guide), and include lunch, a ride to and from Tigre by train, and a boat ride among the rivers of the Tigre Delta, all for about $65 per person. Additionally, **Borello Travel** (☎ **1-800-405-3072** in the United States and Canada or 54-11-5031-1988 in Buenos Aires; borellotravel.com) offers luxury trips to the delta, including stays at the spa resorts.

Where to Stay

Bonanza Deltaventura ★★   If you're looking to get away from it all, head to this adventure hotel on one of the islands in the Río Tigre Delta, with miles of walkways through the grasslands for bird-watching, horses for riding along the shoreline, and a dock out front for swimming. The lodge can accommodate a total of eight people at a time; guests can rent four small but comfortable rooms as either singles or doubles. The living style is communal, with a shared kitchen and bathrooms. The price is for 2 days and 1 night and includes meals and excursions; alcoholic drinks cost extra. The staff also speaks English. You will need to call ahead of time if you want stay here, to ensure that space is available and to make the appropriate boat arrangements. The hotel is on the Carapachay River islands section of the delta, about a 1-hour boat ride from the center of the town of Tigre.

Carapachay River Islands, 1648 Tigre. www.deltaventura.com. ☎ **11/4728-1674** or 11/15-5603-7176 (cell). 4 units for up to 8 people. From $140 a person, including all meals (no alcohol) and trekking. No credit cards. **Amenities:** Shared kitchen; horses; trekking.

Casona La Ruchi ★★   This charming bed-and-breakfast overlooks the waterfront across the bank from the Estación Fluvial. Owners Dora and Jorge Escuariza and their children run the place, treating guests who stay in the six-room, 1893 mansion like family. In the back, guests can enjoy the pool and grill. Rooms are furnished with quaint Victorian antiques, and some have windows looking out onto the waterfront. The place is open year-round, but busiest on weekends in the summer. Guests have 24-hour access, though the family does not have an actual overnight staff person. Call if you're arriving late in the day to verify that someone can let you in. You will enjoy the warmth and hospitality at this place. Some rooms share a bathroom; all have Wi-Fi.

Lavalle 557 (at Av. Libertador), 1648 Tigre. www.casonalaruchi.com.ar. ☎ **11/4749-2499.** 6 units, some with shared bathroom. $60 double. Rates include continental breakfast. No credit cards. **Amenities:** Use of kitchen and backyard grill; outdoor pool; Wi-Fi.

Delta Eco Spa ★★   This resort hotel and spa complex opened in mid-2010. Portions of it, including additional bungalows and year-round residents off the main grounds, are still under construction as of this writing. Built on its own private island, the complex has the feel of a rustic luxury jungle resort. The large spa has several treatment rooms with a view to the grounds, a wet and dry sauna, and an indoor heated pool. Rooms are large, perfect for couples, some with dual sinks and showers, and all come with balconies or patios. The complex is open to the public for day trips, dining, and use of the spa. Bungalows have cathedral ceilings and line a small inlet. We list daily rates, but rooms are usually booked as 2-night packages, including scheduled express transport from central Tigre. Children under 10 are not allowed.

Río Carapachay, western delta, 1648 Tigre, 20–30 min. boat ride from central Tigre. www.deltaecospa.com. ✆ **11/5236-0553.** 20 units, including 4 suites and 23 bungalows. From $165 double; $340 suite; $415 bungalow. Day rate with lunch $96; Spa Day without treatments $155, with treatments $180. Rates include meals and scheduled transport from central Tigre. AE, MC, V. **Amenities:** Restaurant; bar; concierge; outdoor pool; indoor pool; spa w/dry and wet sauna; treatment and massage rooms (additional rates for services); room service; Wi-Fi. *In room:* A/C, TV, DVD, minibar, Wi-Fi.

Rumbo 90 Delta Lodge and Spa ★★★ This small, romantic spa resort with only seven rooms, all with Jacuzzis and balconies, was opened by the Gezzi family on the Canal del Este. The name is a nautical reference, meaning to turn east. Rooms are oversized and filled with antiques, and the honeymoon suite has an enormous balcony and two-person Jacuzzi. The large private island is divided into sections, including the main lodge grounds and a working farm. The spa, with a heated pool connecting to the outdoor pool, dry and wet sauna, and various treatment and massage rooms, is open to the public for day trips on a limited basis, so as not to spoil the low-key atmosphere. The restaurant features an award-winning Menu Tigre, with an emphasis on local fish. I give daily rates, but rooms are usually booked as 2-night packages, including scheduled express transport from central Tigre. Children under 16 are not allowed.

Canal del Este, eastern delta, 1648 Tigre, 30–40 min. boat ride from central Tigre. www.rumbo90.com. ar. ✆ **11/4749-2499** or 11/15-5843-9454. 7 units. From $220 double; $300 suite. Day rate with lunch $88, Spa Day is $120 but does not include treatments. Rates include meals and scheduled transport from central Tigre. AE, MC, V. **Amenities:** Restaurant; bar; concierge; outdoor/indoor pool; room service; spa w/dry and wet sauna; treatment and massage rooms (additional rates for services); Wi-Fi. *In room:* A/C, TV, DVD, minibar, Wi-Fi.

Where to Eat

Don Emilio Parrilla ARGENTINE/PARRILLA A casual atmosphere and a rustic interior with tables in bright Provençal yellow await you in this *parrilla* overlooking the waterfront. The food here is great, and a complete meal will cost you about $15. Unfortunately, it's only open on weekends.

Lavalle 573 (at Av. Libertador). ✆ **11/4631-8804.** Main courses $3–$10. No credit cards. Fri 8pm–1am; Sat–Sun 11:30am–5pm and 8pm–2am.

El Moño Rojo ★ ARGENTINE/INTERNATIONAL An enormous restaurant complex overlooking the waterfront near the Estación Fluvial, this is one of the best places to come for a meal with entertainment. The atmosphere is brilliantly red, festive, and very kitschy, full of posters of tango stars, pictures of Argentine actors and actresses, and old Peronist memorabilia. On Friday they stage a tango show. The food is a mixture of pizzas, snacks, sandwiches, and traditional *parrilla* grilled meat, so there should be something to please everyone here.

Av. Mitre 345 (at Estación Fluvial Tigre). ✆ **11/15-5135-7781** (cell). Main courses $4–$12. No credit cards. Daily 8am–2am.

La Terraza ★ ARGENTINE/INTERNATIONAL This two-level restaurant looks like it was dropped in from a tropical island, with its wraparound verandas and palm tree overhangs. A full *parrilla* offers some of the best steak dining in Tigre. You'll also find chicken, salads, and Italian cuisine. There is a beautiful view to the Río Lujan from the dining room.

Paseo Victoria 134 (at Colon Tigre). ✆ **11/4731-2916.** www.laterrazatigre.com.ar. Main courses $4–$10. No credit cards. Tues–Sun noon–5pm; Fri–Sat 8pm–1am (sometimes later).

SAN ANTONIO DE ARECO & PAMPAS ESTANCIAS

111km (69 miles) NW of Buenos Aires

San Antonio de Areco is a quiet little town about 90 minutes north of Buenos Aires, deep in the heart of Argentina's famous Pampas. The town is best known as the center of gaucho culture, Argentina's version of American cowboy tradition. Few people stay in San Antonio, choosing to visit it as a day trip from Buenos Aires, or as a base for exploring the nearby *estancias* that surround the town.

The city is compact, built in 1730 around an old colonial church dedicated to San Antonio of Padua, from which the town takes its name. Colonial and turn-of-the-20th-century buildings abound, all reached on walkable cobblestone streets that radiate from the church and Plaza Ruiz de Arellano, the town's main square. The Río Areco divides the town in two parts. Here along the river is a monument-lined green space called Parque San Martín, crossed by an old pedestrian bridge to Parque Criollo, where the city's most famous site, the **Museo Gauchesco Ricardo Güiraldes (Museum of the Gaucho),** sits.

The city's main shopping streets are Alsina and Arellano, heading south from Plaza Arellano. A year-round tourism destination, it lives for the annual **Día de la Tradición,** held around November 10. Gauchos, real and wannabe, fill the town, playing gaucho games of skill such as the *sortija,* where they catch rings from poles while riding horses, giving them as gifts to beautiful women in the audience. San Antonio has only a small number of hotels, which fill up fast at this time of year. (Of course, there's always the gaucho's pad, if he gives you his *sortija* ring.) See also the section on *estancias,* below; all are within a short drive of the center of San Antonio.

Planning

GETTING THERE

San Antonio de Areco can be reached by car from Buenos Aires by driving north along Ruta 8. The drive takes about 1½ hours. Most people come by bus, however. **Chevallier** offers hourly bus service from Buenos Aires's Retiro Bus depot (© **2326/453-904** in San Antonio, 11/4000-5255 in Buenos Aires, or 0800/222-6565 toll-free; www.nuevachevallier.com).

VISITOR INFORMATION

The **Dirección de Turismo de San Antonio de Areco** tourism information center (© **2326/453-165;** www.pagosdeareco.com.ar) is in Parque San Martín along the Río Areco waterfront, near the intersection of Avenida Zerboni with Calle Zapiola and Calle Arellano. It is open 7 days a week from 8am to 7pm. The websites **www.visit eareco.com** and **www.sanantoniodeareco.com** also provide more tourism information.

GETTING AROUND

Within San Antonio itself, your feet can take you most of the places you need to go. Even the most distant actual attraction, the **Museo Gauchesco Ricardo Güiraldes,** is a 15-minute walk from the center. Because many people use the town as a base for exploring other parts of the Pampas, such as the numerous *estancias, remises* are a must. Contact the 24-hour **Remis Zerboni,** Zerboni 313, near Alsina

(☏ **2326/453-288**). The town is also great for bike riding; most hotels provide free bicycle loans.

TOUR COMPANIES

Various travel companies in Buenos Aires arrange day trips to San Antonio de Areco, with or without overnight stays on nearby *estancias*. **Borello Travel & Tours** is a travel firm specializing in upscale travel, with offices in New York and Buenos Aires (7 Park Ave., Ste. 21, New York, NY 10016, ☏ **800/405-3072** or 212/686-4911; and in Buenos Aires at Perú 359, Ste. 407, ☏ **11/5031-1988;** www.borellotravel.com). They can arrange visits to San Antonio with stays in local *estancias*. Buenos Aires–based **Say Hueque Tourism,** with two locations (at Viamonte 749, Office 601, 1053 Buenos Aires, ☏ **11/5199-2517;** Thames 2062, Buenos Aires, ☏ **11/5258-8740;** www.sayhueque.com), also provides trips to this area.

What to See & Do

The center of San Antonio de Areco is the leafy **Plaza Arellano,** surrounded by cobblestone streets and overseen by a statue of Juan Hipólito Vieytes, a local involved in the Argentine war for independence from Spain. His memorial sits in an acoustic circle, so it's fun to come here just to talk and listen to the echo of your voice, especially if you bring kids. The statue faces south to Calle Mitre, staring at the church from which the town draws its name, **San Antonio de Padua,** rebuilt in the late 1800s over the original 1730 colonial version. Colonial on the outside, its interior mixes Gothic and neoclassical styles, with frescoes of angels and saints in niches on the walls, all overseen by a coffered ceiling. On the plaza's north side is the Belle Epoque **Municipal Hall,** a long pink building at Lavalle 363 with an attractive central courtyard. Nearby is the **Draghi Museum and Shop,** Lavalle 387, between Alsina and Arellano (☏ **2326/454-219**), open daily approximately 10am to 5pm, though technically by appointment only. Opened by the late Juan Jose Draghi, a master silversmith who began his career nearly 50 years ago making ornamental items for gauchos, it is now run by his son Mariano. The museum is itself a work of art, with its exquisite stained-glass ceiling. The museum also has its own hotel (p. 248). A few blocks away, you can watch other silversmiths at work in the small **Artesano Platero,** Alsina at Zerboni, facing the Parque San Martín (☏ **2326/454-843** or 2325/15-656-995 [cell]; www.arecoplateria.com.ar), open daily 9:30am to 12:30pm and 3 to 9pm.

From here, head to **Parque San Martín,** on the south side of the Río Areco. It's lined with trees and monuments, and full of vine-covered walkways called *glorietas*. It's a place where families picnic and kids play soccer or climb over the small dam constructed in the river. Two bridges cross the park here, but the most picturesque is the **Puente Viejo,** originally constructed in the 1850s as a toll crossing. The other end of the river is the site of Parque Criollo, and here sits the city's most famous attraction, the **Museo Gauchesco Ricardo Güiraldes** (**Museum of the Gaucho,** named after the author of *Don Segundo Sombra*), Camino Ricardo Güiraldes, at Sosa (☏ **2326/455-839;** www.museoguiraldes.com.ar), open Wednesday to Monday 10am to 4:30pm. Written in 1926, Güiraldes's novel immortalized the noble gaucho, making him an honored part of Argentine history. The museum combines an authentic 1830 *pulpería*, or country general store, where gauchos gathered, with a museum designed in a colonial style by Argentine architect José María Bustillo in 1936. Here you will find the author's personal effects, photos, books, and other gaucho memorabilia. It's a bit kitschy (think rooms filled with gaucho mannequins), but if you speak Spanish, a conversation with the museum's guide and historian, Omar Tapia, will help you put the gauchos in their proper historical context.

The Pampas & Estancias

San Antonio is a popular base for exploring Argentina's famous *estancias,* which have a history as both farms and fortresses, built throughout the country along trails from Buenos Aires as a means of conquering and stabilizing territory originally controlled by the Indians. (The fertile lowland plains in this part of Argentina, as well as Uruguay and a small part of Brazil, are called the Pampas.) The majority of Argentina's *estancias* date from the mid- to late 1800s. After General Roca's Campaign of the Desert in the 1870s, in which he murdered most of the Indian population within 150 miles of Buenos Aires, more and more *estancias* sprang up in this area, driving the cattle and grain industries. Despite the bloody history that spawned them, today they're seen as an idyllic retreat from the chaos of Buenos Aires. They are popular among Porteños who come here on weekends or for day trips. With the increase in tourism to Argentina, many foreigners delight in them as well.

Most *estancias* listed here are a half-hour from San Antonio, and no more than 2 hours from Buenos Aires. You can drive on your own, or use a bus service from Buenos Aires to San Antonio, and catch a taxi from there. For a fee in the range of $80 to $120, most *estancias* provide transportation from your hotel or either Buenos Aires airport. Because many *estancias* are accessed by dirt roads, it is advisable to rent a 4WD vehicle if you drive yourself, especially if rain is predicted during your visit. The *estancias* here have detailed driving maps on their websites.

Services and features vary, but the atmosphere at most *estancias* is a cross between a rustic resort and a bed-and-breakfast. Nothing relieves stress like a few days in the country, and horseback riding, trekking, lounging by the pool, and eating and drinking aplenty are all part of a day on the Pampas. In general, the rates for *estancias* include a full board of four meals—breakfast, lunch, afternoon tea, and dinner—and sometimes all drinks, including alcohol. Lunch, the highlight of dining on an *estancia,* is usually an *asado,* or barbecue, where everyone, including the workers, gathers to socialize. Day rates generally include only lunch and limited activities. Most *estancias* are real working farms, with hundreds of acres and cows, horses, and other animals attended by real gauchos (not all of whom dress in the traditional way). If you're in the mood to milk a cow or watch the birth of colt, you just might have the chance.

El Cencerro ★★★   Smaller, cozier, and more rustic than some of the other places listed here, this working *estancia* will make you feel like you're part of the farm's daily goings-on. It's owned by Buenos Aires–based psychologist Liliana Herbstein, who spends her weekends here. The ranch takes its name from the *cencerro,* a bell used by gauchos to tame horses. Rooms and public areas are filled with antiques and odd objects Liliana and her husband Eduardo have collected over the years, including antique luggage from Liliana's family's old store in Buenos Aires. Eduardo is an architect and artist, whose work also hangs throughout the main house. Activities include horseback riding, helping with the animals if you want, carriage rides, bicycle rides, and trekking. The main house was renovated in 2008 to include five bedrooms—three as suites with private bathrooms, and each large enough for a family of four. A gourmet chef cooks dinner, and a new playroom has a game room, small home theater, and other amenities. The 21-hectare (52-acre) property also has a wooded creek, a relaxing place for a nap, having a picnic, or doing some afternoon reading. In 2011, the owners added a *fogón*, or outdoor fireplace, along with a Jacuzzi and a mud oven for more open-air enjoyment. The trip here by *remis* from Buenos Aires, 80km (50 miles) away, is about $75. Only 3km (2 miles) away is historic **Capilla del Señor,** a charming colonial town. (You can also access the *estancia* by taking a bus from Buenos Aires to Capilla del Señor and then a $6 taxi ride.) Similar to San Antonio de Areco in feel, it's virtually unknown to foreigners and walkable from the *estancia*. Real gauchos wander downtown and every second Tuesday of the month, there is an animal auction, which Liliana attends with guests. The area is also a ballooning center, and rides are offered for $150 per person.

Buenos Aires Provincial Ruta 39, 2812 Capilla del Señor. www.estanciaelcencerro.com.ar. © **11/4743-2319** or 11/15-6093-2319 (cell) in Buenos Aires. 5 units, including 3 suites. From $150. Rates include all meals and some drinks. Day rate of $75 includes lunch only. No credit cards. Free parking. **Amenities:** Bicycles; bird-watching; carriage riding; horseback riding; outdoor pool; limited room service. *In room:* Ceiling fan, TV, DVD, A/C.

El Ombú de Areco ★★★ El Ombú takes its name from the tree that dominates the Pampas. It's among the most historic *estancias* near Buenos Aires. General Pablo Riccheri, an Italian military man who came to Argentina during the unification wars, built the original vine-covered house in 1880. The general atmosphere and overgrown row of trees out front will remind you of a Southern U.S. plantation. The rooms in the old house, with high ceilings, are best. But you really can't go wrong here; all the rooms have romantic appeal, decorated with brass beds and floral linens, with a strong country atmosphere. There are two pools: one in a small courtyard, another on the edge of the main garden with a fantastic view of the sun setting over horses in the fields. There are several game rooms on the grounds, with TVs, movies, and other activities, and it's easy to mingle with the very friendly staff. This is a working ranch, with 300 hectares (741 acres) of land and more than 400 cows and other animals. Horseback riding, cattle roundups, sunset carriage riding, bicycling, and many other activities are available, and all four meals and drinks are included in the rate. Some rooms have hydro-massage tubs, others tub/shower combinations. Rooms are not air-conditioned but have ceiling fans. The *estancia* is about 10km (6 miles) from San Antonio and 120km (74 miles) from Buenos Aires. Their *remis* service costs $90 from Buenos Aires and $115 from Ezeiza airport. Taxis from San Antonio de Areco cost about $11.

Buenos Aires Provincial Ruta 31, Cuartel 6, 2760 San Antonio de Areco. www.estanciaelombu.com. © **2326/492-080** or 11/4737-0436 Buenos Aires. 9 units. From $200 single; $340 double. Rates include all meals and drinks. Day rate of $75 includes lunch only. AE, V. Free parking. Pets allowed. **Amenities:** Babysitting; bicycles; carriage riding; concierge; horseback riding; 2 outdoor pools; room service. *In room:* Ceiling fan.

El Rosario de Areco ★★★ Unlike most *estancia* owners, who live in Buenos Aires, Francisco and Florencia de Guevera—distant relatives of Che who only comment that they have a very different political ideology from him—live year-round on their *estancia*, along with some of their nine children. This *estancia* is among the most pleasant to visit, with its barn-red buildings and bougainvilleas scattered among the grounds. The *estancia* dates from 1892, but the rooms, many of which are in former horse stalls, have surprisingly modern interiors. The waitstaff is a little different here, too. Instead of running around in gaucho outfits, they wear chic black uniforms, as if they popped in from Palermo. The owners regularly mingle with guests, and Francisco cooks the lunch *asado*. There are 16 double rooms, all with large private bathrooms. Rooms are not air-conditioned, but have ceiling fans, and some rooms have

San Antonio de Areco

SIDE TRIPS FROM BUENOS AIRES

fireplaces. In early 2011 the owners opened a small luxury hotel with 30 rooms on the 80-hectare (198-acre) grounds. The property offers a small polo field, horseback riding, carriage riding, two swimming pools, several public rooms with TVs, and other recreational activities such as pool and video games. The *estancia* is 7km (4⅓ miles) from San Antonio de Areco and 100km (62 miles) from Buenos Aires. From San Antonio, a taxi is about $11 and the *estancia's remis* service is $112 from Buenos Aires.

Buenos Aires Provincial Ruta 41 (mailing address is Castilla de Correo 85), 2760 San Antonio de Areco. www.rosariodeareco.com.ar and www.pampasdeareco.com. ℰ **2326/451-000.** 16 units. From $380 double in *estancia*. Rates include all meals and drinks. Day rate of $90 includes lunch only (call ahead for day-rate availability). From $300 double; from $370 suite in hotel. No credit cards. Free parking. **Amenities:** Bicycles; concierge; babysitting; carriage riding; horseback riding; polo fields; 2 outdoor pools; limited room service; TV lounges; Wi-Fi. *In estancia room:* Ceiling fan, Wi-Fi, fireplace (in some rooms). *In hotel rooms:* TV, A/C, Wi-Fi, hair dryer, minibar.

La Bamba ★★★ This is one of the most gorgeous and romantic *estancias* near Buenos Aires. The original building opened in 1830 as a stagecoach stop along what had once been the old Camino Real, linking Buenos Aires with other colonial cities. The buildings are Pompeian red with white trim, contrasting with the rich green landscape. The Argentine movie *Camila,* about a forbidden romance in the 1840s, was filmed here and nominated for Best Foreign Film in the 1984 Academy Awards. If you are honeymooning in Argentina, this place is ideal—especially the isolated Torre Room in the main house, on the third floor, in what had been a lookout tower with windows on all sides opening onto the expansive Pampas. Swimming, horseback riding, carriage riding, trekking, and other activities are all available. The 150-hectare (371-acre) property has cows, soy, and wheat fields. The *estancia* is 13km (8 miles) from San Antonio and 123km (76 miles) from Buenos Aires. The *estancia* was recently bought by Frenchman Jean Francois Decaux, who vastly renovated the property—including new wiring, air-conditioning, pool, and polo ground improvements—all while maintaining the historic nature of the location. It reopened in February 2010.

Buenos Aires Provincial Ruta 31, 2760 San Antonio de Areco. www.labambadeareco.com. ℰ **2326/454-895** or 11/15-4444-6560 (cell). 11 units. $530–$600 double. Rates include all meals and drinks. Day rate of $140 includes lunch only. AE, DC, MC. Free parking. **Amenities:** Babysitting; bicycles; carriage riding; concierge; horseback riding; high-speed Internet; outdoor pool; limited room service; spa. *In room:* A/C, ceiling fan, TV, Wi-Fi.

La Eloisa Golf & Polo Lodge ★ This *estancia* runs its operations a little differently from most of the others. Rather than rent rooms or apartments within the *estancia*, guests rent the whole five-bedroom *estancia* for periods of 4 days or longer, essentially having run of the place as if it were their home, with all the staff as personal servants. There are polo grounds, a 9-hole golf course, tennis courts, horseback riding, an outdoor pool, and many other amenities. Guest rooms are rustic and luxurious, with high beamed ceilings, thick white bedding, and antiques. La Eloisa is 90km (60 miles) from Buenos Aires and about 45km (30 miles) from Ezeiza Airport. A taxi is about $90 from Buenos Aires and about $60 from the airport.

Buenos Aires Provincial Ruta 200, Km 7, 1814 Villa General Las Heras. www.pololaeloisa.com. ℰ **11/6333-3333** or 11/911-831-9542. 5 bedrooms, rented together for $3,000 for 4 days, all included. Up to 12 guests. Rates include all meals and drinks. Contact about other pricing and rental options. AE, MC, V. Free parking. **Amenities:** Babysitting; bikes; bird-watching; carriage riding; concierge; golf course; horseback riding; polo fields; outdoor pool; room service; tennis courts; trekking. *In room:* A/C, TV, Wi-Fi.

Where to Stay

Draghi Paradores ★ The Draghi Paradores is a small apartment hotel opened in 2006 behind the Draghi museum and store. One of the nicest of San Antonio's hotels, it has a romantic feel. It's built in a Spanish colonial style, and its entrance is graced by a small pool and fountain in an enclosed courtyard. It looks a little like a miniature of the *Melrose Place* apartment building, minus backstabbing blondes in high heels and miniskirts. The five rooms are clean and decorated in a country style, with a rich use of woods, frilly white bedding, and terra-cotta tiles. Two rooms come with small kitchens, ideal for families or for longer-term stays in San Antonio.

Lavalle 387 (btw. Alsina and Arellano), 2760 San Antonio de Areco. www.paradoresdraghi.com.ar. ℰ **2326/455-583** or 02326/454-515. 5 units, including 2 with kitchens. From $80 double. Rates include breakfast. AE, DC, MC, V. Free parking. **Amenities:** Free bicycle loans; concierge; heated outdoor pool; limited room service. *In room:* A/C, TV, kitchen (in some), minibar, Wi-Fi.

Hostal de Areco This small family-style hotel is in a historic turn-of-the-20th-century red house, set back from the street and surrounded by a small garden. There are seven small, spartan, tile-floor rooms, each equipped with a full-size bed and a bathroom. Dark-green curtains and bedspreads give the rooms an even smaller appearance. The accommodations are basic. Only some rooms are air-conditioned, others have only fans, but all come with cable TV and Wi-Fi.

Zapioli 25 (near the intersection of Zerboni), 2760 San Antonio de Areco. www.hostaldeareco.com.ar. ℰ **2326/456-118.** 7 units. From $45 double, including breakfast. No credit cards. Free parking. **Amenities:** Free bicycle loans; concierge. *In room:* Ceiling fan or A/C, TV, Wi-Fi.

Hotel San Carlos ★ Overlooking the Parque San Martín, you'll find a sun deck equipped with a grill and a Jacuzzi, two outdoor heated swimming pools in the courtyard, and a fountain decorated with a mosaic of San Antonio de Padua. (It's one of the few places where you're likely to see bikini-clad women frolicking in front of religious icons, unless you belong to a particularly liberal church.) Some rooms are on the small side, but they're larger in the hotel's new wing. Many come with hydro-massage tubs or Jacuzzis in the bathrooms, and a few two-bedroom apartments have kitchens. The hotel added a spa in late 2008. Ask about spa packages.

Av. Zerboni (on the west corner, at the intersection of Zapiola), 2760 San Antonio de Areco. www.hotelsancarlos.com.ar ℰ **2326/453-106.** 30 units (25 doubles, 5 apts). From $60 double; from $85 apt. Rates include breakfast. Higher prices for all-day use of spa. AE, MC, V. Free covered parking. **Amenities:** *Asado;* free bicycle rental; concierge; health club; high-speed Internet station; Jacuzzi; 2 heated outdoor pools; room service; spa; Wi-Fi in lobby. *In room:* A/C, TV, minibar, Wi-Fi.

Los Abuelos Alberto Cesar Reyes is your grandfather at this property overlooking Parque San Martín and the Río Areco—the hotel's name literally means the grandparents. The hotel is basic, with a lot of white metal and Formica furnishings in the tile-floored room. The beds are covered with sea-foam green chenille bedspreads. Some bathrooms are tub/shower combinations, while others are only showers. An aboveground pool is surrounded by a small deck in the back of the property, where the parking lot is located. A nice warm touch is a gas fireplace in the front lobby, which is surrounded by simple pine chairs and tables where breakfast is served.

Av. Zerboni on the corner at the intersection of Zapiola, 2760 San Antonio de Areco. www.sanantoniodeareco.com/losabuelos. ℰ **02326/456-390.** 9 units. From $50 double. Rates include breakfast. No credit cards. Free parking. **Amenities:** Free bicycle loans; concierge; outdoor aboveground pool; room service. *In room:* A/C, ceiling fan, TV, Wi-Fi.

Solar del Pago Hotel & Spa ★★   This hotel is unique—not just for San Antonio, but for all of Argentina. It's one of the most wheelchair-accessible hotels in the country, and even has a spa that's wheelchair accessible. The hotel is set on a garden outside of the main part of town, with a restaurant open to the public with Braille menus, rooms with a mix of rustic luxury, with white walls, wooden furniture, and splashes of color, some with doors opening to the patio outside. There's also an art gallery, featuring silver and paintings in gaucho style. The outdoor heated pool also has a hydraulic lift. It's a great hotel on its own, and fantastic for all its specially accessible features for people with low mobility. Nelida Barbeito, already recommended as a specialist in accessible travel (p. 25), is a partial owner of the hotel.

Hipolito Gabino Fiore 232 (at Duran), 2760 San Antonio de Areco. www.solardelpago.com. © **2326/15-410252** (cell) or 011/5941-9694 in Buenos Aires. 10 units. $110–$120 double, including buffet breakfast. No credit cards. Free parking. **Amenities:** Restaurant; art gallery; bikes; concierge; Jacuzzi; library; massage; room service; Scottish shower; spa w/wet and dry sauna. *In room:* A/C, TV, hair dryer, minibar, Wi-Fi.

Where to Eat

Almacén de Ramos Gerelos ARGENTINE/SPANISH/PARRILLA   This restaurant, housed in a turn-of-the-20th-century building, is one of the best-known restaurants in San Antonio de Areco. It has a *parrilla* and international items on the menu, and also offers a broad selection of paellas. Its interior, with rich wooden details, will take you back in time.

Zapiola 143 (at Segundo Sombra). No phone. Main courses $4–$10. AE. Daily noon–3pm and 8–11pm.

Corner Pizza ARGENTINE/INTERNATIONAL   This simple place overlooks the Parque San Martín and the Río Areco. You'll find a selection of fast-food items on the menu, from hot dogs and hamburgers to pizza. Many people just come here to down a beer and look at the park. It's ideal if you're on a budget.

Av. Zerboni at Alsina, overlooking Parque San Martín. No phone. Main courses $2–$6. No credit cards. Daily 10am–11pm.

La Esquina de Merti ★ PARRILLA/ARGENTINE   This restaurant has an old-fashioned feel to it, with exposed brick walls, an ancient copper coffeemaker on the bar, wooden tables overlaid with black-and-white-checkered tablecloths, and shelves full of apothecary jars. But it's all a trick: La Esquina de Merti opened in late 2005, in the location of an old *almacén,* or Argentine general store. In any case, the food, concentrating on the beef the region is famous for, is great. You'll find a beef and chicken *parrilla,* and a selection of pastas and empanadas. The house specialty is *mollejas* with cream, lemon, and champagne (*mollejas* are the softly grilled, melt-in-your-mouth pancreas or thymus of a cow, which might be worth trying for an only-in-Argentina experience). A large wine selection complements everything on the menu.

Arellano 147 (at Segundo Sombra, overlooking Plaza Arellano). © **2326/456-705.** www.esquinade merti.com.ar. Main courses $4–$10. AE, V. Daily 9am–2am (Fri–Sat until 3am).

PLANNING YOUR TRIP TO BUENOS AIRES

A s with any trip, a little preparation is essential before you start your journey to Buenos Aires. This chapter provides a variety of planning tools, including information on how to get here; tips on accommodations; and quick, on-the-ground resources. You'll also find specially tailored travel information for travelers with different kinds of needs.

GETTING THERE

By Plane

Argentina's main international airport is **Ezeiza Ministro Pistarini** (**EZE;** ℂ **11/5480-6111** or 11/5480-2500; www.aa2000.com.ar), located 42km (26 miles) to the west of Buenos Aires. Allow at least 45 minutes to an hour for travel between the airport and the city, and more during rush hour.

Argentina's national airline is **Aerolíneas Argentinas** (ℂ **800/333-0276** in the U.S. and Canada, 0810/222-8652 in Buenos Aires, or 2-9234-9000 in Australia; www.aerolineas.com.ar). The airline uses Miami as its U.S. hub. While it has fewer international connections to Buenos Aires than other major airlines, Aerolíneas Argentinas provides an interesting introduction to Argentina and its culture.

Other operators include **American Airlines** (ℂ **800/433-7300** in the U.S. or 11/4318-1111 in Buenos Aires; www.aa.com), with the most flights to Buenos Aires of any U.S. carrier; **Continental Airlines,** which has connections to Buenos Aires from its Houston hub (ℂ **800/525-0280** or 0800-333-0425 in Buenos Aires; www.continental.com); **Delta** (ℂ **800/221-1212** in the U.S. and Canada or 0800-666-0133 in Argentina; www.delta.com), which has flights to Buenos Aires via Atlanta; **United Airlines** (ℂ **800/538-2929** in the U.S. or 0810/777-8648 in Buenos Aires; www.ual.com); **Air Canada** (ℂ **888/247-2262** in Canada or 11/4327-3640 in Buenos Aires; www.aircanada.ca); **British Airways** (ℂ **0844/493-0787** in the U.K. or 0800-222-0075 or 11/4320-6600 in Buenos Aires; www.britishairways.com); and **Iberia** (ℂ **0870/609-0500** in the U.K. or 11/4131-1000 in Buenos Aires; www.iberia.com). Additionally, **LAN Airlines,** formerly known as LanChile (ℂ **866/435-9526** in the U.S. and Canada or 11/4378-2222 in Buenos Aires; www.lan.com), provides connections from New York and Los Angeles to Buenos

Aires via Santiago, and direct flights to Buenos Aires from Miami, as well as internal flights within Argentina. **TAM** (📞 **1-888-235-9826** in the U.S. and Canada or 0810-333-3333 in Argentina; www.tam.com.br), a Brazilian airline, also has connections to Buenos Aires through Sao Paulo and Rio. **TAM** and **LAN** are currently in a merger process. **Qantas Airlines** of Australia (📞 **13-13-13** in Australia or 11/4114-5800 in Buenos Aires; www.qantas.com.au) has flights to Buenos Aires from Sydney and Auckland, New Zealand.

Most domestic flights and some international flights, including those from Uruguay, arrive at **Jorge Newbery Airport,** also called **Aeroparque** (**AEP,** 📞 **11/4514-1515;** www.aa2000.com.ar), located about 15 minutes north along the river from downtown.

By American standards, domestic flights within Argentina are expensive. Technically, citizens and tourists pay different airfares, but sometimes tourists can get the Argentine rate. **Aerolíneas Argentinas** (📞 **800/333-0276** in the U.S. and Canada, 0810/222-86527 in Buenos Aires, or 1800/22-22-15 in Australia; www.aerolineas.com.ar) connects most cities and tourist destinations in Argentina, including Córdoba, Jujuy, Iguazú, Salta, and the beach resorts. (**Aerolíneas Argentinas** also has a subsidiary called **Austral.**) **LAN** (📞 **866/435-9526** in the U.S. and Canada or 11/4378-2222 in Buenos Aires; www.lan.com) has internal flights throughout Argentina connecting from Buenos Aires, and **TAM** (📞 **888/235-9826** in the U.S. and Canada or 11/3272-6706 or 0810-333-3333 in Argentina; www.tam.com.br) flies from Buenos Aires to the Brazilian side of Iguazú.

If you plan to travel extensively in Argentina from Buenos Aires, consider buying the **Visit Argentina Pass,** issued by **Aerolíneas Argentinas.** You must purchase the pass in your home country—it cannot be purchased once you are in Argentina. This pass offers discounts on domestic travel in conjunction with your international Aerolíneas Argentinas ticket. Passes are purchasable as one-way coupons for flights within Argentina starting at about $120 each, with a minimum of three segments. There are many restrictions on the tickets. **Aerolíneas Argentinas** also has a **Visit South America** package option. For more information, contact the Aerolíneas office in your home country or your travel agent, or visit **www.aerolineas.com.ar**.

Since 2009, Argentina has charged a reciprocity fee of citizens of the United States, Canada, and Australia landing at Ezeiza. The fee can be paid with cash, or Visa, MasterCard, or American Express upon arrival. See "Visas," later in this chapter.

GETTING INTO TOWN FROM THE AIRPORT

Taxis from Ezeiza to the center of town cost about $35. **Manuel Tienda León** (📞 **11/4314-3636;** www.tiendaleon.com.ar) is the most reliable transportation company, offering buses and *remises*. Manuel Tienda León buses operate on a half-hour schedule and cost about $15. These take you to their hub in Puerto Madero, and from there, smaller buses take you to your hotel. The entire trip can take anywhere from 1 to 1½ hours. From Newbery, taxis and *remises* to the city center cost $16 to $25. Manuel Tienda León also operates in Newbery on an approximately half-hour schedule and costs about $12. At both airports, I recommend that you take only officially sanctioned transportation. See "Traveling by Taxi," p. 255.

By Bus

The **Estación Terminal de Omnibus,** Av. Ramos Mejía 1680 (📞 **11/4310-0700;** www.tebasa.com.ar), located near Retiro Station and usually called the Retiro bus station, serves all long-distance buses. You'll use this station if you're connecting in

Buenos Aires to other parts of Argentina, or if you arrive in Buenos Aires by long-distance coach from other countries. Due to the prohibitively high cost of air travel for most South Americans, the continent is served by numerous bus companies offering comfortable, and at times luxurious, service to other capitals, often overnight. This is an excellent, albeit time-consuming, option for student and budget travelers.

Among the major bus companies that operate out of Buenos Aires are **La Veloz del Norte** (℃ **11/4315-2482** or 0800-444-8356; www.lavelozcallcenter.com.ar), serving destinations in the Northwest, including Salta and Jujuy; **Singer** (℃ **11/4315-2653** or 0810-222-1888; www.expresosinger.com.ar), serving Puerto Iguazú as well as Brazilian destinations; and **Chevallier** (℃ **11/4000-5255;** www.nuevachevallier. com), serving points throughout the country.

The **Estación Terminal de Omnibus** is sprawling, enormous, and confusing. Just walking from one end to another takes about 10 minutes, given the ramps, crowds, and stairs through which you have to maneuver. Routes and platform locations rarely make it to the overhead boards, so these should never be relied on as a source of information when you're trying to find your bus. In spite of the chaos readily observable here, there is an overarching order to the confusion. A color-coded system used at the ticket-counters explains, very generally, which destinations of the country are served by which bus lines. Red, for instance, indicates the center of the country, including the province of Buenos Aires, dark blue the south, orange the north, green the northeast, light blue the central Atlantic coast, and gray international destinations. However, at their sales counters, many bus companies indicate on their destination lists names of cities that are no longer served, so you may have to stand in a line and ask. Many companies also have more than one name, adding visual clutter at the ticket counters. To help you make sense of it all, use **www.tebasa.com.ar**, the terminal's website, while planning your trip. Click on the province to which you are traveling and a list of bus companies and phone numbers will come up. Bus tickets can also be purchased at most travel agencies. This can cost slightly more, but can save a lot of aggravation. You can also buy and download tickets ahead of time for select bus companies using the website **www.plataforma10.com**. Another useful site is **www.omnilineas.com.ar**.

By Car

Argentina is a vast country, with enormous distances between major cities. For example, Mendoza is about a 17-hour drive from Buenos Aires, Córdoba is about 9 hours, Puerto Iguazú is about 20 hours, and Ushuaia, in Tierra del Fuego is about 30 hours. (This does not include time for breaks and overnight rests.) I do not recommend driving such distances unless you have an incredible amount of stamina, and a long time to spend in Argentina to enjoy what are undoubtedly quite beautiful drives.

Buenos Aires is surrounded by a radial highway called **Autopista General Paz,** which, like the Beltway in Washington, D.C., or the Périférique in Paris, is seen as the dividing line between the city and its suburbs. **National Route 3** runs from the Southwest and Eizeza airport, intersecting with General Paz, and becomes **Autopista 25 de Mayo** as it runs through the southern portion of Buenos Aires, connecting with **9 de Julio** near San Telmo. The northern end of **9 de Julio** connects with **Autopista Arturo Illia,** towards **Aeroparque** airport, and becomes part of General Paz.

For information on car rentals and gasoline (petrol) in Buenos Aires, see "Getting Around: By Car" (p. 256).

By Train

The privatization and subsequent dismantling of Argentina's national passenger railroad system in the 1990s under President Carlos Ménem means that Buenos Aires is no longer connected by rail to other major cities in the country. A commuter train system is useful for side trips to the river island resort town of Tigre; La Plata, the capital of Buenos Aires Province; and the beach resort of Mar del Plata. See "Getting Around: By Train" (p. 257).

By Boat

Buenos Aires is a port of call for a variety of cruise lines, with follow-ons to Montevideo, Rio de Janeiro, and other destinations. The **Yacht Club of Argentina** (*②* **11/4314-0505;** www.yachtclubargentina.com.ar) is based in Dársena Norte and offers docking for private boats. Most tourists who take side trips to Uruguay will be using boat companies such as **BuqueBus,** which heads from Puerto Madero to Colonia and Montevideo, with bus connections to Punta del Este. **Sturla Viajes** also offers boat connections from Puerto Madero to the Tigre islands. See chapter 10 for more information on these destinations and boat trip details. The number for a nautical emergency is *②* **105.** For more information about cruise ships stopping in Buenos Aires, visit the official port site **www.puertobuenosaires.gov.ar**, contact your travel agent, or see our list of tour companies.

There have been an increasing number of crimes against those entering Buenos Aires by cruise ship. The port itself is very safe, but it is surrounded by what is known as Villa 31—a *villa miseria,* or slum. Although you may have to wait up to 45 minutes for a cab to arrive at the port after your boat docks, under no circumstances should you leave the port and walk through the surrounding area. Recently, a number of tourists have wandered out of the port, either to hail cabs or simply to walk to downtown Buenos Aires (which begins only several long blocks from the port), only to get mugged. Do not leave the port on your own, regardless of the length of time it takes for a cab or other transportation arranged by your tour boat company to arrive.

GETTING AROUND

The Buenos Aires metro—called the *subte*—is the fastest, cheapest way to get around. Buses are also convenient, though less commonly used by tourists. Get maps of metro and bus lines from tourist offices and most hotels. (Ask for the *QuickGuide Buenos Aires* if it's available.) All metro stations are supposed to have maps on hand, but they are rarely in good supply.

By Metro (Subway)

The *subte* is the fastest and cheapest way to travel in Buenos Aires. Six lines connect commercial, tourist, and residential areas in the city Monday through Saturday from 5am to 11pm, and on Sunday and holidays from 8am to 11pm. These are the official hours, but because of budget cuts, many lines stop running by 10pm. However, they don't always close the stations after the trains have stopped, and you could end up waiting for trains that will never come, so ask someone if a train is running in the direction you need during later hours. Service has also been reduced through a lengthening of the wait between trains, even during busy daytime hours, making for extremely crowded trains. A new line, the H or Yellow Line, has been partially built along the Jujuy-Pueyrredón corridor, and existing lines have also been expanded. See the inside front cover of this guide for a map of the system, and be aware that new maps given out or posted at stations might not correctly reflect subway extensions. Visit **www.subte.com.ar** for maps and other information. The interactive site also gives estimated times and transfer information between stations.

The flat fare is 1.10 pesos. Every station has a staffed ticket window. Some stations have ticket vending machines, but they're unreliable. You can also buy a *subte* pass for 11 pesos, valid for 10 trips. The passes are cheap and demagnetize easily, so it's a good idea to buy an extra to have on hand. Trains get crowded during rush hour and are not air-conditioned, so they can be hot in summer. Free subway maps are available, but stations run out quickly. Always be cautious of pickpockets, including tiny pocket-height children who can easily be overlooked. The trains are also full of people trying to sell you odd trinkets.

Try to ride the A line at least once; it's a tourist attraction in itself (p. 98). The oldest line, it runs along Avenida de Mayo and uses some of the system's original rickety wooden cars. Lima station, in particular, retains most of the original ornamentation and copies of advertisements from the turn of the 20th century.

Neither Recoleta nor Puerto Madero has *subte* access. Most of Puerto Madero, however, is accessible via the L. N. Alem *subte* stop on the B line. It's a 5- to 20-minute walk, depending on which dock you're going to. Puerto Madero also has a light rail train running near it that costs 1 peso, but it's slower than walking and thus not particularly useful. If you're going to Recoleta, the D line runs through the bordering neighborhood of Barrio Norte, so you can avoid spending money on a taxi by using this line and then walking 15 minutes to Recoleta.

Be aware that wildcat strikes are common on the system, though workers rarely stop trains between stations. Sometimes these strikes are limited to payment windows, not affecting trains, allowing you to ride for free.

By Taxi

The streets of Buenos Aires are swarming with taxis. Fares are generally low, with an initial meter reading of 5.80 pesos, increasing 58 centavos every 200m (656 ft.) or each minute. (A 20% higher rate goes into effect at night.) Most of the taxi rides the average tourist will be taking will cost $3 to $10. *Remises* and radio-taxis are much more reliable than street taxis (see "Traveling by Taxi," below). Radio-taxis, when hailed on the street, are recognizable by plastic light boxes on their rooftops, though not all will have these. If a cab is available, the word *libre* will flash in red on the windshield. Ordinary taxis, more likely to be run by members of Buenos Aires's infamous taxi mafia, do not have these special light boxes. A rarely enforced law means taxi drivers can stop only if their passenger side is facing the curb. If available cabs are ignoring you, cross to the other side of the street and hail again.

I personally have had few problems in taxis, but it's always best to err on the side of caution. If you speak English loudly with fellow passengers, identifying yourself as a tourist, expect your ride to take longer than it should, with strange diversions ensuring a higher fare than is normal. You can prevent this situation by being discreet about the fact that you're from out of town, having a general idea where you are going, and keeping in mind the one-way street system. Drivers often use traffic problems as their excuse for the longer route. Though most taxi drivers are honest, a substantial number of tourists have been ripped off by dishonest drivers. One common scam among drivers is to say the passenger paid with a smaller-denomination bill than they actually

If you need a taxi, I strongly recommend that you call in advance for a *remis* or radio-taxi (see "Getting Around: By Taxi," above, for numbers). Better yet, ask an employee of your hotel, restaurant, or other venue to call on your behalf, as a representative of that establishment, which will ensure greater accountability from your driver. If you must hail taxis on the street, use only those with plastic light boxes on their roofs, indicating that they are radio-taxis. Since the economic crisis began, robberies by street taxi drivers have increased sharply. *Remises* are only slightly pricier than street cabs, but far safer. Most hotels have contracts with *remis* companies, and they're accustomed to calling for patrons.

did. One way around this is to know in Spanish the value of your bill, announcing it to the driver when requesting change. (Or, better yet, have exact change on hand.) Another scam is to say your bills are counterfeit and then keep them regardless. Tips are not necessary, but many locals round up the fare to the nearest peso.

To request a taxi by phone, call **Taxi Premium** (*©* **11/4374-6666** or 11/5238-0000; www.taxipremium.com), a service used by many top hotels. See "Getting There: By Boat" (p. 256) for warnings about hailing cabs outside of the port of Buenos Aires.

By Bus

Buenos Aires has about 140 bus lines that run 24 hours a day. The fare is 1.10 pesos and up, depending on the distance you're traveling. You'll pay your fare inside the bus at an electronic ticket machine that accepts only coins and provides change. Many bus drivers will tell you the fare for your destination and let you know when to get off, but most speak only Spanish. Locals are just as helpful and will sometimes make an almost comical effort to ensure you don't get lost.

The *Guía T* is a comprehensive if confusing guide to the city bus grid and bus lines that divides the city into quadrants. Buy it at bookstores, newspaper kiosks, on the *subte*, or on the sidewalk from peddlers. (Unfortunately, the city has yet to offer a bus route map that includes city streets and landmarks, which would be helpful to tourists and locals alike.) *Note:* The bus system is notorious for pickpockets, so be very cautious when riding it.

See chapter 2 for bus tours of Buenos Aires.

By Foot

You'll probably find yourself walking more than you planned in this pedestrian-friendly city. Most of the center is small enough to navigate on foot, and you can connect to adjacent neighborhoods by taxi or the *subte*. Based on the Spanish colonial plan, the city is a wobbly grid expanding from the Plaza de Mayo, so you are not likely to get too lost. Plazas and parks all over the city offer wonderful places to rest, people-watch, and meet locals. Sidewalks are in terrible condition and often covered in dog droppings, however, so watch your step while taking in the local beauty. Be aware that most tourist maps of Buenos Aires are not typically oriented with north at the top. To keep a sense of direction, remember that Avenida de Mayo runs east-west, with Casa Rosada and Plaza de Mayo at the eastern terminus and Congreso at the western

NAVIGATING BUENOS AIRES'S GRANDEST BOULEVARD: avenida 9 de julio

Avenida 9 de Julio might be the world's widest boulevard, but finding buildings by their addresses on it isn't so easy. Locals might tell you an office or store is on Avenida 9 de Julio, but then, when you look at the address they've given you, the street will be called something else. That's because instead of being numbered along 9 de Julio itself, buildings take their addresses from their positions on the streets running parallel to 9 de Julio, all of which became part of the boulevard when it was widened. These are: **Cerrito,** on the northwest side of 9 de Julio; **Carlos Pellegrini,** on the northeast side; **Lima,** on the southwest side; and **Bernardo de Irigoyen,** on the southeast side of the boulevard. (Also note that, in the case of Bernardo de Irigoyen, it's the perpendicular street Rivadavia and not the typical Av. de Mayo that serves as the break for name changes in streets running north to south in the city, another source of street position confusion for tourists). Whether the Avenida is referred to by its full name, formalized as Nueve de Julio, or shortened to 9 de Julio, it's the same thing.

terminus, and 9 de Julio runs north-south from San Telmo (at the southern end) to Retiro (at the northern end). See chapter 7 for walking tours of Buenos Aires.

By Bicycle

It's become easier than ever to get around Buenos Aires by bike. The city has an extensive system of protected bicycle routes that traverses many neighborhoods. Look for the map *Red de Ciclovías Protegidas* at tourism kiosks, or visit **www.mejorenbici. gob.ar**. The Ecological Reserve (p. 118) outside of Puerto Madero is also an ideal destination for bicycle enthusiasts. More and more hotels are offering free bicycles or rental bicycles for their guests.

On the fourth Sunday of every month, at 4pm, there is a Critical Mass (Masa Crítica) meeting of bicyclists at the Obelisco. Visit **www.masacriticabsas.com.ar** for more information. The website **www.amigosdelpedal.com.ar** also has more information on group biking excursions. For more information on organized bike tours of the city and surroundings, see "Bike Tours" in chapter 2 (p. 24).

By Car

Buenos Aires is not a place where you need a car. We don't advise that you drive yourself unless you're heading out of the city. If you must rent a car, contact one of the international rental companies at either airport or one of those listed below. Most hotels can also arrange car rentals. Typically, rental cars are manual, and automatic cars are expensive and difficult to reserve, running at about $100 per day. Gasoline is about $2 per liter in Buenos Aires. Most driver's licenses from English-speaking countries are accepted at rental agencies. Visit the **Automóvil Club Argentino,** Av. del Libertador 1850 at Tagle (© **11/4808-4040,** 11/4808-6200, or toll-free 0800/888-9888; www.aca.org.ar) for maps and more information about driving in

Argentina. **Note:** Most local motorists disregard traffic rules except for one—no turn on red.

Rental cars are available from **Hertz,** Paraguay 1138 (© **800/654-3131** in the U.S., or 11/4816-8001); **Avis,** Cerrito (9 de Julio) 1527 (© **800/230-4898** in the U.S., or 11/4326-5542); **Dollar,** Marcelo T. de Alvear 449 (© **800/800-6000** in the U.S., or 11/4315-8800); and **Thrifty,** Carlos Pellegrini (9 de Julio) 1576 (© **800/847-4389** in the U.S., or 11/4326-0418).

By Train

Commuter trains, which run with great frequency and are very cheap, are not ideal for most tourists visiting Buenos Aires. However, the system can be useful for side trips from Buenos Aires, especially to the river island resort town of Tigre; La Plata, the capital of Buenos Aires province; and the beach resort of Mar del Plata. See chapter 10.

The Tigre Delta is best reached by train from Buenos Aires and then a boat or launch from the train station if you're continuing on to the islands. Trains from Buenos Aires leave for Estación Tigre from **Estación Retiro,** Avenida Naciones Unidas and Libertador across from Plaza San Martín, every 10 to 20 minutes along the Mitre Line. Tickets cost about $1 round-trip. Call © **11/4317-4445** or 0800-3333-822 for schedules and information, or visit **www.tbanet.com.ar**. This same train line stops in Belgrano, near Buenos Aires's Chinatown district, and in the wealthy northern suburban towns of Vicente Lopez, San Isidro, and Olivos, where the Presidential Residence is.

A train also runs from the Constitución station, at the intersection of Avenida Brasil and Lima in Plaza Constitución, to **Estación La Plata,** at the intersection of avenidas 1 and 44 in La Plata. Ticket prices are about $3. Trains run about every 15 to 30 minutes, depending on the day, and the trip takes about an hour and 20 minutes. In Buenos Aires, call © **11/4304-0028** for train tickets; in La Plata, call © **221/423-2575;** and call © **0800-3333-822** toll-free nationwide, or visit www. tbanet.com.ar.

Trains from **Constitución** to the beach resort of Mar del Plata run 3 times a day. In Mar del Plata, purchase tickets at the train station, located at avenidas Luro and Italia (© **223/475-6076** in Mar del Plata, 11/4304-0028 in Buenos Aires, or 0800-3333-822 toll-free nationwide; www.tbanet.com.ar.). The train takes about 4 to 5 hours.

A word of caution about trains from Constitución: While the station and surroundings are colorful, they can also be dangerous. The trains connecting to La Plata and Mar del Plata also pass through some of the poorest parts of greater Buenos Aires, and are also often used by rioters coming to the city for demonstrations. Pickpocketing and theft are very common. I do not actually recommend traveling by train to La Plata or Mar del Plata; it's better to use the buses. Traveling by train to Tigre is, however, another story, and while pickpocketing can occur and you should be as cautious in Estación Retiro as you would in any North American or European train station, this train system is nowhere near as problematic as the system connecting to the southern suburbs.

African-American Travelers At the time of Emancipation in 1853, Buenos Aires was a near-majority black city. Argentina's most famous dance, the tango, has its roots in Africa; and Lunfardo (also known as Lumfardo), the rough, slum-based slang still used by tango aficionados, includes many African words. However, specific historical details rarely discussed today in Argentina, such as the placement of black soldiers in the frontlines ahead of white soldiers during the Paraguayan War of the 1860s and the outbreak of yellow fever in the 1870s that disproportionately impacted poor areas where Afro-Argentines lived, mean there is very little of a black presence in the center of the city now. This contrasts strongly with neighboring Brazil and even Uruguay.

With the 2010 Bicentennial and an emphasis on rediscovering the country's various ethnic roots, a black cultural revival is beginning. The theater company **Proyecto 34S** (p. 189) runs African-themed productions, and **Afro-Kitchen,** a *puerta cerrada* (private restaurant), specializes in Afro-Argentine cuisine. The magazine ***Revista Quilombo*** (www.revistaquilombo.com.ar), is an additional source for Afro-Argentine culture. The Argentine term *quilombo,* referring to a chaotic, confusing situation, is a Lunfardo word, originally an African word referring to a place where escaped slaves sought shelter. (In immigrant days the word also meant "bordello.") The island resort **Tigre,** in the Buenos Aires suburbs, was one such place (p. 237).

Today, immigration from Africa itself and increased immigration from neighboring Brazil are increasing the black population of Buenos Aires. Still, blacks are a rather rare sight in Buenos Aires and black tourists may be seen as a curiosity. Since the election of President Obama in the United States, there has been a healthy curiosity among Argentines about the lives and views of African Americans, so don't be surprised if locals approach you with questions.

If you feel you have been discriminated against as a person of African descent, contact **INADI** (Instituto Nacional contra la Discriminación, la Xenofobia y el Racismo; ☏ **0800-999-2345;** www.inadi.gob.ar). You may also report it to Carlos Alvarez of the group **Africa y su Diaspora** (☏ **11/15-6202-9737;** asociacionafricaysudiaspora@yahoo.com.ar; www.africaysudiaspora.wordpress.com).

Area Codes The city area code for Buenos Aires, known locally as a *característica,* is **011.** Drop the 0 when adding Argentina's country code, **54.** The number **15** in front of a local number indicates a cellphone number, though some phones no longer use this code. You'll still need to dial **011** before the **15** if you're calling these numbers from outside Buenos Aires. Calling cellphones from overseas can be complicated. Dial whatever international code you need from your country (011 from the U.S. and Canada), then 54 for Argentina, then 9 to indicate a cellphone, then the area code of the cellphone, then the number. Thus, to call Buenos Aires cellphones from the U.S., you would dial 011-54-9-11 and then the eight-digit number. Be aware that phone numbers in other areas have anywhere from 5 to 7 digits, but always ask if a number seems strange.

Business Hours Banks are generally open weekdays 10am to 3pm, and ATMs work 24 hours. Shopping hours are Monday through Friday from 9am to 8pm or 10pm, and Saturday from 10am to 8pm or 10pm. Shopping centers are open daily from 10am to 10pm. Most independent stores are closed on Sunday, and some close for lunch. Some kiosks selling water, candy, and packaged food are open 24 hours. Most neighborhoods have a 24-hour pharmacy, and *locutorios* or phone centers.

Car Rental See "Getting Around: By Car," p. 256.

Cellphones See "Mobile Phones," later in this section.

Crime See "Safety," later in this section.

Customs Travelers entering Argentina can bring personal effects—including clothes, jewelry, and professional equipment such as cameras and computers—without paying duty. In addition, they can bring in 2 liters of alcohol, 400 cigarettes, and 50 cigars duty-free. Luggage is usually x-rayed upon entering Buenos Aires.

Disabled Travelers Buenos Aires is not a particularly accessible destination for travelers with disabilities. The tiny crowded streets of the Microcentro can often barely accommodate two people walking together, let alone a wheelchair, and sidewalk cutouts do not exist in all areas. Some hotels claim to be equipped for those with disabilities but still have one to two stairs leading to their elevator bays, making wheelchair access impossible, so always ask detailed questions when booking. Four- and five-star hotels; recently renovated hotels; and American, Canadian, and European-owned chains are more likely to have rooms designed for travelers with disabilities.

The city government's special task force **COPINE** (Comisión para la Plena Participación e Integración de las Personas con Necesidades Especiales; © 11/4010-0300, ext. 13407; copine@buenosaires. gov.ar), put out a tourism guide called *Guía Turismo Accesible* in 2009, which might be available at select tourism kiosks or at the airport. The national task force, **COPIDAS** (Comisión Nacional Asesora para la Integración Personas Discapacitadas), Av. Julio Roca 782 at Diagonal Sur, 4th Floor, Belgrano (© **0800-333-2662** or 11/4331-7344; www.cndisc.gov.ar), has a new resource guide available with a small portion on tourism. Other organizations that offer assistance to travelers with disabilities include **MossRehab** (www. mossresourcenet.org), which provides a library of accessible travel resources online; **SATH** (Society for Accessible Travel & Hospitality; © **212/447-7284;** www.sath.org), which publishes the *Open World* magazine and also offers a wealth of resources; and the **American Foundation for the Blind** (**AFB;** © **800/232-5463;** www. afb.org), a referral resource for the visually impaired that includes information on traveling with Seeing Eye dogs. Also check out the quarterly magazine ***Emerging Horizons*** (www. emerginghorizons.com). See also "Disabled, Handicapped & Low-Mobility Tours" in chapter 2.

Doctors Your hotel or apartment service can arrange for you to see a doctor in Buenos Aires. Your embassy can also provide you with a list of English speaking doctors. See also "Hospitals," below.

Drinking Laws The legal age for purchase and consumption of alcoholic beverages is 18 in Argentina, and proof of age is almost never required, meaning that teenage travelers may have easy access to alcohol. Alcohol is available for purchase in grocery stores and convenience stores, and virtually all restaurants serve wine and beer, if not hard liquor. Drinking on the street and in parks is allowed. Drunk driving is illegal and on weekends, especially during holidays, road blocks are periodically set up to identify drunk drivers. Rowdy drunken behavior is not typical in Buenos Aires, but can be observed after football (soccer) games, particularly near the Boca Juniors stadium. Bars generally close anywhere between midnight and 4am, and nightclubs can close as late as 7am on weekends.

Driving Rules See "Getting Around," earlier in this chapter.

Electricity Argentina uses 220–240 volts AC (50 cycles), like most of Europe, Australia, and New Zealand. Travelers from the U.S. will need a converter for any electric appliances or electronic devices they bring with them. Standard electric plugs use a slanted two-prong similar to Australia's, but the round

European two-prong is also common. British-built hotels will sometimes have British outlets, so a universal adapter is useful.

Embassies & Consulates All embassies are in Buenos Aires, Argentina's capital. Embassies have to deal with everything from concerned mothers whose sons have not called home during their Argentina trip, to real emergencies like passport theft, suicide, and murder. While each embassy has different rules and can be limited in providing certain kinds of help, your embassy is your best resource in the event of a problem. Before you leave for Argentina, check your embassy's website for updated information on the country as well as lists of resources, from doctors and hospitals to lawyers. The U.S. Embassy (www.travel.state.gov) provides detailed information, and it's a good idea to register on **STEP** (the Smart Traveler Enrollment Program; https://travelregistration.state.gov/ibrs/ui), so that the embassy and your relatives will be able to contact you in an emergency. Other embassies provide similar help for their citizens.

The embassy of **Australia** is in Belgrano, Villanueva 1400 at Zabala (© **11/4779-3500;** www.argentina.embassy.gov.au).

The embassy of **Canada** is in Palermo, Tagle 2828 at Alcorta (© **11/4808-1000;** http://www.canadainternational.gc.ca/

argentina-argentine/index.aspx).

The embassy of **Ireland** is in Recoleta, Av. del Libertador 1068 at Callao, 6th Floor (© **11/5787-0801;** www.embassyofireland.org.ar).

The embassy of **New Zealand** is in Retiro, Carlos Pellegrini (9 de Julio) 1427 at Arroyo, 5th Floor (© **11/4328-0747;** www.nzembassy.com/argentina).

The embassy of the **United Kingdom** is in Palermo, Luis Agote 2412 at Guido (© **11/4808-2200;** www.ukinargentina.fco.gov.uk).

The embassy of the **United States** is in Palermo, Av. Colombia 4300 at Cerviño (© **11/5777-4533;** www.argentina.usembassy.gov).

Emergencies For an ambulance, call © **107** or 11/4923-1051; for fire, call © **100;** for police, call © **101** or 911. See also "Embassies & Consulates," above, and "Legal Aid," below.

Family Travel To locate accommodations, restaurants, and attractions that are particularly kid friendly, look for the "Kids" icon throughout this guide. If you're traveling with teenagers, be aware that, with a drinking age of only 18, unsupervised minors who look older than they actually are might have easy access to alcohol.

Your children might find it hard to see other children begging on the streets in large cities throughout the

country and helping their *cartonero* (homeless) parents by looking for discarded paper to sell to recyclers to make a very desperate living. The peso crisis has taken a heavy toll on many Argentine children, creating a young, homeless class of beggars. It might be a good idea to explain to your child the inequities within Argentina, and the rest of Latin America for that matter, if he or she comments on this. In theory, your visit to Argentina, in the long run, will improve the economy and the plight of these homeless children. It might be tempting to give money to these kids, but nutritious, wrapped food or school supplies will do them more good in the long run. The nonprofit **Voluntario Global** (p. 28) allows tourists to do charity work while on vacation in Buenos Aires, which might be ideal for helping children understand poverty in Argentina in a constructive way.

Gasoline See "Getting Around: By Car," earlier in this chapter.

Health Argentina requires no vaccinations to enter the country, except for passengers coming from countries where cholera and yellow fever are endemic.

The medical facilities and personnel in Buenos Aires and other urban areas in Argentina are very professional. Argentina has a system of socialized medicine, in which basic services are free. Private clinics are inexpensive by Western standards.

Most drugs requiring a prescription in North America or western Europe do not require one in Argentina. Thus, if you lose or run out of a medication, you may not need to see a doctor and get a new prescription. The same is true if you become ill and know what medicine you need. Many pharmacies in the Microcentro have English-speaking staff. (Be aware, however, that some medicine can be expensive in Argentina.) Pack prescription medications in your carry-on luggage, and carry them in their original containers, with pharmacy labels—otherwise they might not make it through airport security. Also bring copies of your prescriptions in case you lose your pills or run out. Know the generic or chemical name of prescription medicines, in case a local pharmacist is unfamiliar with the brand name. Don't forget an extra pair of contact lenses or prescription glasses.

Buenos Aires's streets and sidewalks can be disgustingly unsanitary. While there is a pooper-scooper law on the books, dog owners seem to take delight in letting their pets relieve themselves in the middle of the sidewalk. Watch where you step, and wash your hands thoroughly after handling your shoes, even if you don't think you stepped in anything. Roaches also

love the city's streets. If you don't want unwelcome visitors in shopping bags or pocketbooks, don't leave them sitting on the ground while you dine outdoors. (This is a good theft-prevention measure as well.)

Dietary Red Flags Water and ice are considered safe in Buenos Aires, though many people prefer bottled water. Travelers should be careful with Argentine steak, however. Because it is generally served very rare, if not almost raw inside, people with delicate digestive systems or immune deficiency should request it well-done *(bien cocido)*. Cross-contamination of uncooked meat with salads and other items is unfortunately common in restaurants. You should also avoid street food and drinks served out of canisters at city festivals. Vegetarians should be aware that with so much leftover cow fat as a byproduct of the cattle industry, lard is commonly used as a cooking ingredient and finds its way into many baked goods. Read labels and ask. We list restaurants with vegetarian options in chapter 5. Kosher and halal foods are also easily found in Buenos Aires.

Bugs, Bites & Other Wildlife Concerns Malaria is not an issue in Buenos Aires, but in summer, and especially in parks and along the Río de la Plata, mosquitoes are everywhere. Wear repellent to avoid bites. Visitors on hiking

trips to the Tigre islands should be aware of saw grass and wear light full-length sleeves and pants to avoid cuts.

Respiratory Illnesses & Allergies Some people with allergies can be affected by the pollution in Buenos Aires's crowded Microcentro, where streets are packed with cars and buses. The beautiful spring blossoms also bring with them pollen, and even people not usually affected by plants might be thrown off by plants different from those in their home countries. It's a good idea to pack a decongestant.

Sun/Elements/Extreme Weather Exposure The summer sun is hot and strong in Buenos Aires. It's best to wear sunblock and carry it with you (it's available in stores and pharmacies throughout the city, so you can purchase it after you arrive).

Tropical Illnesses For advice about shots for various illnesses if you are traveling to other parts of South America, contact **Vacunar,** a chain of clinics specializing in vaccinations and preventative illness, with locations all over Buenos Aires (www.vacunar. com.ar). Keep in mind that many shots require a period of time before they become effective.

Hospitals English-speaking hospitals include **Clínica Suisso Argentino,** Av. Pueyrredón 1461 at Santa Fe (✆ **11/5239-6000;** www.cymsa.com.ar), and **Hospital Britanico,** Perdriel 74 at Caseros (© **11/4304-1081;** www. hospitalbritanico.org.ar). Traveler's insurance is highly recommended. Be aware that in an emergency, you may be taken to a public rather than private hospital. For specific and unlikely traumas such as knife or gunshot wounds or burns, public hospitals are often better than private hospitals, as they have more experience dealing with these sorts of cases.

Insurance As on any trip, traveler's insurance is a good idea. In Argentina in particular, strikes at the airport are common, which can create unexpected expenses (as well as significant delays). In addition, even with a good insurance plan, know that you will likely have to pay all your hospital expenses out of pocket and wait to be reimbursed later. If you plan to visit remote areas of Patagonia or go mountain climbing, it's good to buy increased insurance protection that will cover evacuation or repatriation, the uninsured costs of which can be between $10,000 and $25,000 in an emergency and are the responsibility of those for whom these services have been rendered. For information on traveler's insurance, trip cancellation insurance, and medical insurance while traveling, please visit **http://www.frommers.com/ planning**.

Internet & Wi-Fi Argentina is one of Latin America's most wired countries. You'll see the Wi-Fi sticker on cafe doors and restaurant doors all over Buenos Aires, especially in neighborhoods popular among tourists. Most hotels have Wi-Fi, regardless of the price category. In addition, more and more hotels, resorts, airports, cafes, and retailers are becoming "hotspots" that offer free high-speed Wi-Fi access or charge a small fee for usage. To find public Wi-Fi hotspots in Buenos Aires, go to **www. jiwire.com**; its Hotspot Finder holds the world's largest directory of public wireless hotspots. To find cybercafes in Buenos Aires, check **www.cybercaptive. com** and **www.cybercafe. com**. Most major airports have Internet kiosks that provide basic Web access for a per-minute fee that's usually higher than cybercafe prices. In addition, *locutorios*, or phone centers, usually have Internet stations, available for about $2 an hour. These are all over Buenos Aires and especially concentrated downtown. If you plan to be in Buenos Aires long-term for work purposes, you might want to check out **Area Tres Workplace,** Malabia 1720 between El Salvador and Costa Rica (© **11/5353-0333;** www. areatresworkplace.com), run by Martin Frankel, which rents short-term

office space, complete with Internet connections.

Jewish Travelers Buenos Aires is one of the world's greatest Jewish centers, with an estimated Jewish population of more than 250,000. The historical foci of the community are the neighborhoods of Once and Abasto. They developed in the beginning of the 20th century after immigration of both Ashkenazi Jews fleeing pogroms in Eastern Europe and Sephardic Jews who emigrated after the breakup of the Ottoman Empire at the end of World War I. After World War II, Argentina welcomed Eastern European Jewish refugees (while also allowing the entry of former Nazis). While the Jewish community has dispersed somewhat to the suburbs, replaced here by other immigrant groups, Abasto and Once are still home to kosher restaurants, Jewish businesses, and synagogues. The **Abasto Shopping Center** food court also has the only kosher McDonald's in the world outside of Israel (p. 94).

In 1992, there was a bomb attack on Buenos Aires's Israeli Embassy, killing 29 people (p. 110), and in 1994, an attack on the Jewish community group **Asociación Mutual Israelita Argentina (AMIA)** killed 85 people (p. 118). However, in spite of these attacks, most Argentine Jews feel little discrimination. Argentines of all faiths responded to the attacks with massive candlelight vigils. Visit AMIA's website at **www.amia.org.ar** for more information as well as the **Museo Judio** (p. 123). See also "Jewish-Themed Tours," p. 27.

Language Spanish is the national language of Argentina, spoken with a slight Italian lilt, and with *y* and *ll* pronounced "zhe." With the massive influx of tourism since the peso crisis, English has become ubiquitous on the streets of the city and many young people know some of the language. Shops, hotels, and restaurants are usually staffed by at least one or two English speakers. (A rule of thumb is that less-expensive venues will have fewer, if any, English speakers.) While non-Spanish-speakers should have little trouble getting around in general, those who know a bit of Spanish will be more reliably able to communicate with hotel and restaurant staff, less likely to be ripped off in cabs, and better able for directions and converse with locals in general. For a comprehensive, pocket-size phrase book, check out *Frommer's Spanish PhraseFinder & Dictionary.*

Legal Aid In the event of a robbery or other crime, call ℂ **101** or 911 for the police. If you get into serious legal trouble, or your passport is stolen, call your embassy. The Federal Police also maintains a special division to help foreign travelers, the **Comisaría del**

Turista, Corrientes 436 between San Martín and Florida (ℂ **0800-999-5000** or 11/4346-5748; www.policiafederal.gov.ar; turista@policiafederal.gov.ar). **Javier Canosa,** Montevideo 711 between Viamonte and Córdoba, 4th Floor (ℂ **11/5252-2462;** www.canosa.com.ar), is an English-speaking lawyer who has helped foreigners with legal issues. See also "Embassies & Consulates," above.

LGBT Travelers

Argentina has made immense strides in gay rights in recent years, outdoing North America and Europe to some extent. In July 2010, Argentina became the only country in Latin America, and one of few worldwide, with a national law legalizing same-sex marriage. Buenos Aires had already become the Latin American capital of gay tourism by 2003, when a law legalizing civil unions went into effect. Argentina remains at heart a Catholic country, and the majority of gays and lesbians outside of Buenos Aires live a "don't ask, don't tell" life. Buenos Aires, however, is an exception to this rule and even non-gay venues will go out of their way to express their gay-friendly nature. The neighborhoods of Barrio Norte and San Telmo are particularly gay and lesbian friendly and are home to the city's two main gay hotels, the **Axel** (p. 46) and **El Lugar Gay** (p. 47). Numerous clubs,

restaurants, and even tango salons cater to a gay and lesbian clientele. Be aware of a few rules of thumb in a city where close contact is normal. Women of all stripes may walk hand in hand, and men kiss each other hello. However, when two men hold hands, it means they are gay. Ongoing violence and discrimination against the transgendered is gradually being addressed. See also "Buenos Aires: Latin America's Gay Tourism Capital," p. 207, and "Gay Tours," p. 26.

Mail Post offices can be found everywhere and are open weekdays from 10am to 8pm and Saturday until 1pm. The main post office, or **Correo Central,** is at Av. Sarmiento 151 (ℂ **11/4891-9191;** www.correoargentino.com.ar). In addition, the post office works with some *locutorios,* which offer limited mailing services. At press time, it cost 7.5 pesos to send a postcard or letter to the United States or Canada, and 8 pesos to send mail to the rest of the world outside of the Americas. The purple-signed and ubiquitous **OCA** (ℂ **0800/999-7700;** www.oca.com.ar) is a private postal service that can mail items overseas. UPS has many locations, including Calle Tucumán 300 at 25 de Mayo (ℂ **0800/222-2877;** www.ups.com), and there's a FedEx office at 25 de Mayo 386 at Corrientes (ℂ **11/4630-0300;** www.fedex.com.ar).

Medical Requirements See "Health," earlier in this section. Unless you're arriving from an area known to be suffering from an epidemic (particularly cholera or yellow fever), vaccinations are not required for entry into Argentina.

Medical Tourism Plastic surgery is an obsession for many Argentines. Depending on your view, Susana Giménez, one of Argentina's most famous stars, is an example of either the dangers or delights of that obsession. Botox and breast augmentations are the fashion and are often covered by private health insurance. Because of the exchange rate, Argentina is also becoming a place for plastic-surgery tourism. If you are planning to be here for a long time and have been considering cosmetic procedures, Buenos Aires might be a place to have it done. Two websites with more information on medical tourism are **www. medicinaargentina.com** and **www.argentinahealth care.org**.

Mobile Phones With the right service plan in your home country, GSM smartphones will work in Argentina—in theory. Service is not entirely dependable, and calls are often routed to voice mail. Text messages are more reliable. Most service plans from overseas are very expensive. It makes more sense to use an unlocked phone

that accepts a SIM card, also known as a "chip," and add minutes to this. In general, rates depend on the company, but will run about US50¢ per minute for local calls, and up to US$2 for international calls. The pedestrianized shopping streets Calle Florida and Calle Lavalle are home to numerous stores selling such phones and SIM cards. The phones can be recharged at virtually any newspaper kiosk through an electronic vending system. The cellphone company **Movistar** has a booth in Galerías Pacífico, Calle Florida 750 at Avenida Córdoba (© **11/5555-5287**), as well as at Lavalle 567 at Florida (© **11/4328-5624**). **Altel,** Av. Córdoba 417, 1st floor (at Reconquista; © **11/4311-5000;** www. altelphonerental.com), is a cellphone-rental company aimed at tourists. It offers free rental and delivery, but phone calls cost about $1 to $2 a minute, even locally. With a strong Internet signal, you can also use Skype to call home.

Money & Costs The currency conversions provided were correct at press time. Rates fluctuate, however, so before you depart, consult a currency exchange website such as **www.xe.com** for up-to-the-minute rates.

The peso is the main unit of currency in Argentina. It is indicated with the symbol "$" and is divided into 100 centavos. (Prices quoted in U.S. dollars are often

accompanied by the symbol "US$" or "$US.") Centavo coins come in denominations of 1, 2, 5, 10, 25, and 50. There are also 1- and 2-peso coins; the latter are generally intended as commemorative collector coins but can also be used as currency. Paper money comes in 2-, 5-, 10-, 20-, 50-, and 100-peso bills. The alleged Argentine coin shortages that made media headlines around the world were actually a false, politically motivated rumor. It's true that shopkeepers are hesitant to give change unless you buy something, as they are in cities across the world. Do not accept torn or taped bills with a value over 10 pesos; as a foreigner, you are more likely to have these bills passed off on you by shopkeepers, and they may be difficult to use later.

It's a good idea to exchange at least some money—just enough to cover airport incidentals and transportation to your hotel—at your local American Express, Thomas Cook, or bank before you leave home (though don't expect the exchange rate to be ideal), so you can avoid lines at airport ATMs. If there's no bank with currency-exchange services close by, **American Express** (© **800/807-6233;** www. americanexpress.com) will ship traveler's checks and foreign currency, though, with a $15 order fee and additional shipping costs. At Ezeiza, there's an ATM at the

THE VALUE OF THE ARGENTINE PESO VS. OTHER CURRENCIES

Argentine Peso	Aus$	Can$	Euro (€)	NZ$	UK£	US$
1	A$0.25	C$0.25	€0.18	NZ$0.33	£0.15	$0.25

WHAT THINGS COST IN BUENOS AIRES IN PESOS

Taxi from the airport to downtown Buenos Aires	140.00
Double room, moderate	600.00
Double room, inexpensive	320.00
Three-course dinner for one without wine, moderate	100.00
Bottle of beer	20.00
Cup of coffee	12.00
1 liter of premium gas	8.00
Admission to most museums	10.00–20.00

Banco de la Nación just outside of the arrival terminal.

U.S. dollars are no longer as widely accepted in Buenos Aires as they were before and immediately after the December 2001 peso crisis. However, you can still use them to pay in some business-class hotels, and at restaurants and businesses catering to tourists. For the vast majority of your purchases, however, you will need pesos. You can exchange money at the airport, in hotels, in *casas de cambio* (money-exchange houses), and in some banks. The huge **American Express** building is next to Plaza San Martín, at Arenales 707 (© **11/4310-3000**). In addition to card-member services, the bank offers currency exchange (dollars only), money orders, check cashing, and refunds. You can also withdraw pesos at

ATMs, which are plentiful in Buenos Aires, but use only those in secure, well-lit locations. Even if your bank allows you to make larger daily withdrawals, Argentine ATMs generally only give out pesos in the value range US$100 to $250 maximum at a time or on a daily basis, so plan accordingly. It will be hard to break large bills usually dispensed by ATMs; withdraw money in uneven amounts so that a portion comes in small bills. You can withdraw cash advances from your credit cards at banks or ATMs, but high fees make this a pricey way to get cash. Keep in mind that you'll pay interest from the moment of your withdrawal, even if you pay your monthly bills on time. You can have money wired to **Western Union,** Carlos Pellegrini (9 de Julio) 1365 at Arroyo (© **0800/800-3030**

or 11/4323-4200). Be aware that in 2011, a law was passed in Buenos Aires banning the use or possession of a cellphone while banking, which in theory prevents bank robbers from communicating with each other. You will be asked to leave your cellphone in a locker or with a guard when in a bank.

It is sometimes difficult to exchange traveler's checks outside of Buenos Aires, so plan ahead and bring a sufficient amount of pesos on day trips.

Visa, American Express, and MasterCard are accepted at most establishments in Buenos Aires. Also, note that many banks now assess a 1% to 3% "transaction fee" on all charges you incur abroad (whether you're using the local currency or your native currency). Many places in Buenos Aires will also charge a fee when you use a credit card, often ranging from 3% to 5%, in addition to anything your bank will charge.

For help with currency conversions, tip calculations, and more, download Frommer's convenient Travel Tools app for your mobile device. Go to **http:// www.frommers.com/go/ mobile** and click on the Travel Tools icon.

Newspapers & Magazines Newspaper kiosks abound in Buenos Aires. The main Spanish-language newspapers are *El País* (www.elpais.com.ar), *Clarín* (www.clarin.com), *Página 12* (www.pagina12.com.ar), and *Perfil* (www.perfil. com). Magazines like *Caras* (www.caras.com.ar) and *Gente* (www.gente.com.ar) will keep you up to date on celeb gossip, and *Lugares* (www.lugaresdeviaje.com) is a good source for travel articles in Spanish. If you want to help the homeless, purchase a monthly issue of Hecho en Bs. As. (www. hechoenbsas.com), which has good articles about the music and arts scene and is Buenos Aires's version of London's Big Issue. U.S. and other foreign newspapers and magazines are commonly sold in Buenos Aires, though expensive, along with the International Herald Tribune (http://global. nytimes.com/?iht). The main English-language newspaper is the Buenos Aires Herald (www.buenos airesherald.com), which is an excellent resource for travelers. You might also

want to visit the website for the formerly printed but now Web publication, Argentina Independent (www.argentina independent.com).

Packing Even the most expensive restaurants in Buenos Aires rarely require formal attire, but it's a good idea for men to bring a dinner jacket. Women already know a little black dress will go a long way. If you plan to explore the *milonga* scene, even if you do not dance the tango, wear shoes, not sneakers.

For more helpful information on packing for your trip, download Frommer's convenient Travel Tools app for your mobile device. Go to **http://www.frommers. com/go/mobile** and click on the Travel Tools icon.

Passports Citizens of the United States, Canada, the United Kingdom, Australia, New Zealand, and South Africa require a passport to enter the country. If you do not yet have a passport, see below for passport services by country of origin.

Australia Australian Passport Information Service (© **131-232;** www. passports.gov.au).

Canada Passport Office, Department of Foreign Affairs and International Trade, Ottawa, ON K1A 0G3 (© **800/567-6868;** www.ppt.gc.ca).

Ireland Passport Office, Setanta Centre, Molesworth Street, Dublin 2 (© **01/671-1633;** www.foreignaffairs. gov.ie).

New Zealand Passports Office, Department of Internal Affairs, 47 Boulcott St., Wellington, 6011 (© **0800/ 225-050** in New Zealand or 04/474-8100; www.pass ports.govt.nz).

United Kingdom Visit your nearest passport office, major post office, or travel agency or contact the Identity and Passport Service (IPS), 89 Eccleston Sq., London, SW1V 1PN (© **0300/222-0000;** www. ips.gov.uk).

United States To find your regional passport office, check the U.S. State Department website (travel. state.gov/passport) or call the National Passport Information Center (© **877/487-2778**) for automated information.

Petrol Please see "Getting Around: By Car," p. 256.

Police For police assistance, call © **101** or 911. The Federal Police also maintains a special division to help foreign travelers, **La Comisaría del Turista,** Corrientes 436 between San Martín and Florida (© **0800-999-5000** or 11/4346-5748; www. policiafederal.gov.ar; turista@policiafederal. gov.ar). Police in Argentina are not generally the corrupt figures you may have heard of in other Latin American countries or the merciless characters that patrolled Buenos Aires during the military regime. There is, however, an ongoing dispute between the two police forces operating in Buenos Aires: the Federal Police, controlled by national government (which is headed by the Peronist party), and the Metropolitan Police, created by Mayor Mauricio Macri, a member of the opposition and right-wing conservative party, the PRO. At times, during riots, according to Macri, the Federal Police are called out from the city in order to foment chaotic conditions. This is something to be aware of, but does not generally impact the tourist experience. You will find both police forces in most tourist-heavy areas. The Federal Police are distinguished by the rooster symbol on the medallions of their uniforms. See also "Legal Aid," above, and "Safety," below.

Plastic Surgery See "Medical Tourism," above.

Safety The fact that former U.S. president George W. Bush's daughters were robbed despite being surrounded by Secret Service and local cops says a lot about Buenos Aires. Crime—especially pickpocketing, robbery, and car theft—has increased sharply in recent years with the volatility of the economy and an influx of naive tourists. Visitors need to be aware at all times. Real violence is unlikely; pickpocketing is likely to be your top problem, so be careful in large crowds, on subways, on buses, and while watching street performers. Never leave a bag or purse unattended or on the ground.

(Though official accounts differ and/or deny the Bush daughters were robbed at all, the method by which they were likely hoodwinked was the "soccer" method: A purse on the ground under a chair is kicked to another thief who then takes it away.)

While it's generally safe to walk around Recoleta, Palermo, and the Microcentro day and night, some tourist areas deemed safe by day, such as La Boca, should be avoided at night. While you need not avoid San Telmo by night—many of the best bars and *milongas* are in this area—you should watch out for theft here as well, especially in outdoor restaurants. I would also warn tourists against walking around in Monserrat at night, though with increasing gentrification and tourist spillover from San Telmo, the area has become safer. Visitors should walk in pairs or groups when possible but avoid conspicuous tourist behavior, including speaking loudly in English. Do not flaunt expensive possessions, particularly jewelry. Call for a radio-taxi or *remis* when leaving a place of business. The number-one rule to keep in mind is that thieves take advantage of naiveté and opportunity. See also "Legal Aid," above, and "Police," above.

Because motor vehicle crashes are a leading cause of injury among travelers, walk and drive defensively. Do not expect buses and

cars to stop when you cross the street. Always use a seat belt, which is the law in Buenos Aires, even in taxis.

Senior Travel Argentines treat seniors with great respect, making travel for them easy. The Spanish term for a senior or retired person is *jubilado*. Discounts are usually available; ask when booking a hotel room or ordering a meal. Seniors are often given discounted or even free admission at theaters and museums. **Aerolíneas Argentinas** (⟨✆ 800/333-0276** in the U.S.; www. aerolineas.com.ar) offers a 10% discount on fares to Buenos Aires from Miami and New York for passengers 62 and older; companion fares are also discounted. Members of **AARP,** 601 E St. NW, Washington, DC 20049 (⟨✆ 888/687-2277;** www. aarp.org), get discounts on hotels, airfares, and car rentals. Anyone over 50 can join. The **Alliance for Retired Americans,** 8403 Colesville Rd., Ste. 1200, Silver Spring, MD 20910 (⟨✆ 301/578-8422;** www. retiredamericans.org), also offers discounts on hotel and auto rentals. (Members of the former **National Council of Senior Citizens** receive automatic membership in the Alliance.) **Road Scholar** (⟨✆ 877/426-8056;** www.roadscholar.org) arranges study programs for those ages 55 and over (and a spouse or companion of any age) in the U.S. and in more than 80 countries around the world. Most courses last 5 to 7 days in the U.S. (2–4 weeks abroad), and many include airfare, accommodations in university dormitories or modest inns, meals, and tuition. **ElderTreks** (📞 800/741-7956; www.eldertreks.com) offers small-group tours to off-the-beaten-path or adventure-travel locations, restricted to travelers 50 and older.

Recommended publications offering travel resources and discounts for seniors include the quarterly magazine *Travel 50 & Beyond* (www.travel50andbeyond.com); *Travel Unlimited: Uncommon Adventures for the Mature Traveler* (Avalon); *101 Tips for Mature Travelers,* available from **Grand Circle Travel** (📞 800/221-2610 or 617/350-7500; www.gct.com); and *Unbelievably Good Deals and Great Adventures that You Absolutely Can't Get Unless You're Over 50,* by Joann Rattner Heilman (McGraw-Hill).

Single Travelers Traveling as a single person gives you more flexibility and often makes it easier to meet locals. However, it also means more caution must be taken at times. See also "Women Travelers," below.

Smoking In 2006, Buenos Aires passed a law banning smoking in indoor public spaces, and in general, it is very well adhered to. It's not uncommon, however, to find a few people still smoking in bars or in clubs throughout Buenos Aires, especially as the evening drags on. Although smoking is not allowed in taxis, some drivers will still smoke; it's okay to ask them to stop if it bothers you.

Student Travel Student discounts are common in Argentina, but usually only if one has appropriate ID. **STA Travel** (📞 800/781-4040 in the U.S., 0871/230-0040 in the U.K., or 134-782 in Australia; www.statravel.com) specializes in affordable travel for student and young travelers, and issues the **International Student Identity Card (ISIC),** widely recognized as proof that you are a student. As well as offering discounts on a range of travel, tours, and attractions, it comes with a 24-hour emergency help line and a global voice/fax/e-mail system with discounted international telephone calls. Available to any full-time student older than 12, it costs $21. If you're a student planning to stay long term or study in Argentina, consider also looking at the U.S. State Department's website for student travelers, **http://studentsabroad.state.gov**.

Taxes The 21% sales tax (or VAT) is already included in the sales price of your purchase. Be aware when checking into hotels that the posted or spoken price may or may not reflect this tax, so make sure to ask for clarification. Foreign tourists are entitled to a refund on a portion of the VAT tax for purchases of certain items over 70 pesos, provided that the items are made in Argentina and are intended to be taken out of the country. However, you must request a refund invoice at the time of purchase from participating shops and present this invoice to Customs before departing the country. Check **www.global-blue.com** for more information, or see "Shopping Tips: Hours, Shipping & Taxes," p. 166.

Telephones See "Area Codes," earlier in this section, for information on phone numbers. Public phones take either phone cards (sold at kiosks on the street) or coins (less common). Local calls initially cost 20 centavos and charge more the longer you talk.

Telecentro or *locutorio* offices—found everywhere in Buenos Aires—offer private phone booths where calls to Europe and North America cost about a peso a minute. Most hotels offer fax services, as do all *telecentro* offices. Dial 📞 **110** for directory assistance (most operators speak English) and 📞 **000** to reach an international operator. Direct dialing to North America and Europe is available from most phones. International, as well as domestic, calls are expensive from hotels (rates fall btw. 10pm and 8am). Holders of AT&T credit cards can reach the money-saving **USA Direct** from Argentina by calling $\textcircled{C}$ **0800/555-4288** toll-free from the north of Argentina or 0800/222-1288 from the south. Similar services are offered by MCI ($\textcircled{C}$ **0800/555-1002**) and Sprint ($\textcircled{C}$ **0800/555-1003** from the north of Argentina, or 0800/222-1003 from the south).

Time   Argentina does not have daylight saving time, so the country is 1 hour ahead of Eastern Standard Time in the United States in the U.S.'s summer and 2 hours ahead in the U.S.'s winter. Neighboring Uruguay does have daylight saving time, so be aware of this when making trips across the Río de la Plata.

Tipping   A 10% to 15% tip is typical at cafes and restaurants. Taxi drivers do not expect tips, but many people round up to the nearest peso or 50-centavo figure. If a taxi driver helps you with bags, it's a nice gesture to give a small tip. For help with tip calculations, currency conversions, and more, download Frommer's convenient Travel Tools app for your mobile device. Go to **http://www.frommers.com/go/mobile** and click on the Travel Tools icon.

Toilets   You won't find public toilets or restrooms on the streets in Buenos Aires, but they can be found in hotel lobbies, bars, restaurants, museums, department stores, railway and bus stations, and service stations. It's not impolite to ask to use them in bars and restaurants even if you are not a patron, and even if there's a sign saying not to ask. Many public toilets do not have soap or toilet paper, so it's a good idea to carry hand sanitizer and a tissue packet. Bus and train station bathrooms should be used with some caution; do not, for example, leave pocketbooks on toilet door hooks. Public toilets do not generally cost money to use, but the cleaning people leave tip jars at their cleaning station and it's a nice gesture to leave some change.

VAT   See "Taxes," above.

Visas   No visa is required for citizens of United States, Canada, the United Kingdom, Australia, New Zealand, Ireland, and South Africa for tourist stays in Argentina of up to 90 days. A side trip to Brazil or by boat to neighboring Uruguay will effectively restart the 90-day tourist period. British citizens should be aware that in spite of periodic official rhetoric regarding the Falkland Islands (Islas Malvinas), there is no actual tension between Argentina and the U.K. In addition, all travelers, British or not, should be aware that visiting the Falklands does not jeopardize reentry into Argentina.

Since 2009, Argentina has charged a reciprocity fee of citizens of the United States, Canada, and Australia landing at Ezeiza. The fee covers an entry voucher (not technically a visa) that's valid for 10 years. At press time, the fee is $140 for Americans, $100 for Australians, and $70 for Canadians, which is what Argentines pay for visas to each of these countries, respectively. The fee can be paid with cash, Visa, MasterCard, or American Express upon arrival. Though this may change, at the moment the fee is not charged if you enter Argentina by land or sea.

For more information concerning long-term, work, or other types of visas, contact the appropriate embassy or consulate in your home country (see below).

Australia   Contact the Embassy of the Argentine Republic, John McEwen House, Level 2, 7 National Circuit, Barton, ACT 2600 ($\textcircled{C}$ **02/6273-9111;** fax 02/6273-0500; info@argentina.org.au; www.argentina.org.au).

Canada   Contact the Embassy of the Argentine Republic, 81 Metcalfe St., Ste. 700, Ottawa, Ontario K1P 5B4 ($\textcircled{C}$ **613/236-2351;** fax 613/235-2659; www.argentina-canada.net).

Ireland   Contact the Embassy of the Argentine Republic, 15 Ailesbury Drive, Dublin 4 ($\textcircled{C}$ **353/1-269-1546;** fax 353/1-260-0404; feirla@mrecic.gov.ar; www.mrecic.gov.ar).

New Zealand   Contact the Embassy of the Argentine Republic, Prime Finance Tower, Level 14, 142 Lambton Quay, PO Box 5430, Wellington ($\textcircled{C}$ **04/472-8330;** fax 04/472-8331;

enzel@arg.org.nz; www.arg.org.nz).

United Kingdom Contact the Embassy of the Argentine Republic, 65 Brooke St., London W1Y 4AH (© 020/7318-1300; fax 020/7318-1301; seruni@mrecic.gov.ar; www.argentine-embassy-uk.org).

United States Contact the Consular Section of the Argentine Embassy, 1811 Q St. NW, Washington, DC 20009 (© 202/238-6401 or 202/238-6460; fax 202/238-6471). Consulates are also located in Los Angeles, California (© 323/954-9155/6); Miami, Florida (© 305/373-1889); Atlanta, Georgia (© 404/880-0805); Chicago, Illinois (© 312/819-2610); New York City (© 212/603-0400); and Houston, Texas (© 713/871-8935). For more information, visit www.embassyofargentina.us, with links to the various consulates in the U.S.

Visitor Information

See "Passports," earlier in this section, and "Visas," above, for information on these topics.

The headquarters of Buenos Aires's **City Tourism Office** (© 11/4114-5734; **www.bue.gov.ar**), responsible for all visitor information on Buenos Aires, is located at Calle Balcarce 360 in Monserrat but is not open to the general public. The city runs free tours (for details, call © 11/4114-5791 Mon–Fri 9am–4pm). Most are in Spanish, but a few are offered in English. The City Tourism Office

provides information to tourists at various kiosks throughout the city, which have maps and hotel, restaurant, and attraction information. These are found at the intersection of J.M. Ortiz and Quintana in Recoleta near the cemetery, in Puerto Madero, at the central bus terminal, at Defensa 1250 in San Telmo, on the Caminito in La Boca, and at Calle Florida 100 at Diagonal Norte. Most are open Monday through Friday from 10am to 5pm. Some are also open on weekends as well, including the one at Defensa 1250. The center on Caminito in La Boca is open Saturday and Sunday only, usually from 10am to 5pm.

Argentina's **Ministry of Tourism** has a booth at the Ezeiza airport with information on Buenos Aires and the rest of Argentina, open daily 8am to 8pm (© 11/5480-0192), and one at **Aeroparque** with the same schedule (© 11/4773-9891). The **Ministry of Tourism** is headquartered at Suipacha 1111 between Santa Fe and Arenales, 21st floor (address is also sometimes indicated as Sante Fe 883; © 11/4312-5550), with a street-level information office in the building's shopping arcade open Monday to Friday 9am to 5pm. Government websites **www.turismo.gov.ar** and **www.argentina.travel** have databases and links to hotels and other services, searchable by subject, city, province, and region. The

toll-free hotline number for tourism information on Argentina is © 0800-555-0016. Also visit **http://www.frommers.com/go/mobile** for travel information you can download.

Water See "Health," earlier in this section.

Wi-Fi See "Internet & Wi-Fi," earlier in this section.

Women Travelers

Women travelers will find that Argentine men are extremely flirtatious, and leers and indiscreet remarks are common. While any looks and calls you might get are rarely more than that, drunken men in clubs may occasionally get physical. Women should be cautious when walking alone at night and should take a *remis* or radio-taxi after dark. In the rare and unlikely event of an assault or sexual attack, contact the police immediately. The special 24-hour number for sexual and family violence is © 137. The city of Buenos Aires also maintains a 24-hour police emergency center for victims of sexual violence at Pasaje Angel Peluffo 3981 at Lezica in the Almagro neighborhood (© 11/4958-4291 or 11/4981-6882). The women's group **Centro de Estudios Cultura y Mujer (CECYM),** Guatemala 4294 (© 11/4865-9102; www.cecym.org.ar), recommends **Hospital Pirovano** in the Villa Urquiza neighborhood, Monroe 3555 between Roque Perez and Milian (© 11/4542-5552 or

11/4542-2772; www.talleres delpirovano.com.ar) and its **EVAS** program for women who have experienced sexual assault. Visit the website of the **Eva Giberti Foundation** (www.eva giberti.com) or **www.ecap social.com.ar** for more resources, and **www. buenosaires.ihollaback.org** for specific information on street harassment. In addition, check out the award-winning website **www.journeywoman.com**, a "real life" women's travel information network; the travel guide *Safety and Security for Women Who Travel* (Travelers' Tales, Inc.), by Sheila Swan and Peter Laufer; and the website **www.gutsytraveler. com**, with links to articles for independent women.

Single women, or women whose partners refuse to dance, who want to take advantage of the tango scene should refer to our section on "Tango Tours," many of which can provide a tango dancer to accompany you (p. 204). The tango scene in general, with its strict rules, combining both chauvinism and chivalry, is a safe option for single women to try their hand at dancing. Nothing more than a dance is expected of a woman who accepts an invitation on the dance floor. In spite of tango's brothel roots, misbehavior among men is frowned upon in tango settings today.

Index

See also Accommodations and Restaurant indexes, below.

General Index

A

Restaurants

R.C.L.
WWW.g1.br
DEC. 2011

G